Essentials of World History

REVISED EDITION

Jean Reeder Smith
ENGLISH DEPARTMENT
  AND WRITING PROGRAM
NORTHWESTERN UNIVERSITY

Lacey Baldwin Smith
PROFESSOR OF HISTORY
NORTHWESTERN UNIVERSITY

New York • London • Toronto • Sydney

All inquiries should be addressed to:
Barron's Educational Series, Inc.
250 Wireless Boulevard
Hauppauge, New York 11788

Library of Congress Catalog
Card No. 79-23608

International Standard Book No. 0-8120-637-2

Library of Congress Cataloging in Publication Data
Smith, Jean Reeder.
   Essentials of world history.
   (Barron's essentials : the efficient study guides)
   Ed. of 1966 by L. B. Smith and J. R. Smith published
under title: World history in outline.
   Bibliography: p.
   Includes index.
   SUMMARY: Traces in outline form the major
events of world history from the dawn of
civilization to the present.
   1. History—Outlines, syllabi, etc.—Juvenile
literature. [1. History—Outlines, syllabi, etc.]
I. Smith, Lacey Baldwin, 1922-   joint author.
II. Smith, Lacey Baldwin, 1922-   World history in
outline. III. Title.
D21.S64   1979   909   79-23608

PRINTED IN THE UNITED STATES OF AMERICA
890   510   98765.

CONTENTS

CONTENTS

INTRODUCTION

In organizing the multitude of events that compose world history, the paramount problem is where to begin: 1) with the appearance of humans, the central characters of this story; 2) with the development of civilized society, the absolute prerequisite to recorded history; or 3) with the advent of global history on which the emphasis of this book rests. The last alternative excludes 99.9 percent of recorded history, for world history cannot be said to have begun until the unification of the globe by the Europeans in the sixteenth and seventeenth centuries. The first possibility trespasses upon anthropology and paleontology and falls outside the scope of this book. Through a process of elimination, the logical point of departure must be with the appearance of civilization.

A second major problem is what areas to include in the history of civilization. Presumably world history should encompass the four corners of the earth, but certain peoples and civilizations have played key roles in the unification of the globe and their histories have been emphasized to the exclusion of others, which have been, up until now, on the periphery of world history. For instance, the Eskimo has no place in this history; the Aztec only passing mention; while the Greek, the Chinese, the Arab, the European, and a few others monopolize a major portion of the theme. The book begins with the Middle East, which most authorities regard not only as the cradle of civilization but also as the crossroads from which civilization spread to India, Europe, and possibly even to China.

In revising the text, yet another problem has emerged—what events to emphasize in a global history that continues to accelerate at a mind-boggling rate. During the last 13 years the United Nations has grown from 114 member nations to 150; a human has walked on the moon; a major war in Southeast Asia has ended; and the population of the earth has grown from 2.9 billion in 1960 to 4.1 billion in 1977. It cannot be said that world history stands still.

The Middle East

PREHISTORIC PERIOD   Before 3700 B.C.

Before civilization could develop, people had to learn to communicate, to domesticate animals, and, finally, to farm. Two stages in this process have been named the Old Stone Age *and the* New Stone Age, *which are not strictly chronological but are based on the growing sophistication of tools used and on the introduction of agriculture.*

THE OLD STONE AGE (PALEOLITHIC)

The Paleolithic period, dating from about 500,000 years ago to before 6000 B.C., is considered to be the longest stage of history. Life was sustained by gathering food and hunting, and roughly chipped stone axes were the basic tools. Shelter was generally a cave or a lean-to, and clothes were made of animal skins. It is believed that during this period (about 150,000 years ago), fire was used and language evolved.

THE NEW STONE AGE (NEOLITHIC)

The New Stone Age began in the Middle East about 6000 B.C. but did not come to some parts of the world (Australia and parts of America) until much later, perhaps as late as 1500 A.D.

During this period people began to produce food by domesticating animals—the dog was probably the first—and by cultivating plants—wheat and barley first. Weapons and tools became more refined and were of polished stone.

The production of food resulted in a more settled, less nomadic existence, and this in turn led to the growth of permanent villages (the earliest cities known were Jericho in Palestine and Byblos in Lebanon). A reliable food supply also led to a population increase and, thus, to the development of social order.

From the Middle East, the New Stone Age culture seems to have spread to Africa, Europe, and India. China also developed a Neolithic culture, but historians are not sure whether it was through Indian influence or whether it developed independently. The American Indian seems to have discovered agriculture independently.

ANCIENT CIVILIZATION   3700-1000 B.C.

The word civilization stems from the Greek word civis or city. The arts of civilization—writing, literature, political organization, and science—developed in the fertile valleys of Mesopotamia and Egypt, where people first began to experience an urban life.

THE BRONZE AGE   3700 B.C.

The beginning of what historians call civilization is generally assumed to be the Bronze Age—the era when metal (copper and bronze) was used for tools, when pottery and weaving were developed (about 5000 B.C. in the Middle East), and when the wheel was invented (about 4000 B.C. in Mesopotamia). The use of copper, bronze, and finally iron (1300 B.C.), as Mr. Philip K. Hitti has said in *The Near East in History,* was "responsible for the greatest advances in industry and, until the advent of the

airplane, for the largest measure of progress in transportation."
The wheel led to transportation and communication. The plow
was invented and irrigation was employed; people began to spe-
cialize, becoming potters, carpenters, and smiths.

The Invention of Writing

With the invention of writing, history really begins, for people
were able to record their experiences for future generations. The
oldest known evidence of writing was found in Uruk in Mesopotamia. The script was called *cuneiform* because of the wedge-
shaped characters produced by a stylus. Egyptian writing followed shortly afterward, using picture symbols—*hieroglyphics*.

By 3700 B.C., on the plain of Sumer (Tigris and Euphrates
rivers), civilization had developed. Writing, urban life, political
organization, social classes, and finally arts and sciences had all
evolved. Civilization spread from Mesopotamia to Egypt (3000
B.C.); to the Aegean and the Indus (2500 B.C.); and to China
(1500 B.C.).

Mesopotamia   3000-1200 B.C.

The Sumerians in lower Mesopotamia are considered to have
evolved the first urban culture. The city became a city-state, its
nucleus was the temple, and the ruler, though originally elected,
rapidly endeavored to acquire the attributes of a priest-king.

Mesopotamia was never under the rule of one city-state for
very long. The rich valley of the Tigris-Euphrates was vulnerable
to attack and witnessed many upheavals and conquerors, as peoples fought to gain control of the precious water and land.

The Rulers of the Mesopotamian Area   3000–1100 B.C.

The Sumerians	before 2350 B.C.
The Akkadians	2350–2200 B.C.
The Guti	2200–2050 B.C.

The Sumerians (revival)	2050–1850 B.C.
The Babylonians	1850–1575 B.C.
The Kassites	1575–1180 B.C.

Sargon I, The First Empire Builder

In 2350 B.C. Sargon founded Akkad and conquered the Meso-potamian area, extending its boundaries east through Elam and west into northern Syria. Under his grandson, Naram-Sin (2270–2233 B.C.), the empire was even greater. This was the first time in Mesopotamian history that there was some attempt at an imperial government. Akkadian control was broken by invasions of peoples from the east; by Sumerians who had not been fully assimilated; and then by newcomers from the west, the Babylonians.

Hammurabi (1728–1686 B.C.), One of the Greatest Rulers of Mesopotamia

Under Hammurabi the first national code of laws was cre-ated. There had been earlier attempts at codified law (the code of Bilalama of Eshruma was fifty years older and the code of Lipit-Ishtar of Isim and the code of Ur Nammu were at least 150 years older), but this was the earliest code attempting to govern all peoples in a kingdom. It reveals some interesting things about Mesopotamian civilization: the family was the basis of society; there was a rigid class system and wages were fixed for all jobs; the rights of women were safeguarded; and criminal actions were punished on the basis of *an eye for an eye*.

Mesopotamian Religion

For the people of the Tigris-Euphrates valley, the world was populated with hosts of evil spirits. The ruler of the city-state was believed to be the agent of the gods. The good life consisted of obeying the family, the ruler, and the gods. The greatest piece of Sumerian literature, the *Epic of Gilgamesh,* is the story of the Great Flood, and it reveals a feeling of insecurity, a search for immortality, and a sense of doom; there was no belief in an after-life of paradise and salvation.

Sumerian Contributions

The wheel was a Sumerian invention. In the field of literature the Sumerians far excelled the Egyptians. They led the way in
mathematics by creating a number system based upon the unit
60 and by discovering geometric formulas. The city-state political
organization and business organization also originated in Sumer.

Egyptian Civilization

Unlike Sumer, Egypt developed political centralization. Irrigation and control of the Nile were possible because of the
predictable nature of the river. The need for an organized effort
to regulate flood control was, perhaps, the initial reason for the
pharaohs' great power and political supremacy.

The Dynasties of Egypt   3000–525 B.C.

Pre-dynastic   before 3000 B.C.
Union was attempted between lower and upper Egypt but
was not permanent.

Thinite (dynasties I and II)   3000–2778 B.C.
Under King Menes the second union was accomplished.

Old Kingdom (III–VI)   2778–2263 B.C.
This was the height of Egyptian culture.

Feudal Period (VII–XI)   2263–2000 B.C.

Middle Kingdom (XII)   2000–1788 B.C.

Hyksos (XIII–XVII)   1788–1580 B.C.

The Empire—The New
            Kingdom (XVIII–XX) 1580–1085 B.C.
The eighteenth dynasty was one of the most brilliant, dynamic, and aggressive. During this -period Egypt's empire
was its most extensive.

Rule of the Priests (XXI)   1085–950 B.C.

Rule of the Libians (XXII–XXIV)   945–712 B.C.

Rule of the Nubians (*Ethiopia*) (XV) 712–663 B.C.

Rule of the Natives (XXVI)   663–525 B.C.
Then came the end of independence.

Achievements of Egypt

Despite dynastic change, there was a continuity in Egyptian history, as there was in Chinese history. Almost all of the major advances of Egyptian civilization were accomplished during the Old Kingdom. From then on, achievement was primarily repetitious.

POLITICAL ORGANIZATION

Egyptian government was based on a priestly monarchy. The pharaoh of Egypt was believed to be the child of the sun god. He owned the land and subdivided it among his people, but he maintained direct control of at least one-fifth of the land. The control of wealth as well as religion gave the ruler immense power.

ART AND ARCHITECTURE

The most outstanding aspect of Egyptian architecture was the monumental nature of its buildings, through which the pharaohs endeavored to achieve immorality. The best examples are:

1) the pyramid-tombs (Cheops, built in the fourth dynasty, and the Step pyramid, built in the third dynasty, were incredible engineering feats) ;

2) The Great Sphinx at Giza;

3) the Temple of Amon at Karnak, built during the New Kingdom, is the largest columnar structure ever constructed; a single room, the Hypostyle Hall, covered 54,000 square feet.

RELIGION

Egyptian religion was unlike Mesopotamian religion. Although Egyptians believed in a multitude of evil spirits and gods and although their gods changed with each dynasty, there was optimism in the Egyptian faith. The pyramid, built for the afterlife, represented a belief in eternity. The *Book of the Dead* explains the elaborate system for the preservation of the dead body and the method of embalming; it also states that happiness in the next life is partly dependent upon social behavior in this world.

Cultural Diffusion

The greatest achievements of Bronze Age civilization in Mesopotamia and Egypt were the creation and diffusion through trade and war of the tools of civilization, especially the development of writing systems.

THE COMING OF THE IRON AGE   1300-1000 B.C.

The Iron Age changed the civilizations of the Middle East, for the use of iron tools took control out of the hands of the wealthy and dispersed it. Iron was plentiful, whereas there had been a small and restricted supply of bronze. The creation and spread of the alphabet by the Phoenicians facilitated the use of written communication by more people. The Iron Age also saw the birth of Hebrew religion. As Hitti says, it is "a paradox of world history that the two countries destined to give birth one to the most accomplished system of writing and the other to the noblest system of religious beliefs were not extensive, military and opulent . . . but relatively small, poor and militarily weak."

The Hittites and the First Use of Iron

During the Hyksos domination in Egypt (1788-1580 B.C.), a new empire arose in north central Asia. By 1500 B.C. the Hittites had reached the height of their power. Little is known about these people, but it is believed that they were the first to develop the use of iron. A desperate struggle with Egypt weakened the empire and eventually destroyed the Hittites around 1200 B.C.

The Phoenicians

Origins
When the Babylonians occupied the fertile crescent, the Ca-

naanites were at their southern frontier (in Syria, Lebanon, and Palestine). The group of Canaanites who were not destroyed or absorbed by Semitic hordes, such as the Arameans, Israelites, and Philistines, and who traded with the Greeks became known as Phoenicians for the purple red cloth they sold.

Colonization and Trade

These people were primarily concerned with trade and became the chief agents of civilized life. They founded colonies in Egypt, Cyprus, and Sicily. One of the most famous Phoenician colonies was Carthage (present-day Tunis), founded in 814 B.C. Every colony that they developed was independent yet linked by culture and trade with the principal city-states, particularly Sidon and Tyre. The Phoenicians even reached the Atlantic and possibly England. Legend claims that Europe received its name from Europa, daughter of a Phoenician king. The Phoenicians are believed to have circumnavigated Africa between 600 and 593 B.C. By 727 B.C., however, the principal city-states had fallen to the Assyrians.

The Alphabet

The Egyptians had used in their hieroglyphics forty consonantal signs. The Phoenicians developed twenty-two letters using them as independent signs and then spread this invention throughout the Mediterranean world.

The Arameans

The Arameans settled in the middle Euphrates around 2000 B.C. and soon established states in inland Syria, founding Damascus (Aram). If the Phoenicians carried civilization by sea, the Arameans carried it inland by caravan. In 732 B.C. they also fell before the might of Assyria.

The Hebrews

Origins
Despite invasions and conquests, the small and scattered Hebrew people were able to maintain their cultural unity. Barely civilized in the fourteenth century B.C., they succeeded by 1200 B.C. in forcing their way, tribe by tribe, into Palestine. One migration was connected with the Arameans in the fourteenth century B.C. and one was from Egypt in the late thirteenth century B.C. (1234–1215 B.C.) under the leadership of Moses.

The Monarchy
Faced with a threat from the more advanced and prosperous Philistines, the Hebrews accepted temporary unification under Saul in 1020 B.C. This unity lasted only seventy years. Under David (1004 B.C.) Jerusalem was founded and the Hebrew kingdom extended from Lebanon to the Red Sea. Under Solomon (963–923? B.C.) the monarchy reached its height, but with the king's death it split into the northern kingdom of Israel and the southern kingdom of Judah. Israel was conquered by the Assyrians in 734 B.C. and Judah by the Neo-Babylonians and Nebuchadnezzer in 586 B.C.

Religion
The Hebrews gave the world the concept of exclusive and ethical monotheism as well as an unsurpassed literary achievement —the Torah. By 750 B.C., their God Yahveh (Jehovah) had been endowed by the major prophets with characteristics unlike any other, as a God of justice *and* mercy. The prophet Isaiah gave to the faith a vision of a different world, a world of universal peace "where wolves shall dwell with lambs." The prophet Jeremiah added the doctrine of individual responsibility, not just group responsibility. One was responsible for one's own soul. The prophet Hosea further expanded the theme of a God of love, and the prophet Micah stated that God required nothing more of one than "to do justly, and to love mercy, and to walk humbly with

thy God." Judaism had become a religion of righteousness in which salvation was dependent upon the judgment of a just God who punished evil and rewarded good actions on earth.

CLASSICAL CIVILIZATION 1000 B.C.-500 A.D.

During the classical period of history, the lands of the Middle East were united for the first time under a single empire—first the Persian (sixth century B.C.*) and then the Hellenistic empire under Alexander the Great (332* B.C.*). By the beginning of the first century* B.C.*, however, the countries of the Middle East were once again divided into the Roman Empire in the west and the Parthians in the east. During the classical era, another of the world's great religions was born in the Middle East—Christianity—but it had little lasting influence on the countries of its origin.*

ASSYRIAN DOMINANCE   900–600 B.C.

The introduction of organized cruelty as a political policy, the use of iron for warfare, and the deliberate preservation of the achievements of the past are what the world owes the Assyrians, who began their conquests of the Middle East around 900 B.C. (That Sargon II [721–705 B.C.], one of the greatest of Assyrian rulers, took the name of Sargon of Akkad is an example of the Assyrian preoccupation with the continuity of history.)

In 612 B.C. the Assyrian empire fell, destroyed by a combined army of Chaldeans under the leadership of Nabopolassar (612–605 B.C.) and Medes from Persia led by Cyaxares.

The destruction of the Assyrian empire left four powers to struggle for its legacy: the Medes and the Persians; the Chaldeans or Neo-Babylonians; the Lydians; and the Egyptians.

NEO-BABYLONIANS

The most famous leader of the Neo-Babylonians was Nedbuchadnezzar II (605–562 B.C.) during whose reign the hanging gardens of Babylon were constructed and advances in astronomy were made.

LYDIANS IN ASIA MINOR

Croesus (560–545 B.C.) was the last and greatest king of the Lydians and was responsible for the first use of coinage.

THE PERSIAN EMPIRE

The Conquests

The first modern empire in history was the Persian. Indo-Iranian in language and Zoroastrian in religion, the Persians under King Cyrus (550–529 B.C.) began their conquests. First the Median yoke was thrown off; next the Lydians were destroyed; then the Chaldeans were overthrown. Under Cambyses (529–521 B.C.) Egypt was conquered and the Persians came into conflict with the Athenians and Spartans in 490 B.C., suffering their first defeat.

The Empire

The Persian Empire was divided into twenty provinces, each having a large measure of autonomy yet carefully supervised. Common coinage, a postal system, and well-maintained roads linked the empire together and trade flourished. Compared with the Assyrians, the Persians were lenient, even allowing deportees to return home.

Zoroastrianism

Zoroastrianism began with the Median prophet Zoroaster who is believed to have lived about 600 B.C. *Avesta,* the sacred book, explains the fundamental Zoroastrian belief in the dualism of life. Good and evil, light and dark, are represented by two deities: Ahura Mazda, who is similar to Jehovah, and Ahriman (or

Angra Mainyu), who has the qualities of Satan. A code of ethics is the basis of the faith: good thoughts and good deeds are necessary to stay out of the hands of Ahriman. Later in its history Zoroastrianism became associated with fire worship, for its sacred symbol is the fire that burns perpetually in its temples. The Parsi of Bombay, India, were Zoroastrian, and there are still a few Zoroastrians left in Iran, although Islam has almost destroyed this ancient faith.

HELLENISTIC SOCIETY

Alexander the Great — Conqueror of the Middle East

Alexander's father, Philip of Macedon, had laid the original plans for the liberation of the Greek states in Asia Minor. Aristotle, Alexander's tutor, had instilled in him a devotion to Pan-Hellenic ideals and an appreciation of Greek culture.

Syria fell to Alexander's armies in 333 B.C.; Tyre, the only Phoenician city that put up a struggle, was taken in 332 B.C.; and Egypt, weary of Persian rule, offered little resistance. Then followed Babylon, Afghanistan, and finally northwest India.

In 323 B.C. Alexander died and his empire was divided among four of his generals. Seleucus (312–280 B.C.), the ablest of all of the generals, received Babylonia. He soon acquired most of Asia Minor and encouraged colonization and a standard calendar for the lands he controlled.

Hellenistic Culture

The greatest gift Alexander gave to the world was the blending of Middle Eastern culture with Greek ideas and institutions. Intellectual life flourished. Alexandria, in Egypt, was the symbol of the age—a magnificent city to which scholars from all over the world flocked. The library at Alexandria housed over 700,000 scrolls.

Economic as well as intellectual prosperity was achieved by uniformity in speech, coinage, and laws that created the conditions necessary for a flourishing trade.

THE ROMAN EMPIRE IN THE EAST

By the beginning of the Christian era, Rome had conquered Asia Minor, Syria, Palestine, Egypt, Mesopotamia, and part of Arabia.

Rome carried still further Alexander's efforts to bring Greek ideas and institutions to the Middle East. Neo-Platonism was the attempt to reconcile Platonic and Aristotelian thought with oriental ideas. It combined a contempt for the world of matter with a belief in the purification of the soul, which could be reunited with the godhead through spiritual ecstasy.

During this period of the Roman Empire one of the major religions of the world was born in the Middle East — Christianity (see p. 61). Nevertheless mystery cults continued to flourish, particularly during the third century A.D. They preached that true knowledge of God could be achieved only through mysticism and intuition, not through reason. Paradise could be attained by membership in secret societies that practiced ritualistic and emotional rites. The two most popular mystery cults were the Isis-Osiris cult from Egypt, which was bitterly antagonistic toward Christianity, and the cult of Mithraism (originally a Persian deity).

THE BYZANTINE EMPIRE

Constantine, in 324 A.D., chose the site of the old Greek colony of Byzantium for his capital. Christianity was recognized as the official religion of his empire.

Constant warfare between Byzantine and Persian troops for the mastery of the Middle East was the theme of the Byzantine empire. In 617 the Persians came within one mile of Constantinople but the forces of Emperor Heraclius turned them back. Constantinople itself survived as the imperial center of the Eastern Roman Empire until 1453, despite a massive eleventh-century attack by the Seljuk Turks.

The Christian Middle East

Syria, Lebanon, and Palestine became Christian, although the Syrian church differed in language and ritual from the others. It became known as Nestorian, named after the bishop of Constantinople in 428 who argued the divine nature of Christ. The Egyptian Christian church also deviated from the Imperial church. It used coptic (one of the ancient Egyptian tongues) as its language; and it accepted the Arian heresy, named after a Greek ecclesiastic, Arius (d. 336), who taught that God was unknowable and that Jesus was not God. The church today is known as the Coptic Christian Church, of which there were (in 1964) about 8.5 million members in Ethiopia (one-half of the population) and about 160,000 members in Egypt (seven percent of the population).

MEDIEVAL CIVILIZATION   500-1500 A.D.

The division between the Christian west and the Persian-Zoroastrian east was to disappear at the beginning of the medieval period when once again the lands of the Middle East were united under a single empire and a new religion — Islam. For centuries, the Moslem empire ruled the Middle East, giving to it a common language, a common faith, and a common heritage. By 920, however, the Moslem empire was in decline, and by 1258 it gave way to Turkish invaders from Central Asia. The medieval Islamic period was probably one of the most important in Middle Eastern civilization, for it ended Greco-Roman hegemony and developed the faith and language that are still predominant in the area.

THE ISLAMIC AGE AND EMPIRE

The Birth of Islam

The founder of the Moslem faith was Mohammed (571–632). Born in Mecca, son of a camel herder, and orphaned at six, Mohammed at age twenty-five married a wealthy widow, who gave him the economic means with which to spend a life of meditation.

Around 610, he became aware of the message of Allah (God). His faith was not popular among the pagan aristocracy and his early followers were primarily slaves and members of the lower classes. In 622, because of persecution, Mohammed and 200 followers fled to the city of Medina, a rival of Mecca. The founding of Islam is dated from this flight or *hegira*. Mohammed's faith soon became so popular that by 630 he was able to return to Mecca, defeat his aristocratic enemies, destroy the 360 pagan idols in the Kaaba (holy shrine), and become the head of state.

The Nature of Islam

An offshoot of Christianity and Judaism, Mohammed's faith accepted the basic doctrine of the sole creator and sole judge. The Hebrew prophets of the Old Testament were recognized and Jesus was believed to be a great prophet, but Mohammed was the last and greatest prophet. Mohammed differed with both Christians and Jews, and partly as a result:

1) The sabbath was changed to Friday;

2) The direction faced during prayer was changed from Jerusalem to Mecca;

3) Pilgrimages to Mecca were sanctioned;

4) There was to be neither priesthood (this was later modified) nor sacraments;

5) Eventually the Koran became the word of God.

The Five Pillars

The religious duties and beliefs of a Moslem are known as the Five Pillars of Islam (the word "Islam" means submission to the will of God).

1) The creed of a Moslem is "There is no God but Allah, Mohammed is His prophet." This is chanted from minarets by a *muezzin* when he calls the faithful to prayer.

2) Prayers are required five times a day, kneeling on a carpet, with the head covered, facing Mecca.

3) Almsgiving is necessary and holy.

4) Fasting is also required. The holiest fast, for the entire month of Ramadan, is made in thanks for the Koran.

5) Pilgrimage to Mecca is required of every Moslem at least once in a lifetime. After the pilgrimage is taken, a Moslem may add the title of Hadj to his name.

Another Islamic belief was elevated by some sects to the position of a sixth pillar. From the beginning Islam was a militant faith, believing that the world was divided into two camps, Moslem and non-Moslem, and that Holy War (Jihad) against the infidel was necessary to salvation. Death of a Moslem in Holy War was martyrdom and guaranteed him the privileges of paradise. If the non-Moslem was a person "of the book" (the Old Testament), he need not be forcibly converted but could be allowed to pay tribute instead.

The Koran

The compilation of the sayings of Mohammed was begun under Abu-Bakr (r. 632–634) and completed under Uthman (r. 644–656). The Koran was the earliest prose work in Arabic and to the Moslem was the word of God as revealed to Mohammed. It was (and still is for some sects) the final authority on everything, not just religious matters. It contained civil law, such as rules of inheritance, divorce, and the treatment of slaves and prisoners. It authorized polygamy and concubinage but set the limit at four wives. It forbade most stimulants and it required all good women to practice *purdah* (veiling).

The Two Branches of Islam

The Sunnite Moslem is the orthodox Moslem and believes that the caliph inherited Mohammed's temporal powers only; no one inherited his spiritual ones.

The Shiite Moslem believes that the *imam* (Moslem priest) is the leader of the faith and has inherited Mohammed's spiritual as well as temporal powers.

The Caliphate

When Mohammed died in 632 he left no provisions for a successor. The decision as to who would replace Mohammed as ruler, leader, and commander of the faith led to years of bloodshed within the Moslem world and was never completely resolved. There were three groups who contended for the position:

1) Mohammed's wife's relatives who had fled with him to Medina and those who had supported him in Medina soon joined together to form the Companions. This group at first triumphed.

2) The Legitimists were those who thought that the caliphate should be heir to Mohammed. Ali, husband of the prophet's daughter Fatimah, was named as the legitimate heir.

3) The traditional heads of the community, the Umayyads, felt that they should be allowed to rule.

Caliphates   632–1258

ABU BAKR   (r. 632–634)
The father-in-law of Mohammed and one of his early followers, he was responsible for conquering Arabia and beginning the compilation of the Koran.

UMAR   (r. 634–644)
Like his predecessor, Umar is known for his piety and virtue. He was killed by a Christian Persian slave.

UTHMAN   (r. 644–656)
Uthman was killed during a Moslem uprising.

ALI   (r. 656–661)

At first acknowledged by both Companions and Legitimists, he was killed during a dynastic war.

THE UMAYYAD DYNASTY   (661–750)

Capital at Damascus.

A cousin of Ali's, Muawiyah, governor of Syria, established the principle of succession in his family, the Umayyads. A branch of the Umayyads ruled in Cordova, Spain, from 929 to 1031.

THE ABBASID DYNASTY   (750–1258)

Capital at Baghdad.

This was the height of the empire. The Abbasids succeeded in overthrowing the Umayyads, and from then on the position of caliphate was dependent upon military force.

THE FATIMID DYNASTY   (909–1171)

Capital at Cairo.

The Fatimid dynasty controlled most of North Africa until it was overthrown by Saladin.

Islam Conquers the Middle East   632-750 A.D.

The military campaigns of two of the greatest generals in history—Khalid ibn-al-Walid and Amr ibn-al-As—were responsible for the success of the Moslem armies. The use of cavalry and "camelry" gave the Moslems remarkable mobility.

In 636, Damascus fell to the Arabs and soon all of Syria was in their hands. By 637, the Moslems had defeated the Persians and acquired Iraq; by 643 they were on the borders of India.

The battle against Egypt (642) was one of the most spectacular. The Arabs had about 20,000 men and no ships or siege machines, yet they took Alexandria with its garrison of some 50,000 men and the entire Byzantine navy.

North Africa was overrun by 703, and in 711, under Tariq, half of Spain was conquered. Musa, jealous of his lieutenant, rushed to Spain in 712 and captured the other half.

The first defeat the Moslems suffered was in 720, when they

attempted to push on beyond the Pyrenees; they were finally routed by the French at the Battle of Tours in 732.

The Islamic Empire and Civilization

Under the Abbasids the Islamic empire experienced its golden age. Baghdad was the symbol of the era, and *The Arabian Nights* is an accurate picture of its wealth and splendor, as well as of its corruption.

The Social Structure of the Empire

Social classes were rigidly defined. First were the ruling Moslems, the original Arab conquerors. Second in the social scale were the neo-Moslems (those who had been converted). They were discriminated against politically and yet often outshone the Arabs in their intellectual achievements. Third in the social scale were members of the tolerated sects. They were forced to pay tribute and wear distinctive dress. On the whole they were treated fairly well: Jews were treated better than Christians and often held positions of responsibility.

Contributions of the Empire

One of the greatest contributions was the transmission of civilization. Arabic became the predominant language of the area. Ideas from all over the world were brought together at centers of learning such as Cairo and Gundeshapur (Persia). Greek and Indian influences played extremely important roles. Hunayn ibn-Ishaq (809–873), a prolific translator, was representative of this era during which the major works of other civilizations were translated into Arabic. For example, almost all the surviving works of Aristotle were translated. It was through translations such as these that the European world became aware of the ancient Greek world.

Important transmissions in the field of agriculture also took place during the Islamic Empire, although the Arabs themselves did not believe in working with their hands. New crops such as sugarcane, cotton, rice, and fruits were introduced into Mesopotamia, Spain, and North Africa, and stock-raising was also brought to many parts of the world.

Trade flourished, manufacturing increased (the manufacture of linen paper was brought from China and rapidly replaced papyrus), and cities grew throughout the Middle East.

Not only were the natural sciences of Greece thoroughly studied but the Moslems also made important contributions in the field. Arabic numerals and the zero were adopted from India and spread to Europe, making possible significant Arab discoveries in the fields of trigonometry, geometry, and astronomy.

Some of the most outstanding Moslem achievements occurred in the field of medicine. Hospitals were established throughout the empire; extensive work was done on eye diseases; Al Razi (865–925) wrote a book that was the chief source of chemical knowledge in Europe until the fourteenth century. Ibn-Sina (980 to 1037) wrote the medical guide *Al-Quanun* which served in the East until the nineteenth century. Important discoveries in alchemy and botany went hand in hand with medical progress.

A Spanish Moslem, Ibn-Khaldun (d. 1406), was probably the founder of social science, taking into consideration physical facts such as climate and geography in order to understand historical development.

In art and the humanities the Moslem, influenced by the Persian, created the most exquisite mosaics as well as outstanding mosques across the Arabic world. Moslem philosophers "succeeded," according to Philip K. Hitti in *The Arabs: A Short History,* "in harmonizing and reconciling monotheism . . . with Greek philosophy. . . . Islam thus led Christian Europe toward the modern point of view."

THE DOWNFALL OF THE ISLAMIC EMPIRE

General Causes

The continuous problem of the succession of the caliphate

became more and more serious as rival dynasties claimed control. Internal problems such as the cleavage among social classes, between north and south Arabia, and within the faith itself also tore the empire apart. Luxurious living, overtaxation, and the depletion of manpower through war added to the causes of the downfall of the Moslem empire.

The Seljuk Turks

The Seljuk Turks claimed control of Mesopotamia and placed their leader Tughril on the throne of Baghdad in 1037, although the caliph was allowed to survive. In 1092, however, Seljuk rule began to break up.

Militant Christianity

By 1144, Syria and much of Egypt had fallen into crusaders' hands. Saladin, a Syrian of Kurdish parents and Vizar of Egypt in 1169, recaptured Jerusalem in 1187, and signed a peace with the Europeans in 1192 giving the coast to the Latins and the interior to the Moslems. But his victories were only a temporary reprieve. Saladin was more than a warrior; he devoted his energies to building canals and irrigation ditches and encouraging scholarship.

The Loss of Spain

In Spain, the Christians delivered the death blow to the corrupt Moslem dynasties. In 1031, the Spanish Islamic government had broken up into a conglomeration of Moslem states and then had passed to a Berber dynasty, the Almoravids. At the same time the Christian Spaniards had begun the reconquest of the land. In 1469 the marriage of Ferdinand of Aragon and Isabella of Castile united all Christian forces, and the Moslems were totally eliminated with the fall of Granada in 1492.

The Loss of Sicily

The Moslems had been in Sicily since 827, but in 1060 the Norman conquest began. Contrary to their experience in Spain, however, the Moslems were allowed, until 1154, to retain some of the highest positions.

The Loss of Egypt

The Fatimid Caliphate had established its independence from the rest of the Moslem empire in 909, but it faced the same problems as its cousins.

The Mamluk dynasty was the last medieval dynasty in the Arab world. A dynasty of slaves, they ruled from 1250 to 1517 and were able to defeat the Christian crusaders and check the advance of the Mongols so that Egypt did not suffer the devastation that Iraq and Syria did. The dynasty was noted for its amazing architectural and artistic productivity. Domes, the geometrical arabesque, and Kufic lettering were representative of this period. The Mamluks were finally defeated in a battle by the Ottoman Turks, and Egypt was overrun by 1517.

The Barbarian Invasions

In 1216, Jenghiz Khan and 60,000 Mongolian barbarians invaded the Middle East, destroyed the cultural centers and the irrigation works, and laid waste to the land. In 1253, the second wave of Mongols led by Hulagu invaded. In 1258, Baghdad was destroyed and 800,000 people were killed in a single week. In 1260 Syria was under Mongol control and Hulagu took the title of Il-Khan. The Mongols may have destroyed the Islamic empire, but in the end Islam triumphed; the seventh khan recognized Mohammed's faith as the state religion.

In 1380 Tamerlane (Timur Lang) and his horde of Tartars gained Afghanistan and Persia. By 1393 they were in Baghdad and soon they overran the rest of Mesopotamia. By 1401 they had acquired northern Syria, sacked Damascus, and soon afterward conquered all of Asia Minor.

The Ottoman Turks

The Ottoman Turks had originated in Mongolia and had mixed with Iranian tribes and established a kingdom in Asia Minor by the beginning of the fourteenth century. By 1517 they had conquered Syria and Egypt.

MODERN CIVILIZATION   1500 to the Present

The modern period in Middle Eastern history began with the conquest of the Moslem empire by the Ottoman Turks, but the founder of modern Islamic civilization was Muhammed Ali (d. 1849) of Egypt, who first borrowed Western ideas and institutions. By 1900, the Ottoman empire had become "the sick man of Europe," an invalid state financially under Western control; the only reason it was not totally in Western hands was because the Europeans could not decide how to divide it up. At the end of World War I, however, France and England assumed control under the League of Nations' mandate system. Along with Western influence came nationalism and the demand for independence, and immediately after World War I many of the mandated countries revolted. Order was finally restored and there was uneasy peace until World War II. By the end of World War II the situation had changed. The power of Western Europe, particularly France, had declined; Arab nationalism had been further inflamed by German propaganda; and Russia had become a great power, thus giving the Middle East a chance to play off Western Europe against the USSR. By 1946, most of the Middle Eastern countries were free but divided—more divided than they had ever been in their history. There have been some attempts at Pan-Arabism, but the problem of uneven distribution of wealth and the rivalry for leadership of the movement loom large, and so far there seems to have been very little success in achieving unity. A factor that has solidified antagonism toward the West and strengthened Middle Eastern nationalism is the existence of Israel.

THE OTTOMAN EMPIRE

Government

The government of the new empire was a military dynastic institution. The Turks were the privileged class in society and the entire Moslem hierarchy was headed by them. The chief judge of Islamic law, the *mufti,* soon assumed both religious and secular power. The Ottoman empire trained enslaved Christian boys, "turkified" them, and used them as government officials, army officers, and soldiers. The empire was naturally antinationalistic, for it contained so many different ethnic groups.

The Important Sultans of the Ottoman Empire

Osman (r. 1299–1326), the first of thirty-six sultans, is given credit for the founding of the empire.

Muhammed II (r. 1451–81), however, was the real founder, for it was he who led the troops against Constantinople in 1453, destroying what remained of the Byzantine empire and establishing Ottoman supremacy. Only his death prevented the conquest of Southern Italy.

Salim I (r. 1512–20) conquered Egypt and Syria and brought Arabia into the Ottoman fold. With the addition of Arabia the Ottomans assumed the position of caliph and became heads of the Moslem faith.

Suleiman the Magnificent's reign (1520–66) was the height of the Ottoman empire. Under his rule law was codified, Ottoman sea power was built, and great buildings were constructed (he is given credit for building 312 structures). Most of Hungary was added to the empire; Vienna was besieged for the first time in 1529; and Tunis was invaded in 1534. Ottoman supremacy had reached its height. Thereafter the empire went into decline, subject to foreign pressures and internal revolutions.

THE DECLINE OF THE OTTOMAN EMPIRE

As early as Salim II (r. 1566–74) the decline of the Ottomans had begun. The state was unwieldy; its population was heterogeneous; it was too far-flung in area; and its purpose seemed to be "warfare rather than welfare." There was never an attempt to improve either industry or agriculture. Other problems plagued it: a lack of established rule of succession; corruption; constant warfare in the Balkans; and Russian ambitions to gain a warm water port.

The Ottomans Were Never Able to Control Effectively Their Far-flung Empire

Egypt was semi-independent from 1801 on; Iraq, incorporated into the Ottoman empire in 1638, was ruled by Egyptian Mamluks, although the Ottomans reasserted their authority in 1831; Lebanon developed independently thanks to two of its rulers, Fekhri-al-Din II and Bashir II; Greece declared its independence in 1821.

Saudi Arabia also gave the Ottomans trouble. In the 1700s a puritanical religious revival, led by Muhammed ibn-Abd-al-Wahhab (d. 1792), was befriended by a local chief, Muhammed ibn-Saud (d. 1765). To spread the word of Allah, the Saudi family had to capture Arabia. In 1773 they succeeded in seizing Riyad, and this became the Saudi capital. In 1818 the Ottomans finally defeated the Saudi clan and the dynasty was banished. In 1902, however, twenty-year-old Abd-al-Aziz ibn-Saud returned to Arabia and proceeded to give the Ottomans nothing but trouble.

Abd-al-Hamid II's Reactionary Reign (1876-1909) Contributed to the Downfall of the Turks

He replaced his liberal brother, Murad V, on the Ottoman throne, declared him insane, and abolished his constitution. Repressive measures, such as the Armenian massacres of 1894 and 1895, in which 100,000 were killed, were symptomatic of his fear of assassination at the hands of liberal Turks and his fear for the life of the state, because of uprisings in Bulgaria and Armenia.

He attempted to block Western ideas, to control the nation with an iron hand, and to turn the clock back. This finally led to a coup in 1908 by young army officers demanding a constitution and a homogeneous nation. Hamid was deposed in 1909 and his brother,

Muhammed V (r. 1909–18), was placed on the throne—in name only, for the government was actually controlled by an organization known as the Young Turks.

External Conflicts Leading to the Empire's Disintegration Occurred under the Young Turks

Austria annexed Bosnia and Herzegovina in 1908 and in the same year Bulgaria declared her independence; in 1910 Albania revolted; and in 1911 and 1912 Italy occupied Tripoli and Benghazi. Serbia, Montenegro, and Bulgaria allied against the Ottomans, and in 1913 Bulgaria and Serbia agreed to partition Ottoman Macedonia. This agreement led to war, in which Turkey was stripped of most of Eastern Europe (the First and Second Balkan Wars).

EUROPEANS AND EUROPEAN INFLUENCE COME TO THE MIDDLE EAST

North Africa — the First to Fall into European Hands

During the sixteenth and seventeenth centuries the Turks preyed on Christian shipping in the Mediterranean. At one point there were 30,000 Christian captives in Algiers. This figure had dropped to 100 by the time the French invaded and occupied Algeria in 1830. The French then occupied Tunisia in 1881 and began occupying Morocco in 1906. In 1911, Italy joined the scramble for North Africa and seized Libya. The native Arabs and Berbers, however, successfully resisted and actually limited occupation to the coast. By 1912, the French and Spanish had divided the rest of Morocco between them.

Egypt

From the very beginning of Ottoman rule (1517), Egypt had

been under a system of dual control involving the Mamluk governors *(beys)* and an Ottoman *pasha* or overlord. Corruption, poverty, and heavy taxation were the themes of the administration.

Westernization and Muhammed Ali

With Napoleon's invasion of Egypt in 1798, the situation changed and Western influence began to penetrate Egypt. Muhammed Ali, a Turkish officer of Albanian birth, drove Napoleon's troops out of Egypt by 1801. As pasha, Ali then made his rule virtually independent of Ottoman control.

Recognizing the technological superiority of the West, Muhammed Ali began a rapid program of westernization and centralization. He established state monopolies and improved agriculture and industry. He introduced rice and cotton, Egypt's most important crop, and promoted irrigation projects and native industries. He combatted plagues by rigid quarantines; established the first schools of engineering and medicine and the first Arabic press; sent 311 students to Europe to study; and created a westernized military force that destroyed the Mamluks.

Muhammed Ali had visions of a pan-Arab state and captured Syria (which Egypt controlled until 1840) and the Sudan, and he even knocked on the gates of Constantinople. This led to the first Western intervention in Egyptian affairs, for the British and French preferred a weak Ottoman state to a strong pan-Arab one.

Western Intervention in Egypt over the Suez Canal

In 1859, Said (r. 1854–63) granted a concession (ninety-nine years) for a Suez Canal to the French Engineer Ferdinand de Lesseps; Said was to receive in shares 15 percent of the profits and provide four-fifths of the labor.

Under Said's successor, however, the Egyptian government fell further and further into debt. Ismail (r. 1863–74) set up uniformity of jurisdiction, increased the number of public schools, introduced the first post office in Egypt, and bettered communications. But his projects were expensive and reckless (the debt rose from 250 million francs in 1865 to 2 billion in 1875). Ismail, in order to stave off bankruptcy, was forced to sell his 200,000 shares in the canal to the

British government, but the money from this sale lasted him only a year.

After the Egyptian government defaulted on debts borrowed from French and English banks, two controller generals, one English and one French, were established to protect European investments, and they virtually took over the government. They instigated reforms in the government and forced Ismail to abdicate in favor of his son. This caused rioting against foreign penetration.

War broke out in 1882, and the Egyptians threatened to destroy the canal. Britain sent in troops, seized the canal, and ruled Egypt in all but name until 1914, when it took over total control.

The Sudan

Although culturally the southern portion of the Sudan is a part of Africa, Sudanese history is closely linked to Egypt and the northern half of the country is Moslem and Arab.

From 1896 the British ruled the country by force, and in 1899 a condominium was formed with joint Egyptian and British rule. Great Britain provided the governor-general and the high officers, and Egypt provided the middle-grade officers and four-fifths of the military cost. In 1925, however, the condominium was broken, and Egyptian troops were pulled out of the Sudan.

Lebanon and Western Influence

Under Fekhr-al-Din (r. 1590–1635) Lebanon was virtually independent of Ottoman control. During his reign European Catholic missions, which were later to play a large role in the westernization of Lebanon, were permitted in the country.

Again under Bashir II (r. 1788–1840) Lebanon became independent and open to foreign influence. American missionaries arrived in the 1820s, and the French built the first silk factory there in 1841. Civil wars, following the death of Bashir, finally led to European intervention in the 1860s.

Persia

Persia was one of the first Middle Eastern countries to become a pawn of the Western powers. The Safawid, a native dynasty, ruled Persia from 1501 to 1736, and during this period, the Portuguese seized Hormuz on the Persian gulf, controlling it until 1622, when it was recovered by the Safawids with Dutch and English help. From then on it was Great Britain that received the concessions in Persia.

The Afsharid, a Turkoman tribe, ruled Persia from 1736 to 1746, followed by the Ands, a nomadic Iranian tribe, 1750–79, and then the Qajars, another Turkoman dynasty, 1799–1925. The Qajars ruled the country as an enemy and were far from popular with the people. During their rule the British, French, and Russians bickered among themselves for control of the country.

The Anglo-Persian Treaty of 1814 against Russia put Persia at the mercy of British foreign policy; the Russo-Persian Treaty of 1828 put it at the mercy of Russian foreign policy. From then on it was a pawn in world politics; foreigners controlled its economy; the British and the Russians were given more and more concessions; and the Persian government sank further and further into debt. In 1907, Russia and Britain settled their differences, dividing the country between them—Russia taking the northern half as a sphere of influence and the British the southern half. In 1901, a concession for oil was given to William D'Arcy, a New Zealander. In 1909, the Anglo-Persian Oil Company was formed, which built the Aradan refinery, the largest in the world.

WORLD WAR I AND THE DEATH OF THE OTTOMAN EMPIRE

Turkey entered the war on the side of Germany and Austria-Hungary in the summer of 1914. It was unprepared to fight a war on four fronts: Russia in the Caucasus; Anglo-Iranian troops on the Iraqi border; Arab, British, and French troops on the Palestine-Egypt front; and Australian, New Zealand, and English forces in the Dardanelles. Many of the Arabian countries such as Lebanon and Syria welcomed the Allies, and others such as Saudi Arabia fought vigorously against the Turks.

The armistice ending World War I did not end the war for the Turks, nor did the Peace Treaty of Sevres, signed by Sultan Walud-al-Din in 1920, bring peace. The Ottoman empire was dismembered: Syria and Lebanon became mandates of France; Iraq and Palestine became mandates of Great Britain; the Hejaz and Armenia were to be independent. Turkey's islands went to Italy and Greece; and foreign troops, primarily Greek, landed in Anatolia.

THE CREATION OF THE MODERN MIDDLE EAST

The Ottoman Empire Becomes Turkey

The Turks were in a state of anarchy. In 1920, a national assembly at Ankara set up a provisional government with Mustafa Kemal (Ataturk) as head. The nationalist government refused to accept the terms of the peace treaty, and Turkey was once again at war. In 1923, the Lausanne Peace Treaty was signed: Turkey recovered East Thrace and some of its islands, escaped paying reparations, and freed itself from European control. By 1924, Ataturk and his forces had pushed the Greek army into the sea.

Once Turkish territory had been regained by the nationalists led by Kemal, the Republic of Turkey was established with Kemal as president.

Radical reforms were immediately introduced to change the face of Turkey and create a modern, westward-looking country. Education was taken out of religious hands and made universal; women were granted rights including the franchise; the fez and purdah were outlawed; Islam was disestablished as the state religion; Islamic law was replaced by a new code based on European models; polygamy became illegal; the Arabic alphabet was outlawed and replaced by the Latin one; family names were adopted.

(Kemal took the name of Ataturk [father of the Turks].) The Turkish revolt and radical reforms were the forerunner of similar movements throughout the Arab Mideast.

Persia Becomes Iran

Persia was not part of the Ottoman empire and did not change drastically as a result of World War I. It was not until Reza Kahn (1925–1941) took over the government of Persia that a definite break with the past occurred.

Reza Kahn first brought the tribes of Persia under government control and then set about on a drastic program of reforms similar to those of Ataturk in Turkey. Communications were improved; the Trans-Persian Railroad was built; privileges of the priestly class were curtailed; education was modernized and nationalized; legislation on women's rights was initiated; and in 1933 Reza Khan abolished the capitulations (foreign extraterritorial rights) and acquired more oil royalty for Iran.

Reza Khan was forced by the Allies to abdicate, because he was pro-Axis during the World War II. His son, Muhammed Reza, at the age of twenty-two, succeeded him and immediately declared war on Germany.

Arabia Becomes Saudi Arabia

Between 1902 and 1917 the banished Saudi clan led by Abd-al-Aziz ibn-Saud had fought for control of Arabia. By 1917, they had succeeded in eliminating all but two rivals—Muhammed ibn-Rashid in the north and Hussein ibn-Ali (father of Faisal of Iraq and Abdullah of Jordan) in the Hejaz.

During World War I the British offered Hussein an independent Arabia—there was definitely a question whether this promise included the entire Arab world—if he would fight against the Turks, and he obliged in 1916. Ibn-Saud, however, did little during the war for the Allied cause but instead made ready his troops and consolidated his possessions for the battle that was to ensue for mastery of the peninsula.

In 1921, ibn-Saud succeeded in eliminating the house of ibn-Rashid, thus gaining control of central and east Arabia. Between 1924 and 1926, he defeated Hussein's son, seized Mecca and Medina, and was proclaimed king of Hejaz. By 1932 the Arabian peninsula, with the exceptions of Yemen (an independent principality), Oman, and Aden (both British domains), had been unified as Saudi Arabia. The present ruler is a direct descendent of ibn-Saud.

Egypt

Britain declared a protectorate over Egypt as soon as Turkey had joined Germany, and martial law was enforced throughout the country. Nationalistic hopes and aspirations were raised during the war as a result of frustration with British control and promises made in Wilson's Fourteen Points. Saud Zaghlul led a delegation (the Wafd party) to London demanding independence, and for his efforts he was deported to Malta and then to Aden. Yet in 1922 Britain yielded to nationalistic demands, gave up its protectorate, and declared Egypt to be "independent with reservations" (defense, communications, protection of foreign interests, and the status of the Sudan).

In 1936, after negotiations, riots, and more negotiations, Great Britain agreed to withdraw its military forces except in the Suez Canal zone, but it still retained indirect control through King Farouk. In 1937 Egypt was admitted into the League of Nations.

During World War II Egypt declared a state of siege (not war); Cairo and Alexandria were bombed by the Axis powers; and Egypt was occupied by the Allies. Egypt was strategically important and served as a supply center for the entire region. As a result of the war, the country prospered economically and emerged from World War II as the most powerful Arab state.

Egypt had changed, but the government had not. The monarchy was bound to run into trouble. By tradition and training King Farouk (r. 1936–1952) and his father, Faud I (r. 1922–1936), were instruments of British influence; they were authoritarian in their rule and they had little concern for the welfare of their people. The Wafds (an antimonarchy party) held a parliamentary majority and yet were not in control of the government.

In 1952 General Naguib (hero of the war against Israel) and the army overthrew Faud II, who had replaced his father Farouk. According to Nasser (who overthrew Naguib in 1954), the original cause of the revolution was "the enslavement of the people by the imperialists and their lackeys, the Egyptian feudal lords and politicians."

Syria and Lebanon

The administration of the French mandates was entrusted to the military. The Syrians were opposed to the mandate from the very beginning. Lebanon was in favor, because the majority of its population was Christian and it felt French rule would be a protection from Moslem domination. A Syrian congress declared Faisal, son of Hussein, to be king of Syria, but the Congress party was put down by French arms (and Faisal was installed by the British as king of Iraq). A period of terrorism and reprisal followed. After World War II, however, the French were in no position to argue, and Syria became independent in 1945.

Lebanon followed a different pattern. Although under French mandate, it had a history of independent rule and had thrived for years on trade and tourism. For the first fifteen years following World War I there was peaceful progress. In 1926 Lebanon was proclaimed a republic and given a constitution. From 1936 on, however, there were further demands by the Lebanese for complete independence. In 1943 France finally yielded, but it required UN action in 1946 to force the last French troops from Lebanon's soil.

Iraq

In contrast to French administration in Syria, leadership under the British mandate in Iraq fell into civilian rather than military hands. In 1921 a revolt was put down by the British at the cost of 400 British and Indian and 8540 Iraqi lives. The British quickly learned their lesson and treated Iraq in much the same manner as they had treated Egypt. Faisal was made king of Iraq, and in 1924 it was declared a sovereign state. By 1932 Iraq was totally independent and it joined the League of Nations.

Palestine and Trans-Jordan

The Creation of Jordan

From the outset, Palestine resisted the British mandate, and because of the peculiar wording of the mandate, Britain was able to divide the Palestine and Trans-Jordan area into two separate countries.

Britain made Trans-Jordan autonomous under Amir Abdullah, brother of Faisal of Iraq. An artificially formed state with no geographic unity, no political history, and no economic viability, Trans-Jordan was created by the British as a fortress to guard its oil interests. During World War II the Arab Legion of Jordan supported the Allies, and in 1946 Britain granted independence so long as Jordan agreed to consult Britain on all foreign matters.

The Palestine Issue

In 1917, the Balfour Declaration announced that it should be England's intention to establish a national home for the Jews in Palestine "without prejudicing the rights of non-Jews." At this time the Arabs in Palestine numbered about 700,000, whereas the Jews were a minority of about 70,000.

From 1917 on, Zionists (the organization of Jewish people desiring the reestablishment of a national home in Palestine) encouraged immigration into the country. By 1939, Arabs outnumbered Jews by only two to one.

In 1928 and again in 1936, Arabs rioted; and in 1939 a British White Paper attempted to end Jewish immigration into the country. Throughout World War II immigration continued to be denied, but after the war the sympathies of the world were naturally with those few who had escaped the persecution of Hitler. Britain was in no position to argue and turned the problem over to the United Nations.

Civil war immediately broke out between Jews and Arabs in Palestine. In November 1947, the United Nations voted to divide Palestine and internationalize Jerusalem, but war between Arabs and Jews continued. In May 1948, a provisional government in Tel Aviv declared the independent state of Israel headed by David Ben-Gurion as prime minister. Following statehood, Israel was invaded by neighboring Arab states. In 1949, an armistice was declared, but it was not the end of hostilities (see p. 38). As a result of the war, Israel was in control of considerably more territory than the 1947 partition plan had called for.

Jordan

With the creation of Israel, Arab Palestine was merged with Transjordan to form the kingdom of Jordan, and Jordan became one of the leading members of the Arab League. In 1953 Hussein replaced his father as king of Jordan.

The Sudan

During World War II, the Sudanese agitated for independence, but negotiations reached a deadlock primarily because of Egypt's claim of control over the area. In 1948 the first legislative assembly was granted, and in 1953 the British and Egyptians reached agreement that the Sudan should, in three years, decide whether it wished to join Egypt or be totally independent. When Nasser overthrew Naguib (Sudanese by birth), the Sudan, in 1955, declared its total independence.

Libya

In 1943, as a consequence of defeat in World War II, the

Italians were expelled and Libya was put under British and French military administration. In 1949 the United Nations declared that Libya should be independent by January 1951. The independence of Libya led to agitation in the rest of North Africa.

Tunisia

In the 1930s Tunisia began to agitate for independence from the French. Tunisia suffered as one of the battlefields of World War II. Its trade was paralyzed and it was occupied by the Germans for six months. Between 1947 and 1950 the French agreed to some minor reforms, such as giving more offices in the government to Tunisians, but this was not enough, and from 1951 to 1954 there were riots and troubles.

In 1955 the first all-Tunisian government was granted; in 1956 it became a member of the United Nations; and in 1957 the monarchy was abolished and a republic under President Habib Bourguiba was established.

Morocco

Morocco had had a history of freedom. Before the French and Spanish occupation it had been free for eleven centuries. In 1934 nationalist movements began. In 1943 the Istiqlal party objected to having no voice in the government, no civil liberties, and the fact that foreigners owned most of the fertile land in the country.

The French had established a dualistic rule in Morocco, retaining the Sultan as a tool of their administration. Muhammed V, on the throne since 1927, was forced abroad at the insistence of the French in 1953 because of rioting in Morocco.

In 1955 the French finally agreed to independence and Muhammed V was returned. In 1956 both the French and Spanish pulled out of the country, and in May 1963 elections were held for Morocco's first parliament.

Algeria

The movement for independence in Algeria was complicated by the presence in 1954 of 934,052 French citizens living among 8,595,674 Moslems. Algeria had always been controlled directly from Paris and was economically closely allied to France (40 percent of its exports were wines). The first demands by Arabs for reforms were made in 1926; in 1939 the French agreed to allow Arabs to be elected to an Algerian parliament, but they were never allowed to gain a majority. World War II increased the agitation for independence, and the Free French under Giraud and De Gaulle encouraged the nationalists.

Open war was declared in 1954, and the French, using 70,000 troops, tried to eliminate the extremist section at the cost of $3 million per day. In 1959, De Gaulle offered the Algerians, after a four-year period of pacification, the opportunity to secede from France or to stay with France and be completely integrated. In 1962 he finally negotiated a cease-fire with the nationalists, and Algeria achieved total independence.

THE DEVELOPING MIDDLE EAST

Generally the Middle Eastern countries have moved faster and with more success than developing countries in Asia and Africa. This does not mean that there are not severe economic, social, and political problems; but many of these might be worked out if the question of Israel could be peacefully solved. Israel remains the single most explosive issue in the Middle East.

The Unsolved Question of Israel

The "War of Survival"
In 1949 Israel emerged victorious from the war of survival

against the forces of the Arab League. Its national determination proved stronger than the Arab crusade against it, and its economic, technological, and military strengths were more than a match for the Arab forces. An armistice was signed between Israel and the Arab League, but no peace treaty followed. Raids by discontented Arabs continued into Israeli territory; the boundary question was never resolved; and in 1951 Israel's ships were banned from the Suez Canal.

The Suez Crisis

In 1956, when the United States and Great Britain withdrew the promise of a loan for the building of the Aswan Dam, Nasser retaliated by nationalizing the Suez Canal. In October, Great Britain and France attempted to seize the canal by force of arms. At the same time, Israel invaded the Sinai peninsula and the Gaza Strip, where it claimed concentrations of raiders were located. Under pressure from Britain, the United States, and the United Nations, the troops were withdrawn. But the result of the invasion was to further heighten Arab hatred of Israel.

The "Six-Day War"

After the Suez crisis a UN force in Egypt successfully policed the border between Gaza (annexed by Egypt in 1949) and Israel. In May 1967, however, Egypt (claiming that Israel was about to attack Syria) moved its army to the Israeli border, threatened to cut off the port of Elat, and demanded the withdrawal of UN forces. Since the UN could not stay on Egyptian soil without Egypt's consent, it began to withdraw its forces. That June, in anticipation of Egyptian aggression, Israel attacked Egypt. Jordan and Syria invaded Israel. Six days later, victorious Israeli forces controlled the Sinai, Jerusalem, the West Bank of the Jordan River, and the Golan Heights.

The repercussions were that Egypt, Syria, and Jordan all lost territory and face. Jordan, however, suffered the most—6094 dead or missing; a loss of one-third of its most fertile land; and an influx of 200,000 more refugees. Israel immediately incorporated Jerusalem but treated the other territories as "occupied areas."

The Palestine Liberation Organization (PLO)

The existence of the PLO adds to the volatile nature of the Arab-Israeli conflict. The PLO consists of numerous factions and advocates various formulas for the return of "Palestine" to the Arabs. The PLO usually claims responsibility for anti-Israeli terrorism and the increase of violence throughout the world has been fostered by them. Since 1969, over 35 anti-Israeli terrorists have surrendered after killing nearly 100 people in over a dozen separate incidents. Of the PLO's terrorist activities, the worst examples to date include the burning alive of 30 people in a Pan American aircraft in the Rome airport and the massacre of school children in Ma'alot.

The "Yom Kippur" War

In October 1973, hostilities were resumed by Egypt and Syria, and the surprise attack on the most holy day of the Jewish calendar caught Israel unprepared. Militarily, Israel was again winning by the time a cease-fire was arranged, but the Arabs had recovered their pride and, more important, succeeded in transforming the Mideast into a top international problem largely because of an oil boycott.

A demilitarized zone was set up in the Sinai peninsula, but the issue of the return of Israel to its pre-1967 boundaries remained, and Syria from 1973–75 was rearmed by the USSR at a cost of $2 billion.

Interim Egyptian-Israeli Peace Pact

In the fall of 1975, negotiations between Egypt and Israel showed promising signs. Israel agreed to withdraw from 2000 square miles of the Sinai with the guarantee of U.S. monitors in the area. Egypt's acknowledgement of Israel's existence in the Middle East offered hope for peace, and for the first time in sixteen years an Israeli-bound ship was allowed through the Suez Canal. In 1978, further negotiations were held between Egypt and Israel, but discouraging signs remain. PLO raids from Lebanon continue, and the Third World has succeeded in having the United Nations declare Zionism to be a form of "racism."

The Economic Outlook for the Middle East

The Oil-Rich Nations

Saudi Arabia has one-third of the non-Communist world's oil reserves, and many other nations (Kuwait, Iran, Iraq, Qatar, Abu Dhabi, Algeria, and Libya) possess in abundance this extremely valuable natural resource. In 1973–74 these nations began to exploit their command of oil by quadrupling the price. Whether, in the long run, this will be detrimental to their economies by inducing the industrial world to use other fuels remains to be seen, but in the meantime, they have vast quantities of capital with which to develop and diversify their economies and to use as a political weapon.

The General Picture

The other countries in the Middle East are a study in contrast. Over 70 percent of the region's people live in oil-poor countries.

Although not rich in oil, cosmopolitan Lebanon, which benefits from the oil pipes on their way to the sea, was until recently the center of trade, commerce, and banking in the Arab world. The civil war threw Lebanon's future into doubt.

Morocco is less dependent upon a "one crop" economy than many nations, for it is plentiful in phosphate, cork, manganese, and lead. Iran not only has oil but also has extensive mineral resources and rich agricultural land. In contrast, the Sudan combines a vast area, a scattered population, and a poverty of resources. Measured in terms of gross national product, it is one of the world's twenty-five poorest nations.

Jordan is almost entirely supported by outside funds. It has received over £40 million in aid from Great Britain and over $30 million annually from the U.S. in military support. It has little irrigated land, few resources, little industry, and a small seaport on the Gulf of Aqaba. As a result of the wars with Israel, Jordan, like most of the other Arab League countries, has spent more and more of its national budget on the military.

Agriculture

A basic conflict in all developing countries is the problem of investment in industry or investment in agriculture. Only in Egypt has more money been allocated for industrialization than agricultural improvements, yet this has failed to meet the needs of a rising population.

Farming, even in countries like Turkey which has one of the higher per capita incomes ($300 annually), is still primitive in many areas, and there is a sharp contrast between the archaic countryside and the developing urban areas.

Landholding in the hands of a few was a common phenomenon in most Middle Eastern countries. In 1952 in Egypt, six percent of the landowners held two-thirds of the land. When Nasser came to power, he led the way toward redistribution; as early as 1957, half a million acres had been divided. All of the Arab countries have redistributed land; only a few have paid anything in compensation. Iran completed its "white revolution" in 1971, and all large landholdings, including those of the shah, were divided up among the peasants. Before this, 0.2 percent of the landowners owned 33.8 percent of the land.

The building of the Aswan Dam in Egypt (1970), the Euphrates High Dam (1975) in Syria, and the Litani Irrigation Project in Lebanon have made thousands of new acres available for cultivation. But it is still questionable whether agricultural (and industrial) development can keep pace with the population explosion—except in Iran and Iraq where only 20 percent of the potentially cultivatable land is in use.

Israel is proof of what can be done in an underdeveloped area, given enough dedication, sacrifice, technical knowledge, and money. The Negev desert has been largely reclaimed, production of food has soared, and Israel has the highest per capita income in the Middle East.

Economic Problems

The Population Explosion

The Arab countries had a population of 125 million in 1975;

in 20 years this is expected to double. The past 20 years have seen a significant drop in infant mortality and an increase in life expectancy which have contributed to the rise in population.

Some of the countries, such as Saudi Arabia, look forward to an increase in population but others, such as Egypt (where life expectancy has risen from 46 to 54.5 years), are already badly overcrowded. And still others, such as Morocco and Algeria, face serious unemployment and/or underemployment.

With the introduction of birth control measures, Egypt's annual birth rate has dropped from 4.2 percent to 3.6 percent—but this must be compared with America's 0.6 percent. Tunisia's population has been rising by 2.6 percent since 1969 despite active attempts at birth control; and Algeria has made few efforts to encourage family planning.

The Lack of a Skilled Labor Force

Even the oil-rich nations have serious economic problems. The major problem is the need to create a skilled work force; education is being pushed with varying degrees of success. Saudi Arabia announced in 1975 an ambitious program to invest $140 billion, part of which would be spent on importing technicians, teachers, and workers. But its situation is unique; most nations cannot afford such costly expansion.

Even Israel is faced with a serious shortage of technical skill since new immigrants have come not from West Europe but from the Mideast and Africa.

Instability

Revolution and counterrevolution have brought economies to a standstill. When radical governments assumed power, nationalization without compensation frightened away both local and foreign investors. In traditionally stable Lebanon, the Israeli commando raids and the operations of the PLO have resulted in a costly and deadly civil war. In Iran the removal of the shah has seriously disrupted the economy.

Health, Education, and Welfare

Standards of health and education, of course, reflect the wealth and history of the country, but even in the rich nations improvement is a slow process. There are many reasons for this which are common to all developing nations.

1) Lack of communications and facilities in the rural areas.

2) Shortages of trained teachers, nurses, and doctors.

3) An ever increasing population with half of the people in the Arab world under the age of eighteen (meaning a large investment in education and no immediate productivity).

4) Politics have interfered with Iraq's, Libya's, and Syria's higher education as educators rose and fell with the ideology of the regimes.

5) There are also the historic problems of the segregation of the sexes and the inferior position of women in the Moslem world.

6) The majority of those who go on to secondary education do not pursue the vocational courses that the country needs. In Jordan, for instance, only eight percent choose vocational courses.

Education

The statistics on education show progress but they also indicate the extent of the issue. In Syria today, 64 percent of the labor force is still illiterate, but before independence only 5 percent of the population was educated. By 1974, more than 65 percent of the young were receiving a free state education. In Tunisia only 20 percent of primary pupils go on to secondary school; but in Iraq only 40 percent of the boys and 20 percent of the girls graduate from elementary schools. Egypt, on the other hand, has a tradition of higher education and has eight medical schools which produce more doctors than all other Arab countries together. Education is free and compulsory for ages six through twelve which, with the population explosion, means the government must build 400 new schools a year. Saudi Arabia has four universities but girls are either external students or are instructed through closed circuit television, and job opportunities for women are very limited. Iran has created a "literacy corps," in place of military duty, to be sent into the countryside, but as of 1972, 92 percent of urban children while only 55 percent of rural children were in school. Lebanon had the highest literacy rate in the Arab world: 80 percent.

Health and Welfare

Almost all the nations have some sort of health and welfare plan, but doctors are still in critically short supply and the distinction between rural and urban facilities is extreme.

Egypt's ratio of doctors to people is one of the best in the area, and the state has required doctors to do two years of compulsory service in the countryside. Yet Algeria, where physicians are required to serve as military doctors for two years and then five years in the remote areas of the country, still has a situation where the ratio of doctor to patient is one to 500–600 in the city of Algers and one to 20,000–30,000 in the southern desert regions. The need to import doctors is still a major problem. Of 1500 doctors in Libya, only 90 are Libyan; of 1100 doctors in Saudi Arabia, only 130 are Saudis. Syria has produced, during the last ten years, 5400 doctors, but 4000 of them have left the country.

The Political Situation

The governments of the Middle East vary as much as their economic situations. Certainly Western style democracy is not the rule. Government philosophy ranges from outright Communism in Yemen to unpredictable radicalism in Libya, from what was once a semicapitalist authoritarianism in Iran to a form of feudalism in the sultanates along the Persian Gulf. In an age where monarchy throughout most of the world long ago became figurehead government, it continues to exercise real power in Saudi Arabia, Jordan, and Morocco.

Islamic customs and laws have been abolished or modified in most of the nations, but Saudi Arabia's constitution is still based on the Koran, with all its conservative laws and prohibitions.

Egypt (since Nasser) and Tunisia (since Bourguiba) have had

relative stability; but Syria and Iraq have seen one radical government after another and Turkey has had to rely more and more on military rule.

The Leaders of the Major Countries   1979

Algeria	Colonel Houari Boumedienne
Egypt	Colonel Muhammad Anwar Sadat
Iran	Ayatollah Rubollah Khomeini
Iraq	General Hassan-al-Bakr
Israel	Menachem Begin
Jordan	King Hussein
Lebanon	Elias Sarkis
Libya	Colonel Gaddafi
Morocco	King Hassan II
Saudi Arabia	King Khalid and Crown Prince Fahd
Sudan	General Numeiry
Syria	Hafez al-Assad
Tunisia	Habib Bourguiba
Turkey	Suleyman Demirel

Pan-Arabism

The attempt to unify and coordinate the Arab world has met with mixed success. The United Arab Republic of Egypt, Syria, and Yemen established in 1958 failed in 1961; another attempt with Iraq in 1963 and union with Libya in 1971-72 also failed.

The avowed aim of Pan-Arabism, however, remains the annihilation of Israel. The first really successful example of Pan-Arabism occurred in 1973 when the oil shieks united to pressure the industrial world with an oil boycott if it did not help to resolve the Arab-Israeli conflict.

Except for oil, the Middle East is singularly lacking in economic cooperation among nations. It is the only part of the world without a regional United Nations Economic Commission (because the Arabs refused to include Israel) and a regional development bank. Egypt, however, has signed (1974) an agreement with the Sudan on joint political action and economic integration.

Foreign Affairs

Today, most of the Middle East declares itself neutral—a part of the Third World. This has the great advantage of allowing the solicitation and acceptance of aid from either side.

Egypt, however, reversing earlier policy, expelled Russian "advisers" and paid the USSR in hard cash for military equipment. Lebanon, traditionally pro-West, stayed out of the Arab League until 1973, but the outcome of civil war will determine its future political leaning. Iran and Saudi Arabia are basically anticommunist. Bourguiba of Tunisia has been more pro-West than many Arab leaders and did not break diplomatic relations with the United States in 1967 over the Israeli war. Turkey is the only country directly linked with the West. It is traditionally anti-Russian and a member of NATO. This participation in NATO, however, has been strained by the Greco-Turkish conflict over the control of Cyprus. Libya, under Colonel Gaddafi, announced that its oil money would be used to finance Arab terrorism and in 1975 declared that the Soviet Union would be allowed to use its ports on the Mediterranean.

European Civilization

ANCIENT AND CLASSICAL CIVILIZATIONS
2000 B.C.-500 A.D.

Europe was in the New Stone Age until 2000 B.C., *while the Middle East, Egypt, the Tigris-Euphrates valley, the island of Crete, and the Aegean area had passed the Neolithic Age at least 1000 years before. Toward the close of the Stone Age, invading Indo-Europeans appeared throughout Europe. The first of them to make an imprint on European history were those who settled in Greece. It is here that the story of European civilization begins. From about 900 to 500* B.C. *the Greeks passed from barbarism to the peak of civilization, developing concepts of political freedom, producing great works of literature, and evolving the foundations of modern science. In governmental organization and military defense, however, they were deficient, and in 146* B.C. *the Greek islands were conquered by the Romans, who assembled an empire joining the ancient civilizations of Egypt, Asia Minor, Syria, and Greece to what is today North Africa, Spain, Portugal, France, Switzerland, Belgium, and England. It is to the Romans that Europe owes the transmission of the cultures of the East and of Greece, as well as Roman culture, which emphasized political organization, administration, government, and law. It is also through Rome that Europe received Christianity, for Jesus, being born in Palestine, was a citizen of the Roman world. By the fifth century* A.D. *the entire Roman world was formally Christian.*

47

PRECLASSICAL CIVILIZATION

The Indo-European Invasions   2000-1000 B.C.

Around 2000 B.C. the Mycenean and Minoan civilizations of Crete and southern Greece, which had borrowed heavily from Egypt and Mesopotamia, were confronted with Indo-European invaders. The newcomers to the Aegean area were composed of many separate barbaric tribes. The four main ones were the Ionians, who settled in the area of Athens and went across the Aegean to Lydia; the Dorians and the Acheans, who went farther south, the Dorians who settled in the area of Sparta; and the Aeolians, who stayed in the northern part of the country and crossed the Aegean to Asia Minor.

By 1000 B.C. the expansion into the Greek islands was complete and the older Mycenean civilizations, such as on Crete or at Troy on the coast of Asia Minor, were destroyed.

The Dark Age or the Homeric Period   1000-750 B.C.

The havoc created by the invasions of the Indo-Europeans led to a temporary eclipse of civilization. Tribes were under the leadership of clan kings, wealth was based on land, and plunder and piracy were the main means of livelihood.

Homer wrote of an earlier era (the destruction of Troy by the Indo-European invaders) in his epic poems, the *Iliad* and the *Odyssey,* but he revealed the bitter struggles that marked the transition from the Bronze to the Iron Age of his own era.

HELLENIC CIVILIZATION

The Age of the City-State   750-500 B.C.

By the eighth century B.C. the clan kings had been overthrown by the aristocracy; tribal organization had disintegrated with the increase in landed estates controlled by the nobility; and the city-state had emerged as the political unit throughout Greece.

The Polis (the city-state)

The most famous of the city-states to emerge were Athens, Sparta, Thebes, Corinth, Olympia, Argos, and Delphi. They had developed as separate political units partly because of original tribal settlements and partly because of the geographic isolation of the Greek countryside. People settled in the valleys where fertile soil was available, but in doing so they were completely cut off from their neighbors by the rugged nature of the intervening terrain.

The failure to evolve a single and united Greece resulted in each city-state developing its own local patriotism and independence. This led to different types of political, economic, and social structures; consequently, great differences existed between such city-states as Athens and Sparta.

There were, however, at least two unifying forces in Greece: the Olympic games, in which athletes of all city-states entered; and the oracle at Delphi, which was the center of religious belief for all Greeks.

The Colonization Movement   750–550 B.C.

The Greeks planted colonies, which in turn became independent city-states, from the Straits of Gibraltar to the Black Sea. Marseilles, Naples, Syracuse, Segesta, and Istanbul were all originally Greek settlements.

The motivations behind the extensive colonization movement were half economic, half social. Land was scarce, the population was increasing, the city-states needed markets for their goods, and there was often political and social unrest at home.

The obvious effect of colonization was to spread Greek civilization; perhaps an even more important result was the rise to power of nonaristocratic members of society, for trade led to wealth, and wealth began to rival birth as the basis of political power..

The Age of Tyrants   600–500 B.C.

Opposition on the part of the merchants and the newer elements of society to the power of the nobility led to the rise of tyrants in many city-states. These men were rulers who, with the support of the rising middle classes, overthrew the aristocrats. Although ruthless, they were the first step in the development of democratic government, for they often extended social rights, patronized the arts, and encouraged the development of law and trade. They were the first great "protagonists of freedom"; the most famous were Thrasybulus of Miletus, Peisistratus of Athens, and Periander of Corinth.

The tyrants were eventually replaced either by an oligarchy of landed aristocrats and wealthy mercantile commoners or by democracies where the citizens became the ruling power.

Athens and the Development of Democracy   750-400 B.C.

In the 700s Athens was ruled by a board of *archons,* a council of nobles who had assumed the power of the kings.

In 621 B.C. Draco, the chief archon, established a code of law that was extremely severe (the death penalty was given for stealing a cabbage). It was important, however, because it took punishment for a crime out of private hands and placed it under the control of the state.

In 594 B.C. Solon became sole archon and reformed the harsh system of Draco. Slavery for debt was abolished, nobles were put under the law, and the first steps toward democratic government were taken with the development of a citizens' assembly and a people's court. In addition, the money standard was reformed and skilled artisans were imported into Athens.

From 560–527 B.C. Peisistratus, the benevolent tyrant, ruled Athens. He encouraged the development of agriculture, industry, and the arts. At his death, Athens broke into civil war under the harsh rule of his sons, Hippias and Hipparchus.

Cleisthenes took over the government of Athens, and this was the actual beginning of democracy. In 508 B.C. his constitution was formulated, which placed considerable power in the hands of the citizens.

1) Citizens were given the right to ostracize one man every year by popular vote. Ostracism meant exile for ten years.

2) Citizenship was extended to include all males over the age of eighteen who were native-born. (This was actually only about 10 percent of the population, the remainder being women, children, foreigners, and slaves.)

3) A legislative council of 500 citizens, from whom the administrative officials of the government were chosen by lot for one year, and a popular court of 6000 citizens were also created. The principle of rotation in office was established.

4) The army was set up under a board of ten generals who were elected by the people.

Pericles (461–429 B.C.) was the unofficial ruler of democratic Athens, for he was both chief general and leader of the popular assembly. His rule, called the Golden Age of Athens, is considered to be the height of Athenian democracy, for as Pericles himself said, "Since our constitution considers not the benefit of the few, but the welfare of the many, we call it a democracy."

Sparta — A Military Oligarchy

Sparta's political organization consisted of two figurehead kings, an aristocratic council, an assembly composed of citizens over the age of thirty, and five *ephors,* who were elected annually by the assembly and were the actual rulers of the city-state. Sparta was a military oligarchy that could not afford the luxury of violent party discord or political revolution, because the *helots* (pre-Dorian inhabitants on whom the Spartan society depended for its labor) were always a menace to the security of the area.

In order to safeguard against the corrupting influence of wealth and new ideas, neither commerce nor much outside contact was allowed. Education was state-controlled and emphasized physical training and military discipline. At the age of seven, children were selected for the army and taken away from their homes to be trained in rigorous discipline. This was in contrast to Athenian education, which emphasized personal and intellectual as well as physical development. Although Athenian boys went into the army for two years at the age of eighteen, they were also trained in music, literature, and art. Women in Athens, and in most city-states, were educated in household duties only. In Sparta women had greater freedom and were given physical training; their sole purpose, however, was to breed future soldiers.

The Triumph and Decline of Athens   550-400 B.C.

The Persian Wars

The Persians under Cyrus overthrew the Lydian Empire in 546 B.C. and under Darius (521–486 B.C.) they ruled their Greek subjects with an iron hand. As a result of an Ionian revolution supported by Athens, Persia engaged in two punitive wars against Athens; the Athenians won both.

In 490 B.C. Darius invaded Greece. The Athenians were out-numbered two to one, but the Persians were defeated at Marathon, 26 miles northeast of Athens. It was during this battle that Philippides ran 140 miles to Sparta for aid.

Under Xerxes, who succeeded Darius in 486 B.C., the Persians again tried to conquer Greece. The Persian troops crossed the Hellespont in ships and then marched through Thrace, Macedonia, and Thessaly. At the battle of Thermopylae Pass, 300 Spartans and their king, Leonidas, put up a heroic but futile stand in which they were slaughtered to a man. The Athenians evacuated Athens while the Persians burned the city, but at the Straits of Salamis the Athenians won a brilliant naval victory under the leadership of Themistocles. At the battle of Plataea, a combined Greek force defeated the Persians, forced them to retreat, and liberated Ionia.

Significance of the Greek Victory

1) It meant that the development of Greek culture and political organization had triumphed over oriental despotism.

2) It gave control of the Aegean Sea to the Greeks, allowing their culture and commerce to spread.

3) It led to the growth of Athens as a great power.

The Athenian Empire and Its Downfall

The Delian League was formed in 477 B.C. by the eastern city-states as a defensive measure against the possibility of future Persian attacks. Ships and money were contributed by the member states. The League became the foundation of the Athenian empire, for in 454 B.C. the treasury was moved from Delos to Athens. Athens used force to prevent secession from the League (in 482 B.C. Lisbos attempted to revolt and as punishment its people were sold into slavery), and spent the tribute on the beautification of the Athenian state. (The buildings on the Acropolis—the Parthenon and the Propylaea—were constructed with League money.)

The Peloponnesian League was formed by Sparta and Corinth, who were rivals of Athens. Wars between Athens and Sparta began in 431 B.C. At the same time, the plague raging in Athens killed one-fourth of the population, including Pericles, and led to lawlessness and terror in the city. In 421 B.C. a peace was concluded that lasted until 415 B.C. when Alcibiades, the leader of Athens, led an attack on Sicily and lost all his forces. Persia aided Sparta and in 404 B.C. Athens surrendered, becoming a puppet state ruled by Sparta. In 371 B.C. Thebes defeated Sparta and ruled both cities until 362 B.C.

The Contributions of the Greeks to Western Civilization

Political Science

Systematic political investigation and writing was first set forth by Plato (427–347 B.C.) in *The Republic* and by Aristotle (384–322 B.C.) in *The Politics*.

Plato believed that the state's function was to satisfy the common good, and he outlined the first utopia. It was founded on justice, with workers providing the necessities of life, warriors acting as guards, and philosophers as rulers; there was no private property or family organization, and education was regulated by the state. Aristotle, the student of Plato and tutor of Alexander the Great, classified all known fields of knowledge and founded biology, formal logic, and deductive reasoning. *Politics* is the first analytical examination of politics as a social science.

Philosophy

Plato and Aristotle established the basis of Western philosophical thought.

Plato believed that ideas had an existence apart from matter. He rejected the concrete world as a source of absolute knowledge. To Plato, truth was unchanging and reality was found in abstract ideas.

Aristotle, on the other hand, denied Plato's Theory of Ideas and said that the universe was changing and dynamic. He believed that every concrete object was composed of form and matter and that neither had existence apart from the other.

History

Herodotus (485–425 b.c.), the "father of history," traveled over much of the known world attempting to find out about the past and wrote the *History of the Persian Wars*. Thucydides (460–400 b.c.), one of the ten generals of Athens in 424 b.c. and exiled for twenty years, wrote about the Peloponnesian Wars and was, perhaps, the first scientifically critical historian. He thought of history as utilitarian: one could learn from study of the past.

Drama

Tragedy and comedy, as the western world understands them, were first produced by the Greeks. Aeschylus (525–455 b.c.) introduced dialog by adding a second actor. Sophocles (497–405 b.c.) wrote some of the greatest tragedies of all time, including *Oedipus the King* and *Antigone*. There are about nineteen extant plays by Euripides (480-402 b.c.). Aristophanes (446-385) was best known as the originator of comedy.

Mathematics

The foundations of the mathematical sciences were laid by Euclid, who worked out the principles of geometry, and by Eratosthenes, who concluded by mathematics that the earth was a sphere and computed its size. By the first and second centuries before Christ, writers and encyclopedists passed on the knowledge of Greek science to later generations—Strabo in geography, Galen in medicine, and Ptolemy in astronomy.

Architecture and Sculpture

In the fields of architecture and sculpture, the Greeks reached their artistic zenith in Athens in the fifth century B.C. Moderation, proportion, and poise were the themes of such famous edifices as the Erechtheum, the Temple of Wingless Victory, and the Parthenon. Three types of columns were used—the Doric with no base and topped by a simple capital, the more elaborate Ionic with a base and spiral decorations on the capital, and the Corinthian (employed more by the Romans) with columns topped with acanthus leaves. The human body was magnificently portrayed in sculpture. Polyclitus (430 B.C.) was the first to change the traditional stance of the rigidly upright human figure by putting weight on the advanced foot. Myron's Discus Thrower is famous for its balance and restraint. The greatest of sculptors was Phidias, who carved the pediment statues and the friezes of the Parthenon.

MACEDONIAN ASCENDANCY

Philip II of Macedonia, through a policy of "divide and conquer," was able to control the disunited Greeks. In 338 B.C. he defeated the forces of Athens and Thebes.

After Philip's assassination in 336 B.C., Alexander the Great (356–323 B.C.) succeeded to the throne of his father and led his army into Asia, conquering the Persian Empire in 331 B.C. and reaching India. His ultimate aim was to create a world government, involving the fusion of races and ideas, but his empire broke up soon after his death at the age of thirty-three. Nevertheless, Alexander accomplished a great deal. Greek thought, art, and language were spread far and wide, and a new type of culture was born uniting the Greek and oriental minds.

ROMAN CIVILIZATION

The Migrations into Italy

Italic tribes, probably from central Europe, infiltrated into the peninsula between 2000 and 1000 B.C., followed by Etruscans from Asia Minor in the ninth century B.C. Greek settlers arrived in the south of Italy around 750 B.C. At the end of the sixth century B.C., Celtic tribes invaded the Po valley and destroyed the Etruscans.

Etruscan Rule

From the ninth century to the sixth cenitury B.C., the Etruscans ruled Rome but made no lasting contributions to Roman civilization. Invasions in the north and a popular revolt in Rome destroyed their power. By 509 B.C. the Roman Republic had begun.

The Roman Republic   500-30 B.C.

Two consuls elected annually held executive power and appointed members of the senate; it was this group of men who ruled the republic.

Social and political power were in the hands of the *patricians,* the wealthy landlords who constituted about two percent of the population, and this soon resulted in class struggle with the *plebians* (nonaristocrats). Gradually the plebs won legal and political rights. In 494 B.C. they were granted tribunes to protect their interests; then an assembly was created and empowered to enact resolutions or plebiscites, which could become laws if approved by the senate; and finally in 287 B.C. the Hortensian law was passed, which said that plebiscites were law without the consent of the senate. But government remained essentially aristocratic because office-holding was expensive and, unlike men in Athens, officials received no pay.

Territorial Expansion

In 509 B.C., the Romans controlled only 300 square miles of territory; by 275 B.C. they ruled southern Italy and 10,000 square miles of land.

Conquest of the western Mediterranean was accomplished between 264 and 146 B.C. In the First Punic War (264–241 B.C.), fought for control of Sicily, the Romans defeated Carthage by sea power. In the Second (218–201 B.C.), Hannibal of Carthage achieved the extraordinary military feat of crossing the Alps and reaching the Po valley with 30,000 men. He won every battle until, at last, he was defeated at the battle of Zama. After the Third Punic War (149–146 B.C.), Rome captured and destroyed Carthage, burning the city to the ground, selling its people into slavery, and plowing the land with salt in order to destroy its fertility. During these three wars Rome annexed Sicily, Corsica, Sardinia, Spain, and parts of North Africa.

Conquest of the eastern Mediterranean, including the lands of Macedonia, Greece, Asia Minor, Syria, Judea, and Egypt, was begun in 200 B.C. and was complete by 30 B.C. Almost all of what is today Western Europe was also conquered by the Romans. Caesar seized Gaul (France and Belgium); later, parts of what are today the Netherlands, Germany, and Switzerland were added; Britain was taken by Claudius in 43 A.D. By 117 A.D. the empire had reached its greatest extent.

Results of Imperialism

1) The Roman world was unified by a single imperial administration and code of law. The entire Mediterranean world could claim Roman citizenship, and a system of military roads, a single currency, and one language (Latin) united the empire.

2) The areas conquered gained by the transmission of civilization; but at home, imperialism resulted in economic decline. The small farmer, who had to leave his land to fight in the wars, was driven out of business both by wheat brought into the country from conquered lands and by the growth of the *latifundia* (large estates

owned by senators and worked by slave labor). This led to massive unemployment, and peasants flocked to the cities with no jobs and no homes. Since no one could maintain order in the city of Rome except the army and an emperor (who was always a general), the republic gave way to dictatorial rule.

The End of the Republic and the Beginning of the Empire

The Senate was unable to cope with the political, social, and economic problems caused by the acquisition of an empire. Radical reforms were necessary and benevolent despotism seemed the only solution. Roman society was deteriorating—corruption, brutality, divorce, and idleness were all on the increase.

The reorganization of the army into a professional volunteer army meant that the generals replaced the state in gaining the loyalty of their men and became independent powers able to use military force in politics. Sulla, Pompey, Caesar, Antony, and Octavian all rose to power in this way.

Marius was the first military leader in politics, but it was Caesar who officially ended the republic. The first triumvirate of Caesar, Crassus, and Pompey ruled from 60 to 50 B.C. Crassus died, and Caesar won over Pompey and established himself as dictator.

Despite the fact that Caesar rebuilt and beautified Rome, reformed the administration of the provinces, introduced the twelve-month calendar, and was a great general, politician, and statesman, his rule ended in the same way it had begun—by violence and military takeover.

The second triumvirate consisted of Antony (in Egypt), Lepidus, and Octavian (in Rome). After defeating Antony and Cleopatra, Octavian became Augustus Caesar (29 B.C.–14 A.D.), the first emperor of Rome.

Roman Literature

This chaotic era was the Golden Age of Roman literature.

During the period from 70 to 43 B.C., Cicero composed his oratorical writings, Catullus his lyric poems, and Caesar his historical works.

The era of Augustus brought tight imperial censorship but literary patronage. Virgil (70–19 B.C.), famous for his epic *Aeneid,* Horace (65–8 B.C.), famous for his satire and insight, Ovid, famous for his poetry, Livy, famous for his prose, and Seneca, famous for his tragedy, all flourished during this period.

Pax Romana   30 B.C.-170 A.D.

Two centuries of relative peace started with Augustus and lasted through the rule of Marcus Aurelius. Commence expanded; the speed of travel possible on the highways was not surpassed until about 1800; government armies patrolled and controlled the provinces. Lawyers worked on the body of legal principles known as Roman Law, which was extended to include all conquered peoples. Roman Law favored the authority of the state and argued that the source of law rested with the enlightened intelligence and not with historic custom. Justinian I (527–565), who codified Roman law many years later, said that there could be only "one empire, one law, one church."

The Fall of the Empire

There were many reasons for the gradual collapse of the Roman empire: increasing despotism and suppression of personal liberties, civil war and rebellion, and the decline of Italy as the easten provinces grew in importance. But there were three main causes for the fall.

Economic Problems

The basis of the Roman economy was agriculture. There was little industry, partly because the Romans considered trade degrading and partly because there was no need to invent laborsaving devices since all such labor was done by slaves. Over the years gold was being drained out of the country for the luxuries of the East that Roman industry failed to produce. Eventually this led to the bankruptcy of the Empire and the decline of trade. With the growth of large estates, areas of the Empire became self-sufficient. This decreased trade between parts of the Empire still further and in turn led to increased independence and self-sufficiency.

The Problem of Succession

Three conflicting sources of imperial power existed in the Roman Empire—the election by the senate, the right of inheritance, and the strength of the army. Senatorial sanction became nominal and succession by inheritance was never established absolutely. Increasingly, emperors tended to base their claim on their position as generals. As a result, Rome was often afflicted with civil war.

The Barbarian Invasions

Germanic infiltration began long before the Germanic invasions. Tribes of settlers were allowed into the Empire, particularly in Gaul, and, as the manpower of the Empire declined, German mercenaries were paid to join the army. Even some of the emperors were German.

The barbarian invasions brought the final blow. About 450 A.D., the Angles and the Saxons overran Britain and the Franks moved into Gaul. The West Goths sacked Rome in 410 and reached Spain in 420. In 476 the western kingdom fell to Odovacer and ended the Roman Empire in the West.

In the East, the Empire (Byzantium) successfully resisted the barbarians and, with its center in Constantinople, lasted another thousand years.

The Germans were totally agricultural, thus breaking down trade even further and increasing the tendency toward self-sufficiency and decentralization. They were also tribal; thus, imperial political unity collapsed as the Western Empire broke up into warring Franks, Lombards, Burgundians, Saxons, and others.

Christianity

The Origins of the Christian Faith

There are five major sources of Christianity:

1) Eastern mystery cults from which the Christians received the doctrine of grace, of an afterlife, of personal union with God (the mystical union of the Trinity), and of a universal source of power.

2) The Jews from whom they received the concept of God as a judge and of salvation based on righteousness. The Old Testament of the Christian faith is approximately the same as parts of the Torah.

3) Classical philosophy, which contributed the Platonic concept of the existence and hierarchy of ideas with the good as the highest abstraction. In Christianity the Platonic good became the Christian God.

4) Jesus of Nazareth himself, who revealed the Word of God to the Christians and offered redemption for humanity.

About 4 B.C. Jesus was born in Jerusalem in Palestine. About 28 A.D. he began to preach against the vices of his era, the selfishness of the rich, and the self-righteousness of the Jewish priests. He taught a gospel based upon love of one's fellow human, love of God, and the mercy and righteousness of God. Soon Jesus began to attract followers and when he came to Jerusalem during Passover he was greeted by crowds as the promised Messiah of the Jews.

The crucifixion of Jesus (33 A.D.) has been the subject of endless theological and historical debate. According to the New Testament, Jesus came to Jerusalem knowing that it would mean death. He was tried first by the Jewish high court that enforced the law of Moses for blasphemy and then was turned over to the Roman state for a second trial. His messianic claims were considered seditious and a threat to the stability of Roman-held Jerusalem, but it may have been the demands of the populace which led Pontius Pilate, the Roman procurator, to order his death.

Under the leadership of one of his followers, Paul, a man of

Jewish birth, Roman citizenship, and Greek culture, Christianity began to make converts, for Paul eliminated many of the narrow characteristics of the faith, making no distinction between Jew and Gentile. It was also through his teaching and those of the other disciples that Jesus was recognized as "The Christ, the son of the living God," who had died to atone for the sins of humanity.

5) A number of documents, written by early Christians, were selected in the seventh century to compose the Christian creed or the second half of the Christian Bible—the New Testament.

The Effects of Christianity

Christians taught that there was only one God and only one path to salvation. The idea of the world as a single whole was therefore important, and this sense of human unity meant that Christianity was essentially evangelistic and crusading, since all people were in need of salvation.

Christianity brought to Europe a new sense of human life, for it taught that all people were equal in the sight of God and that beauty, wealth, and power were only superficial.

The Spread of Christianity

Through the efforts of the disciples, Christianity spread from Judea throughout the Jewish communities in Athens, Antioch, Corinth, and Rome. Because of this connection with the Jews, the Christians enjoyed the benefits of their immunities until 64 A.D.

However, the attitude of the Christians toward the Roman Empire led to popular antagonism toward them. The Christians were not concerned with this world; they refused to participate in public and pagan festivals; they excluded non-Christians from their gatherings; and they were monotheistic, thus committing treason by denying the divinity of the emperor. At first accepted mainly by the discontented, the slaves, and the poor, by the second century, many educated and well-to-do people adopted Christianity, and the Roman state looked upon this as even more dangerous.

Christianity in Rome

Under Nero the early Christians were brought to trial on a

charge of arson (the burning of Rome in 64 A.D.), but they were punished in the same manner as magicians and sorcerers—by crucifixion, burning, and wild animals in the arena. Persecutions of the Christians varied from ruler to ruler and province to province, but in 250 A.D. the Emperor Decius began the first attempt to abolish the faith throughout the whole empire by issuing an edict ordering all citizens to perform public acts of worship to the gods of the state. Refusal meant death.

In 303 A.D. Diocletian renewed the persecutions. Edicts were issued calling for the destruction of Christian churches and books, imprisonment of the Christian clergy, and the worship of state gods by all persons. Nevertheless, the majority of Christians remained true to their beliefs, and finally, in 311, Galerius issued the edict of toleration.

Constantine invaded Italy in 312 and defeated the forces of Maxentius, successor to Galerius. According to legend, before the battle at Milvian bridge just across the Tiber from Rome, Constantine had a vision and ordered his men to mark their shields with a Chi and Rho, symbols for Christ. Victory followed, and from then on Constantine looked upon himself as designated by the Christian God to rule the Roman Empire. He thus transformed the empire into a Christian state, although he did not force pagans to change their ideas.

When Christianity became the state faith, it was weakened by the church's growing wealth and power and by its enslavement to the emperor, yet it was the only institution of the empire that survived the collapse of the empire in the West.

As the barbarians invaded the empire, they were converted to the faith. The most important conversion was that of the Franks under King Clovis in 496. In 590, under Gregory the Great, monks were sent to England and Ethelbert of Kent was converted. Bishop Boniface brought about the conversion of Germany in the 700s.

The Organization of the Early Christian Church

At first the Christians formed independent communities directed by an elected committee of elders (bishops) and assisted by deacons. By the third century, the organization became centralized in the hands of a single bishop from each community, who controlled the elders or the priests. The laity gradually ceased to participate in the government of the church. About this time a dispute occurred over the question of whether the bishop of Rome should be supreme or all bishops should have equal authority.

The bishop of Rome was eventually triumphant, acquiring the name of *pope* (father). Leo I (440–461 A.D.) claimed the primacy of Peter. A rival to his power, however, developed in the patriarchate of Constantinople, but the patriarchs never acquired the independence of the popes of Rome, for they were dependent on secular authority and support of the emperors. In the West, the bishops soon had a definite place in municipal administration, and as imperial authority collapsed, they became the leaders of the Romans in their contact with barbarian conquerors. By the end of the sixth century, the pope became the virtual ruler of Rome.

MEDIEVAL CIVILIZATION   500-1500 A.D.

The blows of the barbarians broke the unity of the Roman world and divided it into three parts—Byzantium, the Arabic world, and Europe. Europe was in chaos: the Germans who had overrun the Roman provinces were able to maintain political organization only on the local level. The West broke up into self-sufficient, localized villages with little contact with the rest of the world. Trade withered, cities died, and the Roman roads fell into disrepair— Europe was in the "Dark Ages." Christianity, however, continued and became the cultural foundation of the new medieval society that evolved. The church was the one remaining institution capable of providing unity. It attempted to win protection and reestablish the empire by crowning the king of the Franks, Charlemagne, emperor in 800. Although a certain degree of unity was achieved, his empire did not last. There were more barbarian invasions (Magyars and Scandinavians) in the ninth century, and by the tenth century the church as an institution was fragmented and localized and its creed was a mixture of pagan and Christian doctrines. About

1000 A.D., however, Europe began to change. It developed a system known as feudalism which provided a decentralized defensive system against further barbarian invasion; created a professional and constantly ready military protection; and preserved a minimum amount of political unity. Peace and security were thus maintained. Gradually, technological advances in the field of agriculture led to an agricultural surplus, which in turn led to the growth of towns and new commercial classes who desired independence from the feudal lords. At the same time, feudal kingdoms began to grow in power, and a secularization process commenced that led to a new era of thought and feeling known as the Renaissance. It was then that modern civilization began.

FEUDALISM

Feudalism as a Form of Political Organization

The Feudal Contract

Feudalism evolved slowly out of the dying Roman world. Its purpose was to supply a minimum of political order in a society that was falling to pieces, had no money economy, and had no defense against invaders. Feudalism was a political relationship between two men in which one gave land, and *dominium* over it, in return for military service. This arrangement was perhaps clearest in England. William the Conqueror, who invaded England in 1066, claimed all lands. He kept one-fifth as crown lands, gave one quarter to the church, and gave the rest to 170 Norman barons. In return, the barons had to provide the king with a fixed number of mounted and armed knights. The barons, in order to meet their obligations, gave their land to lesser tenants. This continued on down the line until one knight held one manor (in theory a unit of land large enough to support him and his armed retainers).

FEALTY AND HOMAGE

Feudalism was a contractual relationship in which each party was bound by certain obligations:

1) The obligations of the overlord or baron were to provide justice and protection for his vassal.

2) The obligations of the vassal were to do homage and fealty to his lord, to fight for his lord for forty days a year, to take his disputes to his overlord's court, to pay a form of taxation, and to defray certain costs such as the knighting of the lord's son, the dowry of his daughter, and the ransoming of the lord in time of war. The vassal was also expected to give advice to his lord; this later became the germ of parliamentary government, since vassals claimed a historic right to advise the king.

FEUDAL KINGSHIP

1) The essence of feudalism was anarchy. Real power rested with the baron, and kings had only nominal authority.

2) Kings were often elected by the *curia regis* (great council) of the barons and wise men of the kingdom. In 987 Hugh Capet was chosen king of France; in 911 a German king was elected and crowned emperor in 962. In England, however, there was a more centralized form of feudalism, for William, Duke of Normandy, had not been elected; he had conquered.

Chivalry

Originally, knighthood was a secular ceremony in which the vassal swore fealty to his overlord, but in the twelfth century religious vows were added, which meant that in breaking his feudal oath the knight was endangering his soul. This concept of the ethical duty of the vassal to the lord was absolutely necessary, for there was no effective means by which the overlord could compel his vassal to do his duty. Even a full-scale military attack was not always an effective means, since most castles could resist a siege longer than the normal length of military service (40 days).

Despite the chivalric code, real power rested with the individual baron in his castle who had political, military, and judicial power. This was particularly true in the German empire, which eventually broke up into almost six hundred semi-independent states recognizing only nominal allegiance to the German emperor.

Feudalism as an Economic and Social Institution

The political structure of feudalism rested on an economic structure called *serfdom*. Serfdom was an effort to regulate the labor supply in an era when there was a shortage of labor and an abundance of land. The peasant was not a slave, but he was tied to the land. The lord of the land did not own his serfs, but he did own a percentage of the fruits of the land that were the product of the serf's labor. Thus, he could claim a certain percentage of the serf's labor (often three to four days a week) as well as a percentage of his productivity in the form of wheat, and so on. The serf was at the mercy of his lord and received justice only if his lord cared to give it. It must be remembered, however, that "medieval Europe was the first complex human society not to have slavery as its economic base."

THE HOLY ROMAN EMPIRE AND THE CHURCH

In 962 the Holy Roman Empire was proclaimed. In theory, medieval Christianity was divided between pope and emperor: temporal power wielded by the emperor, spiritual authority by the pope. In actual fact, the emperor's authority was limited to Germany and northern Italy, and even in these areas he was unable to make his rule effective, primarily because of the elective nature of his office and the separatist ambitions of his feudal barons.

Throughout most of medieval history there was a long struggle between pope and emperor over ultimate authority. The great Saxon emperors (919–1039) were able to resist papal supremacy, and Otto the Great (936–973) came close to turning the pope into an imperial appointee. Imperial authority reached its height under Henry III (1039–1056). In the end, however, the popes won and, at Canossa in 1077, Pope Gregory forced Henry IV (1056–1106) to do penance and to accept papal supremacy. After Henry IV, the empire became increasingly decentralized and power was wielded by the states, each controlled by an elector. Eventually it was, as Voltaire said, neither holy, Roman, nor an empire.

Attempts to Reform and Reunify the Church

Pope Nicholas II proclaimed in 1059 that popes should be elected by cardinals. This attempt to keep the church free of secular control was not always successful.

Pope Gregory VII (1073–1085) was responsible for reforms within the church such as enforcement of celibacy and the creation of an independent and self-contained clergy centralized under the leadership of the pope. In effect, the church became a state within a state, having its own laws, government, and jurisdiction.

The height of the medieval papacy was achieved under Innocent III (1198–1216). He succeeded in establishing the papacy as the absolute moral and spiritual leader of the Christian world. The papacy was the major power in Europe; popes intervened in politics and acted as a feudal overlord to kings.

The Position of the Christian Church in the Medieval World

In 1300 Europe was primarily a religious community. Religion and the church were omnipresent. The vows between lord and vassal were religious oaths; the king was crowned by the church; merchant guilds were religious brotherhoods with patron saints; drama and art were all concerned with faith; the church was the largest landowner in all countries; and the clergy was a privileged class.

The church acted as the agency of Christ, the intermediary between God and people. It was believed that the church alone possessed the means of salvation. The church gave to people the sacraments by which they could gain God's grace—baptism, confirmation, the mass, penance (such as prayer, fasting, and pilgrimages), extreme unction at the time of death, ordination (giving the priest spiritual power the common man did not possess), and marriage.

The Church Had Three Principal Weapons with Which It Enforced Its Teachings

1) Canon law to punish crimes such as usury, sorcery, blasphemy, and perjury (the Inquisition began in the thirteenth century as a means of punishing such crimes);

2) Excommunication, the exclusion of an individual from the church and thus from the means of salvation;

3) Interdict, which was excommunication of whole groups. This was first used in 998 against France and then against John of England.

The Scholastic Philosophy

In the twelfth century new knowledge poured into Europe from the Arabs in Spain, who had studied and translated the Greek masters. The greatest of church scholars was Thomas Aquinas, who maintained that faith and reason were not in conflict with one another but led to a greater understanding of God. By "reason" he meant Aristotelian logic and precise definitions of words and concepts. The schoolmen argued that God was a rational deity, capable of being comprehended by human reason. That people could not understand their God and their universe was explained in terms of human failings. Although Scholasticism was not encouraging to the development of natural science, it gave new dignity to intellectual study, philosophies, and universities. The official doctrine of the church was never as extreme as that of some of the scholastics; it insisted that God was beyond human reason and could be accepted only on faith.

THE CRUSADES

The greatest threat to the existence of Europe seemed to be militant Islam, which had invaded Spain but was stopped at Tours in 732 by Charles Martel. Finally, in the eleventh century, Europe took the offensive after the Seljuk Turks occupied the Middle East, conquered the Holy Land, and endangered Constantinople.

The first crusade (1095) was a military success. Asia Minor

was conquered in 1097 and Jerusalem fell in 1099. Afterward, however, the political situation in Jerusalem—which was characterized by political strife, conflict between clergy and laity, and mingling of infidel and Christian—undermined the initial success.

In 1144 after the fall of Edessa to the Turks, the second crusade was organized. This was a military failure.

In 1187 Jerusalem was recaptured by Saladin and this led to the third crusade. Frederick I of Germany, who died before he could play an active part, Philip II of France, and Richard I (the Lionhearted) of England were all involved in the costly failure, which took endless lives and gained only the city of Acre.

As a result of the fourth crusade in 1201, Venice increased in power and wealth and Constantinople declined.

The remaining crusades—Childrens' in 1212, fifth in 1219–21, sixth in 1229, and the seventh in 1270—were all disastrous. The effects of increased contact with the East were, nevertheless, important and were the most significant result of the crusades.

Elsewhere Christendom was also on the move. In about 1100 the Normans won Sicily from the Arabs, and by 1250 the Christians in Spain succeeded in throwing back the Moors and gaining most of the peninsula except Granada. Although there was still to be trouble from the Ottoman empire, Europe had proved itself to be capable of resistance.

THE BREAKDOWN OF FEUDALISM AND THE MEDIEVAL WAY OF LIFE

The Growth of Towns and Trade

Agricultural innovations that created a food surplus were the vital steps in the rise of towns and trade: a heavier plow enabling the farmer to cut a deeper furrow; a horse collar enabling the horse to pull a much greater load; windmills creating a new source of power; and the three-field system of rotation whereby two-thirds of the land was cultivated and one-third left fallow were all introduced. The result was increased agricultural productivity that allowed a larger population and the means to feed urban areas.

The new towns soon demanded freedom from the control of feudal lords. Cities in Italy and the Holy Roman Empire became city-states and often small republics owing only nominal allegiance to the emperor. In England and France the feudal kings were too powerful and the towns received charters of liberties, not complete independence. This difference explains in part the creation of the national states in England and France long before those in Germany and Italy.

Trade took a long time to develop; brigands, tolls, and political instability meant high risks, high costs, and high interest rates— sometimes 30 to 40 percent. The church attempted to establish the principle of a "just price" in all commercial transactions and threatened to excommunicate those who charged usurious rates of interest.

Eventually the growth of trade, towns, and a money economy undermined the feudal structure. They offered freedom and occupation to those who wanted to escape from serfdom. The self-sufficiency of the manor was destroyed and the power of the crown increased.

The entrepreneur began to emerge during this time. Clashing with the conservative, monopolistic town guilds, he usually began as a merchant, buying and selling materials in an extensive market, and often became a banker. Two examples were Giovanni de Medici of Florence (d. 1429) and Johann Fugger (d. 1408) of Augsburg. These two families were representative of:

1) the wealth that would later finance the art of the Renaissance and the commercial revolution;

2) the existence of nonfeudal elements that could buy out the feudal nobles and even determine royal policy.

The Hundred Years' War

This war, fought between England and France during the years 1337 to 1453, made chivalry a mockery. Ultimately, it cost the English all their territory in France except Calais, which remained English until 1558, and led to the centralization of France under the French monarchy.

The Rise of the National Monarchy and the Centralization of Legal and Territorial Power

Slowly kings began to demand money instead of military service from armed knights in payment for the use of land, and they began to supervise their interests by instituting such royal officials as sheriffs and justices of the peace in England and baillis and intendants in France. In addition, they began to extend royal justice and the authority of royal courts. This led to baronial opposition: the Magna Carta in England (1215) was a document requiring King John to reconfirm the historic rights of freedom of his barons.

With the growth of towns, merchant and manufacturing classes began to turn to the king for protection and rights. Representative assemblies were called to explain the king's policy and to ask for money. This occurred all over Europe: the first Cortes met in Spain in 1188; the first Estates-General met in France in 1233; the first diet in the Holy Roman Empire assembled in 1255; and the first parliament met in England in 1295 (the Model Parliament).

The English Parliament

England was the first to develop an effective two-house system in which a very small number of great barons (about fifty to eighty) sat in the House of Lords and the lesser aristocracy (the knights of the shire) sat along with the representatives of the charter towns (the burgesses) in the House of Commons.

England was also the first to have representatives with sufficient authority to commit their constituencies to policies initiated by the king. Therefore the English kings used their parliaments, whereas the other monarchs of Europe did not.

The Unification of the State

THE BREAKDOWN OF RIVAL ALLEGIANCES

With the new wealth from taxation, monarchs were able successfully to demand the total loyalty of all subjects. This was in contrast to the medieval past in which individuals had tended to give their loyalty to their immediate overlord, to their village, to their profession, to their class, or to some combination of these.

THE GROWTH OF MONARCHY

The growth of the feudal monarchs reached a high development in England under Henry II and Edward I and in France under Philip IV. The growth of central power in both countries, however, received serious setbacks—in England, the Magna Carta and the civil wars of the second half of the fifteenth century (Wars of the Roses) and in France, the Hundred Years' War.

THE "NEW MONARCHIES"

In both France and England, monarchy was successfully revived. The "New Monarchs" came to England in 1485 with the Tudor dynasty, and to France with Louis XI in 1461. In Spain, the union of Aragon and Castile in 1469 under Ferdinand and Isabella created a unified Spanish state. In Spain however, the new sense of nationalism had religious overtones, being closely linked to Catholicism and the crusading instinct that led eventually in 1492 to the total defeat of the Moors at Granada.

The Kings of England   1066–1485

*William the Conqueror	1066–1087
William II	1087–1100
*Henry I	1100–1135
Stephen	1135–1154
*Henry II	1154–1189
Richard I (the Lionhearted)	1189–1199
John	1199–1216

*The most important are starred.

Henry III	1216–1272
*Edward I	1272–1307
Edward II	1307–1327
Edward III	1327–1377
Richard II	1377–1399
Henry IV	1399–1415
Henry V	1415–1422
Henry VI	1422–1461
Edward IV	1461–1483
Richard III	1483–1485
*Henry VII	1485–1509

The Kings of France   987–1483

Hugh	987– 996
Robert	996–1031
Henry	1031–1060
Philip I	1060–1108
Louis VI (the Fat)	1108–1137
Louis VII	1137–1180
*Philip II (Augustus)	1180–1223
Louis VIII	1223–1226
*Louis IX (St. Louis)	1226–1270
Philip III	1270–1285
*Philip IV (the Fair)	1285–1314
Louis X	1314–1316
Philip V	1316–1322
Charles IV	1322–1328
Philip VI	1328–1350
John II (the Good)	1350–1364
*Charles V (the Wise)	1364–1380
Charles VI	1380–1422
Charles VII	1422–1461
*Louis XI	1461–1483

*The most important are starred.

Science and Technology Destroy the Medieval Way of Life

Gunpowder, printing, and the compass were doubtless three of the most important inventions that contributed to the breakdown of feudalism.

1) Gunpowder, probably brought from China, meant the end of the power of the feudal castle and increased the ability of the monarch to wage war against the feudal barons.

2) Movable type, invented around 1448, put education within the reach of the masses and made the circulation of the Bible possible (the first printed Gutenberg Bible was set in 1454). Printing influenced not only the Renaissance but also the Reformation.

3) The compass, brought from China through Spain, plus geographical knowledge gained from Arab cartographers made possible the discovery of the New World during the 1500s and the commercial revolution in Europe.

A Change in the Way of Thinking — Humanism

In Italy, a new concept of humanity was evolving. A sense of the tremendous capacities and potential of every human being replaced the concept of the frail creature in need of God's grace: humanity became worthy of study in its own right. This nonreligious orientation can be seen in the development of the writing of history as opposed to theology, in secular biography in contrast to the history of saints, and in portrait-painting as opposed to scenes of religious inspiration.

Though his *Divine Comedy* is the highest literary expression of medieval thought, Dante (1265–1321) broke with tradition by writing in Italian rather than Latin and by stressing happiness on this earth.

Petrarch (1304–1374) has been called the father of humanism, because he was among the first scholars to revive interest in classical literature. His sonnets stress earthly love and physical beauty rather than the glory of God.

In painting, the new concern with things human can also be found. Although art remained more religiously oriented than other disciplines, studies of anatomy by Leonardo da Vinci, concern with perspective, and recognition of individual personalities reflect the new concept of humanity.

Machiavelli produced a handbook of statescraft called *The Prince* (1513), which was the first European secular and pragmatic treatise on politics. In many ways he diagnosed the era in which kings were breaking with the authority of the church and national states were demanding the loyalty of the people.

Humanism outside Italy

Humanism spread into north and central Europe nearly a century after it had begun in Italy. The humanism of the north has often been called Christian humanism because it blended the religious with the secular humanitarian concerns.

The greatest of all northern humanists was Erasmus of Rotterdam. He satirized the scholastic philosophers, called for the reform of the clergy, urged the translation of the Bible into vernacular languages, and placed his faith in education, reason, and laughter. His best-known work is *The Praise of Folly*.

MODERN CIVILIZATION   1500 to the Present

The beginning of modern European history is also the beginning of world history; between 1500 and 1763 Europe unified the world and, from 1763 to 1914, dominated it, spreading Western civilization to the remote corners of the globe, ruling directly Africa, India, and Southeast Asia and controlling indirectly China, the Ottoman Empire, and the Americas. Never before had one small area so influenced the rest of the world. The story of European history up to 1914, therefore, is the story of how Europe came to control the world—the unique features of religious, economic, industrial, scientific, social, and political revolutions that made it possible. The spread of these peculiar qualities of Western civilization was

Europe's triumph as well as its decline, for in giving to the rest of the world science, industry, and western political philosophies, Europe also gave the technological and ideological means to rebel successfully against domination. This is the essence of European history from 1914 to the present. In his article, "Encounter Between Civilizations," A. J. Toynbee says "Future historians will say, I think, that the greatest event of the twentieth century was the impact of western civilization upon all the living societies of that day."

EUROPE   1500–1763

The five basic movements that marked the transition to modern civilization were (1) the achievements in art, literature, and thought of the Renaissance, which emphasized the importance of humanity and this world; (2) the birth of nations, which destroyed the ideal of European political unity and gave rise to a new allegiance to the national state; (3) the discovery and exploration of the New World, which led to an economic revolution; (4) the revolt against the papacy, which destroyed the spiritual unity of Europe; and (5) the scientific discoveries and experiments of the seventeenth century, which led to technological changes that, in turn, made Europe more powerful than any other area in the world.

The Renaissance

The new attitudes led to the breakdown of feudalism and the medieval way of life and also created the conditions that made possible the Reformation and the commercial, scientific, and industrial revolutions.

The height of Renaissance individuality and art was from 1450 to 1559. Politically, the Italian city-states were in the hands of either French or Spanish armies and the peninsula was in chaos, yet it was during this era that Italy produced the greatest figures of the Renaissance.

The Men of the Renaissance

MICHELANGELO (1475–1564)

Michelangelo was a sculptor, painter, engineer, and architect. Examples of his work are the Medici tombs, the dome of St. Peter's Cathedral, the fresco on the ceiling of the Sistine Chapel, and the statues of David and Moses.

BENVENUTO CELLINI (1500–1572)

Cellini was a great artist of the Renaissance, but he is best known for his work in silver and gold.

LEONARDO DA VINCI (1452–1519)

da Vinci was the Renaissance ideal, the universal man, who experimented in mathematics, architecture, geology, botany, physiology, anatomy, sculpture, painting, music, and poetry. Two of his most important paintings are the "Mona Lisa" and the "Last Supper."

RAPHAEL (1483–1520)

Raphael was another of the great painters and artistic experimenters of the Renaissance.

Much of the literature of the period was imitative of Greek and Roman works, yet in England Sir Thomas More (1478–1535) wrote the *Utopia,* the first important book describing conditions necessary for an ideal state since Plato's *Republic;* William Shakespeare (1564–1616) attained new heights in drama and poetry; and Christopher Marlowe (1564–93) wrote *Doctor Faustus.* In Spain, Cervantes (1547–1616) wrote *Don Quixote* and Lope de Vega produced 700 dramas; in France, Montaigne (1533–92) wrote his essays.

The Reformation

Causes of the Reformation

ECONOMIC CAUSES

1) The economic practices of the merchant and the manufacturer clashed with church doctrine, especially on the issues of just price and usury.

2) The fiscal demands of the church were an economic drain on Europe, and monarchs soon came into conflict with the church over the control of ecclesiastical revenues.

POLITICAL CAUSES

The growth of the national state and the resulting clash between the church and the monarch on the question of ultimate sovereignty was another cause of the Reformation. That the Reformation was supported in Germany was due in part to the desire of German patriots to use the religious question to further the cause of nationalism at the expense of an Italian-controlled empire and church.

INTELLECTUAL CAUSES

The vast intellectual revolution was an influential factor in the revolt against the Roman Catholic church. The humanism of the north, religious sincerity combined with secular and humanitarian concerns, played an important part in the desire to find a way of attaining salvation without renouncing life or depreciating the importance of the individual.

FAILURE WITHIN THE CHURCH

1) The conflict between the officially sanctioned ideals of society and actual practice increased the desire for reform. Ideally the church was universal and concerned with things of the spirit, yet in practice it was more involved in worldly affairs. The popes used their spiritual authority to interfere in the political affairs of European nations and depleted national currencies through rents, tithes, and other monies sent to Rome. In addition, moral laxity, the sale of clerical positions (simony), and other unethical practices were condemned by the reformers.

2) From 1378 to 1417 there were two popes, one at Avignon in France, the other at Rome. Known as the Great Schism, this caused doubt about the divinity of the papal office and weakened the authority of the church.

Martin Luther

The Reformation began when Martin Luther (1483–1546), professor of Bible at the University of Wittenberg, posted his *Ninety-five Theses* directed against the selling of indulgences. Luther claimed that the source of spiritual authority was not the church but scripture and the individual reader. The church, he said, was not necessary to salvation, because only faith could save man. This is the famous Lutheran doctrine of "justification by faith alone." After the Diet of Worms in 1520, when he refused to recant, Luther was excommunicated, and Lutheranism was formed in defiance of the Roman Catholic church.

The Spread of Protestantism

A social and political reformer, Zwingli (1485–1531) broke with Luther and in Zurich, Switzerland, formed many of the ideas later to be associated with Congregationalism.

John Calvin (1509–1564) articulated the theory of predestination and the doctrine of the elect. He was the father of the French Huguenots and the Puritans. John Knox founded the Presbyterian church in Scotland but differed little from Calvin in theology.

Henry VIII of England broke with the Roman Catholic church in 1534 because the pope refused to allow him to divorce his wife. Although Henry broke without first adopting any essential Protestant principles, eventually the forces of reform prevailed and the Anglican or Episcopalian church developed.

Protestant Theology

Although Protestants split into Anglicans, Presbyterians, Congregationalists, Huguenots, Baptists, Methodists, Lutherans, and so forth, each sect had certain beliefs in common:

1) All rejected papal authority and the supernatural character of the priesthood.

2) All replaced Latin with the *vernacular* (language of the country) and accepted the authority of the Bible.

3) All believed, with various interpretations, in justification by faith alone.

4) All rejected purgatory, transubstantiation, and obligatory confession.

5) All reduced the number of sacraments, usually to two or three.

The Catholic Counter-Reformation

At the Council of Trent, sitting irregularly in the mid-1500s, the Roman Catholic church was reformed and rejuvenated. In Spain the Renaissance spirit had not taken over, and it was here that Catholicism became most militant. St. Ignatius Loyola founded the Society of Jesus (the Jesuits), a monastic order dedicated to active participation in world affairs and acting as a missionary force throughout Asia and the Americas. The Inquisition was first established in Rome to enforce conformity throughout the Catholic world.

The Wars of Religion

From the middle of the sixteenth century to the middle of the seventeenth century, wars raged in Europe; these were often referred to as the "wars of religion," although in most cases the motives were basically political and economic.

France from 1562 to 1595 was engaged in a civil war between Catholics and Huguenots.

War broke out in Germany (the Holy Roman Empire) in 1546 between Lutheran princes and the Emperor, Charles V. In 1555 the Peace of Augsburg was concluded, recognizing the religious stalemate and giving each individual prince the right to decide whether his territory would be Lutheran or Catholic.

From 1568 to 1609 (or 1648, the Treaty of Westphalia), the Netherlands fought for independence from Spanish control. This was, in part, a religious war between Catholics and Calvinists, but it was also an economic conflict.

In 1588 England defeated its Catholic rival when the Spanish Armada was destroyed by a combination of English seamanship and "Protestant weather."

The Thirty Years' War (1618-1648) was, in part, a German civil war fought over the Catholic-Protestant issue and constitutional issues and, in part, an international war involving most of the continental states, including Sweden. The Peace of Westphalia finally terminated this bloody struggle, recognizing again the religious stalemate in Europe.

In 1642 England's Civil War began, and although the Puritans ruled for a decade, the religious issue was not resolved until 1660, when Charles II and the Anglican church were restored.

The Commercial Revolution

The Discoveries and Explorations

Spain and Portugal led the way in explorations of the New World primarily because they were both politically united.

In 1498 the Portuguese Vasco da Gama rounded the Cape of Good Hope and discovered a new route to Asia, the source of valued commodities such as spices and silk. This new route reduced considerably the cost of Eastern goods because it circumvented the expensive overland routes, with unloadings and reloadings and dependence upon Arab middlemen. Portugal was soon making profits of ten to thirty times the cost of goods in the East Indies.

In 1492 Columbus, sailing under the flag of Spain, thought he had reached the Indies. In reality he had landed in the New World. In 1520 Magellan and a Spanish expedition sailed into the Pacific, discovering the Philippines and circumnavigating the globe. Hernando Cortez of Spain conquered the Aztecs of Mexico between 1519 and 1521, and Francisco Pizarro destroyed the Incas of Peru in the 1530s. Between 1500 and 1660 Spain received 18,600 tons of silver and 200 tons of gold from the New World alone.

Inflation, wars in Europe, corruption, the *hidalgo* spirit (the belief that the gentleman did not work with his hands), internal disunity, and the growth of the northwestern European states led to the decline of Spain and Portugal. The defeat of the Spanish Armada in 1588 was proof that the Iberian powers were no longer masters of the seas.

The Commercial Revolution and Its By-products

The commercial revolution was the change from a self-sufficient town-centered economy to a capitalistic nation-centered economy.

1) The entrepreneur was the first to break with the town and the guild.

2) The putting-out system or the domestic system of rural household industry was another step in the breakdown of the restrictive practices of towns and guilds. The system applied mainly to the manufacture of cloth. Cottagers received the wool and made it into thread or cloth, and the finished article was then collected by an agent who paid the cottager for his work.

3) The first industry to change to a capitalistic economic base was the cloth industry, but certain other concerns were capitalistic from their formation (mining, book printing, and armaments all required large outlays of capital and mass production).

A monetary revolution was one of the by-products of the commercial revolution. With the discoveries of precious metals in the New World, their value declined, prices rose, and inflation resulted. The monetary crisis affected all levels of society:

1) Monarchies soon quarreled with their parliaments over demands to increase taxation. This led to constitutional crises and, in turn, to the rise in royal absolutism throughout Europe (except in England, where Parliament triumphed).

2) In the country the position of the peasant improved and the feudal lord lost ground. (In Eastern Europe the reverse occurred.)

Mercantilism was a direct result of attempts by states to acquire more money. Kings endeavored to assist merchants, force people to work, and create a favorable balance of trade. Companies with exclusive trading monopolies were formed; the most famous were the East India Companies founded by the British in 1600, the Dutch in 1602, and the French in 1664. It was through these companies that northern European nations began to encroach on the Spanish and Portuguese monopolies in the New World and the Far East. These companies enabled England, France, and the Netherlands to establish their commercial empires.

New wealth and prosperity in Europe from the profits of trade led to changes at home, for the commercial aristocracy began to rival the landed aristocracy in social and political power.

The Scientific Revolution of the Seventeenth Century

The essence of science is the union of reason with observation and experimentation: the reasoned postulate or working hypothesis is accepted only as long as it accords with the observed data.

The Men of Science

NICHOLAS COPERNICUS (1473–1543) OF POLAND

In 1543 Copernicus disputed the Ptolemaic theory, which stated that the sun revolved around the earth. He advanced a heliocentric theory that was mathematically simpler than the geocentric.

JOHANNES KEPLER (1571–1630) OF GERMANY

Kepler carried Copernicus' theory further and discovered that the orbits of the planets were ellipses.

GALILEO GALILEI (1564–1642) OF ITALY

In 1609 Galileo built one of the first telescopes, confirmed the Copernican theory, and suggested that planetary bodies were made of the same substance as the earth. Galileo's work threatened existing philosophy and theology, and he was forced to recant by the Roman Catholic church.

FRANCIS BACON (1561–1626) OF ENGLAND

Bacon formalized the inductive method of acquiring knowledge and emphasized the usefulness of knowledge.

RENE DESCARTES (1596–1650) OF FRANCE

Descartes, the developer of coordinate geometry, believed that nature could be reduced to a mathematical formula and advanced "the principle of systematic doubt."

ISAAC NEWTON (1642–1727) OF ENGLAND

In 1687 Newton published the *Mathematical Principles of Natural Philosophy* showing that all motion could be described by the same mathematical formula. Gravitation was the force that moved matter. Until Einstein, his theories remained unshaken, but now it has been proved that they do not apply to subatomic structures.

The Effects of Scientific Discovery

Although the effects of the new science were important in navigation, in the development of calculus, in the science of map-making, and in warfare, the psychological effects were the most profound, for mankind could no longer claim to be the center of the universe. The universe was seen as natural, understandable by natural laws which could also be applied to society. Two of the most important political thinkers of the era were Thomas Hobbes (1588-1679), who wrote in justification of absolutism, and John Locke (1632-1704), who supported constitutionalism.

The Rivalry among the European Powers

With the explorations, commercial exploitation, and wealth of the New World came further conflict on the European continent as well as in the colonies.

At first the Dutch were the most successful in the competition with the Iberian peninsula for overseas control, for they had an efficient merchant ship (the flyboat) that was able to challenge Portuguese control in the East Indies and to establish Dutch interests in the New World. The Netherlands monopolized whaling in the Arctic and trade in the Baltic. Temporarily (until 1664) they controlled New Amsterdam (New York), the northeast coast of Brazil (until 1654), and the Cape of Good Hope in South Africa. But the Netherlands became entangled in a series of wars with France and England, and lacked the manpower and resources necessary to compete with mightier neighbors.

England and France became supreme in the commercial rivalry of the eighteenth century, in part because of their high industrial production and in part because of the fact that their governments were organized on a national scale. Over half of England's trade became transoceanic, whereas only one-third of France's trade was involved overseas—the other two-thirds were in Europe and the Near East.

The decline of the Netherlands and the Iberian powers left England and France to fight for the mastery of the New World and to maintain a balance of power on the European continent.

Conflicts for control of North America, India, and eventually Africa, as well as for supremacy at home, were fought in 1679–89 (King William's War) and 1701–13 (the War of the Spanish Succession or Queen Anne's War). The Peace of Utrecht in 1713 partitioned the Spanish empire: Belgium, Naples, Sicily, and Milan went to the Austrian Hapsburgs, Sardina to the Duke of Savoy, and Minorca and Gibraltar to England. England also acquired Nova Scotia, Newfoundland, and the Hudson Bay area from France.

Then followed the War of the Austrian Succession (King George's War) in 1740–48 and the Seven Years' War in 1756–63. Although there were eight years between them, they were essentially the same war, for their causes were the same:

1) a struggle between Britain and France for colonies, trade and mastery of the seas;

2) a duel between Prussia and Austria for power in Central Europe.

The War of the Austrian Succession did not destroy the Hapsburg empire, but it was forced to surrender Silesia to Prussia. This doubled Prussia's population and more than doubled its resources, thus upsetting the balance of power in Europe. An about-face in allies occurred after this war: in 1756 England and Prussia became allies, and France and Austria joined forces—Louis XVI was married to Marie Antoinette, one of the daughters of Maria Theresa.

The Seven Years' War began in America but soon spread to Europe. On the continent, it was merely another war of partition. France was losing the war and in 1761 made an alliance with Spain; nevertheless England and Prussia prevailed. The situation overseas solved what might have been an endless struggle on the European continent. The Marquis of Montcalm was finally defeated by General James Wolfe at Quebec, and Joseph Dupleix was defeated by Robert Clive in India. The deciding factor in the colonies was the superior strength of the British navy. After the Treaty of Paris was signed in 1763, England was in control of North America and India, supreme on the seas, and, hence, the most powerful nation in the world. France surrendered the St. Lawrence Valley and all territory east of the Mississippi in America. Spain lost Florida to the British, and France lost all her fortifications in India.

The Kings of France   1483–1774

Charles VIII	1483–1498
Louis XII	1498–1515
*Francis I	1515–1547
Henry II	1547–1559
Francis II	1559–1560
Charles IX	1560–1574
Henry III	1574–1589
*Henry IV (the first Bourbon)	1589–1610
Louis XIII	1610–1643
*Louis XIV	1643–1715
Louis XV	1715–1774

The Kings of England   1485–1760

*Henry VII (the first Tudor)	1485–1509
*Henry VIII	1509–1547
Edward VI	1547–1553
Mary	1553–1558
*Elizabeth I	1558–1603
James I (the first Stuart)	1603–1625
*Charles I	1625–1649
The Commonwealth	1649–1660
Charles II	1660–1685
James II	1685–1688
William and Mary	1689–1702
Anne	1702–1714
George I (the first Hanoverian)	1714–1727
George II	1727–1760

*The most important are starred.

The Kings of Spain   1479–1788

*Ferdinand and Isabella	1479–1516
Philip I (the first Hapsburg)	1516–1519
*Charles I (as Emperor, Charles V)	1519–1556
*Philip II	1566–1598
Philip III	1598–1621
Philip IV	1621–1665
Charles II	1665–1700
Philip V (the first Bourbon)	1700–1746
Ferdinand VI	1746–1759
Charles III	1759–1788

The Hapsburg Emperors   1440–1765

Frederick III	1440–1493
Maximilian I	1493–1519
*Charles V	1519–1556
Ferdinand I	1556–1564
Maximilian II	1564–1576
Rudolf II	1576–1612
Matthias	1612–1619
Ferdinand II	1619–1637
Ferdinand III	1637–1657
Leopold I	1658–1705
Joseph I	1705–1711
Charles VI	1711–1740
Charles VII (not a Hapsburg)	1742–1745
Francis I (husband of Maria Theresa)	1745–1765

*The most important are starred.

EUROPE   1763-1914

During the period 1763 to 1914, Europe became the leader of the world. The explanation of how this was possible can perhaps be found in three revolutions, economic, scientific, and ideological, which changed the face of Europe during the eighteenth century and made it physically and spiritually able to dominate the rest of the world. The transmission of these three revolutions to the rest of the globe was Europe's gift to the non-Western world. In 1914 seven European countries held 115 colonies (Britain had 55, France 29, Germany 10, Belgium 1, Portugal 8, the Netherlands 8, and Italy 4) representing a population twice as large as the mother countries and an area almost three times as great. The economic revolution in part inspired the seizure of these colonies, and the scientific revolution, which was an integral part of the economic and industrial change, made it possible to exploit them, to penetrate them, and to subdue those who objected. At the same time ideological changes were taking place: the development of constitutional government, the rise of nationalism, the growth of liberalism, and the development of socialism and communism. But imperialism and nationalism brought conflict to the states of Europe and, ultimately, world war.

Economic Change and Revolution

Commercial capitalism produced new wealth. Huge private fortunes were amassed and governments became more susceptible to the wishes of the wealthy. When rich merchants and financiers withdrew their support, collapse of the government was almost inevitable; this was in part the cause of the French Revolution of 1789.

The Industrial Revolution

According to R. R. Palmer in *A History of the Modern World,* "the process of shifting from hand tools to power machinery is what is meant by the industrial revolution." In the nineteenth century the use of the steam engine and power-driven machinery led to modern industrialization.

The country that led the way was Great Britain, beginning around 1770. There were two primary reasons why the industrial revolution occurred first in England:

1) Improvements in agricultural production (such as fertilization, crop rotation, and scientific breeding of livestock) and the private ownership and consolidation of land (known as "enclosure") had led to a sharp rise in productivity. Improved productivity provided food for the new industrial cities; changes in land ownership produced the necessary mobile labor supply for the new factories.

2) The new markets opened up by the control of India and the Americas combined with growing prosperity at home to produce an insatiable demand for manufactured goods.

Technological improvements were first introduced in the textile industry. In 1773 John Kay invented the flying shuttle, which increased the productivity of the weaver; in 1769 Richard Arkwright introduced the water-frame (spinning machine), and, more important, in the 1780s used the steam engine (first invented by Newcomen in 1702 and improved by James Watt in 1769) to drive the spinning machines.

1) The use of steam necessitated the growth of factories. Since the machine could no longer be taken to the labor supply, labor had to be brought to the machine.

2) The demand for raw cotton led to further inventions: Eli Whitney, an American cotton grower, invented the cotton gin in 1793.

3) At the same time, the wood shortage increased the demand for coal and led to the Darby and the Bessemer processes for the large-scale manufacture of steel.

By 1815 Great Britain had become the workshop of the world. Production in coal rose from 6 million tons in 1770 to 57 million in 1861 and iron production rose from 50 thousand to 3800 thousand tons. After 1870, however, Great Britain faced competition from the major nations of the continent. This competition was in part responsible for the grabbing of the colonies and the scramble for concessions throughout the world, since the great industrial powers were anxious to control markets for their goods.

The Scientific Revolution

Science went hand in hand with economic change and industrialization. In the sixteenth and seventeenth centuries, great progress had been made in physics, chemistry, and mathematics; in the eighteenth century, chemistry was further advanced by Antoine Lavoisier's writing and by Joseph Priestley who isolated oxygen in 1755; but the nineteenth century witnessed the greatest advances in scientific discovery.

In 1830, Sir Charles Lyell did extensive study on the formation of the earth. George Mendel worked in the field of biology and made significant contributions to the principles of heredity in the 1860s. William Wiendt made contributions in psychology in 1872; and Louis Pasteur did important work in medicine—the germ theory of diseases—in 1864. The first modern psychoanalysis was introduced by Sigmund Freud in 1895; and in the field of natural sciences, Charles Darwin's theory of evolution, *On the Origin of Species,* was to have an astonishing influence.

Effects of the Scientific and Industrial Revolutions

International

The industrial and scientific revolutions made possible the exploitation of the globe—railroads, canals, steamships, and armaments made the European mobile and dangerous. Medical science made existence in the tropics possible.

Another international effect was the economic interdependence of the world. The entire globe became a single market which was dependent upon the fluctuation of prices and demand in other parts of the world.

Social and Economic Effects in Europe

At home, the population boomed (in Great Britain and Ireland, it tripled from 1750 to 1850) and new cities rose (steel centers such as Birmingham, shipbuilding in Newcastle, cotton works in Man-

chester). The rapid urbanization and industrialization caused un-
heard-of problems: overcrowding, unparalleled squalor, an incredible sanitation problem, and the breakdown of traditional family life
and authority. Eventually the factory towns improved and became
more desirable than the rural slums. The very concentration of
people ultimately led to the organization of labor unions and
the gradual improvement of living and working conditions.

Another serious effect of the industrial revolution was technological unemployment. The cotton gin, for example, reduced the
number of people required to separate the cotton from fifty to eight.

In the long run, the total increase in wealth led to a general
rise in the standard of living. For example, increased industrial
productivity meant that child labor was no longer an economic
necessity and that an educated labor force was required.

Political Results of the Revolutions

Industrialization meant a further increase in the power of the
bourgeoisie.

At the same time, it led to the rise of labor as a political force.
Ferdinand Lassalle formed the German Socialist party in 1848. In
1871 it had 124,655 votes out of 3,892,160; by 1874 it won 351,952
votes out of 5,190,254. Louis Blanc organized the first socialist party
in France around the same period. The British working class was
more advanced and more successful in forcing collective bargaining
on their employers, and thus they were slower in forming workers'
political parties. The British Labour Party was not formed until
1900 and was less socialistic than those on the continent. The new
ideology of socialism was one of the intellectual and cultural results
of the industrial revolution. (See pp. 100–01.)

The Urge to Imperialism

After 1870, European expansion, which had been going on for
four hundred years, was referred to as imperialism. There were several causes of the scramble for possessions and concessions.

Economic Factors

Surplus capital looking for overseas investment, an expanding population, the need for raw materials, and the urge to find markets for industrial goods contributed to imperialism. Competition with rival European nations and the desire for protection by tariff were other factors.

Political Factors

Rivalry among the European powers eventually led to a projection overseas of inter-European rivalries. Strategic reasons, such as the need for naval bases and coaling stations, were also involved. The newly unified Germany and Italy contributed to the acute competition for power on the European continent.

Personalities Influenced the Demand for Colonies

Without the encouragement of such men as Disraeli, prime minister of England from 1874-80, England might never have entered the scramble. Norway, for instance, whose merchant fleet was second only to Britain's, did not take part. Germany, whose industrial capacity was greater than France's in the 1880s, did not enter the race until the beginning of the twentieth century because of Bismarck's influence.

Political Revolution   (1642-1815)

The Great Rebellion and the Glorious Revolution

The first step in the radical change in relations between those who governed and those who were governed was the Great Rebellion of 1642. Thus, the first country to develop effective representative government was England.

In 1642 conflict between king and parliament led to civil war. At issue was the right of parliament to tax and to control governmental policy. Charles I argued that government initiative rested solely with the king and that parliament was just an advisory body. By 1646 the parliamentary forces were victorious; in 1649 the monarchy was overthrown and Charles was executed.

The period from 1649 to 1660 is called the Commonwealth. It was an era of extremism in politics and religion, culminating in the theocratic dictatorship of Oliver Cromwell.

In 1660 the monarchy was restored; Charles II returned from exile. Parliament's right to raise money was recognized, but the complete victory of parliamentary government and control was not reached until the Glorious Revolution (1688–89), when James II was overthrown and replaced by William and Mary. Although England remained a monarchy in name, it was in fact an aristocratic oligarchy until 1832, ruled by parliament, which in turn was controlled by men of landed wealth.

The Age Of Enlightenment

The Age of Enlightenment took place during the five decades that preceded the French revolution. It was a period of scepticism toward tradition, secularization of thought, a new attitude toward government, a view of the state as the main instrument of welfare, and a profound belief in reason. It had its origins in the works of men like Locke, Bacon, and Descartes, but the heart of the movement was in Paris. The most momentous work of the era was the *L'Encyclopédie* or the "reasoned dictionary," edited by Diderot and d'Alembert; it contained a compilation of much scientific and historical knowledge.

VOLTAIRE, MONTESQUIEU, AND ROUSSEAU

Three writers symbolized the enlightenment—Voltaire, Montesquieu, and Rousseau—and their writings were to have a profound influence on the fate of the French nation.

1) François Voltaire (1694–1778) wrote for the new bourgeois middle class. His main concern was freedom of thought. Around 1740 he became a crusader, preaching religious tolerance and crying out against bigotry, censorship, and the power of the clergy. He held England up as an example of freedom of thought and religious liberty. He attacked superstition and was the first to present a secular concept of world history.

2) Baron de Montesquieu was an aristocrat and his most famous work, *The Spirit of Laws* (1748), advocated constitutional monarchy but conceded that types of government were dependent upon climatic factors as well. He developed an intricate system of separation and balance of power (and, in part, inspired the American constitution). He too regarded England as a model of good government.

3) Jean Jacques Rousseau (1712-1778) was unlike either of his contemporaries. He preached that society was corrupt and that man should return to the state of nature from which he came. In his *Social Contract* (1762) he argued that governments were formed by an agreement among the people themselves and that every person should feel that he belonged to the state, since it was a product of the "General Will." This theory contained within it the seeds of democracy, nationalism, and totalitarianism. His novel *Emile* pointed out the artificiality of aristocratic life and had an immediate effect on his society.

ENLIGHTENED DEPOTISM

Enlightened depotism was a characteristic of the age of enlightenment.

1) It was rational, reformist, and despotic and was caused in part by the writings of the philosophers but also by the wars of the eighteenth century (1740–48 and 1756–63), which increased the need for efficient government.

2) In Spain and Naples, Charles II was an enlightened despot.

3) In Austria, Maria Theresa pushed through internal consolidation and began to attack serfdom; but it was her son Joseph II (who came to the throne in 1780) who abolished it, established equality of taxation and punishment, and permitted toleration of all religions. But in so doing he also built up a police state.

4) In Prussia, Frederick the Great held the title of "enlightened" because of his intellectual and musical abilities. He revised the law and established public education and religious freedom; but he maintained a highly stratified society.

5) Catherine II, the Great, of Russia had a more tenuous claim to enlightened depotism. Nevertheless, she affected a measure of legal codification and consolidated the government apparatus.

6) Enlightened despotism never really flourished in England, but during this era the thirteen American colonies revolted, and American leaders were a part of the enlightenment. Thomas Paine not only wrote *The Crisis* (propaganda for the American Revolution) but also *The Rights of Man* and *The Age of Reason.*

7) Although France was the home of enlightened ideas, its government was one of the most clumsy and inefficient, and this in part explains the downfall of Louis XVI.

The American Revolution   1775–1783

The American Revolution for independence had significant repercussions in Europe. It overburdened the French treasury and thus contributed to the French revolution. It led to revolts for independence and civil rights throughout Europe. It changed the great nations' attitudes toward their colonies, and England, particularly, began to accept the fact that some day all colonies would be independent. It had a decisive influence on the French Revolution. The French Declaration of Human Rights and the constitution of 1791 were in many ways drawn from American models.

The French Revolution   1789–1815

CAUSES

The philosophers' writings, the new ideas about the nature of humans and society, and the new attitudes toward authority were significant causes.

The political and tax structures of France were imbalanced. The bourgeoisie had little voice in a government which was still controlled by the prestige classes (nobility and church). The tax burden rested most heavily on those least capable of paying, and people of great wealth, both noble and bourgeois, escaped their fair share of taxation.

There was general dissatisfaction with the church in France, for it was a political power and the greatest of all landowners.

A rising proletariat (wage-earning group), although not class conscious, provided a necessary ingredient.

The property system was outmoded, for it remained in large part feudal.

The financial bankruptcy of the government precipitated the crisis, although it probably was not a cause in itself. The government's efforts to tax the nobility led to the summoning of the Estates-General (parliament) and initiated the revolution.

THE REVOLUTION

A meeting of the Estates-General was called for the spring of 1789; it had last met in 1614. There were to be three hundred representatives from the first estate (the church), three hundred from the second estate (the nobility), and six hundred from the third estate (which included the upper bourgeoisie—lawyers, bankers, etc.—as well as artisans, peasants, and working men). The issue immediately arose as to whether the estates should sit and vote by estates or as one assembly. The third estate demanded a National Assembly, consisting of all three estates. This led to a two-month struggle in the beginning of July in which the third estate, joined by some members of the other estates, created their own National Assembly.

The battle happened to coincide with severe depression in the countryside, and, on July 14, 1789, a Parisian mob marched on the Bastille to get arms and to demonstrate in favor of the National Assembly. This saved the assembly, for Louis, instead of disbanding it, was shocked into turning the government over to it.

THE REVOLUTIONARY GOVERNMENTS

On August 4 serfdom was abolished and the nobility voluntarily gave up their feudal rights. On August 26 the Declaration of the Rights of Man and Citizen was announced, declaring that "Men are born and remain free and equal in rights" assuring "liberty, property, security and resistance to oppression," and promising freedom of thought, religion, due process of law, taxation only by consent, and separation of powers of the government.

But in September there were disputes over the powers of the

king; insurrection and violence followed. Then the National Assembly moved to Paris and soon fell into the hands of the more radical elements (the Jacobins).

In 1791 a constitutional monarchy was formed. This lasted ten months. The Girondists had precipitated war between France and most of Europe by threatening to export the revolution to the other European monarchies. The government failed to win the support of the masses. It gave the franchise to only fifty thousand landed men.

In 1792 the National Convention was organized, but it lacked control and also failed.

Then, under the guidance of Robespierre, the Reign of Terror began in order to bring about a "republic of virtue." It was due in part to the pressure of war and the acute economic crisis. Seventy percent of the forty thousand who died during the Terror were peasants and laborers. Robespierre died the way he had governed—by the guillotine.

The Directory, under conservative bourgeois control, was placed in power, followed in 1799 by the Consulate.

THE SPREAD OF FRENCH REVOLUTIONARY IDEAS

The three great principles of the French Revolution were liberty (the right of self-determination and self-government), equality (the destruction of all forms of feudal privilege and the equality of all men before the law), and fraternity. French ideas (often enforced by French armies) produced revolutions in the Netherlands, Milan, Naples, Spain, Switzerland, and many of the states of Germany. Though most of these revolutions were in the name of liberty, most ended up in dictatorship. Fraternity tended to deteriorate into nationalism. The only effective ideal was equality, which led to the abolition of aristocratic privileges and the end of serfdom.

Napoleon (1769–1821) was the man most responsible for the spread of the ideas of the French Revolution. He assumed control of the French government first as consul in 1799 and then as emperor in 1804.

At home Napoleon's rule was that of an enlightened despot, standardizing taxation and codifying laws.

He then set out to impose a political unity on the European continent by conquest. The results were to force reforms upon the conquered areas. Religious tolerance was enforced, serfdom was abolished by decree, and guilds were destroyed.

Territorially, the height of the empire was between 1810 and 1811. Napoleon controlled the entire European continent except the Balkan peninsula. Nationalist movements sprang up in protest to Napoleonic rule and became both anti-French and antiautocratic. In England hatred of France and all French ideas eclipsed the misery of industrialism and delayed political reform for thirty years, until 1832. The British fought against Napoleon's Continental System, which was intended to destroy Great Britain by halting commerce and shipping and which aimed at developing the economy of continental Europe, particularly France. In Spain, reaction to Napoleon led to guerilla warfare. In Germany, it made the people acutely conscious of their German origins (nationalism).

Napoleon's power was ended as a result of military defeats in Russia (1812) and at the Battle of Waterloo (1815). The conservative Congress of Vienna, led by the Austro-Hungarian Prince Metternich, attempted to reconstruct the map of Europe prior to the French Emperor's conquests. It did not take into account the new wave of nationalism that had been spurred by Napoleon's dream of a pan-European empire.

Political Revolution   (1815-1914)

Liberalism
Liberalism was essentially the doctrine of individualism in which:

    1) The state was viewed as the aggregate of all individuals.

    2) It was assumed that individuals were responsible for themselves.

    3) All restraints that impeded individuals from realizing

their full capacity and achieving their own self-interest should be abolished.

In government this meant the extension of suffrage and freedom of speech, press, and religion. In economics this meant the doctrine of laissez-faire (no interference on the part of government in the economic life of the nation) and free trade. In philosophy it meant the insistence upon the dignity of humanity and the contention that every minority should have the right to express its ideas.

Liberalism was first introduced in Great Britain. The Reform Bill of 1832 constituted a revolution; suffrage was extended and the seats of parliament were redistributed so that the new business class was as well represented as the old aristocracy. From 1832 to 1872, social reform legislation was passed. Slavery was abolished (1833), a poor law was adopted (1834), local government was modernized, parliamentary votes were allowed to be publicized, and the army and the civil service were open to competitive examination. In 1847 the Ten Hours Act was passed, limiting labor of women and children in industry to ten hours a day. In 1846 the Corn Laws, which kept up the price of food, were repealed, and suffrage was further extended in 1868.

Socialism

Socialism was an offshoot of industrialism and the problems it created. It also developed as a result of new attitudes toward the state and what it should do for the individual.

The early socialists regarded an economic system based on private property, free enterprise, unrestrained competition, and the liberal doctrine of the absolute freedom of all individuals—even to starve to death—as unjust. They all favored communal ownership of the means of production and rejected the doctrine of laissez-faire. They demanded both social and economic equality.

Robert Owen (1771–1858) experimented at New Lanark, Scotland with a cooperative community scheme. In France, Saint Simon advocated a planned society, and the journalist Louis Blanc wrote against the private capitalist and organized the first socialist party. After 1830 socialism spread rapidly, and in France and Germany it became more violent than in Great Britain. All these early socialist movements tended to be highly idealistic, moralistic, and pacifistic, and they were branded by Karl Marx (1848), the father of communism, as utopian and "unscientific."

Although based on theories of surplus value, communism was a branch of the socialist movement and differed essentially in demanding violent overthrow of the existing conditions. (See pp. 183–85).

Nationalism

Modern nationalism was in part the product of the nineteenth century. The French revolution fostered it. The mass army, the indoctrination that every person was a citizen with a duty to serve the state, and the loyalty to the state rather than the estate (class or group) were ideas of the revolution. Nationalism also sprang up as a resistance movement to French imperialism and Napoleonic dictatorship.

Nationalism is an emotion characterized by intense loyalty to the nation, no matter the kind of government; unreasoning love of the land; and extreme pride in the cultural and economic achievements of the state.

In the nineteenth century nationalism was a force for the unification of states whose peoples had been divided into a multitude of states.

THE UNIFICATION OF ITALY

Giuseppi Garibaldi (1807–82) with his one thousand Red-shirts seized Sicily and then invaded the Kingdom of Naples in 1860. He planned to march on Rome and unify Italy by conquest, but he was forestalled by Cavour.

Count Camillo Di Cavour (1810–61), prime minister of the Kingdom of Sardinia, whose liberalism had been influenced by the British, drove the Austrians out of Lombardy in 1859. In 1860 other areas in central Italy joined Sardinia by plebiscite. In 1861 the Kingdom of Italy was proclaimed under the ruler of Sardinia,

Victor Emmanuel. Venetia was then acquired by war with Austria in 1866; the papal state and the city of Rome were not absorbed until 1870.

THE UNIFICATION OF GERMANY

Two German states, Austria and Prussia, had ambitions to unify the German states of the defunct Holy Roman Empire (abolished in 1806 by Napoleon). William I (King of Prussia 1861–88) had grandiose plans of a united Germany, but it was his prime minister, Otto von Bismarck (1815–98), who was really responsible for the expansion of the Kingdom of Prussia into the German Empire.

In 1864 Bismarck gained Schleswig and Holstein from Denmark by military action. In 1866 he went to war against Austria and forced Austria to give up its rights to interfere in the states of Germany.

The ability of Prussia to combine the German states into a unified Germany dominated by Prussia was in large measure a result of prestige. When it became clear that France was trying to prevent German unification, Bismarck tricked France into declaring a war in which it was overwhelmingly defeated. In the wake of military triumph the German Empire was proclaimed in 1871 at Versailles. During the Franco-Prussian War, France lost Alsace-Lorraine and was forced to pay an indemnity of $1 billion.

By the beginning of the twentieth century, however, nationalism was no longer a unifying force, for it had spread into east and central Europe. Here it could only succeed by destroying the old regimes of Austria-Hungary and the Ottoman empire.

THE AUSTRO-HUNGARIAN EMPIRE

The Austro-Hungarian Empire was a collection of peoples in central Europe brought together by the accidents of history and ruled over by the Hapsburg monarchy. The three main national divisions of the empire were the Germans of Austria, the Magyars of Hungary, and the Slavic peoples of Serbia. The history of the empire in the nineteenth century was primarily that of the efforts of the monarchy to prevent these three elements from forming separatist movements and destroying the empire. By 1914 the days of the Hapsburg empire were numbered; separatist movements, particularly in Serbia, were becoming more desperate, and the monarchy was becoming increasingly irresponsible in its handling of the minority elements within the state.

As Europe moved into the twentieth century, nationalism became more and more militant and jingoistic, breeding misunderstanding and hatred among the states of Europe, and leading to the horror of World War I.

Nationalism also spread to the four corners of the globe in the wake of European imperialism and liberal ideas.

The Governments of Europe   1760 to 1918

The Monarchs of England

*George III	1760–1820
George IV	1820–1830
William IV	1830–1837
*Victoria	1837–1901
Edward VII	1901–1910
George V	1910–1936

Party Government in England

Liberal Party—Gladstone		1868–1874
Conservative—Disraeli		1874–1880
Liberal	—Gladstone	1880–1885
Conservative—Salisbury		1885–1886
	—Gladstone	1886
	—Salisbury	1886–1892
	—Gladstone	1892–1894
	—Rosebery	1894–1895
	—Salisbury and Belfour	1895–1905
Liberal	—Campbell-Bannerman	1905–1915
	—and Asquith	
Coalition	—Asquith	1915
	—Lloyd George	1916–1922

The Government of France

Louis XVI	1774–1792
First Republic	1792–1804
The Terror, 1793–94	
The Directory, 1795–99	
The Consulate—Napoleon, 1799–1804	
The Empire—Napoleon I	1804–1814
The Restoration—Louis XVIII	1814–1824
—Charles X	1824–1830

*The most important are starred.

July Monarchy—Louise Philippe	1830–1848
Second Republic	1848–1852
Second Empire—Napoleon III	1852–1870
Third Republic	1870–1940

The Government of Spain

Charles III	1759–1788
Charles IV	1788–1808
Joseph (Bonaparte)	1808–1813
Ferdinand VII	1813–1833
Isabella II	1833–1868
Alfonso XII	1868–1885
Alfonso XIII	1885–1932

The Government of Austria-Hungary

*Maria Theresa	1740–1780
*Joseph II	1780–1790
Leopold II	1790–1792
Francis II	1792–1835
(the end of the Holy Roman Empire—1806)	
Ferdinand I	1835–1848
Francis Joseph	1848–1916
Charles I	1916–1918

The German Government

William I (in 1871 he took the title of Emperor; in 1861 he had become King of Prussia)	1871–1888
Frederick III	1888
William II	1888–1918

The Italian Government

Victor Emmanuel II	1861–1878
Humbert I	1878–1900
Victor Emmanuel III	1900–1946

*The most important are starred.

Europe Overseas

The impact of Europe was in no way limited to the export of its ideas and technology; Europeans were exported in such unprecedented quantities as to make previous migrations pale in comparison. Hundreds of thousands of Europeans went to the New World in the wake of the five great maritime empires of the sixteenth to eighteenth centuries—the English, the Spanish, the Portuguese, the Dutch, and the French. But it was in the nineteenth century that the migration became a deluge. In all, 51,600,000 people left Europe between 1846 and 1932: 18 million from Great Britain, 10.1 from Italy, 5.2 from Austria–Hungary, 4.9 from Germany, 4.7 from Spain, 2.2 from Russia, 1.8 from Portugal, 1.2 from Sweden, and 3.5 from the other countries. They went to the four corners of the earth: 34 million to the US, 6.4 to Argentina, 5.2 to Canada, 4.4 to Brazil, 3.5 to Australia–New Zealand, 1.6 to the British West Indies, and 852,000 to South Africa.

In some areas the racial balance was left untouched, and European control was maintained by relatively few people—the Portuguese in Angola and Mozambique, the English in India and Ceylon. Elsewhere there was a mixture of racial stock—in Brazil and Spanish America, for example.

In North America (Canada and the United States) and in Oceania (Australia and New Zealand), however, Europeans tended to replace the indigenous populations to varying extents. The Europeanization of these areas ranged from systematic or indirect *genocide* (destruction of an entire race) as in the cases of the aboriginal population of Tasmania and many American Indian tribes to cultural understanding and integration as in the cases of the Maoris in New Zealand and the various ethnic groups of Hawaii.

Australia

Settlement

As a result of American independence, the British looked elsewhere for suitable areas to export the undesirables of society (between 1717 and 1776, 30,000 convicts had been sent to North America). In 1769 Captain Cook explored the east coast of Australia and sent home a favorable report recommending colonization. In 1788, 717 English convicts arrived in Sydney (New South Wales). Free settlers followed in 1793. As more settlers and more convicts reached Australia, the continent was opened up. In 1829 Perth was established in the West; in 1834 South Australia and Victoria were founded.

Growth

The primary occupation of the settlers was sheep raising, and Australia's population grew very slowly. In 1840 the last convicts were brought to Sydney. By then the free population greatly outnumbered them. In 1853 transport of convicts to Tasmania ended and in 1870 the last were brought to West Australia.

In 1850 the population was only 400,000 people, but the discovery of gold in 1851 contributed to the rapid growth of the country. Within ten years the population had doubled; Victoria grew from 77,000 in 1851 to 540,000 in 1861. In those ten years the Victoria fields produced 80 million pounds worth of gold.

Not only was the continent wealthy in gold but it was also rich in zinc, copper, and coal. With the invention of refrigerated ships in 1882, meat exports increased immensely. By 1900 the population had reached 4 million.

Government

In 1842 Sydney (New South Wales Colony) was granted a large measure of autonomy, and in 1850, by the Australian Colonies Government Act, the colonies were given virtual self-government. They could elect their own legislatures, could alter their constitutions, and could determine their own tariffs, subject to British confirmation. All the colonies were granted internal autonomy—Queensland, Victoria, South Australia, North Territory, North Australia, and New South Wales. In 1870 the British withdrew their troops from the continent, and in 1901 Australia was given dominion status within the British empire.

New Zealand

Settlement

Unlike Australia, which had few and scattered aborigine tribes, New Zealand was inhabited in the north and south by about 200,000 Maoris (Polynesians) who were socially advanced and warlike. Although permanent settlements were established by convicts who escaped from Australia and the islands were frequented by missionaries who wanted to establish a Christian Maori culture (with very little success), immigration to New Zealand was slight. It was not until 1837, when E. G. Wakefield promoted a New Zealand Association, that settlement really began.

In 1840 the British government reluctantly assumed responsibility for the settlers' protection. In the Treaty of Waintangi, England promised to protect natives' rights and grant them lands. In exchange the Maoris acknowledged Britain's sovereignty. England, however, did not always fulfill its part of the agreement, and this led to several wars with the Maoris.

Government

In 1852 a constitution granted the provincial government's control over most affairs, but New Zealand remained essentially disunited and as yet unable to cope with Maori uprisings. In 1875 New Zealand was unified under one government; in 1907 it was given dominion status within the empire.

The "Great Britain of the South"

New Zealand became the pioneer in labor reform, in social legislation, and in democratic government. In 1855 Victoria Colony introduced the secret ballot; in 1893 women's suffrage, workmen's compensation, and old-age pensions were granted.

As in Australia, meat refrigeration for transoceanic shipment led to prosperity, for sheep now were raised for meat as well as for wool. New Zealand also became a great dairy nation. In 1861 gold was discovered, and the population rose from 100,000 to 250,000 by 1870. Then followed a period of depression and serious efforts to encourage immigration. The result was that the white population rose to about 772,000 in 1901.

Australia and New Zealand in the Twentieth Century

Australia and New Zealand very clearly indicated their allegiance to Great Britain in both world wars. With the military decline of Great Britain, both countries have looked to the United States for defense and, somewhat reluctantly, are dependent upon American support. Although essentially still British in culture and sentiment, Australia (much more so than New Zealand) began to change after World War II as new immigrants came from Eastern and Western Europe. The absolute exclusion of Asians ended in the 1970s.

EUROPEAN CIVILIZATION   1914 TO THE PRESENT

The twentieth century has been given many names. It has been referred to as the Age of Industrialism and the Age of Science and Technology. It has been described by José Ortega y Gasset as the era of *The Revolt of the Masses,* the century of the masses. Others have called it the "Age of the Political Collapse of Historic Europe," for in 1900 Europe ruled over 20 million square miles of non-European territory with one-half billion people, and guided the destinies of countless others. By 1918 Europe was declining; by 1945 it was no longer the greatest power in the world; and a decade later its colonies had dwindled to almost nothing. Another perspective of the period is that of R. Aron, who has called the years following 1914 *The Century of Total War,* and it is around this concept that the other epithets for the twentieth century are best understood and organized.

The war that broke out in 1914 was in some ways more significant than the second one of its kind in 1939. The First World War, lasting over four years, was a momentous and unique situation in human history. War was no longer confined to the battlefield; the total energies of all the citizens of the nations involved were mobilized. The war was a war for survival, fought to the point of exhaustion. It was unbelievably destructive, destroying four empires and wiping out a decade of Europe's growth. It was fought on the land and above it, on the sea and under it; war for the first time in history had become "three-dimensional." The Second World War, lasting six years, was the same kind of war, fought in part for problems that were left unsolved or were caused by the First World War. The period between the wars has in fact been referred to as the "Long Armistice."

Near the end of World War II, nuclear energy was discovered; two atomic bombs were dropped on Hiroshima and Nagasaki in Japan. The advent of atomic warfare has added to the totality of war, making war for the first time in history absolutely destructive. During the twentieth century, the Soviet Union and the United States rose as the greatest powers in the world, yet Western Europe, taken as a whole, surpassed both of them in population and in economic potential. The economic and political future of Europe remains in doubt, but there are signs that a "United States of Europe" may evolve, establishing another force in the balance of power.

Causes of World War I

Nationalism
Nationalism was the primary cause of the First World War. (See p. 101.)

Colonial Conflicts
At the beginning of the twentieth century there were six major collisions in the colonial field. Three of these led Europe to

the brink of war because the nations involved felt that their national interests were at stake.

1) Britain and France clashed over the question of Egypt in 1898. This was resolved when the two nations agreed to a monopoly of British interests in Egypt and French interests in Morocco.

2) Britain clashed with the Boers in South Africa, which led to the Boer War of 1899. (See pp. 410–11.)

3) Britain and Russia argued over control in Persia. Here again a solution was reached by agreement. Persia was divided into two spheres of influence in 1907.

4) Russia and the Austro-Hungarian Empire were at odds over dominance in the Balkans. Austria-Hungary controlled most of the area, but Russia was supporting nationalistic revolts among the Slavs in hopes of gaining access to a warm-water port. This was the particular crisis that led to the World War in 1914.

5) Russia and Japan struggled over which would be the dominant power in Manchuria and Korea. This was solved by war between the two countries in 1905, in which Japan was victorious.

6) Germany and France clashed over Morocco, and this conflict almost precipitated war in 1911.

European Conflicts

Another standing feud between France and Germany was Alsace-Lorraine, taken from France in 1871; much of French policy after 1871 was aimed at getting the lost province back. The growing Anglo-German naval and commercial rivalry, which threatened England's control of the seas, was another European conflict that led to war. The conflict between Austria-Hungary and Serbian nationalism precipitated the war.

The System of Alliances

One of the most important elements in projecting local conflict into total war was the European system of alliances.

Germany, to prevent France from regaining Alsace-Lorraine, entered into a defensive alliance with Austria-Hungary in 1879 (the

Dual Alliance). In 1882, Italy joined the alliance for its own expansionistic reasons, making it the Triple Alliance.

In 1890, Germany failed to renew Bismarck's Reinsurance Treaty tying Russia to Germany, and France saw an opportunity to break out of isolation. In 1894 France achieved its objective through a military alliance with Russia. In 1904, England and France entered into an understanding, and in 1907 England and Russia did the same, thus creating the Triple Entente. In 1914 the great unsolved question was whether England would in fact go to war if Germany invaded France or Russia.

Each crisis tended to tighten the bonds between the members of the two main alliance systems; by 1914 the balance of power was so perfect that neither side could risk the defection of any member of the alliance. This gave great influence to the secondary partners, Austria-Hungary and Russia, just at the moment when both countries were becoming increasingly irresponsible.

The Sarajevo Crisis Turns into War

On June 8, 1914 a young Bosnian revolutionary, a member of a Serbian nationalistic secret society, assassinated Archduke Francis Ferdinand of Austria-Hungary. The Austrians decided to end once and for all the Slavic separatist movements led by Serbia, which were tearing the empire apart. Before commencing any action against Serbia, they obtained from Germany the promise of support no matter what the consequences would be. Austria then sent a drastic ultimatum that demanded Serbian submission. The Serbs, after receiving encouragement from Russia, rejected the ultimatum, and Austria declared war. Russia mobilized its army on both the German and Austrian frontiers. Germany, receiving no answer to its demand for Russian demobilization, declared war on Russia on August 1 and on France two days later. (France had also mobilized on August 1.) Russia dragged France into the battle and Austria-Hungary dragged in Germany.

The Germans, pleading military necessity, marched through

neutral Belgium, and, on August 4, England declared war on Germany. The invasion of Belgium created a justification for Great Britain's entry, but the reasons were much more involved than this. Britain did not dare let one great power control the Low Countries and did not dare interpret the buildup of German naval power as anything but a threat to its supremacy of the seas.

World War I

The First Year

The war, which lasted four years and three months, started out as a European war. It was essentially a war among the great powers over imperialistic and nationalistic interests. No one thought it would last longer than six months. At the beginning of the war, the Central Powers had the advantage of superior organization and strategic position.

The Von Schlieffen Plan, devised by the German chief of staff, was based on the concept of a "swinging hammer" in which both a northern and a southern army would strike France simultaneously. As conceived, it would strike quickly, before Russia could mobilize. In six weeks the Germans had reached the Marne. There they were stopped.

Under the leadership of General Joffre, the French and British threw back the Germans. By the end of September, 1914, the two armies were facing each other along a line that extended across northern France and a corner of Belgium. The weapons of defense (the machine gun, barbed wire, and the trench) were superior to those of offense, and Europe settled down to prolonged trench warfare.

The Central Powers were stronger than the Allies on land, but the British fleet was almost complete master of the seas by the end of 1914.

European War Becomes World War

During late 1914 and into 1915 the battle lines expanded:

Italy, originally a part of the German and Austro-Hungarian alliance, joined the Allies. The Ottoman Empire and Bulgaria sided with the Central Powers, while Rumania opted for the Allies.

On both the eastern and western fronts the war was deadlocked. There were four major battles in 1915 in which the Allies attempted to break through enemy lines but with no success. In 1916 the battles of Verdun and the Somme were costly and futile.

On the sea both Germans and British were cautious (although in 1915 the British liner *Lusitania* was sunk without warning by submarines). The Battle of Jutland in May 1916 confirmed the supremacy of the seas by the British. It was then that the Germans decided to cut off supplies to the island country by waging unrestricted submarine warfare against any and all ships headed toward Britain. They knew that if they did, they risked the United States' entry into the war, but the German high command was overpowered by political pressures in Germany demanding victory.

1917—The Crucial Year of the War

In November the Bolsheviks came to power in Russia, and in December the Russians surrendered to the Germans, liberating German troops for a final drive on the Western front.

The decision to wage unrestricted submarine warfare was part of the reason for the entry of the United States on April 6, 1917; it was sufficient to tip the scales in favor of the Allies, not just in manpower but, more important, in the production of iron and steel. The entry of the US also changed the ideological flavor of the war, for President Wilson declared that the war was a fight for democracy, and for a lasting peace, based on his fourteen points, which included "open covenants openly arrived at," freedom of the seas, reduction of tariffs, disarmament, and self-determination of nations.

Victory

At the end of 1917, with the use of detection devices, depth charges, mines, and the convoy system, the British regained control of the seas.

By the winter of 1917, German airplanes were bombing

London but were more of a nuisance than a menace. The final German offensive came in March–July 1918. It was successfully repelled by the Allies under the command of General Foch. By July the Germans were in full retreat.

On September 30, 1918, the Turks surrendered; on November 3, 1918, the Austrians surrendered; and on November 9 the German Kaiser, Wilhelm II, was forced to abdicate. Two days later the armistice was signed, having been postponed to correspond with the eleventh hour of the eleventh day of the eleventh month.

The Cost of the War

The number of dead has been placed anywhere from 10 to 13 million, with 20 million wounded. The total direct cost of the war is figured at about $180,500,000,000 and the indirect cost at $151,612,500,000. Four great empires disintegrated as a result of the war: the Russian, Ottoman, Austro-Hungarian, and German.

The Treaty of Versailles and the New Balance of Power

There were two basic tasks that faced the victors of the war: settlement with Germany and redrawing of the political boundaries of Europe.

The German Problem

The settlement in Germany immediately led to disagreements among France, the U.S., and Britain. The French demanded total demilitarization of Germany; they would have preferred dismemberment. Premier Clemenceau was under great pressure to achieve military occupation of the Rhine. Both Prime Minister Lloyd George of England and President Wilson of the United States objected. They finally agreed on a settlement:

1) Alsace-Lorraine was returned to France.

2) Germany was not to fortify the left bank of the Rhine, and a demilitarized zone was established on the right bank.

3) Germany was to have a reduced army of 100,000 and was forbidden to build up its military potential. Its navy was also limited

in size, and submarines and military aircraft were prohibited.

4) The coal of the Saar was to go to France for fifteen years with the territory administered by the League of Nations. In fifteen years there was to be a plebiscite to decide the nationality of the Saar.

5) Germany was stripped of all its colonies.

The amount of reparations was never decided but Germany was to begin paying immediately. It was really signing a blank check.

In order to persuade the French to agree to these terms, the United States and Britain promised to sign treaties to protect France. There was, however, a catch: Britain would not aid France unless the United States did, and the U.S. Senate refused to ratify the military guarantee and treaty; therefore Britain was not under obligation and France felt it had been tricked. The defection of the United States destroyed one of the main props of French security and was in part responsible for the next war.

The Reshaping of Eastern Europe

The new states of Poland, Lithuania, Czechoslovakia, Estonia, Latvia, and Yugoslavia were created. Austria lost three-quarters of its area and three-fifths of its population; Hungary gave Rumania more territory than it was allowed to keep.

Evaluation of the Peace

PRO

The aim of the settlement was idealistic, but unfortunately the concepts were rarely achieved. The peoples of Europe did achieve greater self-determination than ever before, and the organization of the League of Nations was an important step.

CON

The peace failed at general disarmanent. The colonial settlements under the mandate system were important from a theoretical point of view but failed to protect the colonies. Self-determination was in many cases impossible, as in Yugoslavia, but the principle was never applied to Germany. The Tirol, which was German in population, went to Italy; the Polish corridor cut Germany in half and caused repercussions; and the western fringe of Czechoslovakia was almost solidly German. The Treaty of Versailles left France feeling that it was not strong enough; the United States not interested in carrying out its commitments in Europe; England with a guilt complex, believing that Germany had been mistreated; and a resentful and bankrupt Germany.

The League of Nations

The League was weak from the beginning: the United States refused to join, and few of the great powers were ever members at the same time.

The League did, however, have specific functions and made some progress between the two world wars:

1) To prevent war: This was obviously unsuccessful except in the case of the Greeks in Bulgaria in 1925. Here it was a matter of two small powers.

2) Disarmament: The only progress made in disarmament was in reducing naval strength at the Washington Conference in 1922, and this was accomplished outside of the League.

3) Social and economic fields: The League had its greatest success in the fields of international communications, health, protection of children, and so forth. Every one of the specialized organizations of the League of Nations was carried over into the United Nations.

The basic problem with the League was that it lacked executive power and did not have the force and authority to back up its goals.

The 1920s

The 1920s were generally a period of optimism; democracy seemed to have triumphed; the League of Nations had had some success, naval armaments had been reduced at the Washington Conference in 1922; peace had been assured by the Locarno pacts in 1925 and the Kellogg-Briand Pact in 1928. As late as 1928 most people were assured and self-confident, yet by 1935 there was a general feeling of despair. Totalitarianism had triumphed in Yugoslavia, Poland, Italy, Germany, and Hungary. Hitler had defied¹ the Versailles Treaty in 1935. In 1931 the Japanese aggression in Manchuria could not be stopped by the League of Nations, and in 1935 Italian aggression in Ethiopia was successful. Part of the explanation for this change was the world depression that began in 1929 and did not run its full course until the beginning of World War II in 1939.

The World Depression

Postwar Economic Conditions Led to Depression

The European economy was in a state of dislocation after World War I; overseas markets were lost (the U.S. began trading heavily with Latin America, and Asia turned to Japan for goods), and inflation of currency was aggravated by a production slowdown.

The breakup of the old empires in central Europe caused economic nationalism. Each new country raised its tariffs, expanded its industry, and wanted to sell but not to buy.

Europe's wealth had declined as a result of the war. Before the war Great Britain had been the largest creditor nation in the world, but during the war it had had to liquidate 25 percent of its overseas investments. After the war, New York became the financial capital of the world.

The position of the United States was more to blame for the depression than any other single factor.

1) Between 1913 and 1924, gold poured out of Europe to the United States (it had half the total supply in the world by 1924). Almost 50 percent of the total war debt was owed to America, and it insisted that the loans be paid in full. Britain and France, in order to pay their debts, had to collect reparations from Germany, but in turn Germany had to borrow the money from the United States or export at a time when tariffs were highest.

2) The world, therefore, depended upon the financial stability of the United States, yet the situation in the U.S. was anything but stable. More was imported than exported, and there was extreme economic imbalance within the country (although industry was booming, agriculture was seriously depressed). Although productivity increased, wages did not rise proportionately; poverty and agricultural depression cut the domestic market. The American banking system was incapable of weathering the storm when it did come.

International financing was unstable. Only short-term loans had been given by the United States, and they were subject to sudden recall. This made capital investment susceptible to whims and prone to easy panic, and it meant that when the United States' market collapsed, the world market did also.

The Depression

On October 24, 1929 the American stock market crashed. The repercussions in Europe were tremendous and immediate. Loans were withdrawn, prices fell, producers of primary goods lost their markets, and workers lost their jobs, further reducing the demand for goods.

Between 1929 and 1932 world production fell by 42 percent and world trade by 65 percent. By 1930 unemployment had increased by 50 percent, and in 1931 came the complete collapse of the financial structure of Germany and Austria—and total depression.

The Consequences of the Depression

The depression resulted in further intensification of economic nationalism. (Great Britain, for instance, abandoned free trade, which it had maintained since 1846.) To meet the economic crisis, more and more power was vested in the state, which in countries with no democratic tradition often led to totalitarianism and dictatorship.

Internationally, it furthered ill feeling among nations, and governments were so concerned with their own affairs that they ignored what was happening in other countries. The colonial world suffered as the demand for raw materials dropped, and their demands for independence grew louder.

In Germany it was directly responsible for the rise to power of Hitler.

The Failure of Democracy and the Rise of Fascism

Italy

The postwar government of Italy lacked experience and was plagued by economic problems; unemployment of servicemen, the decline of tourism, and rural overpopulation all contributed to dissatisfaction. In 1920 came a crisis: workers in Milan seized the factories and the leftists took over the government. But the leftist revolution failed primarily because most of the leftists were orthodox Marxists who were willing to sit and wait for the revolution and also because they were overconfident.

In reaction against the left, industrialists and the army combined. In the election of 1921, this new party known as the Fascist Party carried only twenty-five seats, whereas the leftists captured 122, but the following year the Fascists took over the government.

THE RISE AND RULE OF MUSSOLINI

Benito Mussolini (1883–1945), originally a socialist, broke with the party over the socialist position that the world war was a capitalist-imperialist war and should not be supported by the proletariat. In 1919 his fascist movement began, drawing support primarily from ex-soldiers but also from property owners and intellectuals. These groups had nothing in common except supernationalism and fear of communism. In 1922, Mussolini threatened that "either the government will be given to us or we shall march on Rome." The government resigned and King Victor Emmanuel III turned control over to Mussolini as prime minister.

Order was immediately restored, strikes were suppressed, and unemployment was eased by the building of public works. The government took over industry and labor; the corporate state had been formed. Between 1925 and 1928 all political parties except the Fascist were dissolved, property of dissenters and Communists was confiscated, and communications were taken over by the government.

Germany

THE WEIMAR REPUBLIC

Germany was given a democratic government after the war. The republic was bicameral in structure and based on universal suffrage with proportional representation. The president was elected by the people and he in turn appointed the *chancellor* (prime minister), who was generally the head of the largest party. The power of the president was excessive, for in case of emergency he could dismiss the chancellor and rule by decree, and the judiciary had no power of declaring a law or a decree unconstitutional.

The postwar problems faced by the government could not be solved. The most serious problem was reparations: Thirty-three billion dollars was finally demanded in 1921, but protectionist tariffs in other countries meant no markets for Germany, and no markets meant no money, and no money meant no payment of reparations. By 1923 the Germans could no longer pay reparations, and the French retaliated by invading the iron-rich Ruhr.

1) The Dawes plan in 1924 was one of the first attempts to deal with reparations on an international scale. The decision that reparations be based on world economic conditions and Germany's prosperity eased the situation and set the stage for German recovery.

2) The Young plan in 1929 set reparations at a definite sum to be paid off by 1988.

3) From 1924 to 1930, Germany paid nearly $2 billion in reparations. By 1930, however, reparation payments went into a state of limbo, and they were terminated at the Lausanne Conference in 1932.

Inflation destroyed the German economy. In 1920, one dollar was worth 60-70 marks; by November 1923, the dollar was worth 4,200,000,000,000 marks. This almost destroyed the middle class in Germany by wiping out their savings and investments.

The Weimar Republic failed to win the support of the people, for it was associated from the very beginning with Germany's defeat and it had been forced to sign the Versailles Treaty.

In foreign policy, the republic had the most success. In 1922 the first break in Germany's isolated world position occurred when Germany signed the Treaty of Rapallo with Russia. In 1926 it joined the League of Nations, and in 1928 Allied occupation forces evacuated the Rhine. But the government could not achieve what the Germans demanded—the reannexation of the Saar, a union with Austria, and the end of the Polish corridor.

HITLER AND THE NAZI TAKEOVER

An essential reason for the success of fascism in Germany was Adolf Hitler (1889–1945). Frustrated during early life, he experienced a sense of comradeship and dedication during World War I. In 1920 he formulated his program for National Socialism. This program was a blend of supernationalism, state control of industry, and the offering of the Jews and Communists as the scapegoats for all Germany's troubles and defeats. He demanded the union of all Germans, the revision of the Treaty of Versailles, living space for Germany's surplus population, and a homogeneous state. He listed the three main threats to Germany as Communists, Jews, and democracy. The driving force behind the Nazi revolution, however, was not the program but Hitler himself, who was ruthless, paranoiac, and magnetic, having the ability to use propaganda and to sway the masses. After his unsuccessful coup in Bavaria in 1923, Hitler was jailed, and it was then that he wrote *Mein Kampf,* a clear statement of his intentions. The official title of the party Hitler organized was the National Socialist German Workers' Party; both party and state were means of enhancing the "German Volk" and upholding the superiority of the "Ayran Race."

The depression was an important factor in the Nazi rise to power. In 1929, 1 million out of 20 million were unemployed in Germany; by 1933 there were 6 million unemployed. By 1930 the Nazis had become the second largest party; by 1932 they nearly controlled the Reichstag (parliament). The Communists also gained during this period, and part of the reason for the Nazi gain was middle class fear of a leftist revolution.

During the depression economic recovery programs could not

be passed through the Reichstag because the government was composed of a coalition of conservative and socialist parties. The president used his special power, and parliamentary democracy had in fact ceased even before the Nazis came to power. Between 1930 and 1933, intrigue, party maneuvering, and backstairs politics—along with the skillful use of propaganda and hard work—increased the strength of the Nazis tremendously. Hitler promised a revitalized Germany, jobs for all, and the end of Communism and the Jews. By July 1932, the Nazis had become the largest party; in August, Hitler was offered the vice-chancellorship in a coalition government, which he refused. At the beginning of 1933 Hitler was appointed chancellor.

In February 1933, Hitler moved against his most powerful rival, the Communists. On February 27 the Reichstag was burned, and this was blamed on the Communists. Civil liberties were suppressed and all Communist deputies were arrested. The next power Hitler destroyed was the trade unions. In May 1933, the unions were brought under control by the use of Hitler's storm troopers. The only party that had any strength was the Social Democrats, and in May 1933, their assets and properties were seized by the Nazis; in June the party was outlawed. By July the Nazi party was the only legal one. In March 1933, all state governments were taken over by force and governors were made directly responsible to Hitler. Never before in German history had there been such a degree of political centralization. In August 1934, von Hindenburg died and Hitler became both chancellor and president of the Third Reich, which had been established in 1933. As president, he also became commander-in-chief of the armed forces.

Hitler carried through his plans without any serious opposition. It may be characteristic of the twentieth century that masses can be easily controlled by a shrewd and ruthless leader and that totalitarianism is a phenomenon of mass civilization. Hitler made good his promises; public works created new jobs. The rearmament (1935) further stimulated production. The Nazis, however, were not interested in economic stability for its own sake. Hitler's domestic policy was a step to the ultimate aim of making Germany strong enough to go to war once more.

Spain

During World War I Spain had been neutral, and war had brought tremendous industrial expansion and prosperity; but with the end of the war prosperity ebbed and discontent increased. In 1923 King Alfonso gave in to demands that General Primo de Rivera head the government. Rivera was an absolute dictator: jury trial was suspended, censorship of the press was enforced, the *Cortes* (parliament) was dissolved, and only textbooks approved by the church were permitted. Rivera did, however, build public works and clean up the bureaucracy. The intellectuals rose up against Rivera's educational and censorship policies, and King Alfonso was forced to ask for Rivera's resignation in 1930. General Berenguer, who then took over the government, reversed many of Rivera's policies, and when censorship was ended, the monarchy was flooded with criticism. Alfonso finally had to give in to public opinion, and in April 1931, he allowed elections to be held.

The republican parties (the leftists) were victorious, Alfonso left the country, and Manuel Azana became prime minister until 1933, when the tide swung to the right. In the 1936 elections, however, a coalition of socialists and Communists under the popular-front policy were victorious, and Azana once again became prime minister.

FRANCO AND THE CIVIL WAR

A group of army officers (the Spanish fascists known as the Falange) revolted in 1936 against the program of the Spanish popular front. When neither side was immediately victorious, each received aid from the outside. Italy and Germany aided General Francisco Franco and Russia aided the legitimate republican government. Despite official neutrality on the part of Great Britain, France, and the United States, a certain amount of private aid and manpower was given the republicans. However, not even with Russia's contributions did this aid match the massive military support sent by Italy and Germany. Spain was useful to Germany as a testing ground for its tanks and particularly its air force, where for the first time the mass bombings of cities was used as a strategic method of warfare. In March 1939, the surrender of Madrid to Franco ended the Civil War.

Fascism in Spain meant rule by the army, the Catholic church, and the upper classes. In 1939 Spain withdrew from the League of Nations. Although Spain remained neutral during World War II, it was an important base of supplies for Germany.

The Long Armistice: Basic Causes of World War II

Nationalism

All the causes of the war can be tied to the rise of super-nationalism—the glorification of the state. World War I had heightened jingoism in all the countries of Europe, and Hitler's Germany became the most extreme example.

Imperialism

So called have-not powers—Germany, Japan, and Italy—demanded "living room" for their overcrowded populations and raw materials for their new industries, and Japan wanted a chance to compensate for its sense of inferiority. The British had access to eighteen out of twenty-five essential raw materials in their own empire, whereas Germany had only four and the Italians and the Japanese had almost none. This economic situation was further complicated by mounting tariff barriers and the collapse of world trade after 1930.

Revisionism

Discontent with the Versailles Treaty, and particularly with the boundary settlements, also led to war. Germany was extremely resentful, Hungary was dissatisfied, and even Italy felt badly treated, not getting as much of the alpine Tirol as it had wanted.

The Failure of the League

The failure of the League of Nations was not so much a cause as it was a reflection of the other causes. It failed to protect all nations, disarmament negotiations floundered, and it could do nothing about Japan's aggression in Manchuria, Germany's breaking of the conditions of the Versailles Treaty, or the Italian invasion of Ethiopia.

Division in the West

Without division in the West, Hitler might have been stopped before he got any farther than the Rhine. But France and Great Britain were at odds. The British felt that Germany's eastern frontiers were of little vital significance, that concessions should be made to Germany, and that a strong, prosperous Germany was an asset to English industries. France wanted desperately to keep the status quo of the Versailles Treaty and to keep Germany poor and militarily weak.

The Road to War

1930–1936

Hitler's actions led directly to war, and although Germany's guilt as far as starting the First World War is questionable, there is no doubt about the Second World War. Indirectly, the refusal and/or the inability of England and France to stop Hitler during the early years of his career (the policy of appeasement) also contributed to war.

In October 1933, Hitler withdrew from the disarmament conference and the League of Nations. In 1935, when Germany gained the Saar by plebiscite, he announced that Germany had no more territorial interests in the West. Then in March 1935, he boldly announced the creation of an air force and obligatory military service. In June a naval agreement was signed with Great Britain, although it was a violation of the Versailles Treaty.

In 1935 Mussolini attacked Ethiopia, and although the West imposed economic sanctions, oil and coal—the two vital military commodities—were not included. By May 1936, Ethiopia was overrun. The League had proved worthless. The failure of the League to stop Italy as well as Japan was the last bit of encouragement Hitler needed. In March 1936, he sent his troops into the demilitarized section of the Rhine. In October the Rome-Berlin Axis was signed; in November the Anti-Comintern Pact was signed with Japan, and the following November a similar pact was signed with Italy.

Appeasement

UNION WITH AUSTRIA

In February 1938, the Austrian Nazis were admitted to the Austrian cabinet—after pressure had been exerted. In March, Hitler presented an ultimatum to Austria that the pro-German minister of interior take over the government and that two-thirds of the seats go to Austrian Nazis. A few days later union with Germany was announced. France and England did nothing, even though German occupation of Austria made a mockery of France's military alliance with Czechoslovakia, for French troops could no longer reach the country should it be threatened by Germany.

In April, Britain concluded an agreement with Mussolini, recognizing Italy's position in Ethiopia and pledging mutual friendship.

THE SUDETEN CRISIS

The Sudeten area of Czechoslovakia was the center of the armaments works and the fortifications of Czechoslovakia. It contained, however, 3.5 million Germans and only 300,000 Czechs. The Sudeten Nazi party began agitating for an autonomous province. Czechoslovakia tried to make concessions, and Hitler concentrated his troops on the border. The crisis subsided temporarily when Britain objected, but in September, 1938, Hitler suddenly demanded self-determination for the Sudetens. Four days later, Britain and France backed him with a formal note to the president of Czechoslovakia. Hitler then raised the price, demanding not only self-determination but the incorporation of the Sudetenland into the German Reich. A conference was proposed by Prime Minister Neville Chamberlain.

THE MUNICH CONFERENCE

The Munich Conference met on September 28, 1938. Hitler, Mussolini, Daladier of France, and Chamberlain of England were the only representatives (Czechoslovakia and Russia were omitted). By September 30, an agreement was reached: Hitler got what he wanted—one-fifth of Czechoslovakia, 4 million people, the fortifications of the Sudetenland, and the crucial Skoda armament works. In March, 1939, Hitler violated the Munich Pact and took over the rest of Czechoslovakia.

With the takeover of Czechoslovakia, Britain and France were finally shocked into realizing that appeasement would not stop Hitler. In April 1939, they guaranteed the defense of Poland, but they failed to reach agreement with Russia, primarily because of mistrust on both sides.

The Nazi-Soviet Pact

The Nazi-Soviet Pact was announced on August 23, 1939. This was Hitler's grand strategy of assuring Russia's neutrality and isolating Poland. (The same arrangement had been made in the eighteenth century between Catherine the Great and Frederick the Great.) The pact meant that Hitler could attack Britain and France in the west without worrying about the eastern front; then, when the right time came, he could turn on Russia.

On September 1, 1939, the German army, ignoring a non-aggression pact signed in 1934, invaded Poland. The Second World War had begun.

World War II

The Second World War Differed from the First

Warfare became mobile; airpower was an essential factor in victory. In Europe fewer soldiers were killed in the second war of survival than in the first, primarily because the war was one of movement but also because of new discoveries in medicine.

The Second World War was more truly a world war, for,

with the exception of the American continent, the whole world was a battlefield, and twenty-six nations fought on the side of the Allies. The major nations involved in the war were still the same as they had been in World War I, except that Turkey and Italy had switched sides.

The war also differed from the first in that atrocities were committed that were unparalleled in the history of civilization.

Science and invention played an even more vital role. The British invented radar in 1939; rockets, from the portable bazooka to the German V-2s that fell on London in September 1944, became practical weapons of war; and finally, atomic research and the development of the two atomic bombs, which the Americans dropped on Hiroshima and Nagasaki, inaugurated a new age of warfare.

At the beginning of the war Germany had many advantages. Its military leaders had developed advanced types of tanks and planes, achieving higher speeds, greater mobility, and increased fire power. The Allies, on the other hand, still believed in the World War I theory that well-fortified positions were impregnable; the Maginot Line had been built by France, stretching from Belgium to Switzerland.

The War Begins on the Eastern Front

On September 1, 1939, Germany invaded Poland; on September 17, Russia followed suit; ten days later Poland surrendered and was partitioned. Then the Baltic states were brought under Russian control, and on February 1, 1940, the USSR declared war on Finland. On September 3, 1939, France and Great Britain had declared war, but nothing happened on the Western front until Hitler had settled matters in Eastern Europe.

The Western Front

On April 9, 1940 Hitler began the hot war in the west by attacking Denmark and Norway. Reaction in Britain to this campaign led to the fall of Chamberlain's government and the organization of a National Wartime Government under Winston Churchill.

Then Hitler proceeded to sweep through the European continent: Luxembourg surrendered in three days; Belgium and the Netherlands were invaded on May 10; the Dutch capitulated in five days and the Belgians in eighteen. By May 20, the Germans had reached the English Channel, cutting off the British from the main French forces.

THE BATTLE OF DUNKIRK

Between May 27 and June 4, 1940, almost 340,000 British and French troops were evacuated from Dunkirk by sea with every available boat the British had. This was one of the most spectacular evacuations in military history.

THE SURRENDER OF FRANCE

On June 10, Mussolini joined the war on Hitler's side and invaded southern France. The Germans entered Paris on June 14. There were many who wanted to continue the fight, such as General Charles de Gaulle, who later formed the Free French movement. On June 16, Prime Minister Reynaud was forced to turn over the government to Petain, and on June 22, the treaty was signed; two-fifths of France was left under French control (the Vichy French) and France was to pay the cost of the German occupation of the other three-fifths. The French prisoners of war were to remain hostages.

GREAT BRITAIN ALONE AGAINST THE AXIS—ENGLAND'S "FINEST HOUR"

Luckily for Great Britain, German leadership was divided, Hitler's plans were disorganized, and the German air force could not make up its mind what its strategy should be. The Battle of Britain was won by the British R.A.F. and the courage of the British people who refused to let the bombs break their will to fight. The Battle of Britain started in July and came to a climax in September. It was fought to establish air control over the English Channel, the preliminary step to any invasion. In October Hitler abandoned his invasion plans. The British had the advantage that they could save many of their pilots. By the spring of 1941 Britain was retaliating by bombing Germany.

Africa and the Middle East

In the meantime British forces were spread too thin, for Italy moved into Egypt in the autumn of 1940. The British, however, succeeded in driving them out, in removing Iraq's pro-Axis faction, and in clearing out the Vichy government of Syria. In 1941, Russia and Britain occupied Iran, thus providing a supply route to the U.S.S.R.

The Eastern Front and the Invasion of Russia

The Germans and Russians soon came to blows over the question of supremacy in the Balkans. From December to May, 1941 Germany invaded the Balkans, primarily for the sake of oil and also in preparation for war with Russia. By June 1, Germany had full control of the peninsula. Russia in the meantime had signed a neutrality pact with Japan, which at least secured its eastern front. On June 22, Germany invaded Russia. By December its troops were within twenty-five miles of both Leningrad and Moscow. The Germans were stopped by the cold, the collapse of their supply lines, and the Russian offensive.

The United States Entry

Long before December 7, 1941, the United States had become the "arsenal of democracy"; it had in effect chosen sides and was shipping supplies to Great Britain.

The Neutrality Act of 1937 had placed an embargo on arms to any belligerent nation, and this acted as an aid to the Nazis, but in 1939 the United States passed a somewhat less neutral act which allowed arms to be sold to any belligerent if they were paid for in cash and transported by the warring nations. This in essence meant that the U.S. had chosen to side with Great Britain.

In 1940, President Franklin Roosevelt began to release more arms and some old destroyers to Britain in exchange for naval bases in the Caribbean. Then in March, 1941, the Lend-Lease Act was passed: in effect the act came close to being a declaration of war, since the bill gave the President of the United States the right to lend resources to any nation whose defense was necessary to United States security.

In August, 1941, Roosevelt and Churchill signed the Atlantic Charter, in which they pledged their countries to the spread of democratic principles; it established eighteen points similar to Wilson's Fourteen Points of World War I and also stipulated that a "permanent system of general security" should be established at the end of the war (the origins of the United Nations).

Pearl Harbor

In 1940–41 Japan was obtaining four-fifths of its oil and a great deal of scrap iron from the United States. In 1941, after Japan had taken over Indochina, Roosevelt froze Japanese assets in the United States and placed a severe embargo on Japan.

On December 7, 1941, Japan retaliated by attacking the naval base and the airfields at Pearl Harbor on Oahu Island in Hawaii. The same day it also attacked the Philippines, Hong Kong, and Malaya, and the next day, the American bases on Guam and Wake islands.

On December 8, 1941, the United States, the United Kingdom, Canada, South Africa, the Netherlands, and Luxembourg declared war on Japan. Now the war had become global.

The entry of the United States finally defeated the Axis both because of the addition of American soldiers on the battlefield and also because of United States production. The output of the U.S. between 1943 and 1944 was one ship per day and one aircraft every five minutes. (See also p. 247.)

The United Nations Declaration   January 1, 1942

The U.S., U.K., and USSR (the "big three") along with China and twenty-two other nations signed the United Nations declaration, which pledged them to a common effort to defeat the Axis, promised not to make a separate peace, and agreed to the "common program of purpose and principles" as laid down in the Atlantic Charter.

The Far Eastern Theater

Japan was initially very successful; only the Philippine Island fort of Corregidor held out until May. Malaya and Singapore fell in February 1942, and by March Japan had virtual control of Burma and the Dutch East Indies.

Occupied Europe

Poland's lot was the hardest; almost all its political leaders and its Jewish population were exterminated. All of Eastern Europe suffered, for the area was just behind the battle lines. The brutality of the Nazis was unbelievable.

1) Medical experiments carried on by the Nazis involved the resistance of an individual to air pressure, to cold water, and to inoculation with fatal diseases (100,000 were sacrificed in this way). The tortures employed by the Gestapo (the secret police) were equally brutal although more conventional. To avenge an assassination in Prague, a town was razed to the ground, and in Prague itself the army shot seventy people taken indiscriminately off the streets during a nine-day period.

2) Nazi brutality was even more ferocious against the Jews. In two days in the Ukraine 33,771 Jews were shot. Of 500,000 Jews in Warsaw, only 200 lived to see the end of the war. The concentration camps and extermination camps were first established by Hermann Goering in 1933. At Treblinka B, 10,000 Jews from Warsaw were gassed to death every day for a week. Seventy to 80 percent of the people in these camps died (the other 20 to 30 percent were those who had been imprisoned the day the peace was signed). In all, it has been estimated that at least 10 million people, including 75 percent of Europe's Jewish population, were killed by the Germans in extermination and concentration camps.

The Turning Point—the Winter of 1942–43

AFRICA

In November 1942, under General Dwight Eisenhower, Anglo-American troops landed in North Africa. The British under Montgomery pushed Rommel out of Egypt to Tripoli, and in May 250,000 German and Italian troops surrendered.

THE EASTERN FRONT

By 1942 the Germans had reached Stalingrad. The defense of Stalingrad was crucial to the Russians, for if captured it would have isolated Moscow and Leningrad. Under General Zhukov the Russians made a last-ditch stand, and by January 1943, 300,000 Germans had surrendered. From then on Russia was on the offensive, recapturing Kiev in 1943 and Odessa in 1944.

THE INVASION OF ITALY

In June 1943, the Allies captured Sicily; then they began a long, clumsy invasion and conquest of Italy. In July 1943, Mussolini's government fell, but it was not until July 1944, that the Allies were able to reach Rome. Italy had surrendered, although Italian troops, aided by Germany, continued to fight in the north.

THE BATTLE IN THE AIR

The British flew at night and the Americans by day, bombing cities to break the morale of the German people and destroying strategic bases, ammunition, and supplies. The battle in the air was vital to victory.

THE BATTLE AT SEA

Shipment of supplies was endangered by German submarines. Sometimes over 600,000 tons a month of Allied shipping was destroyed, but the aircraft carrier, the destroyer escort, and the bombing of submarine bases helped alleviate the situation. The other essential reason that the Allies won the battle at sea was the fast production of considerable tonnage of new shipping.

THE PACIFIC THEATER

The Pacific Theater was under three different Allied commands: the Northwest Pacific under General MacArthur, the Pacific Ocean under Admiral Nimitz, and the China–India–Burma command eventually under Vice-Admiral Mountbatten. For a while the Allies played a waiting game in the Far East while they slowly built up supplies and concentrated their troops in Europe. Then in 1942 came a series of Japanese naval defeats: the Battle of the Coral Sea, the Battle of Midway Island, and the Battle of Guadalcanal. The Allies were now on the offensive. Tokyo was bombed for the first time in April 1942, and by September 1944 the Allies were ready to retake the Philippines.

THE WAR IN ASIA

The most important aspects of the war in Asia were the defense of India (Japan penetrated into the Assam valley) and the problem of getting supplies to China. This involved flying over the 17,000-foot Himalayas mountains. The Chinese, nevertheless, were not easy to work with, and General Stilwell and Chiang Kai-shek often came to blows on strategy.

Victory

Victory began with the invasion of Normandy on June 6, 1944. Under the unified command of General Eisenhower, five divisions landed on the Normandy coast. By July, one million had been landed. Six months later the Allies had reached the German frontier. On December 16, 1944, Germany made its last desperate counterattack in northern France. The Battle of the Bulge lasted a full month. At the same time, Germany began to bomb London with rockets. On March 1, the Russians crossed the Oder; on March 7, the Americans and British crossed the Rhine; and in April Vienna fell. On April 30, Hitler committed suicide, and on May 8 victory in Europe was proclaimed.

Victory in Japan came the next year. As defeat followed defeat, the Japanese government was disgraced and began to topple. In July 1944, Prime Minister Tojo resigned. The Battle of Leyte Gulf, the largest naval engagement in the war, was fought in October 1944. As a result, Japan's naval power was wiped out. Then, in January 1945, the Allies captured Luzon. In the spring of that year, Iwo Jima and Okinawa fell, and from there the U.S.

Air Force began the systematic bombing of Japan. Between May and August of 1945 the greatest air offensive in history destroyed the remnants of the Japanese navy and its industry. The Japanese government still refused the American demand for unconditional surrender, so President Harry Truman (Roosevelt had died in April) decided to use the atomic bomb. Hiroshima was destroyed on August 6; on August 9, Nagasaki suffered a similar fate. On August 14, the Japanese accepted the terms of unconditional surrender, and on September 2, 1945, they signed the surrender papers. The second total war had come to an end.

The Cost of the War

By the end of the war forty-six countries were fighting on the Allied side, eight on the Axis. Death count statistics range from 35 to 60 million. The cost of military operations is figured at 1.5 trillion dollars. There was more physical destruction in the World War II than in World War I. Ground fighting ruined western Russia, and air fighting reduced whole cities to debris. Industry and transportation were destroyed, and refugees swarmed homeless over Europe. Most overseas investments were lost, and Europe was reduced to bankruptcy.

The Conferences of World War II and the Peace Settlements

The Foreign Ministers Conference—1943

In October 1943, the foreign ministers of the "big three" met in Moscow. It was decided that Italy, which had surrendered in September, should have a democratic government and that Austria should be liberated and made a free and independent nation. Also, the U.S. was able to get the Soviet Union to agree to a system of collective security after the war. This was the first definite commitment to a postwar substitute for the League of Nations. The conference was relatively free of differences, for the need of military cooperation was still great.

The Teheran (Iran) Conference—1943

Churchill, Roosevelt, and Stalin met for the first time in Teheran in November 1943. Before this, Roosevelt and Churchill had met in Cairo with Chiang to assure China's rights after the war. Russia would not meet with Chiang since the U.S.S.R. and Japan had a neutrality pact. At Cairo it was agreed that Japan would be stripped of all gains in the Pacific since 1914; Manchuria and Formosa would be returned to China; and Korea would be free and independent. The Teheran Conference was essentially military and was the high point of Allied cooperation. It was agreed that a second front would be opened. The question of Poland's boundaries was broached but never solved, and it was agreed that Germany should be eliminated as a strong military power after the war.

The Yalta Conference—1945

The single most important conference was Yalta in February 1945. There was still hope of compromise and Russian cooperation regarding each country's postwar role, and policy had not yet been clearly formulated. The aims of the three major powers were:

1) The United States wanted agreement on the United Nations organization, and this took precedent over all other matters. The U.S. also wanted a definite commitment that Russia would enter the war in the Pacific.

2) Great Britain wanted to arrive at a friendly settlement on specific items and political problems, especially the questions of Greece and the Middle East.

3) Russia wanted territories and rights in the Far East and a buffer zone of pro-Russian nations to secure its western border against Germany.

THE SETTLEMENT

No real agreement was reached on postwar Germany. The stumbling block was, again, reparations. Russia was now taking the position that the French took in World War I (that is, to make Germany pay for the war). It was agreed, however, that until a peace treaty was signed there would be four zones of military occupation, and France was to participate in the zones of occupation.

The fate of Eastern Europe was decided, although the West was unaware of the consequences. The Poles would have a coalition government. This would be a provisional government until free elections could be held—they never were. All the Eastern European nations were to have free elections—they never did.

The settlement in the Far East can be understood only by realizing that the United States felt that Russia was still necessary in the war against Japan. Military advisers had forecast the end of the war in the Pacific to be as far off as December 1946 and were convinced that the invasion of the home islands of Japan would be necessary to bring about Japanese surrender. Russia refused to consent to war without a price and agreed to enter two or three months after the conclusion of the war in Europe. (The USSR did not enter until after the first atomic bomb was dropped.) In return, Mongolia was to remain as it was, a Russian puppet; Manchuria was to be a Russian sphere of influence under Chinese sovereignty; and Russia was to acquire the Kurile Islands and the southern half of Sakhalin Island.

The Potsdam Conference—1945

There was no longer room for diplomacy, for the situation had changed. Germany had surrendered in May, and America was on the way to winning the war against Japan. Most of the agreements were disagreements. There was no fundamental meeting of minds, and all that was settled was a kind of bargain unfavorable to both the Russians and the West.

Two major questions were to be settled: one was Allied economic policy for Germany, and the other, Russia's position in Eastern Europe. Stalin wanted reparations from Germany and recognition of the Communist regimes in Eastern Europe (this was in violation of the Yalta Agreement). Truman and Churchill opposed him. All that could be agreed upon was that:

1) Certain German areas should be placed under Polish administration.

2) A Council of Foreign Ministers was established that would draft the peace treaties for Italy, Rumania, Bulgaria, Hungary, and Finland.

3) It was decided that there would be no central government for Germany; each zone would be different. A control council, however, was set up to decide on joint policies for Germany as a whole. Within each zone Germany was to be demilitarized and de-Nazified. Reparations could not be decided upon, but it was agreed that they were to be paid by the removal of German industrial plants and capital equipment.

4) Berlin was divided into four zones, separately governed by the United States, the United Kingdom, France, and the Soviet Union.

The European Peace Treaties

In 1947, peace treaties were signed with Italy, Rumania, Bulgaria, Hungary, and Finland. Certain territorial changes were made, and reparations were agreed upon, with Russia being the primary benefactor.

Austria was also divided into four occupation zones, with the capital city of Vienna administered in the same way as Berlin. The Austrian peace treaty was concluded in 1955 without the final division of the country into separate nations.

No peace treaty was agreed upon for Japan and Germany. In 1951 peace was made with Japan. Neither of the two Chinas was invited to sign, and the Soviet Union refused to sign.

In 1949 the German Democratic Republic (East Germany) was proclaimed. In 1955 a treaty was signed by Russia that recognized the sovereignty of the republic. In 1951 the British, French, and Americans announced the formal termination of the state of war with Germany. On May 5, 1955, West Germany gained full sovereignty.

The Nuremberg Trials

For the first time in the history of war the men who had led the world into conflict were put on trial for their actions; war had become a crime against humanity.

In October 1946, an international military tribunal was set up by the Allies in Nuremberg to try the top Nazis. These men were charged with causing the war, with crimes against humanity, and war crimes. Three men were freed, seven received ten years' to life imprisonment, and twelve were condemned to death. Most were generals in the SS, the elite guards, and held other positions as well.

There were twelve more trials held in Nuremberg, but these were under United States auspices. As a result of these trials, 185 men were indicted and 24 were put to death. The major responsibility for denazification, however, was turned over to the German tribunals under Allied supervision; in these, 1635 people were judged major offenders and 600,000 received some punishment.

In Japan the leaders of the war party were also tried. (See p. 370.)

The United Nations

The United Nations was formed by the Allies in the summer of 1945 in San Francisco. Like the League of Nations, it was a voluntary organization of sovereign states, dependent upon the cooperation of its members. Unlike the League, it had the support of the United States. At the creation of the U.N. there were 51 member nations; now there are 150.

The General Assembly, in which all nations have one vote, is purely an advisory body. The Security Council, the initiative body responsible for peace and security, consists of five permanent members plus ten nations elected for two-year terms. The five permanent members are the United States, the Soviet Union, Great Britain, France, and China. In 1971, Nationalist China was replaced by the People's Republic of China. Decisions must be agreed upon by nine of the ten nations and all five of the permanent members. This implies a veto power and means that any of the permanent member nations is capable of blocking an action.

The principal organs of the UN are the International Court of Justice, the Economic and Social Council, the Security Council, the Trusteeship Council, and the Secretary-General (and the Secretariat). The secretary-generals of the UN have been

1) Trygve Lie of Norway (1945–1953)
2) Dag Hammarskjöld of Sweden (1953–1961)
3) U Thant of Burma (1961–1971)
4) Kurt Waldheim of Austria (1972–   )

The U.N. has proved valuable as a forum for international discussion and has been used as a peace-keeping (or truce-keeping) agency in the Suez Canal (1956), Lebanon (1958), Kashmir (1949 and 1965), the Congo (1960), Cyprus (1968), and the Sinai (1967 and 1974).

Specialized and related agencies of the UN are involved in many and varied projects around the world. They vaccinate millions against disease, develop new foods and seeds which prevent millions from starving, and send tons of food and medicine around the world. The UN's agencies have saved temples in Egypt, art treasures in Florence, and wildlife all over the globe; they have worked for women's right and have set up a global weather system and a monitoring system for world pollution.

The New Balance of Power at the End of World War II

There were only two world powers after World War II—the United States and the Soviet Union. The rivalry between these two nations has deeply affected Europe's postwar history, for Europe was the center of this rivalry and the prize to be won. Since the seventeenth century there had been a half-dozen nations of relatively equal strength. In the years following the Second World War, however, the old diplomacy broke down because the world was divided into two camps dominated by two giant states, and though certain nations remained neutral, they did not influence the balance between the U.S. and the USSR. It was most important to both the USSR and the U.S. that Europe choose their side, but there was a decisive difference in their approaches—the USSR had more to gain by chaos on the continent and an internationally weak

Europe, while the U.S. had more to gain by rebuilding Europe. This is what the United States set out to do almost immediately after the war.

The Cold War

In March 1946, Churchill announced that "an iron curtain has descended across the continent." Churchill was one of the first world leaders to recognize the new balance of power and Russia's ultimate designs. It took the rest of the West longer to perceive the true nature of Russia's plan. In 1947 the Cominform was established, and there was no longer much pretense about Russia's ambitions. In 1947 the Greek civil war began, and it was primarily Great Britain that had to muster resources to fight against the communists. Then in February, 1948, Czechoslovakia was taken over, and in June of the same year Russia blockaded Berlin. In reaction, the United States inaugurated the policy of containment, seeking to alleviate the chaotic economic conditions on which communism bred through such plans as the Marshall Plan and the Point 4 program of technical aid. America also sought to protect Europe by military aid (the Truman Doctrine in 1947, followed by the creation of NATO in 1949).

The Marshall Plan

The creation of the United Nations Relief and Rehabilitation Administration was the first economic effort at saving Europe. Between 1943 and 1948 it distributed millions of tons of food, clothing, farm equipment, and industrial machinery, saved thousands of lives, and fostered the world's economic recovery.

On April 3, 1948, the European Recovery Program, called the Marshall Plan, was signed by President Truman, and billions of dollars began to flow into Europe. The London *Economist's* comment on the Marshall Plan was that it was "the most straight-forwardly generous thing that any country has ever done for others." The Organization of European Economic Cooperation was set up to distribute the funds according to need. Most of the money was in the form of outright grants. Each nation receiving these grants had to match the amount in "counterpart funds."

NATO

The Truman Doctrine in 1947 was the first step by the United States toward a European defensive alliance. Truman announced that it must be the policy of the United States "to support free people who are resisting attempted subjugation by armed minorities or by outside pressures." In April 1949, the North Atlantic Treaty Organization (NATO) was formed. The member nations were the United Kingdom, France, Belgium, the Netherlands, Luxembourg, Denmark, Iceland, Norway, Italy, Portugal, Canada, the United States, Greece, Turkey (in 1951), and finally West Germany (in 1955). NATO is a defensive military pact. General Eisenhower was the first commander. The counterpart is the Soviet-dominated Warsaw Pact. NATO has switched its emphasis from reliance on conventional weapons to dependence upon the American nuclear deterrent. At the same time, the members of NATO have shown an increasing reluctance to follow American leadership. NATO received a serious blow when France pulled out. However, it has survived for thirty years, which is a long time by diplomatic standards.

Postwar Europe

Great Britain

The major change in the United Kingdom after the war was nationalization and socialization.

Nationalization, or government ownership, was not new in Great Britain; the BBC (British Broadcasting Company) had been taken over by the state in 1927, the telephone had been under post office jurisdiction from the start, the London transport system had been nationalized in 1933, and the government had assumed control of the mineral rights of coal mines in 1938. During the war all aspects of life were regulated and controlled by the government.

In 1945, when the Labor party came to power in England, a far more extensive program of nationalization took place. The Bank of England, the cable and wireless service, and civil aviation were put under government auspices. The operation of coal mines, railroads, canals and docks, electricity, and gas were also nationalized. Steel has been nationalized, denationalized, and renationalized. None of this was done by confiscation; in each case the owners received compensation. In 1946–48, four major acts were passed that changed Britain into a welfare state and provided for health, injury, old-age, and unemployment insurance.

At the same time the United Kingdom began to provide for the economic and social development of its colonies. The British Colonial Development and Welfare Acts of 1945, 1950, and 1955 provided £220 million to be spent by 1960 on colonial improvements (although rationing at home was not completely ended until July 1954).

France

France suffered not only economic but political problems at the end of the war.

In 1944 De Gaulle, as head of the Free French, took over the government, named a cabinet, and governed by executive decree. He too was forced to nationalize certain industries because of the dislocation and disorganization caused by the war. Coal mines, aircraft, banking, gas, and electricity were nationalized.

Between 1945–48 French politics were extremely unstable, and the Communists were often the largest single party.

In May 1958, however, the French army leaders seized power in Algeria and demanded the return of De Gaulle. In June, De Gaulle took over the government on his own conditions. In September a new constitution was ratified that gave dominant power to the president, who would be elected for a seven-year term, could dissolve parliament, and, in emergency, could assume the powers of a dictator (which De Gaulle in fact assumed). The Fifth Republic was proclaimed.

Overseas, France had difficulty adjusting to a postwar world in which there was no place for imperialism. France tried to maintain its control in both Indochina and Algeria but had to give them up eventually (1954 and 1963). De Gaulle was responsible for the

French Community of Nations.   Internal autonomy was granted and the executives of the French Community (the premier of France and the heads of the member nations) controlled foreign affairs, defense, and overall economic planning.

Italy

In 1949, Italy was declared a Republic and ever since has been ruled by coalition governments. Here too there is a very heavy Communist vote, but the Catholic church is also still a strong power.

Germany

At the end of the war, East Germany was firmly under Soviet control. By 1973, normal relations between East and West Germany had been established and the two nations entered the UN.

Berlin, within East Germany, was divided into four zones of occupation in 1945. The western occupied area remained a part of the free world, but the eastern (Soviet occupied) became a part of East Germany.

West Germany contrasts sharply with East Germany, for it has established a democratic government and a prosperous economy. In 1949, a constitution was drawn up in Bonn, the new capital. Power was vested in the chancellor and the cabinet. A combination of direct and proportional representation was used in electing the lower chamber. West Germany in essence became a multi-party nation.

Economic Developments   1950–79

After 1950, Germany made great strides in industrial and agricultural growth and became the major West European economic power with the fourth highest GNP in the world. Although Britain's GNP has almost doubled in ten years, its trade deficit has also continued to rise. Next to Britain, Italy has the highest trade deficit. Just as it appeared that this situation was improving, Italy was hit by increased oil prices. Italy, of all the countries of Europe, is most vulnerable for it has few natural resources.

A major issue throughout Western Europe, and in fact the world, is inflation. Britain and Italy were the hardest hit with a yearly 20 percent rise in the cost of living (this must be compared, however, to many countries in Latin America where the rise was 100 percent). By 1974, there were 4 million people in the Common Market countries who were unemployed.

Europe does not lack resources. In manpower, Western Europe has approximately 485 million people. In industrial potential it is greater than either the U.S. or the USSR. In some fields of food production, however, Europe cannot compete: America and Russia produce more oats, wheat, and cotton than the Common Market countries, and the United States also produces more meat.

Political and Social Troubles   1950–79

Again Communism has been on the increase. Italy in 1975 voted heavily for the Communists at the local level. This may in part have been protest over extremely corrupt and inefficient governmental practices, but the swing to the left is even more pronounced in Portugal where a minority Communist party supported by the military took control. In Portugal, after the right wing dictatorship was overthrown in 1974, it appeared as if the country might take its place among the democracies of Western Europe. The Communists, however, despite an overwhelming socialist vote in 1975, assumed dictatorial control, and although the Socialists regained control, the situation remains highly unsettled.

France, Germany, and Great Britain have been politically stable, despite riots, student demonstrations, and serious labor unrest. The economic situation in 1974 was reflected at the polls. Only three of the Common Market nations (Ireland, the Netherlands, and Denmark) began and ended the year with the same leaders, and only in Britain was the leader the head of a single-party majority government.

Great Britain has had a problem in Northern Ireland where religious and economic controversy led to violence over the issue of political representation and union with the Irish Republic. Between

1969 and 1975 there were over 1000 deaths; and in 1973 the radical IRA (Irish Republican Army) started planting bombs throughout Britain to coerce the government. The situation remains unresolved.

The Governments of Europe   1918–79

The Government of England
The Monarchy

	—George V	1910–1936
	—Edward VIII	1936
	—George VI	1936–1952
	—Elizabeth II	1952–

Prime Ministers

Coalition	—Lloyd George	1916–1922
Conservative	—Bonar Law and Baldwin	1922–1923
Labour	—MacDonald	1924
Conservative	—Baldwin	1924–1929
Labour	—MacDonald	1929–1931
Coalition	—MacDonald	1931–1935
Conservative	—Baldwin	1935–1937
	—Chamberlain	1937–1940
	—Churchill	1940–1945
Labour	—Atlee	1945–1951
Conservative	—Churchill	1951–1955
	—Eden	1955–1957
	—Macmillan	1957–1963
	—Douglas-Home	1963–1964
Labour	—Wilson	1964–1970
Conservative	—Heath	1970–1974
Labour	—Wilson	1974–1976
	—Callaghan	1976–1979
Conservative	—Thatcher	1979–

The Government of France

Third Republic	1870–1940
Vichy France	1940–1945
The Fourth Republic	1945–1958

Presidents of the Fifth Republic

—DeGaulle	1958–1969
—Pompidou	1969–1974
—Giscard d' Estaing	1974–

The Government of West Germany

The Weimar Republic	1919–1933
The Third Reich	1933–1945
Allied Military Occupation	1945–1949

Chancellors of West Germany

Adenauer	1949–1963
Erhard	1963–1966
Kiesinger	1966–1969
Brandt	1969–1974
Schmidt	1974–

The Decline of Europe

After World War II, Europe no longer guided the destinies of the world; its colonies had been reduced to a handful and its prestige had suffered badly. Possibly the most important and certainly one of the last remaining vestiges of European influence is the British Commonwealth of Nations — an enormous but unstructured association of thirty-two states, all of which were originally members of the British Empire.

The Future of Europe

Europe's economic and international difficulties are caused mostly by lack of political unity. There have, however, been steps toward economic unity.

In 1951, France, Germany, Italy, Belgium, the Netherlands, and Luxembourg formed the European Coal and Steel Community—a federalized organization creating free markets for coal and steel. The result was a production boom.

In 1957, the same nations set about a more ambitious plan: they formed the European Economic Community (the Common Market) and the European Atomic Energy Community (Euratom). The Common Market's purpose was to promote free trade among its members by slowly eliminating all tariff barriers. Euratom is a common market for nuclear raw materials, technicians, and equipment. For the first time in history, the European nations surrendered certain portions of their sovereignty willingly. The achievement of free trade (particularly in agriculture) has been slower than anticipated and the events of 1973 dramatized the lack of European political unity. During the Arab-Israeli war and ensuing oil crisis, the Netherlands alone took a firm pro-Israeli stand; France made an independent arms-for-oil deal with Saudi Arabia; Germany and Britain tried to remain neutral.

In 1973, the United Kingdom, Ireland, and Denmark entered the EEC, and industrial free trade agreements with the European Free Trade Association (Austria, Iceland, Norway, Portugal, Sweden, Switzerland, and Finland) were signed. In 1975, the British went to the polls in the first national referendum and voted overwhelmingly to stay in the Common Market. Economic cooperation in the long run may lead to greater political cooperation.

The Heritage of Europe

Despite the fact that Europe is no longer the economic and political center of the world, indirectly its influence has never been greater, for its three revolutions—industrial, scientific, and ideological—have swept the world. Even the United States' and Soviet Union's achievements are in large measure European in origin. Although Europe may be in decline, its heritage remains predominant.

Russian Civilization

ANCIENT AND CLASSICAL CIVILIZATIONS
1000 B.C.–500 A.D.

The civilization of Russia is young compared with that of China, India, the Middle East, and Europe. Consequently, there is no ancient and very little classical history. The history of Russia is usually considered to begin in the ninth century A.D. *with the wave of Viking migrations and conquests that swept over all of Europe including Russia and the Mediterranean area. The history of Russia can just as easily be dated about 1000* B.C., *when Slavic tribes moved in from central Asia; but very little is known about these peoples until 650* A.D.

THE SLAVIC MIGRATIONS

Slavic peoples moved from the foothills of the Carpathian Mountains to the fertile western part of the Eurasian plain. By the eighth and ninth centuries B.C. they had dispersed through the Dnieper River valley as far north as Novgorod and as far south as Kiev.

The Slavs were tribal and had no central organization. Agriculture was the basic economic occupation and all property was held in common. Their religious concepts resembled those of the early Indo-European peoples.

150

The Khazars

The first attempt to unify the land was made by the Khazars. They were essentially a trading empire in the Kiev area. According to most authorities they followed the Jewish faith and were peace-loving people, but in 737 A.D. they were scattered and defeated by constant Arab invasions.

MEDIEVAL CIVILIZATION   500–1500 A.D.

The medieval era of Russian history must be regarded as Russia's first period of recorded history. The age witnessed the migrations, invasions, and settlements of the Vikings (in Kiev) and the Mongols (in Sarai). This period is historically important for the penetration of Byzantine influence and the foundation of the Russian Orthodox faith, as well as the development of a sense of unity among the tribes of Slavic background.

THE KIEV PERIOD   878–1237

The Varangians

Because the western Eurasian plain was exposed to constant Arab invasions, the Slavs turned to the Varangians (or Vikings) for aid and protection. According to legend, Rurik, king of the Vikings, was called upon for help in 862 A.D. The protectors soon turned into conquerors, and it was under the leadership of Oleg, who succeeded Rurik at Novgorod, that Kiev was conquered in 879. Through this period of Varangian rule, however, there was no Russian state, but the name Russia itself was of Viking origin.

Christianity and Vladimir

Vladimir (known later as Vladimir the Saint), who won the throne of Kiev in 977 by murdering his older brother, was converted to Eastern Christianity in 988 after having explored all the other major faiths. He seems to have chosen Christianity not because of its theology but because of the splendor and beauty of its churches. (This concern with the ornamental elements of religion was to remain a characteristic of the Russian Orthodox faith.) For the masses, converted by the sword, Christian ritual was only a thin coating on top of deep pagan superstition.

In 990 Vladimir was allowed to marry a Byzantine princess in return for protecting the Byzantine emperor, thus making the ties with the Eastern world stronger. Although no Russian state was created, a degree of unity was achieved through the introduction of Christianity and of Byzantine civil law.

Church Slavonic became the language of the church in Russia, and during this period a native literature evolved, but the use of the vernacular narrowed Russia's intellectual horizons, for it "closed the door in Russia upon Greek culture."

The Collapse of Kiev

With the death of Yaroslav the Wise (1019–54), any form of centralized state ruled from Kiev came to an end, for he divided the land among his five sons. The growing number of Russian princes struggling for control of land, along with raids by nomads from the east, further weakened the city. In one year there were 64 principalities, 293 princes, and 83 civil wars.

Kiev lost its economic significance once the Mediterranean was opened for trade by the Crusades, and trade with Constantinople was blocked by nomadic invasions along the shores of the Black Sea. Novgorod in the north took the place of Kiev as the main center of trade in Russia.

THE SARAI PERIOD   1237–1472

The Mongol Invasions

In 1237 Batu Khan, the grandson of Genghis Khan, and his Golden Horde invaded Russia and by 1240 had captured most of the great Russian cities. Only Novgorod remained an independent area.

Results of Mongol Rule

The Mongol onslaught was devastating. Towns and settlements were burned (it took eight centuries for the Russian city population to recover), captives were slaughtered, and a huge tribute was exacted. Skilled craftsmen were taken to the Mongol capital at Sarai. Industry and commerce were virtually extinguished. Russia was further isolated from Western Europe and unity was shattered. The fortunes of the peasants were worsened and they fell further and further into debt.

The Mongol state was founded upon the principle of universal service and submission to the ruler. Many of the forms of despotism in the government of the czars were inherited from the Mongols. The Sarai government treated city and country alike (the Kievan period had not), thus strengthening the basis for common subordination of all subjects to the monarch. An efficient system of taxation, which czars were later able to use to their advantage, was introduced.

THE MUSCOVY STATE   1322–1462

Ivan I   1322–1341

From the time of Ivan Kalita (Moneybags), the title of sovereign prince of Russia was held by the princes of Moscow. In 1326 the seat of the *metropolitan* (bishop of the Eastern church) was moved from Vladimir (originally it had been in Kiev) to Moscow, and in 1328 Ivan was made responsible for the collection of tribute for the Mongols. These two events gave the princes of Moscow power to extend their influence and their territory.

The Successors of Ivan

Simeon the Proud	1341–1353
Ivan the Red	1353–1359
Dmitry of the Don	1359–1389
Vasily	1389–1425
Vasily II, the Dark	1425–1462

Under the successors of Ivan, Moscow continued to grow. Each prince added new lands, increased the wealth of the principality, and strengthened the position of Moscow vis-a-vis Sarai. By 1400 Russia comprised approximately a 250-mile radius of land around Moscow.

The War against the Mongols

Divisions within the ranks of the Golden Horde brought opportunities to Moscow. In 1378 the Russians won victories at the Vozha River and in 1380 at Kulikovo, but in 1408 Moscow was ravaged by the Tartar army. During the reign of Vasily II the Golden Horde suffered as Tamerlane advanced and Mongol centralized authority collapsed. However, it was not until Ivan IV's reign that the remnants of Tartar power were driven from Russia. In 1480 Ivan's father had defied the Golden Horde by refusing to pay tribute, and in 1552 Ivan IV conquered Kazan and four years later Astrakhan. In 1583–84 the Siberian Khan was defeated.

MODERN CIVILIZATION   1500 to the Present

Russia's modern history has been divided into three sections: the Creation of Czarist Russia 1462–1703; Growth and Westernization 1703–1917; and the Soviet Union 1917 to the present.

THE CREATION OF CZARIST RUSSIA   1462–1703

The modern period begins in 1462 with the growth of the Muscovy state and the power and influence of Ivan III and his descendants. The capital of Russia became Moscow, and it was during this era that Russia developed many of the characteristics that lasted into the twentieth century. The concept of czardom evolved, and the centralization of government under a despot was established. The church was subordinated to the state; the peasant was tied to the land; the middle class lost all its power and influence and became a tool of the government; and the imperialistic expansion of Russia began. It should also be remembered that this period corresponded in time with the Renaissance in Europe. In contrast Muscovy was uncultured, illiterate, and backward. The same year (1645) that Charles I of England was defeated by parliamentary forces, serfdom was formally acknowledged in Russia.

The Czars of Russia   1462–1689

*IVAN III, THE GREAT (1462–1505)
Known for his consolidation of power and territorial acquisition, Ivan married the orphan niece of the last of the Byzantine emperors, thus establishing his claim to be czar of Russia.
*VASILY III (1505–1533)
Vasily extended the work of his father. When he died he left two children by his second wife. The eldest (aged three) became Ivan IV.

---

*The most important are starred.

*IVAN IV, THE TERRIBLE (1533–1584)

Ivan is known for his cruelty and love of torture, his paranoic cunning, and his establishment of full autocracy in Russia. Two years before his death he struck his eldest son with an iron staff and killed him. Fedor, the second child of his first wife, Anastasia Romanov, was left to rule.

FEDOR (1584–1598)

Fedor was feebleminded and inherited an empire seething with discontent, and power inevitably fell to men behind the throne, first Nikita Romanov and then Boris Godunov.

BORIS GODUNOV (1598–1605)

Friend of Ivan IV, he was the power behind the throne under Fedor and was finally "elected" czar.

THE TIME OF TROUBLES (1605–1613)

When Fedor died in 1598, the line of princes was extinguished, for his brother Dmitry had died in 1591 under shadowy circumstances. When Boris died in 1605, Russia fell part. The crown went from one pretender to another, and the Russian country was in constant revolt.

MICHAEL ROMANOV (1613–1645)

Elected as a compromise candidate, he was not a strong czar. His only importance is that he founded a line that ruled Russia until 1917.

ALEXIS (1645–1676)

Alexis was somewhat stronger than his father but generally both Romanovs were mediocre men.

FEDOR (1676–1682)

PETER AND IVAN UNDER REGENCY OF SOPHIA (1682–1689)

Alexis left two sons, Fedor and Ivan, by his first wife and one, Peter, by his second wife. Both Fedor and Ivan were sickly children. Fedor died six years after he became Czar. Sophia, Ivan's sister, then ruled as regent over the dual czardom of Ivan and Peter. (Peter, however, lived on the outskirts of Moscow with his mother, while Ivan lived with his sister in the Kremlin.)

---

*The most important are starred.

The Establishment of the Russian State   1462–1703

Ivan III, Vasily III, and Ivan IV

Ivan III and his son, Vasily III, referred to themselves as "czar and autocrat by the grace of God of all Russia." In 1547 Ivan IV was officially proclaimed czar, a word derived from "Caesar" like the German word "Kaiser." The Russian state was established during the reigns of these three princes of Moscow. The Tartars were driven from the land; the separate, independent principalities were gathered in; and government was centralized under the czar. The era dominated by the princely family had ended, and the Russian national state was born.

Ivan III and Vasily III ruled Russia in cooperation with the *boyarskaya duma,* a council of hereditary landed aristocrats (boyars). Although this system worked fairly well under Ivan III, the grand prince of Moscow more and more came into conflict with the ancient aristocracy. It was Ivan IV who was to make himself supreme autocrat in Russia by destroying the power of the aristocracy.

1) He struck at the influence of the boyars by dividing Russia into two parts, half controlled (in theory) by the boyar councils and half controlled directly by a new body, the *Oprichnina,* a council of 1000 men personally responsible to the czar. The Oprichniks' main task was to destroy those who represented a challenge to Ivan's power, specifically the boyar class (although all classes were subject to the terror).

2) The landed aristocrats lost their special privileges, such as the right to transfer allegiance to another prince and their hereditary right to their lands. The nobles became merely servants of the state, bound to act as officials for the prince of Moscow, and land ownership was made contingent upon loyalty and allegiance to the czar. In effect, a new landlord class was created.

3) Once the boyars were eliminated there was nothing in Russia to compete with the czar's authority, although the church did offer occasional resistance.

The Time of Troubles and the Zemsky Sobor

Ivan IV's government was totally dependent upon the personality of the czar, and when Ivan died in 1584, having killed the son he had named as successor and leaving his feebleminded son Fedor and the infant Dmitry (the son of a dubious seventh marriage), he bequeathed to Russia years of anarchy and civil war. Dmitry was killed, and with Fedor's death in 1598 the line of succession ended and the Russian state collapsed. By 1611 the Poles controlled the southwest including Moscow and the Swedes had the northwest. There was no government, no leadership, and the land was devastated.

The results of fifteen years of chaos were disastrous. The boyars were extinct as a class, the peasant had no choice but to sink further and further into the clutches of the gentry, and the country was on the brink of economic collapse.

In 1612 the assembly of the land, the Zemsky Sobor, representing all classes, met and elected Michael Romanov czar. Although the assembly of the people had brought the Romanovs to power, the idea of a representative government never took hold. It was never intended that the assembly should assume permanent powers, and it never developed into an independently functioning body because of lack of unity. Consequently, the Zemsky Sobor was not capable of opposing the will of the supreme autocrat and was called upon only when the czar wished ratification of a policy. The Romanovs were new rulers, but they continued the policy of forcing everyone to serve the state.

The Russian Orthodox Church and Its Conflict with the State

The Russian Orthodox church, from the moment of its conception, was linked with the power of the state. During the sixteenth and seventeenth centuries it became subordinate to the state, and in the following centuries it deteriorated into a mere tool of the czar.

The Moscow Patriarchate

The creation of the Moscow *patriarchate* (archbishopric) was Boris Godunov's achievement in 1589. It was the patriarch Job who assisted in Boris' election as czar. The patriarchate, from its creation, was therefore closely allied with the state.

Nikon

Within the ranks of the clergy there was a desire to reform the Russian church by drawing it into closer unity with the Eastern (Greek Orthodox) church. In 1652 Nikon was elected Russian patriarch and began the revision of the service books. The church split over the issue: the old believers refused to accept the reforms. Nikon triumphed with the aid of the state, but in doing so he forecast the destruction of the independent power of the church and its subordination to the state.

With ambition similar to that of the great Western ecclesiastics, Nikon attempted to make the church stronger than the state. He was finally deposed and exiled. The effect of his efforts was to precipitate the decline of the power of the church and to identify religious dissent with movements against the government's authority. No other patriarch in Russian history ever again challenged the authority of the state in secular matters.

The Peasant and Serfdom

Once an independent farmer, the peasant became a tenant during the fourteenth century primarily because he had been driven into debt by Mongol taxation and felt the need for protection. At first he was free to move, although there were agreements among landowners not to accept him. By the middle of the fifteenth century the peasant could leave the land only during a two-week period in November. Vasily II, however, forbade the peasants on certain monastic estates to move at all.

Although serfdom did not become official until 1645, the peasant was in bondage much earlier. As a tenant, he soon fell further into debt, since he was paying exorbitant rates of interest. Those who were not in financial bondage to a lord were nevertheless subject to fines for leaving the land and were forced to pay annual rent amounting to one-quarter of the capital value of their homestead, which meant they could not afford to leave their land either.

In 1645, under Alexis, a new legal code divided the people into rigid classes. Townspeople were bound to the towns, the church and the nobility were declared closed classes, and most peasants were bound to the land by law. Thus the condition of serfdom that had existed for so long was made official.

The landlord exercised judicial, fiscal, social, and legal authority over his serfs, but the peasant did not accept his fate submissively. Russian history from this period on is characterized by peasant uprisings. In 1650 a rebellion raged in Pokov; during the plague of 1655 constant revolts occurred in the central regions of Russia; in 1662 there was revolution in Moscow and 7000 were executed. In 1670 one of the most famous rebellions of all took place: this uprising, led by Stenka Razin (whose ultimate fate was torture and quartering alive), was symptomatic of peasant dissatisfaction and anarchy.

The Imperialistic Expansion of Russia

Ivan III, Vasily III, and Ivan IV

The extent of Moscow-controlled lands was trebled during the reign of Ivan the Great (1462–1505). This was accomplished by both war and diplomacy. By 1489 the northeast was under Muscovy domination, but the campaigns in the west were less successful. Ivan III was not militarily strong enough to challenge Poland–Lithuania.

Control of the prosperous city of Novgorod and its lands was one of Ivan's objectives. Under his son the *veche* bell, symbol of Novgorod's independence, was removed to Moscow, and leading families were exiled.

Ivan defeated the last remnants of the Golden Horde by 1556. The conquest of Kazan opened up for colonization the fertile land of the middle Volga. Western Siberia was claimed in 1584, but in the west Ivan lost a twenty-year war against Sweden and Poland.

The Time of Troubles and the Romanovs

During the time of troubles (1605–1613) Russia lost much newly acquired land, and during the reign of the first Romanov remained militarily weak and on the defensive. It did expand eastward across Siberia, however, and southward into the Amur basin. (This led to conflict with China.)

It was not until Alexis' rule (1645–1676) that Russia again went on the offensive. It moved against Poland's control of the Dnieper in 1649, and in 1667 the Ukraine was split. The right bank of the Dnieper was to remain Polish and Moscow gained the left bank and Kiev. Russia had not controlled this part of the Ukraine since the Mongol invasions of the thirteenth century.

GROWTH AND WESTERNIZATION   1703–1917

This era's most outstanding characteristic was contact with, influence from, and reaction to the West. The period commences when Peter the Great moved his capital to St. Petersburg on the Baltic, which he called his window to the West because he hoped it would be the port into which would flow Western ideas and culture. Beginning with this first attempt at westernization, the period ends with the greatest manifestation of Western influence— the Russian Revolution.

The Czars of Russia   1689–1917

*PETER I, THE GREAT (1689–1725)

At the age of seventeen Peter, the fourteenth child of Alexis, became czar by military coup, although his mother controlled the reins of government until her death in 1694 and Ivan (his

---

*The most important are starred.

half brother) was nominal co-czar until his death in 1696. As cruel as Ivan IV (he put his own son Alexis to death by torture and executed nearly 2000 during the revolt of the Streltsy), as autocratic as any of the previous czars of Russia, Peter had one characteristic that made him different from his ancestors: he was aware of the West. Educated by foreigners in the German suburb of Moscow, he became acquainted with western techniques. And here he played at war with children who were later to form the nucleus of his army and navy. War, expansion, and westernization were the themes of Peter's reign.

CATHERINE I (1725–1727), widow of Peter I
When Peter I died, the only male Romanov who could claim the throne was his grandson Peter, son of Alexis. However, it was Peter's palace guards who were to determine policy until 1801, and they decided that Peter's widow, the Baltic servant girl Catherine I, should rule.

PETER II (1727–1730), grandson of Peter I
Died of smallpox at the age of 15.

ANNA (1730–1740), daughter of Peter's half brother, Ivan

IVAN VI (1740–1741), son of Anna's niece
The newborn boy reigned for a year and was then deposed.

ELIZABETH (1741–1762), daughter of Peter I
and Catherine I

PETER III (1762), son of Elizabeth's sister, Anna

*CATHERINE II, THE GREAT (1762–1796), wife of Peter III
A palace revolt put Catherine, a minor German princess who had married Peter III in 1745, on the throne of Russia. Peter died a few days later in a futile fight with his captors, and Catherine announced that her husband had died of a hemorrhage.

PAUL (1796–1801)
The son of Catherine the Great and a dubious father, Paul was

*The most important are starred.

mistreated by his mother, and he spent most of his reign trying to undo everything she had done.

*ALEXANDER I, THE GREAT (1801–1825)

Paul was assassinated during a palace revolution and was succeeded by his son. Alexander I was called "the sphinx" by Napoleon, and with good reason, for his motivations were never clear nor his actions consistent. He wavered between a desire for reform and a fear of revolution.

*NICHOLAS I (1825–1855)

When Alexander the Great died at the age of forty-eight, he left two brothers. Constantine, the elder, had had a common law second marriage, and therefore Alexander had left a manifesto naming Nicholas, the younger brother, czar. It was not until almost a month after Alexander's death that Nicholas agreed to rule. His reign witnessed an intensification of the police state, censorship, and tyranny.

*ALEXANDER II (1855–1881), son of Nicholas I

Although famous for his "liberation" of the serfs, Alexander II was the friend and ally of the nobility and of conservatism.

*ALEXANDER III (1881–1894)

Alexander II was assassinated, and this had a marked effect on his son's personality and political attitude. Since reform had ended with murder and treason, he reasoned that it was time to undo what his father had accomplished and set the clock back to the good old days before 1861.

*NICHOLAS II (1894–1917)

Alexander III was a strong enough czar to halt the revolutionary tide, but the last Romanov and the last czar of Russia, Nicholas II, only inherited from his father the principle of autocracy, not the ability to maintain it.

---

*The most important are starred.

The Growth of Autocracy

Peter the Great strengthened autocracy by further subjugating the church, the nobility, and the serfs to the will of the sovereign. Everyone owed service to the government and anyone who resisted faced brutal punishment. Service, in any form, was demanded for life, and the Table of Ranks established a hierarchy of fourteen grades based on merit. If a man achieved the eighth rank, he was allowed the privileges of a nobleman, owning serfs and property. The gentry were educated at the command of the czar. It was not until Peter III's reign (1762) that a manifesto was proclaimed emancipating the nobility from military, administrative, and economic obligations to the state.

Despite Catherine II's liberalism, she was as autocratic as any of the rulers of Russia. By the end of her reign, landlords had more control over their serfs, the peasant's bondage was extended, literary censorship had begun, and minorities were forced to conform to the Russian mold. Paul attempted to amend Catherine's charter of the nobility by dissolving their assemblies and once again subjecting them to corporal punishment. Further than this he dared not go, but he succeeded in alienating the mainstay of autocracy, and in 1801 he was strangled by his guards. His son Alexander (who was involved in the plot) was placed on the throne.

Alexander I, Nicholas I, Alexander II, Alexander III, and Nicholas II all attempted to maintain autocracy and the power of the despot, with varying degrees of success. In 1864 Alexander II did reconstruct a system of local self-government by issuing the Zemstov laws, giving considerable freedom in local law, education, and taxation. Nevertheless the principle of unqualified absolutism remained, and after an attempted assassination Alexander quickly changed this policy. In 1905 Nicholas II was forced by revolution to grant a constituent assembly, but it was allowed very little control over Russian affairs, domestic or external.

The Russian Orthodox Church

The church as an independent power in Russia no longer existed after the 1700s. First Peter the Great outraged religious orthodoxy by cutting all noblemen's beards (symbols of piety), and then he humbled it by abolishing the office of patriarch in 1721 and creating in its stead the Holy Synod, a council of ecclesiastical members subject to a layman, an overprocurator, who was in turn subject to the will of the czar. This was the final step in ensuring that the church would be identified with the autocrat's wishes. (It also ensured that the church would suffer the same fate as the monarchy in 1917.) The church could no longer oppose the czar's reforms, and Peter now had control of its wealth.

The Peasant and Serfdom

The Extension of Serfdom

PETER THE GREAT
The fate of the peasant was to finance the czar's schemes of westernization and war. Serfdom was tightly enforced, and the law was extended to new classes of free peasants. Taxes were levied on all males, and thus distinctions among different categories of bondsmen were obliterated. The building of St. Petersburg in 1721 is the classic example of treatment of the serfs. Thousands of lives were sacrificed to clear the swamps and build the parks fountains, cathedrals, and palaces.

Between 1704 and 1711 there were three peasant revolts, but, as in most agrarian revolutions, they failed because they lacked program, unity, and organization.

CATHERINE THE GREAT
Catherine's liberalism in no way extended to the peasant. It stopped short with affairs of state and was totally extinguished by the French Revolution and the Russian peasant revolt of 1773–

1774. Serfdom was further extended under her reign—by 1783 the whole of the Ukraine was subjected to it. The peasants of the Don country and most of the Caucasus were no longer free either. In 1767 an imperial decree prohibited complaint by a serf against his master. There was no redress except revolution.

Of a total population of 36 million, 34 million were peasants, of whom 20 million were serfs on private estates and 14 million were state or crown land peasants (legally not serfs but certainly in bondage). On the majority of private estates there were at least 100 serfs, and usually the figure was closer to 1000.

The Pugachev Rebellion 1773–1774

Of all peasant uprisings in Russian history perhaps the Pugachev rebellion was the most important, for it was to leave a scar that no reform healed. The suppression of the rebellion left behind a desire for revenge; peasants did not soon forget the punitive measures of Catherine II.

Led by the revolutionary leader Emelian Pugachev, peasant serfs, serfs in the mines of the Urals, minorities opposed to russification, and religious dissenters wreaked havoc for a year in the countryside of Russia. Landlords were tortured, farms were burned, officials and priests were hanged. Even the regular detachments sent to put down the revolt turned against their officers and slaughtered them. But in 1774, with carefully picked troops, Catherine had her revenge. The revolt was crushed, and Pugachev himself was carried off to Moscow in an iron cage and executed.

The "Emancipation" of the Serfs 1861

Despite his liberal tendencies, Alexander I made no attempt to emancipate the serfs. In 1801, however, he extended the right to own land to all free classes and to state peasants. In 1802 he passed a law granting serfs the right to purchase land from their masters (of course this was rare), and he also banned the sale of serfs on the open market.

During Nicholas I's reign some peasant reforms were attempted, but they had very little effect. There were 556 peasant uprisings during his rule.

Alexander II, after the humiliation of the Crimean War, recognized the need to reform and in 1856 announced that it was "better to abolish serfdom from above than wait until it begins to abolish itself from below." But the act that came in 1861 was too little and too late. Moreover it was done for military rather than humanitarian reasons. By the Terms of the Emancipation Act of 1861, a peasant was allowed to purchase land from his landlord on credit supplied by the government and repaid over a period of forty-nine years.

THE RESULTS OF EMANCIPATION

1) The land was overvalued and peasant holdings were of uneconomic size. Nor did the land really become the peasant's private property; it was transferred from the landlord to the village commune, which became responsible for the collection of payments due the government for the land and became, in fact, the peasant's master.

2) The peasant was now free but not equal. He continued to pay a poll tax, he alone was subject to corporal punishment, and he was bound to the commune by an internal passport system whereby written permission was necessary before a peasant could move.

The Influence of the West—Liberalism and Revolution

Liberalism and revolution in Russia went hand in hand with the influence of Western culture and ideas; they cannot be separated.

Borrowing from the West

Peter the Great brought the Russian state into contact with the West, but it was superficial contact from the beginning. His interest was primarily in Western military might, not in Western culture and thought, and piecemeal innovations were forced upon the Russian people.

In 1697 Peter, in the company of 200 nobles, went abroad to

study shipbuilding and Western techniques. He returned to Russia and promptly reorganized the military and created a navy.

In order to equip his new army and navy, the czar expanded small mills and foundries, laying the foundations of Russia's industrial development in the Urals and Central Russia. Foreign technicians, engineers, and teachers were brought to Russia to train and advise. But the continuation and strengthening of the bonds of serfdom along with the commanding economic leadership of the nobility were obstacles to further westernization of the Russian economy.

Fundamentally the reforms under Peter were concerned with the expansion of Russian power, although he did reduce the alphabet to thirty-six letters, create a new calendar beginning with January 1 instead of September 1, and sponsor the first newspaper.

The superficial quality of Peter's reforms, however, was revealed when the czar decreed that everyone should wear European dress and shave their barbarian beards. This he felt would make the Russians equal to Westerners. Even Peter's educational reforms indicate that he failed to understand the basis of the superiority of the West: he in no way encouraged intellectual training—only specific technical objectives.

The Enlightenment

Catherine the Great is traditionally grouped with the enlightened despots of Europe, but her claim is dubious. Although the cultural and court life of Russia were brilliant, her armies conquered the northern shores of the Black Sea, and the nobility spoke French and read Voltaire, Catherine did nothing to improve the lot of the majority of her people, and her reforms remained largely on paper. As R. D. Charques in his *A Short History of Russia* said, "Enlightenment in Catherine was, indeed, not much deeper than her vanity; despotism, on the other hand, was implicit in her ambition."

In 1766 Catherine summoned a legislative commission to prepare a new codification of the laws. After a year and a half of work an impressive liberal document was produced—but that was all, and when war broke out with Turkey the commission was disbanded. The commission, however, did bring to the attention of the czarina local abuses and corruption, which Catherine remedied in part by reforming provincial governments.

In 1785 Catherine's charter of the nobility reinforced the privileges that they had won since Peter the Great's death. The aristocracy was exempt from service, taxation, loss of rank, and corporal punishment. Authority in local government was reserved for them.

The First Liberal Czar

Educated in the philosophy of the "enlightenment" by his grandmother, Catherine II, and his Swiss tutor, La Harpe, Alexander I was perhaps the only true liberal to sit on the throne of Russia. During the first years of his reign he restored civil rights to thousands, closed down the secret political police, granted permission for students to travel abroad, and allowed the importation of foreign books. He attempted to grant certain freedoms to the serfs but never dared emancipation.

In 1809 Michael Speransky was commissioned by the czar to devise a system of constitutional government. The draft that was drawn up was a remarkable piece of work but remained on paper only. A *duma* (parliament) was to be created for each district. On the top of the local institutions was to be an elective duma for the entire country and a state council of advisers appointed by the crown. (The Bolsheviks adopted this as their system of representation by soviets.) Speransky was, of course, a threat to bureaucratic vested interests, and he was accused of treasonable relations with France and exiled in 1812.

Although Alexander did fulfill his liberal promises in foreign parts, a period of reaction set in after 1812 when war broke out against Napoleonic France, and most of the reforms he had made were undone. Military colonies were established in 1816. Nearly 500,000 peasants were made exempt from taxation and were trained for military service in colonies where every aspect of their life was dictated and regimented. Illiberalism in education was also manifest.

Dangerous thoughts were rooted out of the classrooms by purging university faculties and by strict censorship of materials, but this came too late, and it was among the group of educated lower nobility that disturbing and unorthodox ideas were spreading.

The Decembrist Revolt   December 14, 1825

The revolt led by a secret society of the young educated lower nobility and junior military officers who had served in the army of occupation in France during the Napoleonic wars was in one sense the last of the palace revolutions, but, more important, it was the beginning of a new revolutionary tradition. It was a rebellion not only to overthrow the czar but also to establish a more representative government.

Paul Pestel, one of the influential leaders, sought revolution and a republic, elimination of the czar, and a temporary dictatorship. The revolt failed because of lack of planning and initiative. One hundred and twenty plotters were brought to trial and 36 were condemned to death; five were actually executed.

Reaction

NICHOLAS I

The Decembrist Revolt was to have a definite influence on the internal policy of Nicholas I. As he declared, "a revolution stands on the threshold of Russia, but I swear it will never enter Russia while my breath lasts." His purpose, he said, was to retard the development of Russia by fifty years. Under Nicholas I the secret police were allowed to rule Russia, disciplined conformity was required of all subjects, secondary and higher education were restricted to the nobility, the universities were brought under control, and censorship was strictly enforced. Ironically, Russian literature was at its height.

Western influence manifested itself in the quasi-philosophical arguments between the Westerners and the Slavophiles, who believed in a unique Russian inheritance. The Westerners triumphed but in doing so became infected with Slavophile notions, and out of the mixture of the two there developed a new social movement called the populist movement.

ALEXANDER III

What liberalism there had been in the years between 1825 and 1881, such as the Zemstov laws and the emancipation of the serfs, was destroyed by Alexander III. Antiwestern, antiliberal, and authoritarian to the core, Pobedonostsev, procurator of the Holy Synod and Alexander III's tutor, became the principal ideological influence of the reign. *Russification* (assimilation accompanied by intolerance and persecution of minorities, particularly the Jews) was increased. Nevertheless, there were limited economic concessions made to the peasants, and industry was expanded during Alexander's reign.

The Revolution of 1905

Nicholas II continued the paternalistic rule of Alexander III, but he did not have the strength to control the revolutionary forces at work in Russia. With the humiliating defeats that Russia suffered during the Russo-Japanese War, liberal demands for reform (freedom of speech, industrial and agricultural legislation, and an elected national assembly) became louder and louder.

The spark that set off the revolution was Bloody Sunday—January 9, 1905. A priest, Father Gapon, led 200,000 unarmed workers to the palace gates in St. Petersburg in order to demand an eight-hour day, a minimum wage of a ruble a day, and a constituent assembly. The workers were fired upon by the guards, and over 500 were killed and thousands wounded.

Bloody Sunday united the dissatisfied bourgeois, proletariat, and peasants. By the end of 1905, 1500 government officials had been assassinated, peasants had seized estates, a strike committee had been set up by Leon Trotsky, and one of the most complete general strikes in history followed. The life of the country came to a standstill. *Soviets* (councils) of workers were established all over Russia and pressed the demand for a representative assembly.

The czar finally gave in and by the October Manifesto granted a legislative duma, but Nicholas maintained control of foreign policy and was allowed to disband the assembly and pass decrees when they were not in session. The duma, therefore, had little power.

Expansion and Foreign Policy   1695–1905

Peter the Great

Under Peter the Great, expansion and westernization went hand in hand. It was for the purpose of military conquest that he borrowed European technology and skills, industry and administration. His main interest was the establishment of two warm-water ports, one on the Baltic and the other on the Mediterranean. (This meant war with the Turks over the control of the Dardanelles and with Sweden over the command of the Baltic.)

Peter's first attempt at conquest was Azov on the Black Sea. In 1695 he moved against the city unsuccessfully, but when in 1696 he built a fleet of ships in order to blockade the fortress, Azov surrendered. His dream of possessing Constantinople and an outlet to the Aegean was the reason for his travels in Europe in 1697, where he sought technical knowledge and military aid.

The Great Northern War against Sweden (1700–21) was the czar's next step. Failure to convince the West of the desirability of dismembering the Turkish empire turned Peter's attention to another warm-water port and outlet to the Baltic. In order to achieve victory against the Swedes, the local and central government of Russia was reformed, a new standing army was created, and the iron foundries in the Urals were developed. Three years of preparation ended in twenty-one years of tragic war.

The Swedes were initially victorious at Narva, and if they had not postponed the invasion of Russia in order to fight a six-year war with Poland, the final outcome of the Great Northern War might have been very different. As it was, Peter had time to recover, reorganize his army, and seize the marshland on the eastern tip of the Gulf of Finland. It was here in 1703 that a fort was built, named St. Peter and St. Paul and in 1721 that Peter constructed his window to the West—the city of St. Petersburg.

Victory at Poltava in 1709 (followed by the conquest of Livonia, Estonia, and Karelia) turned Peter's eyes once again toward the Crimea and the Turks. He was defeated and lost Azov as well as his ambition in the south. The war continued in the north against Sweden. The first Russian naval victory in history was won in 1714, and finally in 1721 the Treaty of Nystadt was signed. The Baltic coast from Viborg to Riga was gained by Russia. Peter then turned his ambitions toward Persia and won, temporarily, the western coast of the Caspian Sea.

1725–1762

Russian diplomacy and expansion were erratic during the years between Peter and Catherine. In 1757 Russia invaded East Prussia. What saved Frederick the Great of Prussia was the death of Czarina Elizabeth and the subsequent reversal of Russian foreign policy. It was clear that Russia was a power to be contended with.

Catherine the Great

Russian territorial aggrandizement was greater during Catherine's reign than any since Ivan IV. She took on first the Poles and then the Turks—her main objective was the outlet to the Mediterranean, Constantinople.

In 1767, by armed force, Catherine established a protectorate over Poland, allowing the country to maintain a loose aristocratic constitution, but in 1772 the czarina had to agree to end the protectorate and to a partial division of the country with Austria and Prussia. In 1793 Poland was partitioned for a second time, and this time Austria did not share in the spoils. Russia gained White Russia and most of the remaining Polish Ukraine. Poland's constitution was annulled and once again she became a Russian protectorate. In 1795 a third partition wiped Poland off the map. Russia gained the rest of the Ukraine and Lithuania.

In 1770 Turkey was incited by France to declare war on Russia. The Pugachev revolt put Catherine in a position where compromise peace was the only solution. By the Treaty of Kuckukkainardji (1774), Russia lost Walachia and Moldavia (trans-

Danubian provinces) but gained the whole northern shore of the
Black Sea, except Crimea. In 1783 Catherine annexed the Crimea,
and in 1787 Turkey and Russia were again at war; in 1792 Turkey,
by the Treaty of Jassy, was forced to confirm Russian control of
the Crimea.

The Napoleonic Wars

In 1799 Russia joined the brief second coalition against
Napoleon and invaded northern Italy. Paul, however, came to
terms with Napoleon, for the czar was convinced that it was England, not France, that was the real threat to his ambitions, and
in 1801 a force of 20,000 unprepared troops marched on India.
Paul died and the campaign ended.

Alexander made peace with the English, and in 1805 he
joined the third coalition against France. In 1807, after defeat at
Friedland, Alexander signed the Treaty of Tilsit with Napoleon
(compare with the Nazi-Soviet Pact of 1939). During this period
of uneasy truce, Russia overran Finland and incorporated it as a
grand duchy. Russia then resumed war with Turkey, gaining only
Bessarabia in 1812.

By 1812 Russia was again at war with Napoleon. The war
bears certain similarities to 1941. The Russian front was over-
extended, Alexander had no coherent strategy, and if Napoleon
had attempted to please the civilian population by liberating the
peasantry, perhaps the conclusion would have been different. It
was only after Moscow was occupied that the war became a "war
of the fatherland." The French forces were primarily defeated by
the Russian winter, and the collapse of their supply lines.

At the Congress of Vienna, Russia's aims were clear—the
Balkans, the Baltic, and the issue of Poland were her chief concerns. Russia allied with Austria, Prussia, and England in the
Quadruple Alliance to enforce the Vienna peace treaty. Later in
1815 Russia signed the Holy Alliance with Austria and Prussia to
preserve monarchy, aristocracy, and godliness in Europe, which,
according to the English Lord Castlereagh, was a piece of "sublime

mysticism and nonsense." Alexander did keep his promise to grant Poland a liberal constitution and to emancipate the peasants in the Baltic.

Nicholas I

In 1831 Poland was absorbed into the Russian empire and brutally russianized. Nicholas then turned his eyes toward the Ottoman Empire and control of the Dardanelles. In 1829 Russia gained a protectorate over the Danubian provinces but soon came in conflict with British and French interests in the Middle East. In 1833, the Turkish sultan accepted Russian aid against Mohammed Ali, but in 1841 Russia had to abandon its privileged status in Constantinople and all foreign warships were banned from the Dardanelles.

In 1853 Nicholas' army invaded Moldavia and Wallachia; war between Russia and Turkey ensued, and in 1854 France and Britain entered on Turkey's side. The Crimean War was disastrous for all concerned, and incompetence, intrigue, lack of supplies, and inferior equipment led to a Russian defeat. In 1856 Alexander II asked for peace.

Russia Turns East

In 1860 China lost the lower course of the Amur River to Russia, and Vladivostok was built. (In 1867, however, Russia sold Alaska to the United States.) In central Asia, Tashkent was captured (1865) and Samarkand fell to Russian troops in 1868. In 1891 the Trans-Siberian railroad was begun. In 1877, however, Russia was again at war with Turkey, and the map of the Balkans was transformed as a result.

After the Boxer Rebellion in China in 1900, Russia's lease on Port Arthur became in actual fact annexation, and Russia became more and more concerned with Japanese penetration in Korea. Nicholas II made no attempt at compromise with the Japanese, and the Russo-Japanese War broke out in February 1904, and Russia suffered an overwhelming and humiliating defeat.

The February Revolution—the Liberal Revolt   1917

Causes

World War I: the February Revolution was a direct outgrowth of wartime conditions.

POOR LEADERSHIP

There were few generals who were trained in modern warfare, and they clung to the concept of positional old-style fighting dating back to Napoleon. Most of the generals were jealous of each other, and there were incidents in which they refused to fight together. The situation was made worse when the czar took over personal command at the front in February 1915.

LACK OF INDUSTRY

At the beginning of World War I Russian industry was hardly capable of taking care of a peacetime economy, let alone wartime demands. (By 1917 men were going to the front with one rifle for every ten men.) What industry there was was located in the Ukraine and was quickly overrun by the advancing Germans.

THE AGRICULTURAL SITUATION

Russian agriculture was based on manual labor, and once the war began to take the peasant from the land, the country was faced with starvation. Most of the rich agricultural land lay in the vulnerable Ukraine, and poor transportation further aggravated the problem, for the cities were soon starving (By 1916 the government had no grain reserves left.)

THE SCORCHED EARTH POLICY

The policy of burning everything as the enemy approached had defeated Napoleon's army, but it did not prove as effective in World War I because of modern transportation. An already acute food shortage was made worse by the burning of wheat, and social discontent was increased by the addition of starving peasants who flocked to the cities.

The ineffectual government of the czar was another cause of the revolution. Nicholas II was more concerned with his family than with the management of the government, and once he had decided to go to the front, St. Petersburg was left in the hands of his wife, Alexandra. She was completely under the control of Rasputin, a man who professed to be a monk. Even after Rasputin's murder by members of the aristocracy in December 1916, the czarina continued to hold seances with him and continued to persuade her husband not to listen to the cries for reform.

The Course of the Revolution

The revolution began as a strike and a demand by the people of St. Petersburg for bread. Government troops were sent out to break up the demonstration but instead they joined the strikers. The arsenal was seized, prisons were opened, and police headquarters was fired upon. A soviet of workers and soldiers was organized.

The government collapsed, and the duma was the only body left capable of taking over. The duma was the third and most conservative in Russian history (the only socialist was Kerensky). The conservative Prince Lvov was made head of the provisional, "liberal" government, and on March 15, Czar Nicholas II abdicated.

The Failure of the Liberal Government

The major weakness of the government was its failure to end the war. The government felt that it must keep the bargain with the Allies and not make a separate peace.

It was a provisional government until elections could be held. Therefore the members felt that they could not put through any of the necessary economic and social reforms until they had received popular sanction.

In the end its very liberalism defeated it, for the new government allowed complete freedom to all groups. There was no censorship of the press, there was little control within the army, and the leftists could do what they pleased.

The Kornilov Affair was the final act that undermined the power of the provisional government. In September General Kornilov, commander-in-chief of the army, decided to restore order in St. Petersburg at the cost of overthrowing the Kerensky government (Kerensky had replaced Lvov as head of the government.) The only place the provisional government could turn for help was to the soviets (controlled by the Bolsheviks). The Bolsheviks were thus armed and became the heroes of the city.

THE SOVIET UNION   1917 to the Present

This era begins with the end of 450 years of czarist rule and the establishment of the Union of Soviet Socialist Republics. Change is the dominant theme as Russia moved from what is called today an underdeveloped area with an agricultural economy based on serfdom to a modern industralized nation; from a highly inefficient form of absolutism in government to a twentieth-century totalitarian state; and from a society led by an aristocratic elite based on land and blood to a state led by another elite—the Communist Party. Yet if there was change, there was also continuity; the peasant problem still exists, the concept of russification is carried even further than under the czars, and the imperialistic desire to control the Black Sea and the Baltic has remained.

The October Revolution—the Bolshevik Revolt   1917

Rival Political Creeds

THE SOCIAL REVOLUTIONARIES
This was a group supported by the great majority of the people; their appeal was primarily to the peasantry. (In the 1918 elections they captured 410 seats out of 707 in the constituent assembly.) They had no organized plan of action and often resorted to terrorism and assassination. Their leader was Yevno Azev, who was for years the head of the Social Revolutionary fighting organization as well as a czarist police spy.

THE LIBERALS

Only a small minority of the population were liberals. Their very moderation and tolerance were their greatest weaknesses. The main body of liberals was called the Constitutional Democrats led by Miliukov, who advocated parliamentary government.

THE MENSHEVIKS

In 1903 the Social Democratic Party of Russia (Marxist) split into the Mensheviks and the Bolsheviks. The main issue was the question of the immediacy of the revolution. The Mensheviks believed that Russia had to go through the stage of bourgeois capitalism first. They were more inclined to be orthodox Marxists, believing that the revolution would be inevitable—so why create it? The Mensheviks also advocated a freer organization with looser control than did the Bolsheviks. At the time of the revolution in Russia they were more popular and numerous than the Bolsheviks.

THE BOLSHEVIKS

The Bolsheviks were a small, tightly knit group of professional revolutionaries who advocated "democratic centralism," whereby there could be no disagreement once a plan had been accepted. They were Marxists who believed in an immediate and violent revolution.

Reasons for the Bolshevik Triumph

The organization itself and its ideology were the primary factors for success. Their leader, Lenin, born Vladimir Ulianov (1870–1924), was a dedicated revolutionary who was willing to "eat, sleep, and breathe" the revolution. Lenin urged, in his pamphlet, *What Is to Be Done?*, the formation of a compact and strongly centralized party whose membership would be strictly confined to active revolutionaries. It was Lenin who was chiefly responsible for the split between the Bolsheviks and the Mensheviks. Lenin, aided by the Germans, returned from exile in Switzerland in April 1917 and immediately took command of the Bolsheviks. At the railroad station he delivered his blueprint for revolution called the April Thesis. By this time Stalin had returned from exile in Siberia, and a month later Trotsky returned from New York. The blue-print stated that the Bolsheviks should refuse support to the pro-visional government and demand that all power go to the soviets; they should gain control of the soviets from the Mensheviks and the Social Revolutionaries, advocate the goal of "peace, bread, and land," and spread propaganda at the front and in the industrial centers.

The Revolution

The actual takeover of St. Petersburg was almost bloodless. On October 25, 1917, the Bolsheviks seized the principal buildings in the capital. In other large cities the same procedure was fol-lowed. The only place where there was active resistance was in Moscow, by a body of about 3000 military cadets who fought for a week. The Bolsheviks did not control the greater part of the Ukraine, the Cossack lands, the Transcaucasus, or the Russian countryside. Control of these areas was to come later with the civil war.

The Lenin Era　1917–1927

Founding a New State

In December 1917, the first general election in Russian his-tory was held. The Social Revolutionaries won the greatest number of votes, but in January 1918, at the command of the Bolsheviks, the soldiers dissolved the Constituent Assembly, and the newly created Bolshevik secret police (Cheka) was ordered to arrest, try, and execute anyone who was an "enemy of the state."

THE CIVIL WAR　1918–1921

The Bolsheviks then began to tackle the problem of taking control of the Russian countryside. The civil war was a military triumph. The reasons for Bolshevik success were:

1) Militarily they had control of the major cities.

2) Trotsky reorganized the Red Guard into an effective fighting force, secured by the Cheka in the rear.

3) The forces opposing the Bolsheviks had no organization and were not united.

ALLIED INTERVENTION

Lenin had to fight western troops as well as his own people in order to secure his hold on Russia. In February 1918, the Soviet Government cancelled all debts and nationalized all foreign property, and in March it signed a separate peace with Germany. In the autumn of 1918 Allied troops invaded Russia in the north, the south, and the east. Allied motivations for intervention were mixed:

1) The Americans wanted to protect Allied munitions supplies in north Russia.

2) The Japanese were imperialistically interested in Russian territory in the Pacific.

3) Britain and France wanted to prevent the Germans from transferring their troops to the western front.

By November the military reasons for intervention had ended with the surrender of the Germans, yet the Allies remained. By 1921, however, Western attempts at organizing the forces opposing the Bolsheviks had failed, and the only foreigners who remained were the Japanese in Siberia (until 1922).

THE NEW ECONOMIC POLICY

After the military takeover of Russia, Lenin still had problems. Industry was in a disastrous condition since the workers had been given control; peasants were refusing to grow crops and miners to mine. In March 1921, the Kronstadt sailors revolted, demanding freedom of speech and the abolition of the specially privileged position of the Communist Party. The primitive mixture of Communist theories and practical necessity used during the civil war was not working: the proletariat was revolting against the dictatorship of the proletariat. Lenin realized that concessions must be made if his government was to last.

The New Economic Policy (NEP) was introduced in 1921. Private ownership of land was restored and private retail trade was recognized. (By the end of 1922, three-quarters of retail trade was in private hands. Heavy industry, however, remained in the hands of the state.) Taxation in kind replaced forcible exaction of produce from the peasants. The industrial proletariat and the landowning peasant were to work together in harmony (a most un-Marxist innovation). The NEP produced results. By 1923 overall agricultural production had risen to nearly three-quarters of that of 1913.

COMMUNIST CONTROL

Despite economic concessions there was little freedom in Russia. Mensheviks and Social Revolutionaries were tried and imprisoned; liberals suffered the same fate. Kerensky and many other political leaders fled to the United States. Artists such as Stravinsky and Rachmaninoff were among the great exodus of creative talent. Artists did remain, however, and some fine works were produced during the 1920s, but after 1928 cultural revolution took place.

The Soviet leadership created a monopoly of the interpretation of ideology. A single source of ideology was absolutely necessary to the maintenance of power. This was the heart of the struggle between Trotsky and Stalin, for the man who laid down the party line would be the man who controlled Russia. (This was also the heart of the battle for Mao, Tito, and Brezhnev.)

International Affairs

THE TREATY OF BREST-LITOVSK

Lenin had come to power promising "land, bread, and peace." Peace had to be achieved on any terms, and in March 1918, one of the harshest treaties in history was signed. Russia agreed to the evacuation of the Ukraine, Finland, the Baltic states, Poland, and the Transcaucausus. It lost three-quarters of its iron and coal, one-quarter of its arable land, one-quarter of its population, and one-third of its manufacturing and also had to pay a large war indemnity. Since Russia concluded a separate peace, almost all the countries of the world broke diplomatic relations, but Lenin succeeded in saving the revolution.

THE SEARCH FOR INTERNATIONAL RECOGNITION

Russian foreign policy from 1921 to 1924 was aimed at:

1) the establishment of relations in order to reduce economic and political isolation,

2) friendship agreements with neighbors to prevent further Allied intervention,

3) the encouragement of colonial countries to revolt.

In January 1921, the Chinese granted *de facto* recognition to the Soviet Government; then Iran and Great Britain followed suit, but it was not until April 1922, that Russia ended isolation by signing the Treaty of Rapallo with Germany. By 1924 Britain gave *de jure* recognition to the Soviet Government, and the rest of Western Europe followed. The United States did not recognize the Soviet Union until 1933.

THE COMINTERN

Despite the fact that Lenin's era was a "soft" period in international relations, the Third Communist International (the first from 1864 to 1876; the second from 1889 to 1914), or what was termed the Comintern, was established in 1919, setting up an international organization with its main objective the establishment of communism in all countries. Orders were taken directly from Moscow, and the Comintern became a fifth column instrument of Soviet foreign policy. It was agreed that "unreserved support of Soviet Russia is the very first duty of Communists of all countries."

THE THEORY OF IMPERIALISM

Lenin's theory of imperialism was to have repercussions around the world. He explained that Marx had not foreseen the possibility of the capitalist saving himself from a revolution by the proletariat. The capitalists had eased the situation at home by exploiting the backward countries of the world. Therefore the communist revolution would occur first in these nations under imperialist domination —the "weakest link" (for example, Russia)—and then spread to the industrialized nations.

Lenin's Death and the Battle for Power

By the end of 1921 Lenin was working only half time; in 1922 he suffered a stroke and was an invalid until his death in 1924, when Stalin and Trotsky began the struggle for leadership of the Soviet Union. The battle between the two men was personal as well as ideological. Trotsky, the brilliant historian, politician, orator, and military leader, had the army and the youth of Russia on his side. On the other hand, Stalin, the son of a Georgian cobbler, common, calculating, and coarse, had the great advantage of being a consummate manipulator of men. His position as secretary of the Party gave him control over party affairs and access to secret files of information.

The victory was an ideological one. Stalin's theories were appealing to the mass of the people; Trotsky's were not. According to Trotsky, the Communist revolution had occurred in a country that had a predominant number of peasants, who were petty bourgeois. The proletariat in Russia was a small minority in a hostile sea of peasants. Therefore the Russian revolution was doomed unless there was a Communist revolution in Europe that could support the proletariat in Russia. The Soviet Union's chief aim should be to continue and encourage revolution outside of Russia. Trotsky's theory proved unpopular. For one thing, Russia's energies badly needed to be directed toward improvements at home. For another, revolution was failing in Europe and all over the world. The German Communist revolution in 1923 had failed, and in 1927 the Chinese Communists were slaughtered by Chiang Kai-shek. Trotsky also believed that the Communist Party should be less tightly knit than Lenin had advocated. Here his philosophy was contradictory, for if a minority were to stay in power it had to be tightly organized and disciplined. This theory was to brand him as the romantic of the revolution and a Menshevik.

According to Stalin the Russian revolution was not unique; it was the pattern of all Communist revolutions. Russia, in fact, was the vanguard of the revolution, therefore the more rapidly Russia built socialism the better. It could then act as a lever for the disintegration of imperialism. Socialism could exist in Russia without the aid of a world revolution, and revolutions throughout the world should be supported only if they were in the interests of the USSR. The Party was the dictator of the vanguard, and until 1928 Stalin maintained that the peasants and the proletariat were allies.

In 1929 Trotsky fled to Mexico, and in 1940 he was assassinated.

Stalin and the Second Revolution   1928–1938

This period is often referred to as the second Bolshevik revolution, for it was during this decade that cultural, political, and economic changes took place that transformed Russia and created the state that exists today.

The First Five-Year Plan

As soon as Stalin was firmly entrenched in power he introduced a program that had two purposes:

1) to force peasants to give up privately held land and to join in collective or state farms,

2) to increase the output of heavy industry.

Stalin's first step in creating Russian socialism was to declare that the peasants were bourgeois and enemies of the proletariat. The peasants were holding back on produce, inflation was resulting, and capital was badly needed to increase industrial production.

In 1929 an extensive drive was begun in the country to force the peasants into collective farms. The peasants resisted; they slaughtered cattle, burned their crops, and killed as many officials as they could. The process of collectivization was bloody and violent; armed troops were sent into the countryside; millions of peasants were exiled; war was declared against the kulak (wealthy peasants), and most were either slaughtered or sent to prison camps. Figures are doubtful, but probably nearly 3 million peasants died of starvation. By 1939 collectivization was almost universal.

Most land and livestock were owned by the collective farm *(kolkhozy)*, although the peasant was allowed an individual patch of land. Machine tractor stations controlled by the Party managed all mechanized farm equipment and thus controlled the collective (these stations were abolished by Khrushchev). By 1940 there were 250,000 collective farms, but according to Leninism-Stalinism, the ideal organization of peasants was the state farm *(sovkhozy)*. It was owned and operated by the state, and peasants worked for wages and had no freedom to dispose of surplus as they did on the collective. By this means the peasant was to be proletarianized. By 1940 there were only 4000 state farms.

The First Five-Year Plan was to control and direct the entire resources of the nation toward a particular set of goals. Steel was to be increased from 4.2 million to 10 million tons (in 1940 the United States produced 66.9 million tons), coal was to be increased from 35 million to 150 million tons (in comparison, the United States produced 62.4 million tons in 1930); and electric power was to be increased from 5 million to 22 million kilowatt-hours (by 1957 the United States was producing 715.7 billion and the USSR 210 billion kilowatt-hours). All industry was nationalized and directed by the state.

The heart of Marxism is the doctrine *from each according to his abilities, to each according to his needs.* The Russian Communists, however, maintained that equality was alien and detrimental to socialism. Under Stalin wage differentials and rewards such as bonuses and vacations for overfulfilling quotas of production were introduced. The worker's freedom was taken away. The power of trade unions was curbed, and they became tools of the Party. The internal passport system was reintroduced, and labor books containing a full record of a worker's employment were necessary to get a job. By 1940 a state decree bound all workers to their jobs. Thus the worker and the peasant were bound to state service under conditions resembling serfdom in seventeenth-century Russia.

The State

Hand in hand with the First Five-Year Plan came a reinterpretation of the role of the state. According to Marxist doctrine the state would wither away, but according to Stalin it would get stronger and stronger because of the danger of foreign capitalistic military attack. Not until socialism was triumphant all over the world would the state disappear.

The Stalin Constitution (1936) granted unrestricted universal suffrage (formerly there had been unequal representation of workers over peasants) and secret elections, but this meant nothing because the system called for a single party. As Stalin said, "in the USSR only one party can exist, the Communist."

Socialist Realism

More than force was needed to meet the demands of the First Five-Year Plan. Propaganda was thrown into the battle for production, and a cultural revolution was forced upon the Russian population. The press, the radio, and the arts were now to be dedicated to the purpose of ideologically remaking the people in the spirit of socialism. All art was to depict Soviet reality — optimistic and happy. No experimentation was allowed, jazz was outlawed, artists were arrested and even executed. The purges in art reached their peak between 1936 and 1938. In 1937 alone sixty authors were attacked; many Jewish authors were shot. History was rewritten to inspire nationalism; names of liquidated men were eliminated from all records. Western books were removed from shelves, and history became merely a pawn of politics.

The Great Purge

The purpose of the purges was to eliminate those groups of people who might form power factions and oppose the existing regime. The excuse was the murder of Kirov, henchman of Stalin, in 1934. (Khrushchev said Stalin had Kirov assassinated.) The groups eliminated included the Old Bolsheviks (the idealists), the army (the Trotskyites and the old guard), those who had had contact with the West (particularly prisoners of war in World War I), and the technical intelligentsia. Seventy percent of the Central Committee of the Party was eliminated and 25 percent of the army.

International Affairs

From 1928 to 1933, Stalin did not concern himself with the affairs of the world, but when Hitler became chancellor of Germany in 1933 and Japan was threatening Russia's defenseless Pacific flank, he began to look to the West for help. In 1934 the USSR even joined that "capitalist club," the League of Nations, and Stalin vigorously made efforts at negotiating security agreements.

The "popular front" tactic of 1935 was an effort to make it appear that Communist parties were just ordinary political parties and to get all nonfascist parties to work together with one another. The popular front had two purposes:

1) to rally support against Nazism,

2) to create new governments that would lead eventually to Communist triumph.

The West did not trust Stalin. His aid in the Spanish Civil War (1936–1939) and his actions at home did not produce confidence. Stalin's policy of collective security had failed when in 1938 England and France refused his offer of military aid against Germany and gave in to the demands of Hitler for the partition of Czechoslovakia.

The Soviet Union in World War II   1939–1945

The Nonaggression Pact with Germany

In 1938 a new foreign policy was signaled by the appointment of Molotov—the "hammer"—as foreign minister, and in 1939, Hitler and Stalin agreed to remain at peace for ten years and to divide eastern Europe into two spheres of influence. Russia was to have eastern Poland, the Baltic states, and Bessarabia.

When Germany invaled Poland in 1939, the Red Army occupied eastern Poland. Treaties were forced upon Latvia, Lithuania, and Estonia in 1940, and both Poland and the Baltic states were incorporated into the USSR. The Russo-Finnish War was fought from November 1939, to March 1940. The Russian army took a terrible beating but won control of Finland in 1940.

On June 22, 1941, the uneasy truce ended and Germany invaded Russia. Stalin had been warned by Churchill and others that Hitler planned to attack, but he refused to believe that his policy would fail, and it was two days after the invasion before he was finally convinced.

The War

In the first year the Germans blockaded Leningrad and came within twenty miles of Moscow; they drove deep into southern Russia in 1942. The Russians played a waiting game until winter, and Stalin appealed to his people to fight for their homes (not for Communism). The Germans created their own destruction by being more cruel and more merciless landlords than the Communists.

At Stalingrad in 1943 the Nazi war machine stalled and the Russian counterattack began. From 1943 to 1945 Stalin drove the Germans from Russian soil and pressed for political concessions in eastern Europe from the Allies. At the Yalta Conference (1945) the "big three" agreed to settle the problem of eastern Europe by free elections, a coalition government of Communists and non-Communists in Poland, and recognition of the 1941 Soviet–Polish frontier. These agreements were ignored by Stalin.

Internal Policy

During the war all propaganda was directed at increasing nationalism, and there was some diminution of police terror in Russia. Yet there was little pro-Western propaganda—only two or three times did news of Western feats come to the Soviet population's attention.

Recovery and the "Cold War"   1946–1953

Policy in Eastern Europe

Immediately after the war East Germany, Bulgaria, Rumania, Poland, Yugoslavia, Hungary, Albania, and Czechoslovakia became Soviet satellites. (Today Yugoslavia is not considered a satellite and Albania has also deviated from the Russian path.)

Eastern Europe was vital to Russia as a buffer zone against the West and as a source of raw materials and manpower. East Germany and Czechoslovakia had enormous industrial capacity; Czechoslovakia had important munition industries as well as rich agricultural and forest lands. Rumania had oil; Hungary had bauxite and fertile plains for agriculture; Poland had raw materials, particularly coal; and Yugoslavia was rich in natural resources. In 1962 for instance, these nations produced 150.9 million metric tons of coal and the USSR 517 million; in steel they contributed 24 million metric tons and the USSR 76; in electricity the satellites' share was 134 billion kilowatt-hours and the USSR's 369 billion.

Most of the satellites were "liberated" by the Russians, and along with Soviet troops came the police and the Party. (Austria was also occupied by the Soviet army but developed an independent multi-party system.) Generally there was a pattern of takeover: first, the Communists would gain control of the key posts of foreign minister, minister of the interior (police), and/or minister of defense. Then, with the Red Army to back them, they would push out the moderate socialists from the government and push through nationalization of industry and land reform, gaining the support of labor and peasants. Finally opposition would be outlawed and, if necessary, destroyed by force. Then friendship, military, diplomatic, and economic pacts would be signed with the USSR.

International Policy

In 1946 Stalin declared that as long as capitalism survived the world was not safe from war. International policy changed abruptly from the "soft" tactics of 1941–45 to the hardest period in Russian foreign affairs. Aggression was the theme of the cold war.

In 1943 the Comintern had been disbanded, but in 1947 the Cominform (Communist Information Bureau) was established. It was a Europe-wide espionage, foreign policy, and economic coordination center. In February 1948, the Czechoslovakia *coup* (the takeover of the country by armed force) finally awakened the Western world to the ultimate purpose of the USSR. Shortly afterward, Greek and Turkish Communists increased antigovernment agitation, and in China Moscow openly supported Mao Tse-tung and gave moral support to Communist activities in French Indo-China.

THE BERLIN BLOCKADE

In the spring of 1948 Stalin decided to drive the West out of Berlin, and he closed all surface access routes to the city. A massive airlift was the West's answer to this threat. From June 1948 to May 1949 planes flew night and day, saving Berlin by bringing in over 2.5 million tons of food and coal. Stalin finally surrendered and lifted the blockade.

THE KOREAN WAR

In 1950 Stalin signed the Sino-Soviet Treaty and then encouraged the North Korean army to attack South Korea. His "forward" policy failed due to the military intervention of the UN.

TROUBLE IN THE SOVIET BLOC

Marshall Tito (Josip Broz) of Yugoslavia was one of the few Communist leaders in the satellites who was not under direct control, and in 1948 Stalin tried to get rid of him. Tito was expelled from the Cominform, but Stalin was unable to shake Tito's grip on his party or on Yugoslavia because Tito turned to the West for aid and received it. Numerous other eastern European Communists of the same independent leanings as Tito were purged. Executions were brutal: Gomulka of Poland was arrested; and Kostov of Bulgaria, Slamsky of Czechoslovakia, and Rajk of Hungary were shot.

Internal Policy

The trend toward national patriotism was reversed; Party membership was tightened; and a police crackdown under Beria was instigated (at least 100,000 were deported). Stalin's personal ascendancy became so great that the Politburo rarely met, and the Party was simply an instrument used to carry out orders.

The Death of Stalin

In 1953 a group of Jewish doctors who were accused of trying to poison Stalin were arrested, and it looked as if a new purge were in the making. The wave of terror was just in the planning stage when Stalin died. It has been argued that his death was not accidental, but so far there is no conclusive proof of this.

Domestic Progress and Détente   1954–1979

The Struggle for Power and Khrushchev

The battle for Stalin's power was similar to the 1924 struggle at the death of Lenin and was an ideological, economic, and personal war. The contenders for power were Beria, chief of the secret police and in charge of all atomic installations; Bulganin, leader of the army; Malenkov, leader of the government; Molotov, foreign affairs minister and vice-premier; and Khrushchev, secretary of the Party. The key post, as in 1924, was that of secretary of the Party, which was held by the son of Ukrainian serfs, Nikita Khrushchev.

Beria was arrested and executed a few months after Stalin's death. Malenkov was the next victim; head of the government from 1953 to 1955, his power was based on the state apparatus. Next to be defeated were Molotov and Kaganovitch (the man responsible for Khrushchev's rise to power during Stalin's rule). Both were old-line Stalinists, and Krushchev almost lost this battle. He was outvoted by the Presidium on the question of agriculture and foreign policy, but saved himself by bringing the issue to the Central Committee and relying heavily on the support of the army in the form of Marshall George Zhukov, popular hero of World War II. When Zhukov had done his work, he too was removed from office. In 1958 Bulganin "resigned" as head of the government, a post he had held since 1955, and Khrushchev was made both premier and general secretary of the Party. He now had the power that Stalin had once held and had successfully played his rivals against one another, but unlike Stalin he did not find it necessary to execute them.

Brezhnev and Kosygin

In October 1964, Khrushchev quietly retired (died 1971), and Leonid Brezhnev became first secretary of the Communist Party, while Aleksei Kosygin assumed the title of premier. The transition was accomplished smoothly. The cited cause was a repetition of the charge against Stalin—"the cult of personality"—but was more fundamental; Khrushchev was out of tune with the *apparatchniki* (organization men who were beginning to dominate the Soviet Union).

The son of a Ukrainian steelworker, Brezhnev rose to power first as a Red Army political commissar and briefly as a member of the Communist Party Central Committee. Under Khrushchev, Brezhnev was put in charge of the virgin lands program; in 1956 he was reinstated in the Central Committee; and in 1957 he was made a full member of the Presidium. In 1960 he was given the honorary title of soviet president, but he resigned in 1963 to give full attention to the secretariat. By this time he was slated as Khrushchev's successor.

Kosygin was the son of a Leningrad lathe operator and had no formal education except the Leningrad Textile Institution. He received his political training under Stalin, and after many setbacks he became Russia's top industrial expert. In 1957 he returned to the Politburo, and in 1960 he was made deputy premier.

For the first time the job of premier has not been absorbed by the party chief, but the problem of succession remains. In 1979 Brezhnev was 72 and Kosygin 75.

The Ruling Elite

The central committee of the Communist Party makes decisions from the cost of wheat to the building of nuclear submarines. Although the pay in 1975 was only $400 a month (Brezhnev made $1200), there are many fringe benefits. Members have special doctors, clubs, and apartments, receive priorities for automobiles and universities, and about 10 percent of their salary is in the form of coupons to buy Western goods at low prices from stores which are not open to the general public.

Economic Changes

One of the main ideological battles on which Khrushchev rose to power was decentralization. Under Stalin the soviet economy had been incapacitated by overcentralization and lack of local initiative. Khrushchev wanted to decentralize industrial management and thus eliminate the serious waste, confusion, and duplication of functions under the State Planning Commission. He also advocated decentralization of agriculture. His main ambition was to decentralize government control and tighten Party control.

During the first two five-year plans and postwar reconstruction, the GNP rose between 15 and 18 percent; from 1950 to 1960 the rate of growth was between 10 and 12 percent. By 1961 the GNP was $264 billion; by 1964, $287 billion; and in 1972, $400 billion. (The United States during the same years was $540 billion; $632 billion; and over a trillion.) Despite low wage levels and high prices, real wages have more than doubled since World War II.

Under Brezhnev and Kosygin emphasis was placed on increased efficiency through modernization and new technical skills. Exchanges with the West were encouraged, trade with the U.S. burgeoned, and western firms participated in industrial projects in the USSR. In 1973 there was a record harvest of 220 million tons of wheat (50 million more than 1972). This helped produce a 7.3 percent increase in industrial output when the target was only 5.8 percent, and the GNP grew by 6.3 percent. Demographic change in part reflects expanding industrialization: in 1939 the urban population was 32 percent; by 1970 it was 56 percent. The USSR has at least 25 percent of the world's total energy resources.

The "Thaw" and the Effects of Detente at Home

The "thaw," named after a novel by Ilya Ehrenburg, began in 1953 with the death of Stalin and reached its high point in 1956 with the announcements of the Twentieth Party Congress. At the congress Khrushchev announced that Stalin had been a villain, for he had established the cult of personality and allowed no contradiction and no freedom. Khrushchev then declared his opponents to be anti-Party for following Stalin's notions. There was to be a cultural and intellectual as well as an economic change in Russia:

1) Educational reform was passed in which the best students were allowed to go to school full time instead of working part time.

2) Cultural exchange was begun in 1958, and there was a general relaxation of censorship and police control.

3) The Communists were attempting to awaken the intellectual life of the USSR without relaxing their control over creativity. Creative impulses in all fields had been hampered by fear and restriction. In Soviet science, for instance, creativity was minimal. Between 1901 and 1962 only five Russians won Nobel prizes for science. (The United States' total during these years was fifty-eight.)

With the thaw, voices of protest against Party dictators got out of hand and even cultural exchange caused problems. The USSR wanted to exhibit its cultural advances, but it was very difficult to control the ideas foreigners brought into Russia. In 1958 the leash was pulled tighter, and Khrushchev was forced once again to restrict the intellectuals.

Détente was more an extension of "peaceful coexistence" (see p. 196) than a loosening of controls within the USSR, but as a gesture to promote the détente Brezhnev in 1971 permitted small numbers of Jews to emigrate to Israel after lengthy formal procedures. Attempts to repress Western thought, however, continue.

The clearest examples of this have been the extension of the prison term of author Amalrik, the denial of citizenship to biologist Medvedev, the jailing for twelve years of writer Bukovsky, the attacks on nuclear physicist Sakharov, and the expulsion of novelist Solzhenitsyn.

Dissension and Revolt in the Soviet Bloc

The revolutions in Hungary and Poland in 1956 were direct results of Khrushchev's de-Stalinization campaign and of tremendous economic discontent.

POLAND

Poland's revolution began with workers demanding bread. Ochab became first secretary of the Party in 1956 and was wise enough to move with the demands of his people, quickly eliminating Stalinists and bringing back Gomulka as first secretary. As a result, Poland became the freest satellite in the Soviet bloc.

HUNGARY

Hungary's revolt began when intellectuals drew up a manifesto demanding the removal of First Secretary Rakosi, the curbing of the secret police, and the end of radio jamming. For a while it seemed as if the Hungarians would have their way, but on October 23, students demonstrated in favor of Polish demands, and the new First Secretary Gero called in the Soviet army. Although Nagy was made premier and Gero forced to resign, the regime had not moved in time. Soviet divisions poured in on November 1, and the revolt ended in bloodshed and terror.

CZECHOSLOVAKIA

The loosening of control brought trouble with Czechoslovakia in 1968. The country demanded more freedom and drove the Stalinists out of power. Russia's answer was to send in 600,000 troops. By 1970 most of the liberals had been purged, and Czechoslovakia signed a new treaty of "friendship," recognizing the Brezhnev doctrine under which the USSR can invade any satellite that threatens to change its political structure or leave the bloc. The most recent example of this doctrine is the invasion of Afghanistan.

International Affairs

With the death of Stalin a thaw took place in foreign relations—the Korean war was ended; Soviet demands against Turkish areas were dropped; a naval base was returned to Finland; a peace treaty was signed with Austria in 1955 and Russian troops went home; and rapprochement with Tito was achieved.

PEACEFUL COEXISTENCE

With Khrushchev's rise to power it was announced that antagonism toward the West would be modified. Because of the strength of the Communist bloc the capitalist world would be afraid to start a war; therefore war was not inevitable in all areas. Communism would triumph by socialist competition—cultural, political, and economic. The shattering of Western confidence and alliance systems was a fundamental aim of this period. In 1955 the Communists tried to combine NATO and the Warsaw Pact. This would have totally undermined NATO. The USSR has also attempted to sway neutral African and Asian nations by guerrilla warfare advisors and "aid-plus-trade" tactics, at the same time keeping the West aware of Russia's military might.

The most serious crisis between the U.S. and the USSR was the Cuban Missile Crisis in 1962. The U.S. announced that an unarmed Cuba was vital to national security and that Russia must withdraw the missile bases. In the face of United States anger Khrushchev backed down.

POLITICAL DETENTE

The period 1972–73 saw political détente with the West—particularly West Germany and the United States. Trade agreements were reached and the SALT talks on limitations of nuclear weapons took place during the 1970s with some degree of success. The Middle East crisis would have been even more serious without détente, but Russian influence has continued to grow in the Arab world, except for Egypt's reversal of position vis-à-vis the Soviet Union.

RELATIONS WITH CHINA

There were many disagreements between the Chinese and the

Russians, but few authorities thought that there would be a major break between the two countries. Presumably the two Communist giants had too much in common, but geographically they are back to back; one an underpopulated nation, the other overpopulated, and their early histories reveal long periods of animosity.

In July 1963 came the first decisive clash. Five "undesirable" members of the Chinese embassy in Moscow were evicted, and Khrushchev was outspoken in his denunciation of China. Since then relations have become further strained (see p. 349), and part of the reason behind the détente with the West is Russia's desire to devote her energies to the problem of China.

North America

Since there is only modern history in North America, this chapter has been divided into the Settlement of North America (1492–1775); the Establishment (1775–1783) and Growth of the United States (1783–1865); Developing Canada (1867–1917); Change in the United States (1865–1917); the United States and Canada as World Powers (1917–1945); Postwar United States and Canada.

THE SETTLEMENT OF NORTH AMERICA   1492–1775

It is traditional to begin North American history with Christopher Columbus' voyage of discovery in 1492. Actually, however, European expansion into the New World was largely limited to the West Indies, Florida, and Latin America for the next hundred years.

Individual Spaniards and Frenchmen explored Florida, the Mississippi River, the St. Lawrence River, and the Great Lakes region. The first settlement in North America was established by the Spanish at St. Augustine in 1565 as a military base to prevent French seizure of Florida. But it was not until 1607, when three ships commanded by Captain Christopher Newport anchored in Chesapeake Bay, that the development of North American civilization really began.

The English settlers who came to the northern portion of the New World faced a very difference situation from that encountered by their Iberian counterparts who penetrated south into Mexico, Peru, and the Argentine. There were no advanced civilizations to

198

plunder, no cheap labor force to exploit (the Indians numbered only about 200,000 east of the Mississippi), and the explorers were there for a different purpose—they came to settle and had to wait for a long-term investment in men and money to pay off.

The English Arrive

Between 1585 and 1587 Sir Walter Raleigh had engineered two expeditions to the New World to found a settlement on Roanoke Island (North Carolina). His failure was in part responsible for the organization of joint stock companies to administer English colonization, which had proved too costly for any one adventurer to handle.

The Settlement of Virginia

In 1606 the London Company was chartered by James I to settle Virginia, and in 1607 Captain John Smith founded Jamestown. By 1619 there were 2000 settlers, a representative government had been formed, and the first twenty black slaves had been imported.

By 1625, 5500 people had been sent to Virginia, 4000 of whom had perished and 300 of whom had returned. That year Virginia was made a royal colony. During the 1650s, 15,000 settlers took the two to three month ocean trip to Virginia and some of them moved south to the Carolinas. Prosperity was assured with the discovery of tobacco; exports rose from 20,000 pounds in 1619 to 60,000 in 1624.

The Pilgrims

Pilgrims who had fled to Holland from England entered into commercial negotiations with the London Company: in return for passage to Virginia, they were to give the Company seven years of labor. In 1620 the *Mayflower* sailed with 102 people aboard (half of them died within a year). Instead of landing in Virginia, they disembarked at Plymouth (Massachusetts) and formed an independent colony.

Massachusetts Bay Colony

In 1629 a group of Puritan merchants founded the Massachusetts Bay Colony and sent John Winthrop with 900 settlers to establish eight cities, one of which was Boston. That same year, Archbishop Laud began a heavy-handed campaign of enforced Anglicanism against all Englishmen, and many Puritans decided to emigrate. By 1640 there were 25,000 people in the new colony. Boston grew from 1200 in 1640 to 6700 in 1700. In 1636 a college was founded to train the clergy of the Society of the Saints; in 1638 John Harvard gave it his library, half his estate, and his name. Public education was established by law throughout the colony, but there was no religious tolerance for the non-Congregationalists, and many dissenters were expelled. In 1691 Plymouth was absorbed into the Massachusetts Bay Colony.

The French Arrive

In 1535 Jacques Cartier discovered what was to become the site of Montreal, but he did not succeed in his attempt to colonize the territory. It was not until 1608, when Samuel de Champlain laid the foundations of Quebec, that the French began to come to North America. In 1628 the Company of New France was formed by Cardinal Richelieu, and the colonies were vigorously supported by Louis XIV. In 1663 New France was made a royal colony. The French, however, came to America only in small numbers, and their chief interest was to trade in fish and furs.

The Dutch Arrive

The Dutch, whose sea power rivaled that of the English and exceeded that of the French, arrived in North America in 1614, establishing an armed fur trading post near Albany, New York. Trade with the Indians failed, but in 1624 the Dutch returned, and the Iroquois, the most powerful Indian confederation, agreed to support the Dutch in return for the exclusive use of Dutch firearms.

In 1626 the Dutch West India Company bought Manhattan Island from the Indians and established the prosperous community of New Amsterdam (New York).

The Thirteen British Colonies

The colonial experience in each of the thirteen colonies differed considerably. Geography contributed to the growth of small colonies rather than large ones, but equally significant was the fact that many of the new colonies were established by dissenters from the old. This initial diversity accounts, in part, for later emphasis on states' rights. However, with the exception of Connecticut and Rhode Island, the colonies all eventually developed much the same kind of political structure. A governor was appointed by the king (if the colony was chartered by the crown) or by the proprietor (if the colony was controlled by individuals). Except in Massachusetts where the council was elective, the governor ruled through an appointed body, which in many colonies developed into an upper house. Below the council was generally an elected assembly which looked upon itself as the equivalent of the English House of Commons and, as in the mother country, increased in power.

The New England Colonies

MASSACHUSETTS

Massachusetts Bay Company was, in its early growth, the most independent of the English colonies, and it was not until 1691 that it was brought directly under royal control. In Massachusetts there developed the most distinctive attribute of New England life—town settlement and government (compared to parish government in the southern colonies).

RHODE ISLAND AND CONNECTICUT

Among the dissenters expelled from Puritan Massachusetts Bay Colony were Roger Williams, who founded Providence, Rhode Island, in 1635, and Anne Hutchinson, who established Portsmouth,

Rhode Island, in 1638. The area was joined into a single colony in 1644 and granted a very liberal crown charter in 1663.

Religious dissenters also migrated into the Connecticut River Valley under the leadership of Reverend Thomas Hooker. In 1662 the colony of Connecticut was formed, also with a liberal charter.

Connecticut and Rhode Island were completely self-governing commonwealths choosing all their own officers. In 1639 the freemen of Connecticut drew up the Fundamental Orders of Connecticut—the first written constitution in the Western world.

Only in Rhode Island, however, was there complete religious freedom. In all the other colonies of New England the Congregational church was the established church.

NEW HAMPSHIRE, VERMONT, AND MAINE

Northern New England was also settled largely by Puritans from Massachusetts who exercised political control over New Hampshire until 1680 and over Maine until 1820. Vermont was disputed between New York and the new colony of New Hampshire.

The Middle Colonies

The Middle Colonies were more tolerant, varied, and cosmopolitan than New England. By the time of the Revolutionary War, New York, New Jersey, Pennsylvania, and Delaware had about 700,000 people, many of whom were small farmers.

NEW YORK

The Dutch settlement of New Amsterdam was autocratic and a constant commercial and military menace to the English. In 1664, during the Anglo-Dutch war, three warships were sent against the settlement. The Dutch gave in without a struggle and New Amsterdam was given a government by the Duke of York.

NEW JERSEY

The Duke of York also created New Jersey when he sold it to two friends in 1664 who ruled as proprietors. It became a royal colony in 1702.

Pennsylvania was unusual from the start. Most of the other colonies were formed by commercial companies as business ventures, but the Carolinas, Maryland, and Pennsylvania were given by the English crown as estates to private individuals. British, Dutch, and Swedish settlers had come into the area of Pennsylvania and Delaware, and in 1681 William Penn, the Quaker son of an admiral, was given the charter to form the "perfect commonwealth." Pennsylvania was based on Quaker principles, representative government was established, freedom of religion was allowed, and Philadelphia became the "city of brotherly love." Delaware was made an independent colony in 1704.

The Southern Colonies

Almost exclusively rural, the South revealed more class distinction. Socially and religiously these colonies tended to be patterned after England. By 1775 the Anglican church had become the established church in all the southern colonies, and the parish (not the town) became the basic unit of local government.

MARYLAND

Maryland was a proprietary grant land, given to Sir George Calvert, Lord Baltimore. His first settlers arrived in 1634. Maryland was free of religious intolerance but slow to receive any form of popular government.

VIRGINIA

(See section "The English Arrive.")

NORTH CAROLINA AND SOUTH CAROLINA

These too were proprietary grant lands. The proprietors attempted to populate the area with tenant farmers, but in 1729 a combination of economic problems forced the proprietors to sell Carolina back to the crown. The country was then split into two royal colonies.

GEORGIA

The convict colony of Georgia was created in 1735 for those

who were in trouble or debt in England. This action infuriated the Spanish, and Georgia's boundaries were not finally settled until Florida was purchased in 1819.

Population Statistics

The Blacks

Dutch traders brought blacks to Virginia in 1619 even before the arrival of the Pilgrims, but it was not until the increase of plantation farming in the South after 1700 that slaves became essential as a labor force. By 1770 a little less than half the population of Virginia were slaves, and in South Carolina blacks outnumbered whites two to one. By 1775 one-fifth the population of the American colonies was black.

The English

By 1688 there were 300,000 English in North America and only 20,000 French. By the time of the Revolution, the population of the colonies came close to 2 million—or about one-third that of the mother country. Philadelphia by 1760 had 40,000 people and was larger than any city in the British Empire except London.

Anglo-French Conflict for Control

In northern Canada the Hudson Bay Company was formed in 1670 as a challenge to the French trading monopoly. The fur business proved so profitable that the company continued to intrude upon French trading, and the Iroquois in New York were persuaded to support the British and to strike at pro-French tribes around the Great Lakes. This led to King William's War (1689–1697).

The French continued expansion into Illinois and Louisiana (1699), contributing to the outbreak of the War of the Spanish Succession, or Queen Anne's War (1701–1713). Again the British won, and by the Treaty of Utrecht in 1713 the French surrendered the Hudson Bay country, Newfoundland, and Acadia (Nova Scotia).

War broke out again in 1744 (the War of the Austrian Succession, or King George's War), but the final struggle came in 1754 with the Seven Years' War. French and Indian raids along with the struggle for the control of the Ohio valley were the chief causes of the war in America. By the Treaty of 1763, England gained all of Canada from the French and Florida from the Spanish.

THE ESTABLISHMENT OF THE UNITED STATES OF AMERICA 1775–1783

The Causes of the Revolution

The Seven Years' War

One of the major effects of the Seven Years' War was to lessen colonial dependence on Great Britain because of the disappearance of the French threat. Another major effect of the war was the change in Britain's attitude toward the colonies. The English felt that the Americans had not been paying their fair share of the cost of defense. Moreover, only three colonies had fulfilled their quota of troops during the war. At the end of the war England's administrative control over the colonies tightened. The mercantile system that had long been in existence was suddenly enforced and the British began searching for taxes which would be acceptable to the Americans in an effort to put the empire on a truly productive and rational economic foundation.

Economic Grievances

The mercantile or navigation acts injured the colonies. They were designed to raise revenues for defense of the empire and stop smuggling which had become highly profitable to American merchants. They also required all duty payments in *species* (gold or silver currency). Since the colonies imported far more than they exported and were required to pay for the import of manufactured goods in species, the new duties exacerbated an already serious problem. In 1764 Parliament prohibited the issuing of colonial paper money.

That same year the Sugar Act was passed which decreased the customs duty but increased the efficiency of the collection on such items as sugar, wine, coffee, silk, and molasses.

A more general economic grievance involved a conflict of interests—debtor (colonist) vs. creditor (British); rural (colonist) vs. metropolitan (London). In 1715 the total colonial debt was £50,000; by 1760 it was £2 million.

Parliament

Misunderstanding over Britain's desire to centralize also caused problems, and a fundamental theoretical disagreement over the power of Parliament led to war. Parliament maintained that all the colonies were subject to its decisions and laws. The colonies, on the other hand, said that the crown alone had authority and could get money only by asking for it from the colonies themselves—in other words, from the colonies' own legislatures, which they regarded as the equals of the British Parliament. As the colonies grew in political and economic strength they became more and more opposed to regulation from England.

The Steps to War

The Stamp Act

Again in an attempt to find revenue, Parliament introduced the Stamp Act of 1765 (a tax on legal documents and newspapers) which led to violence in Massachusetts, New York, Virginia, and North Carolina. The Sons of Liberty were organized to ensure that no one paid the stamp tax.

The Townshend Act

The Townshend Act of 1767 placing duties on tea, paper, glass, and printers' colors hit Massachusetts the hardest and resulted in an economic boycott followed by violence in which four Bostonians were killed in March 1770 by British soldiers. The reaction to the "Boston Massacre" caused Parliament to repeal the duties except those on tea.

Revolutionary Committees

The next step toward war was the establishment of committees of "correspondence," or propaganda societies, by men determined to keep the revolutionary spirit alive. Sam Adams of Massachusetts established the first intercolonial committee.

The Coercive Acts

On December 16, 1773, the Boston Tea Party occurred. Over 300 chests of tea were dumped into Boston Harbor in reaction to Parliament's granting of the monopoly of trade to the East India Company. Boston was once more in rebellion. Reaction to the destruction of private property scandalized even the pro-American members of Parliament, and by way of discipline the British government passed the Coercive Acts (the Intolerable Acts) in 1774, which included the quartering of troops in private homes, the right to try offenders in England, and the closing of the port of Boston.

The Quebec Act

Colonial resentment was further outraged by the Quebec Act. Its purpose was to prevent an uncontrolled land grab of the Northwest Territory, but it was looked upon as pro-French and pro-Catholic, and defined the boundaries of Quebec as including all the areas north of the Ohio River (what is today Wisconsin, Michigan, Illinois, Indiana, and Ohio).

The Continental Congress

Revolutionary legislatures were established by the colonists. The first was in Virginia in 1774. Then came the first Continental Congress, with an agreement to boycott British goods. A Continental Association was created to supervise the boycott, and munition dumps were established by the Association. Britain sent troops to Boston, and General Gage marched to destroy a munition dump at Concord. On April 19, 1775, the Minutemen (called out by Paul Revere) met the Redcoats at Lexington Green. The Revolution had begun.

The Revolutionary War

In May 1775 the second Continental Congress met and appointed George Washington commander-in-chief of the patriots' forces. By January 1776 there was no turning back. Thomas Paine had published his book, *Common Sense*, which proclaimed the growing revolutionary attitude on the part of the Americans: "There is something absurd in supposing a Continent to be perpetually governed by an island." By May of that year most of the colonies had set up independent state governments and were at war with Great Britain. On July 4, 1776, the Declaration of Independence was adopted.

The war was characterized by great bravery, brilliant if sometimes absurd military maneuvers, treason, brutality, and difficulties on both sides in getting men to fight. The Americans' greatest advantages were:

1) They were fighting on home territory.

2) The British would have to use extreme measures to subdue them and this they would not do.

3) The British did not understand the kind of war being fought and were badly divided at home about the war.

The decisive battle of the war was Saratoga (1777), for the Americans were able to keep the British forces divided and the victory led to the entrance of France into the war on the side of the colonists. After 1780 the war became a world conflict in which Great Britain had to fight the French, the Spanish, and the Dutch. In October 1781, General Cornwallis, blockaded by Washington on the land and a French fleet on the seas, capitulated, and the war in the colonies was over.

By the Treaty of Peace (1783), America south of the Great Lakes and west to the Mississippi was proclaimed independent. Two concessions were made by the Americans: British creditors were allowed to sue for debts and loyalist property was to be restored. Congress could not control the states, however, and most loyalist property was not regained. Canada remained an English colony until 1867, but Florida was returned to Spain.

The Growth of Canada

Almost as if they had had a crystal ball, the British in 1774 had passed the Quebec Act which granted French Canadians religious freedom and protection under French civil law, for the French were soon to need that protection. During and immediately after the war for independence, English loyalists (approximately 60,000) fled from the United States and settled in the Maritime Provinces and what is today Ontario. What was to be one of Canada's most enduring problems began—the conflict between French and English.

THE GROWTH OF THE NEW NATION   1783–1865

In many ways, as Robert Wiebe has pointed out, American society was founded on a series of negatives. Republicanism meant no monarchy; democracy was based on the lack of entrenched privilege; the concept of economic freedom meant no government interference; the Bill of Rights was a list of what the government could not do. But the United States also started out with many positive advantages and concepts.

Advantages to Development

Americans were "born free"—they had no feudal past, no entrenched institutions or privileges to smash.

North America had a vast expanse of land and resources which offered unlimited opportunity, and its geographical location gave it a sense of security from military invasion which would last until the twentieth century.

Independence freed the United States from British restrictions on economic growth; lands held by the crown or by one man were distributed to many (the Land Ordinance Act of 1785); primogeniture was discontinued; church and state were separated (except in

Connecticut and Massachusetts) ; and with the end of British rule came the unrestricted migration westward across the Appalachians.

The Government of the United States

The Articles of Confederation

In March of 1781 the Articles of Confederation were adopted by the states. The new congress was little more than a conclave of ambassadors representing sovereign states and had very little authority. There was no uniform system of courts, no true national executive, and the government could not levy taxes or enlist troops. States joined the union and ceded from it at will.

The only real authority that the new congress had was over the territory between the Appalachians and the Mississippi, and the Northwest Ordinance, passed in 1787, was its only achievement. The ordinance divided the territory into five potential states, which would be admitted to the union on the same basis as the original members once any state had a population of 60,000 people. This was to become the precedent for all future states admitted to the United States.

Economic chaos caused by inflation, tariffs, lack of coordination among states, and no control over the printing of paper money finally led to the summoning of a constitutional convention.

The Constitution of the United States

The second convention (the first failed) met in May 1787 and included delegates chosen by each of the state legislatures. The most learned men present were Benjamin Franklin, James Madison, and Alexander Hamilton; George Washington's presence was important to the success of the convention. Many of the men most active in the Revolution (Jefferson, Paine, Sam Adams, John Adams, and Patrick Henry) were absent, and this was significant, for it meant that the more radical elements were not represented.

Three distinct branches of government were established by the Constitution. The eighteenth-century concept of a balance of governmental power was employed. Judicial, executive, and legislative branches were formed, each equal and each checked by the other two.

1) The legislative branch consisted of two houses—the Senate and the House of Representatives. The small states were given equal representation with the larger states in the Senate. The House was elected by direct popular vote and the Senate—until 1812—by the state legislatures. All laws passed by Congress had to be approved by the executive branch of the government.

2) The executive consisted of the President and Vice President, elected by an electoral college in which each state had as many representatives as it had Senators and Representatives. Most appointments and all treaties signed by the President had to be approved by the Senate, and the executive could be impeached by Congress.

3) The Judiciary, the Supreme Court, consisted of judges appointed for life (on good behavior) by the President with the consent of the Senate. Their task was to judge the constitutionality of the law. They could also be impeached.

The variety in terms of office (two years in the House of Representatives, six years in the Senate, four years in the presidency, and life in the Supreme Court) was also a check, for no complete change in personnel could be accomplished except by revolution.

The powers of the Federal Government were carefully specified, and (by the tenth amendment) all residual powers were granted to the states. Taxation, the borrowing of money, control of imports and exports, the coining of money, the fixing of weights and measures, copyrights and patents, post offices, the creation of an army and navy, and control over interstate commerce and international relations were granted to the federal government. Its strength was also added to by the amending process and by the vagueness of phraseology of the Constitution, which did not spell out the powers of the chief executive and said nothing about the cabinet or the committee system of Congress.

The Bill of Rights

The Constitution was passed on the understanding that ten amendments would be included. These amendments guaranteed to all Americans freedom of worship, speech, press, and petition, the right to bear arms, protection against the quartering of soldiers and from search and seizure, the right to jury trial and a speedy trial, the sanctity of private property, protection from cruel punishment, and the rights of the States to the residual powers of the Constitution.

The Presidents of the United States 1789–1865

George Washington	1789	Federalist
John Adams	1797	Federalist
Thomas Jefferson	1801	Democrat-Republican
James Madison	1809	Democrat-Republican
James Monroe	1817	Democrat-Republican
John Quincy Adams	1825	Democrat-Republican
Andrew Jackson	1829	Democrat
Martin Van Buren	1837	Democrat
William Henry Harrison	1841	Whig
John Tyler	1841	Whig
James Knox Polk	1845	Democrat
Zachary Taylor	1849	Whig
Millard Fillmore	1850	Whig
Franklin Pierce	1853	Democrat
James Buchanan	1857	Democrat
Abraham Lincoln	1861	Republican

Political Parties

No date can be named for the beginning of political parties in the United States, and the names of the parties are confusing. At the outset the Federalists (those who supported the Constitution) had no effective opposition. It was Thomas Jefferson who came out violently against the Federalist policies (particularly on the issue of support of the French treaty). It was in part due to party strife that Washington retired in 1796. Thomas Jefferson's party was originally called the Republican and then the Democratic, but neither term should be confused with the present Republican and Democratic parties.

The Democrats did not enter the political picture until 1825, when Andrew Jackson became their leader. The ancestor of the

Republican party was formed in 1854 in opposition to the Democrats and the Kansas-Nebraska Act.

Third parties (such as the Whigs) have sprung up over various issues throughout United States history, but they have generally lacked popularity, organization, money, or staying power.

Democracy and the Federal Government

Under Washington

Washington, the only president of the United States who has ever received a unanimous electoral vote, set several precedents in the development of the executive branch, the most important of which was the creation of the presidential cabinet.

Hamilton played a major role in the movement toward a centralized and stronger federal government. As Washington's Secretary of the Treasury, he set up the first Bank of the United States and the National Mint, and the Federal Government took over the state debts. He encouraged the development of national industries, taxed liquor, and made propertied men dependent upon the federal government for their continued well-being. There was no justification in the Constitution for his acts, but he asserted that it was "an implied power" of the executive. He further strengthened the national government by sending out a force of 1000 national militiamen to smash the Whiskey Rebellion.

Under Adams

The Alien and Sedition Acts of 1795, however, went too far and led to the defeat of John Adams and the Federalists. These acts included censorship of the press, the extension to fourteen years of the residency requirement for citizenship, and an attempt to make a crime of political opposition.

Under Jefferson

Thomas Jefferson posed as the champion of the common man, but his championship tended to be highly aristocratic and paternalistic in form. He did, however, encourage immigration, favor agricultural interests over commercial and financial ones, and seek to abolish honorific titles.

Although Jefferson was doubtful about the extent of the authority vested in the federal government by the Constitution, he was responsible for the stretching of the powers of the government by the purchase of the Louisiana Territory (for $15 million). No clause in the Constitution permitted this, and he acted without the consent of Congress.

Under Jackson

Jackson, one of the "common people," used his position to promote economic and social equality. He destroyed the eastern monopoly of control of finance (the Second Bank of the United States). He reduced the working day in Massachusetts to ten hours, and the ballot throughout many of the states became freer during his administration.

John Marshall and the Supreme Court

Chief Justice of the Supreme Court John Marshall (1800–1835) probably did more to strengthen the federal government and the Constitution than any other single man. He established, among other things, the right of the Supreme Court to review any law of Congress or of a state legislature and the right of the federal courts to have the final judgment on any case. He stood behind Hamilton's insistence that the Constitution gave to the government powers that were not necessarily stated (implied powers).

Economic Growth

The Beginnings of Industrialism

In 1750 the industrial revolution—the use of heavy machinery powered by water or steam and operated by a disciplined factory labor force—had begun in England, especially in the spinning and weaving industries. The introduction of Eli Whitney's cotton gin, which allowed the mass production of cotton for spinning and weaving in English factories, was a key step in the industrial process, which by 1820 was beginning to appear in New England and the Mid-Atlantic states.

Eli Whitney played a major role in forwarding the concept of industrialism in the United States. More significant than his invention of the cotton gin was his introduction of the principle of mass production. The first successful American factory (1791) was small, but by 1812 there were hundreds like it. The first "new model" factory was opened in 1816 by the Boston Manufacturing Company, a totally integrated textile factory, employing young women whom they sheltered and fed. It was an instantaneous success.

America's Economic Advantages

1) The revolutionary war spurred the growth of manufacturing. With new lands and the abolution of old systems of land tenure came agricultural advances.

2) The United States was endowed with a plentiful supply of raw materials including coal, oil, iron and eventually hydro-electric power.

3) A good transportation system linked the Ohio River basin with both the Mississippi and the Hudson.

4) Originally a labor shortage existed, which required the increased use of labor-saving machines, and then a labor supply developed along with an increased demand for goods that was constantly renewed through immigration.

5) The government encouraged industry as well as protected it against foreign competition and prevented the growth of inter-state barriers.

The Pace of the Industrial Revolution

Between 1820 and 1837 investment in industry rose from $50 to $250 million. The Middle West became the leader in the manufacture of agricultural machinery, and this machinery ranked above any in the world. (In 1854, in a thresher competition, an American machine threshed 740 liters of wheat in a half-hour, an English machine 410, and a French machine 250.)

The 1840s and 1850s saw the introduction of the sewing machine, the vulcanization of rubber, and the production of inexpensive steel and petroleum.

By 1820 the republic had grown to twenty-four states, had more than doubled in area, tripled in population, and quadrupled in wealth. By 1860 the United States had become the fourth industrial country in the world (by 1894 the first).

Railroads and Urbanization

Hand in hand with industrial progress and invention went the railroad. In 1840, with 3000 miles of track, the U.S. led the world; by 1850, 5500 miles more were added, and by 1860 another 21,000 miles. By that year $1.5 billion had been invested; 10 million acres of land had been granted to 54 railroads; and Chicago had become the railroad center of the United States.

Urbanization was an immediate result of the industrial revolution. New York had over a million people by 1860, and Philadelphia, Baltimore, and Boston were not far behind. Chicago had 110,000 and St. Louis and Cincinnati 160,000 each.

Cultural and Educational Growth

Culturally the United States remained dependent on Europe; scholars went abroad to study and as late as 1820, 80 percent of books read in the country were imported from Britain. Although Ralph Waldo Emerson announced in 1837 that "our long apprenticeship to learning of other lands draws to a close," it was not until the end of the nineteenth century that American literature became essentially "American" (Mark Twain is as obvious an example as any).

The concept of compulsory public-supported education for all was unique to the United States, and Michigan led the way. It was not until the late nineteenth century, however, that this principle was generally applied to high schools.

Education for women was also exceptional, and Oberlin College was the first to open its doors to both sexes in 1833. From the end of the revolution to 1860, 500 colleges were founded.

The Movement West

People flooded to the northwest and southwest after the revolution. Hunters and trappers went first, followed soon afterward by farmers and, finally, doctors, shopkeepers, preachers, land speculators, and others.

Chicago was a trading village in 1830. Within a lifetime it had become a wealthy metropolis. The city grew from 500 to 4000 between 1830 and 1840; the price of land rose from $1.25 an acre to $100 in 1832, and a few years later to $3500.

The movement west accelerated in the 1840s. Until 1840 fewer than 1000 people had settled in Oregon. By 1843 the Oregon trail had become a great highway from the Missouri River to the Columbia; and in that year alone 1000 people came. The boundary line between the United States and Canada was established at the 49th parallel.

The settling of Utah was much in the tradition of the early colonies, for it was settled by a dissenting group—the Mormons. Led by Brigham Young they fled from Illinois and established what Clarence Ver Steeg calls "a desert Zion."

The War with Mexico

In 1835 settlers in Texas revolted and finally won their independence from Mexico, but Mexico never officially acknowledged this independence, nor the Rio Grande boundary. The American element in California was also growing and the United States took advantage of their dispute with Mexico. War began on April 25, 1846; in September 1847, American forces captured Mexico City.

By the Treaty of Guadalupe Hidalgo, the border at the Rio Grande was established, New Mexico, Arizona, Colorado, Texas, and California were ceded to the United States, and $18 million was paid to Mexico. (New Mexico was enlarged by the Gadsden purchase for $10 million in 1853.)

States Admitted to the Union   1787–1865

Alabama	1819	Mississippi	1817
Arkansas	1836	Missouri	1821
California	1850	Nevada	1864
Connecticut	1788	New Hampshire	1788
Delaware	1787	New Jersey	1787
Florida	1845	New York	1788
Georgia	1788	North Carolina	1789
Illinois	1818	Ohio	1803
Indiana	1816	Oregon	1859
Iowa	1846	Pennsylvania	1787
Kansas	1861	Rhode Island	1790
Kentucky	1792	South Carolina	1788
Louisiana	1812	Tennessee	1796
Maine	1820	Texas	1845
Maryland	1788	Vermont	1791
Massachusetts	1788	Virginia	1788
Michigan	1837	West Virginia	1863
Minnesota	1858	Wisconsin	1848

Population Statistics

There were 3,250,000 people in the new republic in 1783, of whom about one-third (not including the Indians) were either slaves or in jail. By 1850 the total population had reached 30 million.

By 1870, 435 out of a thousand people were native-born whites with native parents; 292 were native-born with foreign-born parents; 144 were foreign-born; 127 were black; one was Indian; and one was Chinese.

The Black

Although the blacks had fought in the revolutionary war, human rights granted by the Declaration of Independence, the Constitution, and the Bill of Rights did not extend to the slave. Even Thomas Jefferson, who felt that these rights should apply did not free his slaves. George Washington at his death was one of the few who did.

The Indian

The government's policy in response to the westward movement was ruthless, and white settlers with superior military equipment drove the Indian farther and farther west, in many cases driving tribes to extinction.

The Immigrant

Between 1851 and 1860, 2,598,000 immigrants came to America. The greatest number came from Ireland and Germany. The South attracted fewer immigrants than the North and this was reflected in the population statistics during the Civil War.

Foreign Affairs

The War of 1812

The United States' policy of neutrality and the British policy of searching neutral ships and taking deserters (and sometimes aliens) during the Napoleonic wars resulted in misunderstandings on both sides. Between 1804 and 1807 United States' ships lost 6000 men, and reluctantly President Madison asked for war.

Sectional dissension within the United States delayed the invasion of Canada, and it was not until September of 1813 that Toronto was invaded and the Canadian parliament houses were burned. In turn, in August of 1814, the British burned the White House and the Capitol. The war was fought badly and mishandled from the beginning, and the Treaty of Ghent did very little except to bring peace.

Eventually commissions set up by the Treaty of Ghent did determine the eastern boundary between the United States and Canada (except for Maine) and ensure the demilitarization of the Canadian-United States border.

The Monroe Doctrine

The most outstanding example of American diplomacy between

1787 and 1860 was the Monroe Doctrine of 1823. Two ideas were presented by President Monroe in his annual address to Congress in 1823—one, that Europe should be forbidden to establish any new dependencies in the Western hemisphere, and two, the older doctrine of American nonintervention in the affairs of Europe. The address was prompted by Russia's claim to territory south of Alaska and by the threat to Latin America by the Quadruple Alliance. Also standing behind the Monroe Doctrine was Great Britain's encouragement and navy.

The Pacific

As early as 1843 the United States was showing interest in the Pacific as an outlet for trade. In 1844 the U.S. received trading rights from China and then in the 1850s Japan was opened up to Western trade. In 1856 the United States government allowed naval officers to raise the American flag on Pacific islands where *guano* (fertilizer) was found.

THE CIVIL WAR   1861–1865

The main theme of the years between 1840 and 1860 was the growing division within the United States. The split between the North and South had been on the increase since 1830.

Background to Division

Economic Priorities

Division was not solely caused by slavery. The industrial revolution had affected the North and South quite differently. The South, which was dependent upon its export of raw cotton to England and which had almost no industry, wanted manufactured goods as cheaply as possible and therefore favored free trade. The North, where industry was developing, wanted protection—in other words, high tariffs.

The Antislavery Movement

A slave rebellion in Virginia in 1831 organized by Nat Turner led to increasingly more and more rigid slave codes in the South at the same time that the North was becoming more and more outspoken in its denunciation of slavery. In 1833 the British Empire abolished slavery and that same year the antislavery movement in the North opened up "underground railroads," illegal channels by which more than 700,000 slaves were transported to freedom.

The Slave Population

The number of slaves rose from 1,500,000 in 1820 to almost 4,000,000 by 1860. Although the South had a total white population of about 6 million in 1850 only 347,725 people owned slaves. Yet it was with the large slave owners (three or four thousand) that wealth and, more important, political power rested.

Slave States

The westward movement brought the issue to a head. The South wanted new states for sugar, cotton, and tobacco plantations. Therefore they were increasingly worried by the introduction of anti-slavery states into the union and the consequent upset of the political balance within the Senate. The schism was artificially mended by the Missouri Compromise of 1820 which permitted Missouri to enter the union as a slave state if Maine were brought in as an antislavery state and slavery excluded from the remaining portion of the Louisiana Purchase, north of 36°30'.

The proposed annexation of Texas and the southwest, however, raised the problem once again. Texas already had slavery, but the issue arose over California, New Mexico, and Utah. The Wilmot Proviso that these territories be admitted only on condition that slavery be prohibited raised the constitutional issue of whether Congress had the right to regulate the existence of slavery in the states. The South threatened to secede from the union if the Wilmot Proviso were passed. Henry Clay's compromise of 1850 that California be free and Utah and New Mexico be organized as territories without qualification and that a law enforcing the return of fugitive slaves to their masters be passed satisfied no one but brought temporary peace.

The Road to War

The Kansas-Nebraska Act

In 1854 the South demanded the right to open up the entire Missouri valley to slavery (forbidden by the Missouri Compromise). On Stephen Douglas' instigation the Kansas-Nebraska Act was passed in 1854. It repealed the Missouri Compromise by opening up the area to popular sovereignty on the issue of slavery. The effect of the act was to:

1) Turn Kansas and Nebraska into a hotbed of contention between the North and South as freeholders and slave owners poured in to grab territory.

2) Eventually kill the Whig party and make it possible for the Republicans to rise to power. The Republicans, appealing to eastern business as well as western farmers, demanded that slavery be excluded from all territories.

The Dred Scott Case

By treating fugitive slave Scott as property that should be returned, the Supreme Court in 1857 decided that Congress had no power to exclude slavery from the territories, and abolitionists were outraged.

Increasing Awareness

In 1858 Lincoln and Douglas, running for a seat in the Senate from Illinois, debated the issue of slavery and did much to awaken the country to the constitutional as well as the moral problem.

In 1859 John Brown and a small band of followers invaded Virginia to liberate the slaves and were hanged for their efforts.

The Rise to Power of the Republican Party

In 1860 the Democratic Party split when radicals demanded that Congress pass laws protecting slavery and nominated John

Breckinridge as their candidate for president. (The other half of the party nominated Douglas.) The split in the party was disastrous not only to victory but also to union. In the election Lincoln won a clear majority of the electoral votes but not the popular votes.

The Confederacy

In December 1860 South Carolina seceded from the union, then Mississippi did the same, and in the following February seven southern states organized the Confederate States of America with Jefferson Davis as provisional president. In April of 1861 the South fired on Fort Sumter.

The War between the States

In reply to the fall of Sumter, Lincoln called out 75,000 volunteers and the uncommitted states chose sides. Maryland, Delaware, Kentucky, Missouri, and the western part of Virginia stayed with the union, and North Carolina, Virginia, Tennessee, and Arkansas filled out the ranks of the rebels. Kinsmen were divided from kinsmen: Mrs. Lincoln's three brothers died on the side of the confederacy; Robert E. Lee's nephew fought for the North.

The South's hope for victory lay in immediate triumph, the North's in delaying tactics until it could mobilize its superior industrial and human resources. During the first year and a half of war the South, better led and fighting on inside lines, was generally the victor, but inconclusively so, and time was running in favor of the North. On September 22, 1862, the Emancipation Proclamation was announced by Lincoln, which changed the conflict from a constitutional one (that is, defending the integrity of the union) into a moral one. Then, in July 1863 the turning point came when General Grant took Vicksburg and split the Confederacy and General Meade conquered Lee's army at Gettysburg. By September 1864, Sherman had begun his march through Georgia. On April 2, 1865, General Lee evacuated Richmond, which had held out for nearly a year, and on April 9 he surrendered to Grant at Appomattox.

The Results and the Cost of the War

The war was one of the most destructive that the world had yet experienced. Union deaths reached 360,000 and Confederate deaths 260,000 (which was one-fifth of the South's white male population). Many southerners died of malnutrition, epidemics, and riots as a result of the aftermath of the war. The war cost the North $4 billion, but much of this had been invested in industries. The Confederacy, on the other hand, had spent about $2 billion but lost everything.

The South was in economic chaos. No compensation was paid to the southern slave owners (a man who owned 500 slaves had an investment of about $500,000). The labor system was totally disorganized, the area was bankrupt (between 1868 and 1874 the southern states' debt rose to close to $125,000,000), factories were forsaken, and ex-slaves wandered homeless. In Mississippi alone there were 10,000 orphans, and there was no one to alleviate the situation or to assume the reins of government.

The blacks were free; they could leave the plantation; they could take on a second name (often Lincoln or Washington) but in many cases their position was more desperate, for landowners had no money to hire labor, and the blacks generally had to become share-croppers.

One of the most tragic events of the war's fanatic aftermath was the assassination on April 14, 1865, of Abraham Lincoln. Hatred between North and South was another tragic result of the war. Not for twenty years would a Democrat (Grover Cleveland was the first) live in the White House, and not for fifty years would a southerner by birth (Woodrow Wilson was the first) become President of the United States.

But the war had achieved its purpose. The Union was preserved, and the Thirteenth Amendment (ratified at the end of 1865) abolished slavery forever.

DEVELOPING CANADA   1867–1917

At the same time that the United States was facing problems of division, Canada was having sectional difficulties.

Background of the Canadian Government

The Canada Act—1791

The French, although protected by the Quebec Act, were increasingly concerned as more and more immigrants from Great Britain poured into the area after 1780. By the Canada Act, Parliament attempted to alleviate the situation by creating two provinces in Canada—one French (Lower Canada) and one English (Upper Canada). Like the thirteen colonies, each province had its own governor, an appointed legislative council, and an elected assembly. Colonial laws could be disallowed by Great Britain within two years of passage.

In 1837 revolts broke out in both Lower and Upper Canada. The primary cause was the constitutional conflict between governor and legislative council on the one hand and the elected assemblies on the other. The grievances were over revenue, church control, and the judiciary. The situation was much worse in Lower Canada, for here the British minority controlled the governor and the legislative council.

The following year the Earl of Durham was sent to Canada as governor, and in 1839 he published a report asking for unification of Canada politically by granting what amounted to virtual self-government and geographically by building roads and canals.

The Union Act—1840

As a result of Durham's report, Canada was reunited, given one governor and an elected national assembly. But the legislative council appointed by the governor was retained until 1856, when it too was made elective. The government had autonomy in internal matters only, and the Union Act failed to solve the French problem. Federalism had to be the final answer.

The British North America Act–1867

Federalism was partly a decentralizing move, for it would divide the French element from the English, but it was also a unifying move, for it combined the provinces of British North America with the St. Lawrence and the Great Lakes region.

A federal constitution was drafted in Canada by Canadians and finally passed through the British Parliament in 1867 as the British North America Act. The passage of the act was hastened by the civil war in the United States, which revealed how destructive separatism could be. It provided for provincial governments, a federal government with a parliament of two houses elected by the people, a prime minister from the majority party, and a governor-general representing the British crown. Partly as a result of the civil war, the constitution created a strong central government with all powers except those specifically reserved for the provinces.

It was the British who suggested that Canada be called a dominion and not a kingdom because the U.S. was touchy about "kingdoms." (The concept of dominion status in the Empire was applied later to Australia [1901], New Zealand [1907], and South Africa [1910].)

Canadian Prime Ministers	1867–1917	
John MacDonald	1867–1873	Conservative
Alexander MacKenzie	1873–1878	Liberal
John MacDonald	1878–1891	Conservative
John Abbot	1891–1892	Conservative
John Thompson	1892–1894	Conservative
MacKenzie Bowell	1894–1896	Conservative
Charles Tupper	1896	Conservative
Wilfried Laurier	1896–1911	Liberal
Robert Laird Borden	1911–1917	Conservative

Canada Expands

Nova Scotia and New Brunswick joined the new union of Quebec and Ontario with the understanding that a railroad be built to connect them with Quebec. The Hudson Bay Company in 1869 gave up its rights to the Northwest territories (for $1,500,000) out of which were carved Manitoba (1870) and British Columbia (1871). In 1873 Prince Edward Island was added to the union. With the completion of the Canadian Pacific Railroad (1881–1885), the prairies were opened up, and in 1905 Saskatchewan and Alberta joined the dominion. In 1949 Newfoundland was added.

The Canadian Economy

Agriculture remained Canada's primary industry, although fishing, forestry, and mining played an important role in development. In the nineteenth century Canada could not compete with the United States. Its natural resources were not accessible, and it was not until the arrival of the twentieth century and the airplane that they were fully tapped. Canada had no fertile midwest, no southern climate, and no industrialized east coast. Between 1881 and 1891 (when Canada had less than 5 million people) one million Canadians moved to the United States.

Relations with the United States

Between the United States and Canada is the largest undefended border in the world. The demilitarization of this boundary was assured after the War of 1812, but it was not until 1842 that Maine's boundary was determined, and as late as 1866 Canadians had to defend themselves against Irish American invaders from the United States.

By the Treaty of Washington in 1871 the Canadians ironed out the remaining obstacles in their relations with the United States, but there is little doubt that there was a residue of fear for a neighbor who was industrializing and growing much faster.

CHANGE IN THE UNITED STATES   1865–1917

The change and growth in the United States following the civil war was even more rapid than it had been during the previous decades. Between 1860 and 1900 the number of industrial establishments increased three times, the number of wage earners four times, and the value of manufactured products seven times. This was the legendary land of promise come true, where the immigrant Andrew Carnegie could start as a bobbin boy at $1.20 a week and become a leader in the steel industry with an income of $20 million per year. But industrialism was not without its problems, and the end of the nineteenth century witnessed the growth of large combines and trusts and the virtual control of the United States by the "robber barons." This was also the era when many immigrants were not welcome and during which there was no improvement in the social and political status of the blacks.

It was also a period in foreign policy of economic and political imperialism. Japan was opened up, Latin America came under United States economic domination, the United States went to war with Spain, and the Caribbean became an "American sea."

Economic Change

Scientific Advances and the Creation of New Industries

Oil was struck in Pennsylvania in 1859, and in five years production had increased to more than 2 million barrels. The oil industry was organized by John D. Rockefeller, who, in 1870, established the Standard Oil Company. The steel industry grew because of the enterprise, skill, and capital of Andrew Carnegie who entered the steel business in 1872. The electrical industry began with the telephone in 1876. Then in 1879 came Edison's breakthrough and in 1882 the first generating and distributing station was built in New York. By 1900, 75 percent of Iowa farmers had phones, while in rural Europe there were almost none. The development of the automobile in the 1890s revolutionized transportation in much the same way as it had been transformed by the steam engine and would once more be revolutionized by the airplane. Along with the growth of new industries came greater and greater scientific progress. Between 1860 and 1900, 676,000 patents were granted.

The Agricultural Revolution

The conquering of the Great Plains by the farmer was a part of the industrial revolution—the application of science to agriculture. Without barbed wire, better plows, irrigation methods, and deep-drilled wells it could never have been done.

Between 1860 and 1900 land held by farmers doubled from 407,000,000 acres to 841,000,000 acres, and the acreage of land under cultivation trebled. This was made possible by the new land that was opened up but even more by the new inventions.

The plow was faced with steel in 1837 and improved steadily from then on. The reaper was first introduced in 1840, and in the 1880s came the reaper-thresher (the combine). Four people could now do the work formerly done by 300.

The agricultural revolution took place west of the Mississippi. In 1920 the farmers of Iowa alone had a larger investment in machinery than did all the farmers in New England and the Mid-Atlantic states combined.

Nevertheless, as the farmer produced more and fed more cities, the agricultural debt began to rise. Farmers were heavily mortgaged for farm machinery. This precipitated the growth of the Populists and the presidential battle between the silverites (cheap money and easy credit terms) in 1896, represented by William Jennings Bryan, and the advocates of the gold standard (hard money). Although Bryan lost, the United States was not to hear the end of the problem.

The Growth of Monopolies and Trusts

During this period almost every product on the market became a monopoly. Meat-packing was dominated by Armour, Wilson, Swift, and Cudahy; the reaper business by the McCormicks; sugar by the Havemeyers; tobacco by the Dukes; milling by the Pillsburys and the Washburns; copper by the Guggenheims.

The United States Steel Corporation absorbed close to 600 iron and steel establishments and controlled two-thirds of the steel products of the country. By 1879 Rockefeller had made a deal with the railroads and controlled 90 percent of the oil refining capacity of the country.

The most spectacular examples of consolidation (and of speculation and manipulation) were the transcontinental railroads. J. P. Morgan, for instance, was able to use the capital of the New Haven Railroad to monopolize all other forms of transportation in New England.

By 1912 the money trusts, dominated by Morgan and William Rockefeller, held 341 directorships in railroads, coal, copper, steel, oil, and other industries with resources of $22 billion. By 1904, 319 industrial trusts had destroyed 5300 independent concerns, and 127 utilities had absorbed more than 2400 smaller ones.

Businessmen dominated Congress and voted in high tariffs and hard money. As early as 1865 it was reported that in New York there were several hundred men worth a million dollars and some worth 20 million. America might not have grown as fast without the Morgans, Rockefellers, Vanderbilts, Carnegies, and others, but there were serious side effects as a consequence of huge trusts. Price-rigging, political lobbying, and lack of concern for conservation, high accident rates, child labor, long hours, and dreadful working conditions, along with the growing dehumanization of industrial machines, were characteristic of the giant corporations.

Labor

The organization of labor in the United States was slow. There was always a supply of cheap labor coming into the country every year. Between 1850 and 1870, 5 million immigrants came to the United States, and they were willing to work for almost any wages and under almost any conditions. (Yet, fortunately for labor, there was an escape valve—the west—and many left the industrial cities for the open land.)

States, not the federal government, had control over labor conditions, and this meant that although there was labor legislation in some states, the majority of states did nothing.

By 1898 more than 17,000,000 worked in American factories, and only 500,000 of these were members of labor unions. In 1881 the first labor union organized for the welfare of labor rather than for political goals was formed by Samuel Gompers. The American Federation of Labor started out as a union of craft unions, and by 1900 it had a membership of 550,000 and had won many rights for its workers.

Between 1881 and 1905, 37,000 strikes occurred. Even as late as 1900 only a small segment of labor had won basic rights, and these did not include any welfare plans.

The Progressive Movement and the Federal Government

Two trends emerged in the growth of the federal government:

1) The fluctuating war for control between Congress and the executive became more and more an issue in the nineteenth and twentieth centuries. In 1861 Lincoln assumed powers never authorized by the Constitution and in response Congress created a joint Committee on the Conduct of the War. The battle between Congress and President Johnson over reconstruction was in part a reflection of this issue.

2) The question and advisability of government interference or intervention in the economy and well-being of the country became an important issue. The general attitude of laissez-faire prevailed, but by the 1870s, as trusts grew larger and working conditions did not improve, protests became louder, particularly among the middle classes.

The Progressives began to realize that the root of the problem was in the political system, the various machines that were running the country, especially in the big cities. They began agitation for the direct primary, and by 1916 forty-five states had adhered to it. Then came demands for the direct election of United States senators, and in 1912 the Seventeenth Amendment was passed through Congress. By 1914, however, women's suffrage was permitted in only eleven states. (It was finally achieved through the Nineteenth Amendment in 1919.)

The first successful regulation of big business concerned the railroads. Midwestern states had passed laws limiting rates of railroads going through their territory. These laws were upheld by the Supreme Court in 1876. Next came the Interstate Commerce Act of 1887, which set up a commission to supervise rates, pools, services, and so forth on the railroads. This law was for a long time ineffective.

To keep the Progressives quiet, the Sherman Antitrust Act was passed in 1890 but remained ineffective for years.

Under Roosevelt

Theodore Roosevelt was the hope of the Progressives, but when he became President in 1901 he actually did very little. The Pure Food and Drugs Act of 1906 was passed but remained useless. Roosevelt, however, did have some success:

1) Arbitration for the workers in the mines of Morgan's Reading Railroad settled the strike with a 10 percent increase in pay.

2) It was during Roosevelt's administration that the Hepburn Act of 1906 was passed. This set up an interstate commerce commission with the authority to set maximum railroad rates.

3) The Aldrich-Vreeland Act of 1908 was the forerunner of the Federal Reserve Act of 1933.

Under Taft

William Taft, it has been said, was "an immense figure physically, [but] as a symbol of Progressivism he was an uncomfortable and uncomprising pigmy." Yet the Progressives in Congress were able to push through more reforms under him than under Roosevelt.

1) The Mann-Elkins Act, passed in 1910, gave the Interstate Commerce Commission the right to suspend objectionable rates on railroads.

2) The parcel post and the postal savings bank were established.

3) A separate Department of Labor and Commerce was created.

4) The most important event, however, was the passage of

the Sixteenth Amendment, making the income tax legal. In the long run this gave the federal government its greatest power—money—and its ability to help alleviate economic differences.

The Presidents of the United States   1865–1917

Andrew Johnson	1865	Republican
Ulysses S. Grant	1869	Republican
Rutherford B. Hayes	1877	Republican
James A. Garfield	1881	Republican
Chester A. Arthur	1881	Republican
Grover Cleveland	1885	Democrat
Benjamin Harrison	1889	Republican
Grover Cleveland	1893	Democrat
William McKinley	1897	Republican
Theodore Roosevelt	1901	Republican
William H. Taft	1909	Republican
Woodrow Wilson	1913	Democrat

Social and Cultural Change

Education

Education during the period 1870–1917 took great strides. Public high schools numbered 500 in 1870; by 1910 the number had jumped to 10,000. In 1869 there were 8000 female undergraduates in college; thirty years later 20,000.

In the South during reconstruction and its aftermath a public school system was founded in almost every state; in contrast it is estimated that before reconstruction only one out of eight children had been educated.

Urbanization

Continuing urbanization was also characteristic of this era. In Chicago in 1850, for example, there were 30,000 people; fifty years later 1.7 million.

Reconstruction and Segregation

Reconstruction has had its critics. Among the criticisms have been the use of the military to enforce congressional acts, the fact that Congress interfered in the composition of state legislatures, and the activities of the *carpetbaggers* (Northerners who moved into the South for both good and bad reasons) and the *scalawags* (Southern whites who cooperated with the reconstruction for both good and bad reasons). On the positive side of the picture, however, it should be remembered that the "radical Republicans" in Congress passed the Civil Rights Act in 1866 (contained in the 14th amendment) and in 1869, the 15th amendment. Some progress was also made in education and, temporarily, in political rights for blacks. Two blacks served in the United States Senate, and they were the only two to do so until 1966 when a black senator was elected (from the North not the South).

Nevertheless, the status of blacks in the South gradually worsened, and segregation evolved during the 1880s and 1890s. In 1890 Mississippi led the way to disenfranchising the black by introducing a literacy test and a poll tax. Louisiana had had 130,324 black voters in 1896; by 1904 the number was down to 1342.

Booker T. Washington's compromise—wait for political rights and concentrate on educational and economic progress—was challenged by W. E. DuBois with the formation of the National Association for the Advancement of Colored People in the beginning of the twentieth century. A great deal of progress toward educating blacks was made in the North, but in the South in 1910 there were only 141 black high schools. Economic, social and political improvement, however, were negligible in both the North and the South.

Population Statistics

About 75 million people lived in the United States in 1900; by 1920 the number had risen to 105 million. During the 1880s the United States swelled with "new" immigrants, many coming from southern and eastern Europe. Between 1900 and 1915, 9.5 million immigrants flooded the country. Many found adjustment more difficult than immigrants whose background was western European. The most serious situation developed with Chinese immigrants who by the 1870s in California were posing a threat to the native American workingman. In 1882 the Chinese were barred, and in 1908 a "gentlemen's agreement" was reached with Japan to keep Japanese workers out.

Despite unpleasant prejudices, most immigrants were considerably better off than in their homeland, and in the end contributed to a cultural diversity and variety that made the United States the "melting pot" of the world.

The End of the Frontier

In 1860 California had 400,000 people, Oregon about 50,000, and Utah about 40,000, and most of the rest of the western lands were occupied by the Indians—the Sioux, Blackfoot, and Crow in the north; the Ute, Cheyenne, and Kiowa in the middle areas; the Comanche and Apache in the south; and the Pueblo in the Rio Grande valley. Thirty years later the frontier was gone; the buffalo were extinct; the Indians had been defeated and all but exterminated; and the Great Plains had been conquered by the farmers.

The miners came first, in search of gold in California, Montana, Dakota, and Wyoming. With them they brought wealth and, most important, the railroads.

The cattle barons were next, claiming the grasslands as their own, but they could not keep out the farmers who crossed the Great Plains. The Homestead Act of 1862 opened the plains to free settlement, but it was under Presidents Arthur and Cleveland that cattlemen were ordered to stop fencing off water rights and to leave the grasslands open to homesteaders.

States Admitted to the Union   1865–1959

Alaska	1959	New Mexico	1912
Arizona	1912	North Dakota	1889
Colorado	1876	Oklahoma	1907
Hawaii	1959	South Dakota	1889
Idaho	1890	Utah	1896
Montana	1889	Washington	1889
Nebraska	1867	Wyoming	1890

Foreign Affairs—the Imperialistic Era

"Manifest Destiny" by the 1880s was no longer confined to the American West; it had been transformed into world imperialism. American businessmen were laying financial empires in Latin America, and the United States began building a navy "to be second to none." By 1898 only Britain and France outranked the U.S. in naval power, whereas earlier it had been twelfth.

Hawaii

The acquisition of Hawaii smelled suspiciously of Texas. Missionaries from New England settled in Hawaii in the 1820s. The native population began to decline, and at the same time the French and British began to show an interest in the islands.

After 1876 sugar was admitted free of duty to America, and in return, in 1887, Hawaii agreed to yield Pearl Harbor to the United States as a naval base.

American missionaries virtually controlled the government and three-quarters of Hawaii's arable land. In 1891 Queen Liliuokalani tried to stop Americanization. She was quickly overthrown and Hawaii was annexed in 1898 as war with Spain broke out.

The Spanish-American War

The Cuban insurrection against Spain in 1895 created anti-Spanish feeling in the United States. Rebels deliberately attacked American property in order to force the United States to intervene, and McKinley became president on a platform calling for Cuban independence.

It has never been proved that the blowing up of the *Maine* in Cuban waters on February 15, 1898, was the fault of the Spanish, but nevertheless it was the justification for the war that was declared on April 25.

The Spanish-American War lasted four months and cost the Americans about 5000 men (over 90 percent of whom died from diseases). The United States acquired, for $20,000,000, Guam, Puerto Rico, and the Philippine Islands and virtual control of Cuba.

Latin America

Troubles in Latin America began in 1891 when rioting occurred in Chile between American sailors and Chileans. This almost led to war. More serious yet was the boundary dispute between British Guiana and Venezuela in which the United States interfered.

President Harrison's Secretary of State, James Blaine, brought the Latin American nations together at the first Pan-American Conference in 1889. His purpose was to get trade concessions. He failed, and as a consequence the United States raised the tariff on Latin American goods.

Under Taft "dollar diplomacy" (the interference on the part of United States private business concerns in the political affairs of South America and the United States' support of those businesses) became even more extreme. Under Wilson United States intervention in Mexico was probably one of the most unwarranted examples of American interference.

The Panama Canal

Theodore Roosevelt's determination to build a canal that the United States alone controlled led to an American-initiated revolution in Colombia, aimed at separating Panama from Colombia. (After Roosevelt's death, the United States paid an indemnity of $25,000,000 to Colombia.)

The canal cost $375,000,000 to build and was opened to ships in 1914. The existence of the canal made United States policy more and more interventionist in the Caribbean.

The Pacific

The port of Pago Pago on the Pacific island of Samoa was acquired by the United States in 1899 as a result of an agreement among the United Kingdom, Germany, and the United States.

In China, Secretary of State John Hay advocated the Open Door Policy, leaving the country free for trade, but the United States still participated in the smashing of the Boxer Rebellion (1912). The U.S. contributed 2500 men and received an indemnity of $24,000,000.

At the end of the Russo-Japanese War (1905), Roosevelt negotiated the treaty because, he said, it was vital to American interests in the Philippines and to the open door policy in China.

WORLD WAR I   1917–1918

"Neutrality"

Unlike Canada who immediately pledged her support to Great Britain and who, by the end of September 1914, had 30,000 volunteers ready to go abroad, the United States hoped to remain neutral during the "European" war. It initially became irritated with Great Britain's naval blockade and seizure of neutral ships. Sentiment, however, remained sufficiently pro-British that the United States did not follow its policy of 1812 and quietly acquiesced to the British blockade of Germany. This was the first step away from neutrality.

By the end of 1916 United States business with the Central Powers had almost totally disappeared, and its investment in the Allied cause in terms of loans stood at $2.5 billion. Although the U.S. had, in fact, if not in theory, committed itself to the Allies, Wilson was able to win reelection on the slogan "He Kept Us Out of War." As soon as he was reelected, he doubled the size of the army and started a three-year naval building program.

Entry into the War

In 1915 the British vessel *Lusitania* was sunk without warning by German submarines and 128 American passengers died. Germany then promised to stop unrestricted submarine warfare but early in 1917 reopened it in order to starve England into submission. Eight American vessels were sunk within the first month, and in February 1917 the United States severed relations with Germany.

Wilson then asked Congress to arm merchant vessels, and when it refused, an old law was found permitting the president to arm vessels without congressional approval, and in March he did so. Then came the news of the "Zimmerman telegram" which indicated Mexican complicity with Germany. The final inducement to the American public was the removal of Nicholas II of Russia. It appeared that Russia would now become a democracy and all the allies could be viewed as "good guys."

On April 2, Wilson asked for war; on April 4th the House agreed; and on April 6, the Senate followed suit.

The War Front

Although only a handful of troops arrived in June 1917, this was sufficient to raise the morale of the Allies. By the time the Germans made their final assault, some 300,000 Americans were on the continent (Canada in contrast sent 640,886 men). American deaths came to 112,000 compared to the cost in Europe of 10 to 13 million. Manpower was significant but it was America's industrial production that tipped the balance in favor of the Allies. For example, American pig iron production tipped the ratio from 50/50 to 50/15.

The Home Front

The mobilization of public opinion by the use of propaganda and advertising was a unique aspect of the war. It was motivated by the need to convince the American public of the righteousness of the Allied cause, but it had serious side effects.

Everything German was suddenly despicable—German-Americans found their liberties curtailed; hamburgers became liberty burgers—and anyone who spoke or wrote against the American government, the American flag, or the American serviceman was liable to prosecution.

THE UNITED STATES AND CANADA AS
WORLD POWERS   1918–1945

By 1918 the United States and, to a lesser extent, Canada had become world powers. Emotionally, however, the United States remained isolationist and in March 1920 rejected the League of Nations and the Treaty of Versailles and pledged itself to a return to "normalcy," which meant "business as usual" with no entangling alliances. In doing so, the U.S. played a major role in the coming of the Second World War, for the League was helpless without the backing of the nation that had inspired it and United States' economic practices contributed to the economic decay of Europe. The Second World War brought new and greater responsibilities to the United States. The rehabilitation of the Western world, the strengthening of democracy, and the sustaining of those nations who wanted to be free fell squarely on its shoulders. Generally, the United States accepted these burdens but the Vietnam War and trouble with European allies over NATO have made many Americans seriously question the United States' "proper" role in the world.

The Return to "Normalcy"

The Defeat of the Treaty of Versailles

Wilson made a series of mistakes at the end of the war; one was in not taking a Republican (the majority party in Congress) to the peace conference with him; another was in not being willing to compromise on Article 10 of the League Covenant (to submit all disputes to arbitration and to employ military and economic sanctions against nations resorting to war in disregard of the League's orders), which was regarded by the Senate as an abridgment of United States sovereignty. These two errors led to the defeat of the Treaty of Versailles in the Senate and kept the United States out of the League of Nations. Legally the war did not end for the United States until July of 1921 when Congress passed a joint resolution so stating.

The Effect of World War I on Society

Immediate reaction was against all things foreign: Americans wanted nothing further to do with Europe or Europeans. Partly as a result of a surplus labor situation in the early 1920s, but partly as a result of this anti-foreign feeling, a series of immigration restriction laws was passed.

One of the greatest effects on American blacks was the move to the cities. During the war 400,000 blacks served, but thousands more moved to the cities in the North enticed by jobs in war industries. Here they encountered ghetto conditions and racial prejudices, and the year 1919 saw the beginning of several years of racial violence. Despite opportunities, rising aspirations led to further disillusionment.

Economic Isolationism

In 1920 an emergency high tariff bill was passed which Wilson vetoed on the grounds that economic nationalism would endanger the peace. But after the Republican victory of 1920, first the Fordney-McCumber tariff and then the Smoot-Hawley tariff were passed, both of which raised duties to the highest they had ever been in American history.

The United States had become, as a result of the war, the creditor nation of the world. It tended to ignore the mounting economic distress in Europe and demanded the payment of all war debts—$10 billion. As President Coolidge put it, "They hired the money, didn't they?"

The Great Depression

Although American industry prospered as an aftermath of the war, agriculture suffered. Between 1920 and 1932 farm income decline from $15.0 billion to $5.5 billion.

Never before had American society been so interested in making money. Sinclair Lewis' *Babbitt* was the symbol of the era. Yet much of the prosperity of the 1920s was specious. By one reckoning, in 1929 a family needed a minimal income of $2000 to buy basic necessities, but almost 60 percent of all American families earned less than $2000.

There are many causes for the Great Depression that struck the United States and the entire world in 1929, but in America two causes were fundamental:

1) Loss of confidence in the industrial growth and prosperity of the land, which was reflected in the collapse of the stock market.

2) The failure to find some way of distributing the wonders of mass production to the people who were making them. Such a small percentage of the profits of industry was finding its way into the pockets of the workers that the laborers were unable to buy (except on time) the products of industry.

By the end of October 1929, Americans had lost $51 billion on the stock market; by the end of that year the total reached $40 billion. By 1932, 12 million people were unemployed in the United States, 5 thousand banks had crashed, and 32 thousand commercial businesses had failed. The national income declined from over $80 billion to $40 billion.

The New Deal and the Federal Government

The Hoover administration did not take drastic action against the effects of the depression, although it did attempt to spend money on public projects, appropriating $300 million for farm loans and lending $2 billion to industry, banks, insurance, and railroads. But these measures did not alleviate the situation.

In 1930 the Democrats captured Congress, and in 1932 Franklin D. Roosevelt was elected president by a landslide victory with a popular majority of 7 million votes.

Government legislation associated with the New Deal was not new. Farm relief, conservation, labor legislation, trust regulation, even judicial reform had all been attempted before, and many of the laws were already on the statute books. The thing that made the New Deal new was not the laws themselves but the philosophy that stood behind them—the doctrine that the government can and should interfere in the affairs of individuals and the unrestricted economic laws of supply and demand in order to create a society in which all men would be able to profit. By the 1930s it had become the responsibility of the government to direct the economy (especially finance) of the country; and poverty became the responsibility of the state, not of the individual.

Relief

The new administration immediately began loans to business, to housing projects, and to public works. Unemployment relief was the first problem tackled. By 1940, $16 billion had been spent on direct relief and $7 billion on public works. The Civil Conservation Corps provided hundreds of jobs; cultural sponsorship kept artists from starving; and public works and the Tennessee Valley Authority provided jobs for thousands.

The Farm Problem

Farm relief was finally achieved by payments to farmers who would devote part of their land to "soil-conserving crops." By 1939 farm incomes were double what they had been in 1932. The greatest boon to the farmer, however, was the Rural Electrification Administration. In 1935, when the program of providing power lines at low interest rates was introduced, only one in ten farms had electricity; by 1941 four out of ten had it (by 1950 nine out of ten).

Banks

All banks were closed and then reopened under stricter supervision and with the government's guarantee of bank deposits.

Labor

The acts passed concerning labor were to have lasting effect.

WAGNER ACT

The Wagner Act of 1935 gave labor the right to collective bargaining and union organization and set up a Labor Relations Board to hear disputes.

UNIONS

In 1932 there were 3,000,000 Americans in labor unions. Then, in 1937, a group within the A.F. of L. (American Federation of Labor) led by John L. Lewis formed the C.I.O. (Congress of Industrial Organization), a union for the unskilled laborers that was organized on the basis of entire industries and not individual crafts. By 1941 the C.I.O. had a membership of 5,000,000, whereas the A.F. of L. had 4,500,000 members. In 1955 these two unions were united and had a total membership of 16,000,000.

FAIR LABOR STANDARDS

The Fair Labor Standards Act of 1938 placed "a ceiling over hours" (a forty-hour week) and "a floor under wages" (a minimum wage of 40 cents per hour).

SOCIAL SECURITY ACTS

In 1935 a series of Social Security Acts was passed that provided unemployment insurance, aid to dependent mothers, and pensions for the aged. With the Social Security Acts, the United States had committed itself to the concept of a "welfare state."

The Supreme Court

In 1936, Roosevelt was dissatisfied with the Supreme Court's unfavorable attitude toward certain New Deal measures, but he failed in his proposal to enlarge the court (with liberal members). Once again the problem of how far the executive could go was at issue.

The Depression in Canada

Canada suffered equally from the depression and was also hurt and irritated by the American tariff legislation against Canadian products in 1929. In 1930 it in turn passed the Dunning tariff, giving Great Britain preferential treatment.

During the depression the Liberal Government failed to provide relief for the unemployed and the Conservatives came to power. By 1936 Canada as well as the United States had achieved a form of welfare state.

In 1930, $20,000,000 was voted for relief of the unemployed.

Tariff duties were again increased, and in 1931 a tariff revision cut off two-thirds of the goods previously imported from the United States. In 1932 preferential tariffs were agreed upon by members of the Commonwealth. In 1934 came a series of acts regulating the prices of marketing and investing and shareholding, and the Bank of Canada was formed under Government supervision. Social legislation was carried through in 1935. A wheat board was established, legislation against monopolies was passed, and the Employment and Social Insurance Act provided unemployment insurance, while the Limitation of Hours and Work Act established an eight-hour day and a forty-eight-hour week.

The End of Depression in the United States

As late as 1939 there were still 10 million unemployed in the United States, and it was World War II and government spending on an unprecedented level which really returned the United States and Canada to prosperity.

Foreign Policy

Latin America
The year 1934 saw a reevaluation of American policy in Latin America and an end to dependence upon military intervention (see the "Good Neighbor Policy" p. 277).

Europe
The United States still viewed Europe with disdain and suspicion. There were too many problems at home to be concerned with what was going on abroad, and the depression intensified traditional American isolationism. When Italy invaded Ethiopia the United States passed the first of several neutrality acts (see p. 131).

Japan
The 1924 immigration restriction law had humiliated Japan, and relations were further strained during the depression. A showdown with Japan was definitely on the horizon in 1941 (see p. 367).

WORLD WAR II   1941–1945

Once again Canada immediately pledged her support to Great Britain, and once again the United States' reaction was to stay out of European involvement. This attitude was a result of disillusionment from the last war, fear of involvement, and a policy of peace at any price.

In 1940 Britain stood alone and Churchill announced that "we shall never surrender" and that if the Germans were to invade and conquer England "our Empire beyond the seas . . . would carry on the struggle, until, in God's good time, the New World, with all its power and might, steps forth to the rescue and liberation of the Old." The Americans' hatred of nazism in Germany; the realization that should England fall the United States would stand alone in a world dominated by fascism; and the efforts of Roosevelt to reeducate the American people and bring them out of isolationism led to a reevaluation and change in American policy.

Steps to War

Rearmament was hastily begun, and Roosevelt called for 50,000 planes to be built in 1940. A joint board of defense was established with Canada. Fifty old destroyers were given to Britain in exchange for leases on naval bases extending from Newfoundland to British Guiana. At the end of 1940 came Lend-Lease (see p. 131) and at the same time the United States was pursuing a policy in the Far East which would ultimately mean war with Japan.

On December 7, 1941, Pearl Harbor was bombed and on December 8th war was declared.

The War

The story of the war is told in the European chapter. The United States provided 16 million men, and all records of production were broken. In 1942 Roosevelt called for 45,000 tanks, 8 million tons of shipping, and 60,000 new planes (48,000 were actually built). The following year the United States built 85,930 planes and 19,396,000 tons of new shipping, and in the last year of the war 300,000 planes and 55,000,000 tons of shipping. The war cost the United States $350 trillion ($50 trillion of which went to Lend-Lease). The Americans at their peak strength had 12,300,000 men in arms (and suffered 291,557 battle deaths); the Canadians numbered 780,000 (with 10,033 battle deaths).

POSTWAR UNITED STATES AND CANADA

As world powers, most of North American postwar history has been directly concerned with world affairs and has been explained elsewhere in this book.

Economic Change

After World War II the United States was the greatest creditor nation on earth. In 1945 it was reported that an American's standard of living was three times as high as an Englishman's, six times as high as an Italian's, and forty times as high as an Indonesian's. The U.S. remains today the richest country in the world with over a trillion dollar gross national product, a higher per capita income than anywhere in the world ($4492 in 1974), and together with Canada has 22.6 percent of the world's food but less than 7.5 percent of the world's population.

An unfavorable balance of trade in 1971-72, the collapse in the value of the dollar on the world market particularly in relationship to the mark and the yen, and increasing inflation have weakened the American world economic position. The dollar continues to fluctuate and inflation has continued at its highest peak since the Korean War and the land of plenty has witnessed shortages and an unstable stock market. The oil crisis (the United States imports almost 50 percent of its oil) has brought home how dependent industrial nations are on countries which control energy resources.

In area, Canada is the second largest country in the world, has immense wealth in undeveloped resources, but has a population of under 22 million. It is the largest exporter of nonferrous metals, the largest producer of nickel, asbestos, zinc ore, and silver, second in cobalt, third in lead, and fourth in uranium and iron. In 1921 Canada was by a slight margin agricultural; by 1951 it was overwhelmingly industrial. It is self-sufficient in gas and oil and second only to the United States in hydro-electric power. Within a decade Canada rose from being an insignificant producer of petroleum to one of the leaders of the world, and the oil crisis suddenly put Canada in a stronger position vis-à-vis the United States. This must be balanced, however, by the fact that 80 percent of investment in Canadian industry is American, and 70 percent of Canada's trade is with the United States.

Social Change

The most important social development in the United States was the Supreme Court's decision in 1954 that racial segregation must end. Much of the nation's domestic interest and legislation has been devoted to the problem of segregation and to the effort to achieve a reasonable degree of equality between blacks and whites. These aims were incorporated into the Civil Rights Act of 1964, but racial strife has by no means ended; the assassination of Martin Luther King in 1968 was a blow to the forces of moderation and led to unprecedented urban disorders and the increase of radical black power groups. Statistics, however, indicate progress. Between 1948 and 1963 the percentage of nonwhite males earning $6000 to $10,000 annually went up twenty-five times.

Growing violence in American life can be measured in terms of the dangers of politics. Not only was President John Kennedy assassinated on November 22, 1963, but presidential candidate Robert Kennedy was killed in 1968 and George Wallace was shot and crippled during the campaign of 1972. In 1975, two attempts were made on the life of President Gerald Ford.

Political Developments

Canada, which is 26.9 percent French and 60.2 percent English, faced a major political crisis in 1967 when President Charles de Gaulle of France fanned the flames of separatism in Quebec. For many years there had been agitation for varying degrees of autonomy; De Gaulle, however, actively supported an independent Quebec. However, with the election of Pierre E. Trudeau, a French Canadian, as prime minister in 1968 and again in 1974, the movement toward separatism, if not greater autonomy for Quebec, receded.

In the United States a crisis occurred in 1973 which threatened to undermine the whole system of government and yet proved that the structure was resilent enough to survive. President Richard Nixon was elected for his second term with the second largest majority in history, but by December of 1973 he was facing the possibility of impeachment. Vice President Spiro Agnew was forced to resign or face charges of bribery and corruption. The president himself came under serious attack not only for income tax irregularities but for his handling of the break-in and bugging of the Democratic National Headquarters at the Watergate Hotel. He was accused of deliberate cover-ups and obstruction of justice, and during Senate committee hearings he refused to turn over tapes and records until ordered to do so by the courts. Nixon resigned the presidency in 1974 after admitting his complicity, and for the first time in United States history, the presidency and the vice-presidency were held by non-elected officials.

In 1973 Congress further challenged the power of the executive by passing legislation denying the president the right to commit armed forces to hostilities abroad without congressional consent. The specific issue was the U.S. invasion of Cambodia. The issue of how far Congress should go in limiting the power of the executive remains an unresolved question.

The Presidents of the United States 1917–1979

Warren G. Harding	1921	Republican
Calvin Coolidge	1923	Republican
Herbert C. Hoover	1929	Republican
Franklin D. Roosevelt	1933	Democrat
Harry S. Truman	1945	Democrat
Dwight D. Eisenhower	1953	Republican
John F. Kennedy	1961	Democrat
Lyndon B. Johnson	1963	Democrat
Richard M. Nixon	1968	Republican
Gerald R. Ford	1974	Republican
Jimmy Carter	1976	Democrat

The Prime Ministers of Canada 1917–1979

Robert Laird Borden	1917–1920	Unionist
Arthur Meighen	1920–1921	Unionist
W. L. MacKenzie King	1921–1926	Liberal
Arthur Meighen	1926	Conservative
W. L. MacKenzie King	1926–1930	Liberal
Richard B. Bennett	1930–1935	Conservative
W. L. MacKenzie King	1935–1948	Liberal
Louis S. St. Laurent	1948–1957	Liberal
John Diefenbaker	1957–1963	Conservative
Lester Pearson	1963–1968	Liberal
Pierre E. Trudeau	1968–1979	Liberal
Joe Clark	1979–1980	Conservative
Pierre E. Trudeau	1980–	

Foreign Policy

The United Nations

The United Nations, a creation of Roosevelt and Secretary of State Cordell Hull, came into being in 1945, and both the United States and Canada pledged their support. The new organization (see p. 140) was considerably stronger than the old League but still faced many problems. Nevertheless, action was taken during the Korean War (1950–54), during the Congo civil war (1960–64), and in the Middle East almost continuously, and both the United States and Canada provided troops on numerous occasions.

The Cold War

The United States took a strong international stand immediately after the war. The Marshall Plan appropriated $12,000,000,000 for European recovery; between 1947 and 1950, thanks to the Truman Doctrine of containing Soviet expansion and subversion, $660,000,000 went to Greece and Turkey. In 1949 NATO was formed, and by 1954, $400,000,000 had been spent by the Point Four Program to bring modern medicine and technology to underdeveloped areas.

In 1948 came the crisis of the blockade of Berlin (see p. 190) and in 1950 the Korean War. Both the United States and Canada sent troops and United States casualties were extremely high. But the policy of *containment* (keeping Communism contained to the area it had acquired after the war) had temporarily succeeded.

United States policy in China, however, was a failure: $2,000,000,000 was spent on the shaky and corrupt regime of Chiang Kai-shek before 1949. The Marshall Mission failed to bring peace. Chiang fled the country before the war was over, yet the United States pledged support to Chiang's government on Formosa and refused to recognize the Communist government until the early 1970s.

The 1950s saw a reversal of United States policy in Latin America with active intervention in order to stop the spread of Communism (see p. 277).

In another effort to contain Communism in Asia, the United States became involved in the Vietnam War. In 1961 the escalation of American participation began with the introduction of combat troops instead of military "advisers." By the end of 1965, 100,000 American soldiers were in Vietnam and bombing of the North had begun; by 1966 the figure rose to 389,000 and bombing was extended to the Hanoi area. The mid-1968 total came to 525,000 men, and in 1969 alone $21.5 billion were spent on the war. The war was disastrous to the morale of the American people and political protests tore the United States apart. American casualties were over 360,000 (deaths over 56,000). A very uneasy "peace," which at least allowed the Americans to withdraw, was finally settled in 1973, but the war went on until April 1975 when Saigon fell and Vietnam was formally reunified.

Policy Changes

Because of détente, the United States has drawn closer to the USSR, and efforts have been made to impose treaty limitations upon nuclear weapons (the SALT treaty). Europe and the United States have been estranged by fear of possible American reductions in NATO forces. In April of 1972 an American president for the first time visited China, and in 1979 the U.S. established full diplomatic relations with China.

North American Relations

Relations between Canada and the United States have been basicly friendly. During World War II many mutual agreements were reached over defense, production, and so forth. In 1958 by the North American Air Defense Act radar warning lines throughout North America were established.

During the Cuban missile crisis in 1962, however, Canada's confidence in the United States was shaken, and a related dispute over guided missiles with nuclear warheads located in Canada led to the downfall of Prime Minister Diefenbaker. Relations were also strained during the Vietnam War when Canada became the home of many thousand American draft evaders and conscientious objectors.

Science since 1945

Although science knows no national boundaries, the United States, the Soviet Union, and Europe have been the major contributors to modern industrial and scientific research.

Scientific discoveries since World War II have moved at an ever accelerating pace. In the field of electronics the transistor was introduced in the early 1950s, followed by the computer (there were 15 in the United States in 1954; ten years later, 17,000); in the field of molecular biology in 1967 the discovery of the mechanism by which the action of the basic genetic code (DNA) was controlled; in the field of medicine, polio and small pox were controlled, the first heart transplant was carried out in 1967 in South Africa, and the widespread use of antibiotics has had a profound effect on life expectancy throughout the world.

The Space Age

The Space Age was ushered in on October 4, 1957, with the Russian Sputnik I, and once again modern technology has moved so fast that it is impossible to record it. The Russians placed a man in earth orbit in April 1961; the Americans in 1962. In 1968 three American astronauts orbited the moon and in July 1969 Neil A. Armstrong in Apollo 11 was the first man to walk on the moon. Skylab was launched in 1973, Venus, Mars, and Jupiter have been photographed, and a joint U.S.-Soviet space project, Soyuz-Apollo, was launched in the summer of 1975.

Latin America

ANCIENT, CLASSICAL, AND MEDIEVAL CIVILIZATION
500 B.C.–1500 A.D.

Historical periods in Latin America do not correspond with the arbitrary dates of ancient, classical, and medieval periods. The great Indian civilizations overlap these eras. It makes things much clearer to talk about the entire pre-historic period as a unit. Before the Spanish came to Latin America in 1500, there were three levels of development on the continent. The lowest comprised the food collectors and nomads on the plains of Argentina; the next in development were those who practiced a primitive form of agriculture in the Amazon valley; and the highest level of civilization was attained by the Mayas of the Yucatán peninsula, Guatemala, and Honduras, the Aztecs of Mexico, and the Incas of the Andean highlands (from Ecuador to Chile). Despite the high level of development, all the Indians lacked draft animals, iron tools, and knowledge of the wheel and the keystone arch. All three civilizations were authoritarian with well-organized and controlled economies, pioneering in the field of agriculture. The Aztecs and the Incas were destroyed by Spanish guns and cunning, but the Indian has remained an important part of the Latin American scene.

THE MAYAS

The first civilization in the Americas that historians have knowledge of is the Mayan. (November 4, 291 B.C., the earliest date in

254

American history, was found on a Mayan altar.) Yet little is known, for only three books escaped the burning of the Mayan library at Yucatán by the Spanish. "Because they contained nothing but superstitions and falsehoods about the Devil, we burned them all."

Copán (Honduras) was the capital of the Old Empire, but in approximately 700 A.D. the Mayans moved northward to the Yucatán peninsula and established the New Empire. No one knows why they abandoned huge cities and made this move.

The Mayans have been called the Greeks of the New World, for they reached a high point of development in the arts and sciences, particularly sculpture, painting, architecture, and astronomy. They were a peaceful farming and trading people. Some say their roads were superior to those of the Romans. They measured time more accurately than the Europeans of their day (instead of a decimal system of nine numbers and a zero, they used nineteen numbers and a zero) and developed a calendar with 365 days (also used by the Aztecs). They wrote in *hieroglyphics* (picture language) and from about 700 A.D. began to record history. With the use of stone tools they created temples similar to the Egyptian pyramids.

The Mayan empire fell apart around 1200 A.D. They were probably conquered by the Toltecs.

THE TOLTECS

Almost nothing is known about this tribe, but according to legend they were the traditional founders of civilization in central Mexico. Their capital was Tula (fifty miles north of Mexico City), and they were skilled in agriculture, weaving, architecture, and carpentry. It is supposed that they destroyed the Mayan civilization and were in turn absorbed by the Aztecs.

THE AZTECS

The Aztecs, unlike the Mayans, were a nation of warriors, merchants, and organizers. They were probably the first Americans to use swords, and their religion was bloody and warlike. (Human sacrifice was the basis of the faith.) Trade was a prestige profession, and the civilization flourished. Tenochtitlán, their capital, was a remarkable city with a population of around 300,000 and a system of canals.

Wandering Aztecs reached Anahuac about 1200 A.D. and learned a great deal from their predecessors, the Toltecs. In 1325 the Aztecs founded Tenochtitlán and gained a foothold in central Mexico. In a hundred years they were the strongest tribe in the valley, and by 1440, under Montezuma I, they had moved east and south and controlled most of central Mexico in a confederation of tribes.

Between 1519 and 1521 Hernando Cortés and 400 Spanish troops defeated them.

THE INCAS

The "children of the sun," the Incas of the Peruvian Andes, were a peace-loving people like the Mayans. A great deal is known about their civilization because they buried their dead in mummy bundles and interred them in the dry desert.

The Incas were empire builders, giving a common language and a communications system to the territories they controlled. By 1492 their empire extended 2300 miles along the west coast of South America. Their government was a type of benevolent despotism. There was a strict labor code, for example, that forced all to work for the state but exempted the nobility, the army on active duty, males under twenty-five or over fifty, women, and all who were incapable of hard labor. Land was owned by the state and there seems to have been abundance for all. The Incas were skilled in domesticating plants, pottery, inlay work, alloying, tapestries, and surgery. They had no system of writing, however.

The faith of the Incas was sun worship with a missionary zeal, but it was because of this faith that the Spanish became interested, for the temple of the sun in Cuzco was described by the Spanish explorers as literally a mine of gold. The face of the sun-god looked down from a massive gold disc, encrusted with emeralds. All trees, flowers, vases, and other objects were wrought by hand in pure gold. By the sixteenth century the Incas had reached the peak of their development and controlled the largest area ever united under one government in pre-European America. But in 1527 civil war broke out at the same time as Francisco Pizarro's expedition, and this led to their destruction.

MODERN CIVILIZATION   1500 to the Present

In the 1500s the Spanish arrived, destroyed the Indian civilizations, and created a colonial empire in the New World. The Spaniards, however, were more interested in "gold, God, and glory" than in colonization, and conquest did not mean effective occupancy everywhere. In some areas of Latin America, Spanish influence was minimal. Even the Catholic church did not penetrate, although its authority and influence went farther than any other European institution brought over by the conqueror. "The church ruled while the state governed." The Indian, when allowed to survive, remained an Indian, and even today some have not yet become westernized. In the twentieth century there are Indians who continue to fight the whites. These are the Huichol, the Lacandón of Mexico, the Indians on the Magdalena River in Columbia, and the Aucas in Ecuador.

The Spanish maintained an authoritarian regime in which there was no room for native representation or experience, and in doing so they in no way prepared Latin America for independence or for democratic government. Three centuries of isolation under Spanish rule also left its mark by encouraging separatist traditions and eventual political fragmentation. Today much of Latin America is underdeveloped, yet it started out with advantages over North America, for it was rich in gold and silver and had a relatively advanced native population. Here too the Spanish left their mark, for the feudalism they introduced and the systems of land tenure and labor relations they developed in part explain the situation today.

The movements for independence began about 1804 in Haiti, and by 1825 almost all of Latin America had become independent of European rule. Simón Bolivar had dreamed of a Latin America both united and free. The first was certainly not achieved, for the eight Spanish colonies became eighteen separate countries, and the accomplishment of the second is doubtful. It has been said that independence day was "the last day of despotism and the first day of the same thing."

THE SPANISH COLONIAL PERIOD   1492–1804

The Spanish Arrive

After Columbus' voyage in 1492, the Spanish established an outpost in the Caribbean Islands.

From there, in 1519, Hernando Cortés led an expedition onto the mainland and with 400 men destroyed the Aztec confederacy and incorporated Mexico into the Spanish empire. (In 1535 Mexico became the Viceroyalty of New Spain.) There was no united resistance by the Indians, for there was strife within the empire and Cortés was clever enough to play upon the jealousy of rival cities, persuading many of the neighbors of the Aztecs to join him. Also, the fear and superstition of the Aztec people played a part in the Spanish victory. European firearms were magic, and horses (never before seen in America) were terrifying.

From Mexico Spanish forces moved south and north. Vasco Nuñez de Balboa discovered the Pacific in 1513 and thus opened the way to the conquest of Peru by Francisco Pizarro.

In 1532 Spanish troops encountered the divided Inca empire. Civil war was raging between the two sons of Huayna Capac. When Pizarro captured the Inca emperor, he demanded a ransom of a room twenty-two by seventeen filled as high as a man could reach with silver and gold. He got the ransom but strangled the emperor. The Inca territory became the Viceroyalty of New Castile (later Peru). Pizarro captured the Inca empire with only 200 troops, but the feat was not as extraordinary as Cortés, since the Incas were not warriors.

Although the Spanish had conquered, their control remained uncertain until the eighteenth century. British, French, and Dutch pirates raided their ships and their seaports; the war against the Apaches in North Mexico went on until the late nineteenth century as did the war against the Indians in Argentina and Chile. It was not until 1717 that the Spanish were able to create the Viceroyalty of New Granada (Colombia, Ecuador, Venezuela, and Panama), and the Argentine was not conquered until late in the colonial period. (The Viceroyalty of the Rio de la Plata, established in 1776, included Argentina, Paraguay, and Bolivia.)

By 1575 some 32,000 Spanish families had settled in the New World, but they were more interested in mining than in colonizing. Between 1500 and 1660 Spain acquired 18,600 tons of silver and 200 tons of gold from the New World, exclusive of smuggled wealth.

Territories Not Controlled by Spain

Portuguese Brazil

By the Treaty of Tordesillas in 1494, Pope Alexander VI had drawn a north-south line running 1300 miles west of the Azores. All lands west of this line were to belong to Spain and all lands east of it to Portugal. Brazil became Portuguese when Pedro Cabral landed there in 1500.

The Caribbean

The political and cultural confusion in the Caribbean today is in part the result of the scramble to control the New World. France acquired Haiti in 1697; the British took over Jamaica in 1670; and the French, British, and Dutch split up Guiana after the Napoleonic Wars.

Authoritarianism

Spanish Government

The Spanish government in the colonies reinforced the authoritarian tradition in Latin America. As the Aztecs and the Incas had been divine-right monarchs, so were the Spanish kings. As life for the Indian had been controlled by indisputable law, so was it now under the Spanish conquistadors.

The chief officer in the New World was the viceroy, who held civil, religious, and military power. The captains-general were of lesser power. Cuba, Santo Domingo (later the Dominican Republic and Haiti), Chile, and Guatemala (which included Guatemala, El Salvador, Honduras, Nicaragua, and Costa Rica) were captaincies-general. All offices were appointed by the king of Spain. Not only were most officials Spanish, but also most were not permanent residents of the colonies. Of 672 viceroys, captains-general, and governors, only eighteen were permanent residents.

The difference between the English colonies in North America and the Spanish colonies in South America in part explains the difference today in their respective political institutions and practices.

The Roman Catholic Church

The church was itself an instrument of authoritarianism. The tradition of militant Catholicism of the Counter-Reformation was carried to the New World. No religious freedom was allowed, and officers of the church were Spaniards (of 706 bishops, only 105 were permanent residents). The religion of the Indian was destroyed and with it the very soul of Indian civilization. The church, however, built its cathedrals where the old temples had stood. In some ways the church was the only force that gave the conquistador and the conquered something in common and gave the Indian a sense of identity with the European (although it required a papal edict to make it clear to the Spanish conqueror that the Indians were human beings).

The Class System

THE INDIANS

The Indian was in the lowest class. Whenever he managed to retain his land he remained Indian in his ways and attitudes. He was deprived of leadership, religion, and learning and was forced by the Spanish into service and to pay tribute. The result of this policy created a nation within a nation.

Nevertheless, it should be noted that Spanish policy toward the Indian was very different from that of the British in North America. The Latin American Indians were more numerous than their North American neighbors and were generally agricultural and urban rather than nomadic. The Spaniards, unlike the English, needed the Indians as a labor force in the mines.

Population figures are inaccurate, but today Latin America is about 30 percent Indian.

THE BLACKS

The blacks were brought to the New World as slaves but were treated quite differently from the way the Indians were handled. The blacks became closer to and more dependent upon the white man and eventually became Europeanized. The position of the slave in the Iberian countries gave him a legal personality, rights, and duties. He was allowed to buy his freedom; unusual punishments could be taken to court; and the killing of a slave was murder. There has never been the problem of segregation in Latin America for blacks.

Today Hatii is 90 percent black, the Dominican Republic and Cuba about 35 percent.

THE MESTIZOS

The child of a European father and an Indian mother, the mestizo was one of the most important by-products of the Spanish conquest, for he became the leader after independence. During the colonial period he was looked upon with hostility and suspicion—a misfit in society. "He had no tradition, no invariable rules, no place in the community comparable with his ambitions" (which were to emulate the role of his Spanish father). The civil wars after the wars of independence gave him his opportunity. Since the Spanish and Portuguese aristocrats were so far removed from the masses and generally more concerned with events in Europe than at home, the leadership of the new nations fell to the mestizo, who had "neither the tradition, the education, nor the experience for the task."

THE WHITES

The whites themselves were divided in colonial Latin America. The *peninsulares*, those who were born in Europe, had the influence and the power, and the *criollos*, those who were born in the New World, were resentful. This resentment was one of the factors in the wars of independence, for it was the criollos who led the revolt.

Economic Policies

Spanish Feudalism

A feudal landowning aristocracy patterned after Spain's was created in Latin America. With the wars of independence, the serf became a *peon* and the landlord a *patron,* but the system did not change, for the peon was tied to the land by debt servitude.

The Urban-Rural Split

The Spanish system of viewing Latin America as a group of cities led to important divisions between urban and rural areas. Laws regulated the cities where the Spanish settled but not the rural areas. The cities, therefore, became linked with the events of Europe—the decline of feudalism and the loss of the economic and political power of the church—but the countryside did not.

The Class System

The Spanish cultural tradition that the gentleman did not work with his hands meant that the mestizo became the artisan, but educational restrictions limiting education to the upper classes caused a situation in Latin America in which there was little or no skilled labor.

THE INDEPENDENCE MOVEMENTS   1804–1825

Causes

The Napoleonic Wars

In 1807 French troops invaded Spain, and Napoleon placed his brother Joseph Bonaparte on the throne of Spain. Whether the colonies refused to accept this "Intruder King" or whether they grabbed the opportunity to overthrow Spanish rule is a matter of opinion. Revolts, however, broke out in 1809 in Argentina, Ecuador, and Mexico, and when Ferdinand VII was restored in 1814, the revolutionists refused to turn the clock back to 1807.

The Role of the Criollo

Discontent with Spain was developing among the criollos, who resented Spanish commercial restrictions (heavy taxation and extremely restrictive mercantilism) and the fact that the government of the colonies was controlled by peninsulares. Despite Spanish censorship, political liberalism had been filtering into Latin America for half a century. Great Britain successfully exported the writings of Locke, Voltaire, and Rousseau.

Liberation

Northern South America (Venezuela, Panama, Colombia, Ecuador, and Bolivia) was led into revolution (1810–1825) and freedom by General Simón Bolívar.

General José de San Martín, known as the George Washington of Argentina, won the battle against Spain in Argentina in 1816. Then in 1817 he led 5000 men across the Andes to free Chile and Peru. This campaign is considered to be one of the great feats of military history.

In 1822 Bolívar and San Martín met at Guayaquil (Ecuador), and San Martín withdrew from political and military activity, leaving Bolívar to determine Latin America's future (which he did until his death in 1830).

Mexico claims as heroes of her independence Miguel Hidalgo and José Maria Morelos, both of whom were executed by the Spanish. Liberation actually came as a result of the leadership of Augustín de Iturbide who styled himself Emperor Agustin I, was exiled by the Mexicans, and, when he attempted to return, was executed.

Brazil declared independence from Portugal in 1822 and achieved it without bloodshed. The French had occupied Portugal in 1807, and the Emperor Joao VI established a government in exile at Rio de Janeiro. Returning to Portugal in 1821, he left his son Dom Pedro in charge. Dom Pedro, rather than return to Lisbon, declared Brazil's independence in 1822, and his father preferred not to send troops against his own son.

By 1825 Spain had lost most of her colonies in Latin America. Only a few islands in the Caribbean remained in its hands. The most important, Cuba and Puerto Rico, were lost during the Spanish-American War of 1898.

LATIN AMERICA SINCE INDEPENDENCE   1825–1979

Political Developments

The Question of Democracy

All the Latin American countries are nominally republics, and almost all have a form of government similar to what Bolívar advocated: the president of the republic should be "the sun, which, firm in the center, gives life to the universe"; he should be the "supreme authority"; this authority should be perpetual; and he should name his successor.

Very few of the countries are actually democratic. In 1964, Uruguay, Chile, Costa Rica, the Dominican Republic, Mexico, Argentina, and Venezuela were the only countries which could be called democracies. The number has diminished: by 1973 Argentina had seen the return of the dictator Perón; Chile's president had been killed in a right-wing military coup; Mexico had become in essence a one-party state; and by 1975 it was questionable whether the president or the military ruled Uruguay, where in 1974 hundreds of professors were fired for refusing to sign a government-dictated "Declaration of Democratic Faith." Most countries are military dictatorships basing their rule on controlled elections.

Militarism

Militarism is the key to power in almost every Latin American nation. In Peru, for example, 80 percent of the presidents have been soldiers. In 1965 President Belaunde held the first municipal elections in 45 years; three years later he was ousted by the military.

Throughout Latin America the rise of the army has been a result of the independence movement and also due to the fact that the army was the only secular institution with a national interest and outlook. Brazil's president justified military control by explaining that "no civilian doctor would open a practice in desolate country"— so an army doctor does—and "the schoolteacher there may be an army man too." In other words, the military know at first hand what their nations need.

The military come from and reflect different backgrounds. Some are from the political left: when the Peruvian armed forces took control they introduced radical land reform and took over the United States oil concession.

After 1965 the increase of guerilla activities in many countries further strengthened the military's position.

ARGENTINA

Juan Domingo Perón's rule in Argentina (1941–1955) was both typical as a military government and atypical because Perón aimed at total control and achieved the nearest thing to fascism on the American continent.

The great grandson of an Italian immigrant, Perón's chief pillars of support were the army and labor. Despite army-supervised elections and ecclesiastical influence, Perón seems actually to have been the choice of the people in 1946. Once firmly established in power, Perón aimed at social and economic revolution, attempting to rid Argentina of United States and British investments and to establish state monopolies. Industrial progress was made during the years 1946–1951 but often at the expense of agriculture. By 1951 the press was brought completely under control, and in 1954 Perón broke with the church and legalized divorce and brothels.

In the end Perón was supported by the United States, and he granted the rights to the oil resources of Argentina to the California

Oil Company. This aroused nationalistic antagonism toward his regime, which, combined with a drastic economic crisis, led to Perón's downfall. Like many Latin American dictators, the army's revolt brought his fall from power. He fled into exile, taking with him an immense fortune. He returned to power two decades later, however. Since his death in 1974, Argentina has been primarily in the hands of military governments.

Instability

Most of the Latin American governments are unstable; coup d'etats follow coup d'etats. Ecuador is the extreme example. From 1931 to 1940, fourteen presidents were in office; there were twelve foreign ministers in a two-month period in 1933; and September 1947 saw three successive presidents. Palace revolutions are a common picture in Latin America. Bolivia has had so many coups that it averages one president per year. Generally the coups cost few lives and affected only the elite.

In the 1970s economic difficulties further heightened political instability, and guerilla actions caused terror and counter-terror. Colombia in 1975 declared a state of "siege" because of economic problems. The situation has been described as "Latin America's classic vicious triangle"—discontent with economic reforms leads to violence; violence leads to military intervention and authoritarian rule; and authoritarian rule leads to discontent. All the nations have two policies which act as a political safety valve but are disruptive of stable government:

1) political asylum: in other words, dictators can escape the consequences of their policies by fleeing to other countries.

2) the exiling of political enemies: this is better than execution but often leads to the failure to mitigate the cause of political discontent.

Communism and Radicalism

By 1959 only in Cuba had Communism become the accepted political creed. Since then Communist ideology has been spreading. Castro's comrade, Che Guevara, after his death by Bolivian troops in 1967, became a folk legend, but guerilla activities in the remote regions of Colombia, Peru, and Bolivia have been too far distant from the majority of the population to have much effect. More serious has been the guerillas' penetration into the cities where they have been better protected, have found more financial support from liberal and "anti-imperialist" elements, and where they exploited a successful source of political blackmail: foreign diplomats were kidnapped and released in exchange for political prisoners. Examples of this have been the kidnapping of the U.S. ambassador in Brazil in 1969 who was released in exchange for 15 political prisoners; the slaying of the U.S. ambassador (1968) and the West German ambassador (1970) in Guatemala. Since 1967, Guatemala has had nothing but trouble; 4000 people may have been killed in what amounts to undeclared civil war (600 labor leaders died in 1970).

In 1970 Salvador Allende became the western hemisphere's first constitutionally elected Marxist president. Allende advocated state ownership of resources, abolition of minority class privileges, and a "republic of the working class." He promised to govern with traditional Chilean "democratic decency." By September 1973 Allende was dead, thousands were arrested, and constitutional Marxism and 45 years of democratic government in Chile had ended.

Social and Cultural Change

Education

In 1960 two out of five people in Latin America were illiterate. Because of the rapid population growth, this figure has not changed. In fact, in Mexico, although more and more children go to school every year, the literacy rate is dropping.

Argentina can boast of an adult literacy rate of 90 percent; Uruguay, Chile, and Venezuela of about 80 percent; Colombia of 60 percent. But Bolivia, El Salvador, and Guatemala have only a 30 percent literacy rate; in Haiti and Honduras it may be as low as 10 percent.

Urbanization

Urbanization and all its consequences are in many ways much

worse than in the United States. The most extreme examples are in Uruguay where 49 percent of the people live in Montevideo and in Argentina where 34.5 percent live in Buenos Aires.

Problems of Race and Population

Ronald Hilton explains Latin America's lack of concern over the population explosion by stating that "Latin American culture is still more aesthetic than scientific." But the problem is real enough. The rate of population growth varies from 3.5 percent in Venezuela and Mexico to 1.2 percent in Guatemala and Bolivia. El Salvador has the highest population density of 400 people per square mile.

Only in a few countries are any real attempts being made to slow down population growth. It is estimated that by the year 2000, Latin America will reach a total population of 624 million while the United States and Canada will be less than 300 million.

The whites still dominate in most areas. They own the land, dominate the church, which in turn dominates the people, and control the army. There is still a caste-like racial and cultural distinction that divides the urban and rural areas and makes popular sovereignty almost impossible.

The Indian who has never been assimilated into Spanish culture remains a problem in many Latin American countries. Bolivia, Ecuador, and Peru face the most serious dilemma, with 80 percent of their inhabitants Indian and 10 percent to 15 percent considered white. In Paraguay, on the other hand, the amalgamation of white and Indian has gone the furthest, and the country today is essentially mestizo and is the only bilingual country in Latin America, where both white and Indian speak two languages— the Indian language of Guarani and Spanish. In Peru, on the other hand, in the village of Hualcán, only 200 miles from Lima, only eight out of nine hundred people could speak Spanish in 1964.

The Church

The role of the church in state affairs is a situation that has not been solved in many countries. Although there is legal separation of church and state in Brazil, Chile, Cuba, Ecuador, El Salvador, Guatemala, Honduras, Mexico, Nicaragua, Panama, and Uruguay, the church is so strong in Ecuador and Colombia that it can initiate legislation; and it has the power of veto in El Salvador and Peru. Yet how much influence it has on the people of Latin America is doubtful—young men are not going into the priesthood at the same rate as they used to.

Economic Problems

In 1960 it was reported that two-thirds of the people of Latin America were undernourished; two-thirds were working under semi-feudal conditions; millions were landless; and there was serious unemployment.

It is difficult to make generalizations about the economic situation, for diversity is the theme, as it is in Africa and the Middle East. Countries range in size from Brazil, with a population of over 100 million inhabitants and a land area greater than the continental United States, to El Salvador, the size of New Hampshire with over 4 million people (New Hampshire's population in 1977 was 849,000). In 1960 Venezuela had a per capita income of $500 a year, Peru of $250, and Haiti, on the other end of the scale, of $85. By 1973 Venezuela's per capita income was $1037 but Brazil's, potentially one of the richest countries, was $360. Costa Rica has the highest per capita income in Central America ($431) and the most evenly distributed national income. Economic statistics are meaningless in a country like Brazil where if you move one hundred miles into the interior you have moved one hundred years back in time.

Natural Resources

The possession of resources also varies. Mexico and Venezuela have oil; Venezuela and Brazil, an abundance of iron ore; Bolivia, tin; Chile, nitrate and copper; Mexico and Peru, gold and silver; and Colombia produces 90 percent of the world's emeralds and is the largest producer of gold in Latin America. Paraguay has rich agricultural and timber lands and is predominately a cattle country. Argentina is also a farming and stock raising nation but must import almost every mineral it uses. Venezuela, on the other hand, is the third largest producer of crude petroleum in the world but agriçulture has not kept pace with the population.

Agrarian Reform

Much of the land in Latin America was controlled by a very small percentage of the population and the *hacienda* system (great estates) was in existence. The remainder of the land (about half) was hardly capable of subsistence agriculture.

Mexico led the way toward land redistribution when it placed 1,900,000 families on 110,000,000 acres. In Bolivia in 1959, 669,441 acres were distributed at an average of fifty-nine acres per person. In Guatemala between 1955 and 1959, 284,694 acres were redistributed, and in Venezuela in 1960, 620,000 acres were given to 5000 families. The redistribution of land, however equalitarian it may have been, did not improve agricultural production and has not substantially bettered the lot of the peasant. In Mexico the most prosperous farms are large-scale ones on the west coast which have circumvented the law.

Economic Cooperation

A five-nation Central American Common Market has virtually collapsed. The Andean Group (Bolivia, Chile, Columbia, Ecuador, and Peru), however, was organized in 1969 and has met with success.

Inflation and Unemployment

The most serious problems in the 1970s were inflation and unemployment; they threaten to disrupt country after country. Bolivia and Chile saw 100 percent inflation in 1973; in Argentina, one of the more affluent countries in Latin America, inflation rose from 40 percent in 1974 to over 334 percent in 1975.

Atypical Countries

Mexico

THE REVOLUTION

The revolution that began in Mexico in 1910 brought fundamental social, economic, and political change.

General Porfirio Díaz was dictator of Mexico from 1877 to 1911. One percent of the population owned 70 percent of the land; Catholicism was the state religion; church and state worked hand in hand; the Indian had no rights and had been forced into peonage; foreign companies controlled most of the natural resources of the country.

The revolution began in 1910, led by Francisco Indalecio Madero whose main complaint was fraudulent elections and who forced the overthrow of Díaz. But the revolution soon got out of hand, for the people wanted more than honest elections. Emiliano Zapata was one of the leaders whose cry was for "Land and Liberty."

CHANGES

1) Land tenure was changed radically. Large estates were divided up, particularly during 1934–1940. Between the years 1915 and 1950, 76,570,000 acres were redistributed. The *ejido* (collective system), where the land was held by the village, was established by 1950 on 27 percent of the land in Mexico.

2) The church lost most of its power over education and government. Church lands were taken away and the government no longer forced people to *tithe* (pay one-tenth of their income to the church).

3) The Indian and the mestizo gained the right to vote and to own land.

4) Foreign investors lost, for the government declared that everything that was beneath the surface of the land belonged to the government and the people of Mexico. Oil was nationalized in 1938.

5) Political change eventually meant the fall of military

dictatorship. No president could be reelected, and in 1946 President Alemán became the first civilian president of Mexico.

Brazil

Brazil's political, economic, and social history differs from the rest of Latin America. One reason for this is that its colonial background was Portuguese and not Spanish. There were few settlers, and they were mostly confined to the coast; the church was relatively weaker and poorer and there was no Inquisition in Brazil. The church today does not interfere in politics, so the country is neither violently clerical nor anticlerical. As one student of art remarked, "In Brazil, even Christ hangs comfortably on the cross."

Another reason for the difference between Brazil and the rest of Latin America seems to be attitude toward life and politics. There is optimism and a desire to improve, no matter what the cost and inconvenience. The new capital of Brasilia, built in an underdeveloped area 500 miles in the interior, is a symbol of this energy. Brazil is the largest country in Latin America, the Amazon is the largest river in the world, the country grows most of the world's coffee and bananas, and one-quarter of all known plant species can be found in its interior.

Even Brazil's dictators have been unique. Vargas ruled from 1930 to 1945. Between 1930 and 1937 his rule was not dictatorial, but with the heavy migration between 1890 and 1937 (by 1937 one-fifth of the population of Brazil consisted of Italians, Germans, Spaniards, Syrians, and Japanese), he met the crisis by establishing a dictatorship. Yet, as Lewis Hanke says, "it was a most Brazilian kind of dictatorship, with little of the harshness usually found in such regimes." In 1945 Vargas surrendered power peacefully at the army's command. He did not flee with millions of dollars as Perón and many others had; instead he ran for the Senate and won, and in 1950 he was elected President at the age of sixty-seven. (He committed suicide in 1954.) Brazil continues to fluctuate between degrees of constitutionalism and dictatorship.

Cuba

HISTORY

In 1898, as a result of the Spanish-American War, Cuba was placed in the hands of the United States; in 1902 the United States withdrew, and Thomas Estrada Palma was inaugurated as the first president of the Cuban republic. By the Platt Amendment of 1903 the United States, however, had the right to intervene in Cuba's defense and also acquired the naval base of Guantanamo Bay.

THE CUBAN REVOLUTION

The republic came to an end in 1952 when General Fulgencio Batista seized control and set up a dictatorship. Under the leadership of Fidel Castro, revolutionary cells opposed to Batista's reign were formed. The revolt staged on July 26, 1953, failed, and Castro was imprisoned. Castro announced total war against Batista in March 1958. More and more supporters rallied to his cause; Batista resigned; and Castro marched into Havana on January 3, 1959.

CUBA UNDER CASTRO

In February of 1959 Castro became premier. Batista's supporters and any who opposed the new regime were killed or imprisoned. Then Castro set about badly needed agrarian reform. The size of farms was restricted to 1000 acres (farms of 3300 acres were allowed for sugar, cattle, and rice). Cooperatives were set up on half the land of Cuba; 2200 "people's stores," 1215 new schools, 1000 "alphabetization centers" (for adult illiterates) were established. In 1960, Castro confiscated all American property (the sugar mills alone were worth about $275,000,000). Turning to Moscow and Peking for economic and technical aid, he was assured that the Communists would give military assistance against any "invasion" from American soil. In 1965 Cuba was officially proclaimed a Communist state.

Venezuela

Romulo Betancourt, president of Venezuela from 1959 to 1964, was a marked contrast to Castro. Betancourt was a revolutionary during his university days and he was among the military junta that made possible Venezuela's first free election in 1947. When Jiménez became dictator, Betancourt fled. Jiménez was overthrown in 1958, and at the end of that year Betancourt was elected president. He immediately set about to solve the economic situation, balancing the budget by cutting expenditures, adopting a program of public works and diversification of the economy, and introducing a land-reform program by purchasing land holdings from absentee landlords. In 1960 his government defeated the attempt of left-wing students to create disorder, and his successors have so far promised and given civil rights and free elections.

Uruguay

Uruguay is unlike any other Latin American country: its population is predominantly white; it has complete religious tolerance; all education, including college, is free; and it has no mountains, no deserts, and no aboriginal Indians. Uruguay's forty-year-old constitutional government, however, came to an end in 1973.

Foreign Relations

The Latin American nations generally do not view themselves as a part of the third world—more accurate would be a "separate" world. They are fundamentally isolationist and view themselves as American and European. During World War II, Brazil was the only Latin American nation to actively participate on the side of the Allies, while Argentina was pro-Axis and a hot bed of Nazi activities.

Until World War II British investments (sold to pay for the war) played the major role in the development of Latin America and came to be criticized in the same way as later American investments were to be.

The most important country that Latin America deals with is its neighbor to the north. A two-way trade exists between them of over $32 billion, and as early as 1975 American investment came closer to the $23 billion mark.

Relations with the United States

The No-Transfer Resolution
From 1810 to 1824 the United States supported Latin America's fights for independence but was cautious, for it was purchasing Florida from Spain at the time. In 1811, the No-Transfer Resolution was passed, stating that the United States would not "without serious inquietude see any part of the said territory pass into the hands of any foreign power."

The Monroe Doctrine
The doctrine presented by President Monroe in 1823 stated that the United States "should consider any attempt on [Europe's] part to extend their system to any portion of this hemisphere as dangerous to our peace and safety." This was not interpreted immediately to mean the right of United States intervention in the affairs of Latin America, because the inspiration for the Monroe Doctrine came from Great Britain, and the defense of South America was predicated upon the existence of the British fleet. By 1895, however, the United States position had changed.

In 1875 Great Britain and Venezuela had a boundary dispute, and in 1895 the United States wrote a series of strongly worded letters to Great Britain and forced it to settle the controversy by arbitration. This was the first step in intervention, and it also led the United States into a hasty rearmament program.

In 1904 the Roosevelt Corollary led to a reinterpretation of the Monroe Doctrine to mean the right of the United States to exercise police power in Latin America.

United States Intervention
There were five occasions between 1900 and 1940 when the United States intervened in the Caribbean because the United States felt it was necessary to its security to restore and maintain order.

1) Under Theodore Roosevelt, the U.S. gave its blessings to a revolution in Panama, arguing that control of the isthmus was necessary to its security.

2) The U.S. intervened in the Dominican Republic in 1904, in 1912, and from 1916 to 1924. In doing so it ultimately placed political power in the hands of the military and was indirectly responsible for the rise of Trujillo to power.

3) In 1909 the marines landed in Nicaragua and came again in 1912, staying until 1933. Here military dictatorship was also the result.

4) Haiti found itself under the control of the marines in 1915.

5) The United States could have annexed Cuba at the end of the Spanish-American War in 1898 but chose an indeterminate status for the island.

Intervention was also practiced by manipulating the diplomatic instrument of recognition. The United States' delay in recognizing a new government in Cuba in 1933 led to the collapse of the government, and its speed in confirming the Mendieta government in 1934 led to the power of Batista.

The earliest example of American intervention was the war with Mexico (1846–1848). (See p. 217.) According to Herbert L. Matthews in the *United States and Latin America,* the years between 1913 and 1917 witnessed "the most blatant, inexcusable and futile attempts at interventionism in the history of our [United States] relations with Latin America."

The United States had 40,000 nationals in Mexico and investments worth a billion dollars, and with the Mexican revolution in 1910 there was bound to be trouble. In 1907 Secretary of State Root had referred to the dictator Díaz as "one of the great men to be held up for the hero worship of mankind." When Huerta, a conservative, came to power in 1913, President Wilson refused to recognize him, because his government rested on force. In 1914 American sailors were arrested by Huerta, and the United States occupied Vera Cruz in retaliation. Huerta refused mediation and fled. Carranza then became president of Mexico, and in 1915 Wilson gave him full recognition. Pancho Villa, a former bandit who had been attacking the Carranza government, retaliated by raiding New Mexico, killing seventeen Americans. At this point the United States sent a military expedition into Mexico. The United

States, however, did past a resolution in 1927 to settle all disputes in Mexico by arbitration.

The Good Neighbor Policy

Presidents Coolidge and Hoover and Secretaries of State Hughes, Kellogg, and Stimson attempted to be good neighbors, but the formulation of the doctrine of nonintervention came in 1933 with President Roosevelt.

In 1934, the marines were drawn out of Haiti; in 1939 the United States abolished its protectorate over Panama; and in 1941 treaty rights with the Dominican Republic were abolished.

The Cold War

Since 1945 the United States has been afraid of Communist penetration into Latin America, but whether the U.S. has followed a rational and enlightened policy remains to be seen. Any dictator in Latin America has been able to win support by saying he is anti-Communist. In 1954 the Order of Merit was conferred on the Venezuelan dictator Marcos Pérez Jiménez and he was named "Honorary Submariner" by the United States Navy. In 1955, Secretary of the Navy Thomas compared Juan Perón to George Washington.

In several cases the United States has tried military intervention again; in Guatemala in 1953; in Cuba in 1961; and in the Dominican Republic in 1965. In 1965 the "Johnson Doctrine" was announced: the United States "cannot, must not, and will not permit the establishment of another Communist government in the western hemisphere."

Nationalization of Industry

The nationalization of oil, copper, and other industries which have a large amount of American capital investment has caused serious problems in the 1970s. In 1971 Chile's government nationalized the copper industry and refused to compensate American firms. In retaliation the United States blocked economic aid to Chile and through the CIA aided the forces that eventually overthrew the Allende government. Again, when Peru's military took over the oil industry, the United States followed a similar policy of economic embargo until compensation was paid.

Aid from the United States

From June 1946 to June 1963 the United States gave Mexico $0.4 billion, Brazil $1.2 billion, Chile $0.4 billion. This does not compare, however, with aid to Europe: France $9.6 billion, the United Kingdom $7.7 billion, Italy $5.1 billion, and Germany $4.0 billion.

Under the Alliance for Progress more emphasis was placed on practical aid to Latin America. In 1961 the United States agreed to provide the major part of $20 billion needed over the next ten years for economic development. In 1965, for example, Peru was granted $86.6 million which was four times the 1960 figure. In 1975 Brazil was receiving the largest share of American aid—$250 million a year.

The Organization of American States

From 1889 on, inter-American conferences have taken place in an effort to solve many of the mutual problems facing Latin America and the United States. In 1947 a collective security pact was signed at Rio de Janeiro. In April 1948, at the Ninth International Conference of American States at Bogotá (Colombia), the charter of the Organization of American States was signed by twenty-one nations. The purposes of the OAS are to settle disputes that may occur between member nations, to achieve economic cooperation, and to promote economic and social welfare. The doctrine of collective security states that any attack by a non-American country would be considered an attack upon all, and each nation would be obligated to assist.

In 1965 OAS troops were sent into the Dominican Republic and in 1970 an OAS police force was stationed between Honduras and El Salvador until a peace settlement was negotiated.

In 1965 the OAS voted to break diplomatic relations with Cuba. Only Mexico retained ties with Castro's government. But in 1975 diplomatic relations were resumed by most Latin American nations (but not the U.S.). The O.A.S. has not been altogether successful, and the U.S. tends to deal directly with the individual nations.

Panama Canal Treaties

United States relations were improved by new canal treaties in 1978, whereby the canal will be turned over to Panama in the year 2000, at which point the canal will become "neutral," open to the world's shipping.

India and Southwest Asia

ANCIENT CIVILIZATION   2500–1500 B.C.

Little is known of the ancient history of India, and no scientific research was done until the 1920s. Evidence seems to indicate that a civilization called the Harappa, named after the city near which the excavation was conducted, did exist in the Indus Valley. Historians believe that this civilization of dark-skinned Dravidians was thriving by 2500 B.C. and reached a high level of development before it was overwhelmed by Aryan invaders from the north. By 1500 B.C. the Aryans were masters of northern India, the Dravidians had been driven into the south, and Hindustan history began. The ancient period of Indian history contributed one fundamental aspect of Indian society: the Dravidian-Aryan schism. This division has caused problems throughout Indian history and continues to do so today. In modern India people speak either a dialect of the Dravidian or of the Aryan tongue and are not able to communicate with one another. (The Aryan tongues are related to Sanskrit and the most important of these are Bengali, Hindi, and Gujarati. The most extensive Dravidian languages are Tamil, spoken in Madras, and Telugu, spoken in Hyderabad). Throughout Indian history the south has been divided from the north not only by the geographical division of the Deccan Plateau but also by the traditional rivalry between Dravidian and Aryan. The caste system of Hinduism may even have originated from the desire of the Aryans to preserve their identity as a ruling class by remaining isolated from their darker subjects.

HARAPPA CIVILIZATION 2500–1500 B.C.

In the 1920s archaeologists excavated a site known as Mohenjo-Daro or Place of the Dead and found evidence of at least seven ancient cities that had been destroyed by floods and then rebuilt on the ruins. Since then they have uncovered two major cities and some seventy towns in the vicinity, but still little is known of this civilization, for as yet the language has not been deciphered.

The Harappa empire was far larger and more tightly ruled than either Sumer or Egypt, encompassing possibly 100,000 people probably ruled by priest-kings. There appears to have been a uniform system of weights and measures unknown in other ancient civilizations, and the civilization seems to have remained unchallenged and unchanged for a thousand years. It had a bronze age technology with a central government strong enough to keep peace and organize the economy.

Probably the fact that the civilization had been peaceful and unchallenged by invaders made it unable to cope with the Aryans, who invaded the land around 1500 B.C., for the empire seems to have fallen almost immediately.

CLASSICAL CIVILIZATION   1500 B.C.–500 A.D.

During this period information is also scarce, for the Indians, unlike the Chinese, were not interested in governmental history and failed to keep full historical records. Yet this is an extremely important era, for it was during these two thousand years that India developed its social system, its philosophy of life, and its religion, all of which were based on Hinduism. It was during this period that another powerful faith evolved, that of Buddhism, which was to be significant in Indian history only briefly but was to have a profound effect on the rest of Asia. From 1500 B.C. to 500 A.D. numerous empires—the Maurya, the Kushan, and the Gupta—rose and fell, but none of these was able to establish effective rule over wide areas

*and remain in power for more than a few generations. India's failure
to achieve political stability was perhaps the major reason for the
persistence of regional, linguistic, and racial differences.*

INDIAN PHILOSOPHY AND RELIGION

Hinduism

Hinduism, the oldest of the major religions of the world,
developed sometime after 1500 B.C. The faith of the Aryan conquerors of India had at first been based on the worship of personified
natural forces such as rain gods and sun gods, and very early
religious ideas were written down in a series of hymns called the
Rig-Vedas. By the tenth book of the *Rig-Vedas* the idea of a single
god had evolved, and with this began the development of Hinduism.

As a Philosophy and a Religion

BELIEF IN ONE GOD

This is perhaps one of the least understood aspects of Hinduism.
A Hindu believes in one god, Brahma, but, in contrast to Western
religions, he believes that the creator and what he creates are one
and the same thing and that therefore Brahma is present in every
particle of life.

Brahma can be represented by many gods, as many gods as he
has characteristics. The two most popular forms of Brahma are
Vishnu, who is Brahma when he becomes the god of life, of love,
of mercy, and Siva, when he becomes the god of change, of destruction, of recreation. Siva, in turn, is usually worshipped not as himself but as one of his characteristics—one of his wives. Many tribal
gods, local deities, nature gods, and household gods are also worshipped and in theory are part of Brahma.

REINCARNATION

Since all things are part of the divine creator, the soul never
dies but is reborn into another body. To the Hindu the particular

body the soul takes on depends on the past lives the soul has led. (The record of past deeds is known as *karma*.) If the record is good, the individual may be reborn as a holy person; if it is bad, the individual may be reborn as a member of a lower caste or an untouchable or an insect or a dog, depending on how evil the record. Since all things have a human soul, an orthodox Hindu regards all life as sacred and is, therefore, a vegetarian. Although Hindus have for this reason often been pacifists, they do believe that certain lives are more valuable than others, and in the animal kingdom the cow is the most sacred.

THE CASTE SYSTEM

The Hindu word for caste is *varna*, which means color, and many historians believe that this must have been the original distinction among the peoples of India.

Caste is similar to strict class distinction but is more restricted, for people marry only within their caste, associate only with people of their caste, and live according to the rules, ceremonies, and rituals of their particular caste.

There were four major castes in India—the Brahmin or priestly caste, the Kshatriuas or warrior, the Vasiya or merchant, and the Sudra or laboring caste. There were, however, thousands (perhaps 7000) of subcastes, and the division was made on professional or occupational lines. The castes were not socially or religiously equal. The Brahmin was the elite. All caste was a matter of birth.

The untouchable was below and outside caste and could not be associated with. There were between 45 million and 50 million such people in India. They were barred from temples, schools, village wells, restaurants, and elsewhere. The only jobs they were allowed were those the Hindu would consider unclean, such as tanning, latrine duty, and street cleaning.

Today caste and untouchability are officially abolished, but old habits die slowly.

MYSTICISM AND THE RENUNCIATION OF THE WORLD

The desire of the Hindu is to achieve union with God. This can be done only by renouncing the body and the material world and concentrating upon the soul. Denial of the material universe takes two main forms:

1) Mortification of the flesh; the attempt to prove, by putting the body through physical tortures such as sleeping on a bed of nails and starvation, that it means nothing.

2) Yoga, which means yoking of the mind to God, is another attempt to have such complete control over the body that it becomes almost superfluous to existence. A yogi has been known to stop his heart beat for a minute and to hold his breath for over an hour.

As a Way of Life

THE SACREDNESS OF ANIMALS

This has caused many problems in India: pious men allow poisonous snakes and rodents to live, and the cow, even if diseased and no longer a source of milk, is permitted to live and roam freely. More than half the cows in India are worthless and destructive beasts.

THE JOINT FAMILY

In India, as in China, the individual owed his first loyalty to his family. All needs, such as unemployment and illness, were taken care of by the family. A joint purse was administered by the oldest member of the family.

The position of women was inferior to men. They could eat only after their husbands, could not appear in public, and their primary function was to bear sons. If this was not done, the husband could take a second wife. *Suttee* was a Hindu practice whereby a wife of a dead man, in order to show her devotion, would throw herself alive onto her husband's funeral pyre. This was outlawed by the British. Marriage was arranged by the family, and a woman's worth was based on her dowry. Many families went heavily into debt in order to pay for the dowry, and, as a result, there was a high rate of female infanticide. Child marriage was also customary. Girls of eight would be married to husbands of thirty. (Today the law limits marriage age to eighteen for males and fourteen for females.)

MEDICINE

There were many taboos against medicine, first because the human body was not regarded as important, and second because Western medicines and treatments often contained animal fats, which were anathemas to good Hindus.

The Ganges was the source of laundry and drinking water for thousands of Indians, and sanitation problems often resulted, since Hindus believed in throwing dead bodies of holy men into the sacred Ganges River and bathing the sick and dying in the river in order to cleanse them of their sins.

Buddhism

Gautama Buddha

According to legend, Gautama was born in 563 B.C. into the second caste of India, the warrior, and brought up in the luxury of warrior aristocrats. At the age of twenty-nine, while on a journey, Gautama is reported to have seen an old man, a sick man, a dead man, and an ascetic. This worried him, for he could not understand why there should be so much misery in the world. For six years he sought a solution. He tried all the Hindu methods, such as asceticism and mortification of the flesh, in order to understand God. Finally, he seated himself under the sacred Bodhi tree and meditated for forty-nine days. He then achieved enlightenment and became known as Buddha, the enlightened one. For the next forty-five years of his life he traveled, preached, and spread his religion.

Buddhism is similar in many ways to Hinduism, advocating reincarnation, the doctrine of *karma,* and renunciation of the world, but Buddha disagreed with the methods of achieving these objectives. He did not believe in mortification of the flesh or in caste distinctions, since all men were to him equal in spiritual potential.

As a Philosophy

The Four Noble Truths: (1) suffering is universal, (2) the cause of all suffering is selfish desire and cravings, (3) the cure to the problem of suffering therefore is to eliminate all selfish desire, and (4) the way to do this is to follow the Noble Eightfold Path.

The Noble Eightfold Path for eliminating selfish desire consists of (1) right views or knowledge, (2) right ambition, (3) right speech, (4) right conduct, (5) right means of livelihood, (6) right effort or self-discipline, (7) right thoughts, (8) right meditation or concentration.

The achievement of enlightenment is the fundamental aim for the Buddhist, as it is for the Hindu. Once one achieves enlightenment, he is said to have reached *nirvana* and is finally released from the wheel of death and rebirth.

Divisions of Buddhism

Hinayana, the Lesser Vehicle, is the original faith, relying solely on one's own introspection and faith to achieve enlightenment. It became the dominant form of Buddhism in Ceylon, Burma, Thailand, and Cambodia.

Mahayana, the Greater Vehicle, is the Chinese adaptation of Buddhism, and the primary difference is that it relies on other Buddhas and gods to achieve enlightenment or *nirvana*. It incorporates the use of saints called *bodhisattvas,* praying to them for aid. Gradually more emphasis was put on good works than on contemplation. Mahayana Buddhism became the dominant form in China, Japan, Vietnam, and Korea.

Buddhism in 272 B.C. was the state religion of India; by 65 A.D. it had spread to China; by 600 A.D. it was introduced into Japan and became the state religion during the 700s. By 800 A.D. the faith had spread all over the Far East, but a hundred years before that date it had died out in India. The main reason for its demise in India was its renunciation of the caste system, which challenged the existing social structure.

Islam, the other important faith in India, was not introduced until the medieval era.

THE EARLY ARYANS   1500–400 B.C.

Unfortunately, the early Aryans left only literary records—the four *Vedas* and two epics, the *Mahabkarata* and the *Ramayana* (1000–500 B.C.). Consequently, historical records are minimal up to the fourth century B.C.

By the time of the epics, the Aryans had settled in villages, expanded eastward along the Ganges, and fused their culture with that of the Dravidian. It was during this period that Hinduism was fully developed.

Alexander the Great invaded India in 326 B.C. and occupied the northwestern part of the country. There was little Hellenistic influence, however, since Alexander himself died in 322 B.C., and this part of his empire was soon reconquered by non-Westerners.

THE MAURYA EMPIRE   321–184 B.C.

This dynasty, founded by Chandragupta Maurya at the death of Alexander the Great, was the first in Indian history to unite all of Hindustan under one effective imperial authority.

The Mauryan empire was a police state with an efficient revenue system, taxing trade and land and controlling all mines.

The reign of the emperor Asoka (273–232 B.C.) was the height of the empire. Although essentially a Hindu, Asoka was devoted to the Buddhist faith and became a missionary of peace, goodwill, and compassion by helping to spread Buddhism into Southeast Asia. His empire at its zenith extended as far south as Mysore.

The dynasty was weak after Asoka's death, and with the assassination of the last Mauryan emperor (184 B.C.), India was once again plunged into a period of anarchy and constant invasion.

THE KUSHAN EMPIRE   50–220 A.D.

The Kushans from central Asia were the next group of people who were able to conquer and successfully hold a large area of

India for over two centuries, but their rule did not extend as far as Asoka's nor was it as influential.

Under Kanishka (62?–120 A.D.?) the state reached its height, for Kanishka was a patron of arts and learning. The school of art called the Grandharan developed one of the traditional images of Buddha and influenced both China and Japan.

THE GUPTA EMPIRE   320–647 A.D.

The Gupta dynasty, founded by Chandragupta II, was much less despotic than the Mauryan and is known as the high point of India's classical period. Medicine, literature, and the arts (particularly sculpture) flourished. Great universities were established, and mathematicians and astronomers were as accurate and advanced as their contemporaries in the rest of the world. The decimal, the zero, and Arabic numerals all originated in India. During this dynasty nearly all of north India was united.

In 455 A.D. the Huns struck a deathblow at the Gupta empire, and this was probably the most destructive of all barbarian invasions of India. It was part of the same movement that set the Germanic tribes moving into the Roman empire, looting the city of Rome in 410 A.D.

MEDIEVAL CIVILIZATION   500–1500 A.D.

During the medieval period the most important single development was the appearance of the Moslems. India had not developed the concept of a single empire; it had not succeeded in unifying the peninsula or in healing the diverse elements within its people. The coming of the Islamic faith created still another division in Indian society, which in 1947 was to split the peninsula into two sovereign nations. The Hindu-Moslem rivalry was not just a matter of two different religious creeds but also two widely divergent cultures. Islam was a proselytizing faith that demanded doctrinal uniformity with only one deity, one book, one duty, while the Hindu allowed latitude, tolerance, and diversity and was nonmissionary. The Moslem had a sense of community and state and believed that Moslems should be governed only by Moslems, while the Hindu's utopia was "philosophical anarchy." Another, and for many years irreconcilable, division was the Hindu belief in caste and the Moslem belief that all men except heathens were equal.

The Moslem invasions occurred in three stages—first, the invasion of the Sind region by the Arab Moslems, second, the Turkish-Mongol invasions, and finally the conquest by the Moguls.

The Arabs invaded the Sind in 712 but were not able to push far inland, for they were checked by the desert terrain. They did retain the area near the mouth of the Indus River as a Moslem foothold in India.

THE TURKISH-MONGOL MOSLEMS

These people from Afghanistan began raiding India across the northwest mountain passes. The terrible and bloody raids were begun in 998 by Amir Mahmud and continued for over four centuries.

One of the most famous invaders was Tamerlane, who massacred thousands of Indians and transported the artisans of the land to his capital, Samarkand, Russia.

The rite of *janhar,* which was practiced by the Indians when they felt there was no hope left, is proof of how devastating the raids were. Men burned their wives and children and then went forth with sword in hand to meet the Moslems and their death.

The result of the invasions was that numerous Moslem kingdoms were established in northern India. The Moslems became the ruling class, the military aristocrats, and the Hindus were used to perform physical and clerical work. The Moslem strongholds were in central and eastern Bengal, where they had the greatest success at conversion since the area had been Buddhist and resented its Hindu overlords, and the Sind, the west Punjab, and Baluchistan.

MODERN CIVILIZATION   1500 to the Present

The beginning of the modern period in Indian history coincides with the establishment of the Mogul Empire, which, according to Edward Gibbon, was "one increasing round of valour, greatness, discord, degeneracy, and decay." The empire contributed very little that was new, and the fact that it ended in 1707 in civil war was nothing unique to India either. But the Mogul's decay also corresponded in time with the arrival by sea of Western Europeans, and this proved extremely significant, for England was able to divide and conquer. From 1857 to 1947 Great Britain ruled India, and during those ninety years India changed fundamentally. It was unified for the first time in its history with a single law and language for all subjects as well as a single government for the entire peninsula. The British also gave to India a sense of nationalism, and the Indian struggle for freedom after 1900 proved to be one of the most spectacular mass movements in the history of political nationalism. Under the leadership of Mahatma Gandhi every Indian was united in a common demand for independence, and on August 15, 1947, the British Union Jack was hauled down and replaced by the flags of two new nations, India and Pakistan (and eventually Bangladesh). It was at this point that British rule passed the acid test: both new states remained in the Commonwealth and in India a constitutional form of government survived. Whether Western ideas of liberty and democracy can endure under conditions of extreme poverty and overpopulation is still problematical.

THE MOGUL EMPIRE   1526–1707

Babur

The founder of the Mogul empire was Babur, a Turk from what is today Russian Turkestan, who claimed descent from both Genghis Khan and Tamerlane. At the head of 12,000 Moslems he swept down on India, conquered Delhi in 1526, and made it his capital.

Akbar and the Golden Age

The reign of Akbar (1556–1605), the grandson of Babur, is considered the golden age of the empire. An outstanding administrator, scholar, and artist, Akbar was the equal of contemporary monarchs such as Elizabeth I of England and Suleiman the Magnificent of the Ottoman empire. His administrators were well paid and competent, and although he was illiterate he was considered one of the best-read (best-read-to) men of his time. He held a meeting every day for discussions of literature, art, religion, philosophy, and politics.

The central purpose of Akbar's administration was to unite Hindus and Moslems. Thirty percent of the officials of the Government were Hindu, and he even attempted to found a new religion that would combine both faiths.

Despite his tolerance and wisdom, another of Akbar's main objectives was the expansion of the empire, and it was during his era that the empire reached its greatest size, extending from central Asia to southern India, and from Persia to the Ganges.

Successors of Akbar

Akbar's son, Jehangir (1605–1627), was indolent, ineffectual, and a drunkard. Jehangir's son, Shan Jehan (1628–1658), was intolerant and came to the throne by blooodshed. He is particularly remembered for his building of the Taj Mahal for his favorite wife, and, although a magnificent piece of architecture, it involved an extremely heavy tax on his people.

Aurangzeb (1658–1707) was the last Mogul emperor to control all of India. Aurangzeb was a man of great courage and talent, but he was also a fanatical Moslem, determined to conquer the entire peninsula and to convert all his subjects to Islam. The Hindus naturally objected, and Hindu princes organized the Mahratta Confederacy, with its power centered around the city of Poona.

In his attempt to conquer the south of India, Aurangzeb over-extended his resources, and ultimately the viceroys of the empire broke away, establishing independent principalities in Hyderabad, Mysore, Bengal, and Oudh.

By 1707 India was divided into separate Hindu principalities combined in the loosely organized Mahratta Confederacy, separate Moslem sultanates, and smaller independent warring groups. The Sikhs in the northwest were an independent power, advocating no caste, no idolatry, and forming a strong militant brotherhood. Although the Mogul emperors continued to claim dominion over all of India, their effective rule after 1707 was limited to the Delhi sultanate, a small area around the capital.

THE COMING OF THE WEST   1498–1600

In 1498 Vasco da Gama reached Calicut and the Portuguese asserted their authority in southern India, controlling trading posts and naval routes. They did not develop a political empire, but they did establish an empire of Indian commerce. It was the sense of security which the mastery of the seas gave them that was their undoing, for soon their power was broken by the Dutch and they retained only Goa, Damao, and Diu. Portuguese influence was considerable, for India became the most Catholic country in Asia outside of the Philippines.

The Dutch encountered interference from the Mogul government during the seventeenth century and therefore concentrated on the East Indies and not on India. This left France and Great Britain to battle for control of India.

THE BRITISH CONTROL OF INDIA   1600–1858

The British East India Company

In 1600 Elizabeth I of England granted the sole right to trade with the East Indies to a group of businessmen and merchants. This was the organization that was eventually not only to trade but also to govern India.

Steps toward Complete Control

The British East India Company established three major posts for its trade. In 1639 St. George Fort (Madras) was built; in 1660 Bombay was gained when Charles II married a Portuguese princess; and in 1690 present-day Calcutta was acquired. This was "the tripod on which England" was to achieve "supremacy in India," for from these points British power fanned out.

Victory over the French

The French and the British had become the main competitors for power in India. Before 1754 the French had had the advantage due to the leadership of Joseph Dupleix, governor of the French East India Company. The French began to intervene in native politics in order to extend their own commerce and limit that of the British, and they were extremely successful. But they pushed the British too far when control of Madras was threatened, and the British regained the initiative and mastery in 1754 under Robert Clive. Dupleix was called back to France because of his costly policies.

The Battle of Plassey (1757) occurred when a British force of 3000 men (2000 were Indians) under the leadership of Clive defeated a large (50,000) native force under the Newab of Bengal (directed and financed by the French) and thus won control of Bengal.

In 1759 the French fleet was driven from Indian waters by the British navy; in 1760 the British defeated them at Wandewash, and in 1761 at Pondicherry. The struggle against France ended in 1763 with the conclusion of the Seven Years' War waged in Europe, America, Canada, and India. France was pushed out of India politically and militarily and was limited to merely commercial operations.

The Defeat of the Moguls

Reasons that a handful of English merchants were able to overthrow the Mogul dynasty:

1) Superior Technology. As in China during the Opium Wars, British artillery and muskets soon proved too much for the archaic Indian means of warfare. The British also controlled the sea, for the Moguls were not seamen, and this gave the English the advantage of being able to move troops freely and quickly from one part of India to another.

2) Political Reasons. Indians were divided and had no sense of nationalism, so that many were willing to fight on the side of the British against the hated Moslems. The decline of the Moguls had left India a hodgepodge of small states usually at war with one another. This meant that the East India Company could conquer India principality by principality.

The Battle of Buxar (1764) brought the rich province of Bengal completely under control of the East India Company, giving it a strong base from which to conquer the rest of India. In 1765 Clive obtained from the Newab of Bengal the right to administer the revenues (known as *dewani*) of Bengal, Bihar, and Orissa, and this meant that the East India Company had in effect become a sovereign power on the mainland of India.

Defeat of the Mahratta Confederacy

In the Battle of Assaye (1803) the British defeated the main Mahratta forces and thus removed the last serious rival to control of India. There was, of course, more fighting. For example, the Sikhs of the Punjab offered bitter resistance from 1845 to 1849 before they were finally brought under control. But in the end the East India Company ruled three-fifths of India directly and the other two-fifths indirectly, through alliances with local princes.

The Exploitation of India

The period from Robert Clive to Warren Hastings has been called the era of the grand conquistadors. Profits were tremendous;

princes were forced to pay heavy tribute; and the Company facilities were often used for private trade. India was ruthlessly exploited, yet what is remarkable is that it caused a reaction in Great Britain. For the first time in history a conquering nation experienced pangs of conscience, and from the start Great Britain maintained the position that its rule was for the benefit of the subject peoples.

Robert Clive, the hero of Plassey and the man who had forecast that "tomorrow the whole Mogul power" will be "in our grasp," was brought before the House of Commons in 1767 for his actions in India and accused of graft and extortion. In 1774 he committed suicide.

Warren Hastings, the first governor-general of Bengal from 1773 to 1785, was a remarkable man, who learned Urdu, Bengali, and Arabic and who laid the basis for order in India. He was also brought before the House of Commons for impeachment but was acquitted and quietly retired.

India Becomes a Crown Colony

By the Regulating Act of 1773 Calcutta was made the seat of government. A governor-general was created and put in charge of three provinces and given much of the East India Company's political power.

By the India Acts of 1784 and 1786, the British Government took over the control of policy-making by establishing a board of control appointed by the crown. Lord Cornwallis was made governor-general (1786–1793) with orders to reform the administration.

In 1813 the government abolished the East India Company's monopoly of trade and in 1831 took away its authority over all territories. The final blow to the Company's power came in 1833 when the government of England demanded that all laws made in India be laid before Parliament.

In 1858, after the Sepoy Mutiny, the Company and the Delhi sultanate were both abolished. From then India was ruled by two British officials, a secretary of state for India, who operated from London, and a viceroy (or governor-general), who functioned in

Delhi (or Calcutta). In 1877 Queen Victoria was declared Empress of India.

THE IMPACT OF BRITISH RULE IN INDIA   1858–1947

The Unification of the Subcontinent

The British established a government that ruled the entire peninsula. All of India was not ruled directly; some 562 semi-independent princely states were governed indirectly, with the English having control only in matters of defense and foreign policy. (It was up to the Republic of India to abolish these.) The viceroy of India not only governed British India in his capacity as governor-general but also represented the crown in its relations with the princely states.

The Establishment of Law

A single law for all was created in 1859. This was truly revolutionary, for now all people and all castes were equal in the eyes of the law. England also passed legislation that prevented brutal punishments and the worst aspects of family law. As early as Bentinck (governor-general 1825–1835), *suttee* had been abolished (1829), the *thugee* (ritualistic stranglers) had been suppressed (1830), and infanticide had been counteracted. Murderers could no longer be turned over to the dead man's family for revenge, and child marriage was forbidden, although this was difficult to enforce.

Improved Transportation

Reform of the communications system was vital to a unified India and was begun under Dalhousie (governor-general 1848–1856). A network of roads, a canal system, and railroads were built. By 1949 India had one of the largest state-owned railway systems in the world. As John Bowle says in *The Imperial Achievement,* "the Romans brought law; the British brought steam as well."

The English Language

The English language was established as the official language of the country in 1835, thus giving Dravidians and Aryans a common and international tongue.

Other Effects

The British undermined not only Hindu customs but also the village and the joint family. The government's police force weakened the authority of the elders of the village, and linking India to world markets destroyed the economic independence of the village. The economic self-sufficiency of the village was also upset by the British demand for taxes in cash, not in kind.

The ancient landholding system of India was destroyed, and a class of ruthless and absentee landlords was created. During the Mogul empire the amount of taxation was elastic, depending on the needs of the empire and the nature of the harvest. The tax collector or *zemindar* gathered the taxes and kept one-tenth. In 1793 the British converted the *zemindar* from a tax collector into a landlord. He could then charge the peasants what he wished, thus driving them into bankruptcy. Forty-nine percent of the agricultural land was controlled by the *zemindar* system. The other 51 percent of the land was somewhat better off, but even here taxes were not adjusted to the harvest, and in bad years the peasant was driven into debt.

Cheap manufactured cloth from England destroyed the domestic handicrafts, and England tended to keep India an agricultural nation and a closed market for its industrial goods. Despite the fact that England did not go out of its way to industrialize India, the industrial achievement was certainly not inconsiderable. In 1947 India was the seventh greatest producer of iron in the world, third in the output of cotton yarn and cloth, and fourth in extent of railroads.

By 1947 India was the most heavily irrigated nation in the world (70 million acres of land under irrigation). Famine had been greatly relieved both by better communications and irrigation, and also by a government Famine Administration established in 1883. (From 1660 to 1750 there had been fourteen major famines in India and countless minor ones.)

The structure of education from primary education to the university level was one of Britain's lasting gifts to India and the rest of its colonies. The British also introduced the idea of nationalism itself, and at the same time created the conditions of political unity in which the idea of nationalism could develop. They thus helped to create the force that in the end destroyed their power in India.

THE RISE OF NATIONALISM 1857–1947

The Sepoy Mutiny

The Sepoy Mutiny did not begin as a nationalistic uprising. It occurred when a new kind of cartridge was adopted by the British army (the army consisted of British officers and Hindu and Moslem soldiers or *sepoys*). These cartridges were smeared with grease and had to be bitten before being placed in the rifle. The rumor spread that the grease was a mixture of cow and pig fat, and religiously neither Hindu nor Moslem could touch it. This was the cause of the mutiny among the *sepoys*. In June of 1857 they revolted, released military prisoners from jail, burned the garrison, and killed any European they could find.

Soon the mutiny spread, and Indian civilians joined because they feared and hated the Westerners and what they were doing in India. (The same superstitions that led the Boxers to war in China also influenced the Indians.) There were over 40,000 mutineers in Delhi alone. The mutiny was finally put down by the British but not until a great deal of blood had been shed on both sides.

Although the causes of the mutiny had not been nationalistic, the results led to a growth of nationalism in India, for after the mutiny the British became less sympathetic to the idea of local self-government and more impersonal, developing a color bar, monopolizing high posts in government, and refusing to share with the Indians in the formulation of public policy. Also, civil service examinations were created, and Indians could not be members of the government unless they passed a test given in England before reaching the age of nineteen. This, of course, eliminated most candidates from the competition. In 1870 there were only seven and in 1880 only two candidates.

The Nationalist Congress Party

In Bombay in 1885 an Englishman by the name of Hume called a meeting of Indians who were interested in the introduction of democratic and parliamentary government into India. Seventy delegates appeared (only two were Moslem) and the aim of the Congress was stated: "Indirectly this conference will form the germ of a native parliament and . . . will constitute in a few years an unanswerable reply to the assertion that India is still wholly unfit for any form of representative institutions."

After 1907 the Congress split between moderates who wanted to cooperate with British rule and radicals who demanded complete independence. But as the British failed to reform, all groups insisted upon independence and British withdrawal.

The Congress party's membership consisted of the educated classes of India—the lawyers, merchants, students, and journalists. It was not a mass movement until Mohandas Gandhi's return to India in 1919.

Lord Curzon's Reforms

After 1900 nationalism increased in India. Famines, plagues (particularly severe in 1897), and British unconcern made the

Indians restless. The humiliating victory of the British in the Boer War (1899–1902) and the defeat of Russia by Japan in 1905 tended to make the Indians more vocal and more militant in their demands for independence.

Lord Curzon was governor-general of India from 1899 to 1905. He was honest and hardworking and he was determined to rule India efficiently, but he had absolutely no understanding of Indian attitudes. Curzon put through many useful reforms. Establishing rural banks, reorganizing agriculture, strictly enforcing measures against British soldiers who abused Indians, and encouraging the study of Indian history (of which he himself was a student) were all to his credit. Yet there were two reforms that were badly needed but totally misunderstood by the Indians.

THE UNIVERSITY ACT OF 1904

One was a reform of education. Universities were overcrowded and suffered from poor discipline and poor teachers, and their sole objective seemed to be cramming for exams. So the University Act of 1904 was passed, giving the British government more control of the school system. This "convulsed educated India from one end of the country to another," for the Indians felt that the aim of the British was to control the last semi-independent institution in India.

THE PARTITION OF BENGAL   1905

The second item that was needed concerned the administration of Bengal, which was terribly overburdened by 78 million people in the provinces, while the area east of the Ganges was neglected. The partition of Bengal into two administrative units was the final blow to the Indian nationalists, for it divided Bengal into the East, which included 18 million Moslems and 12 million Hindus, and New Bengal, of 42 million Hindus and 12 million Moslems. This not only split an area which had a linguistic patriotism but it also outraged the Hindus since the Moslems now had the majority voice in East Bengal. (The Moslem League was formed in part to maintain the partition, which was reversed in 1911 and so outraged them in turn.)

The good feeling caused by the reunification of Bengal in 1911 and the Morley-Minto Reforms of 1909 (allowing one Indian to six British on the executive council and twenty-seven Indians to thirty-six British on the legislative council) was completely nullified by the announcement in 1911 that the capital would be moved from Calcutta to New Delhi. This again outraged Bengal nationalists, for they felt it was an insult to their prestige. Also, there was hard feeling, for the Morley-Minto Reforms did not go far enough for most nationalists and the Moslems were given more representatives than they deserved as a result of pressure by the Moslem League.

World War I

During World War I, 800,000 Indian volunteers fought with the British against the Germans. India provided foodstuffs, and twenty-seven of the princely states provided troops and money. (The Maharaja of Mysore gave £1,600,000, Nepal gave all its troops, Hyderabad gave £400,000 plus expenses for two regiments overseas.)

At the beginning of the war the moderates were in control of the Congress Party, but even this period was not free of violence. Riots broke out in the Punjab when Sikhs and Moslems were denied admission into Canada under immigration laws of 1914. The Moslem League was anti-British, since Turkey was on the side of Germany. By 1918 the moderates had lost control of the Party and a revolutionary situation had developed.

The Amritsar Massacre

In order to curtail lawlessness, particularly in Bengal, the Rowlatt Acts (1919) permitted the jailing of suspects without trial and took away the right of counsel and the right of appeal. This led to so much agitation that the laws died stillborn, but they had done their harm.

Because the northwest region was aflame with tribal struggles while the Third Afghan War was in process, military rule was established and a ban on assemblies proclaimed. A crowd of 10,000 Indians nevertheless gathered in a walled courtyard to listen to speeches against the British administration. General Reginald Dyer, who was in charge of the area, ordered the group machine-gunned without word or signal. The walls were too high to scale, the only exit was blocked by British troops, and as Dyer said, "the targets were good"; 379 were killed and 1200 wounded.

The massacre itself outraged nationalists and so did its aftereffects. Martial law was strictly enforced; a section where two Englishwomen had been killed in the riots was roped off, and all Indians were forced to crawl by it. General Dyer not only escaped punishment but also became a hero to some Britons in India who presented him with a sword of honor as the "Savior of the Punjab."

Mahatma Gandhi and the Road to Independence

Mohandas Gandhi (1869–1948) was a product of two worlds. He studied law in England, practiced in South Africa, and was a journalist who had been trained in Western party politics and mass propaganda techniques. Yet he was also a deeply devout Hindu who believed that industrialization was evil, that violence was wrong, and that an Indian spiritual revival was necessary to save India. The only aspect of Hinduism that Gandhi did not believe in was untouchability. (He is usually referred to as "Mahatma" which means great soul.)

In 1919 Gandhi returned to India from South Africa (where he had been a part of the movement against discrimination) and became the spiritual and political leader of India's fight for independence.

Nonviolent Resistance

Economic strikes and general noncooperation with the British, such as renunciation of titles and honors, the boycotting of law courts, schools, and all British manufactured goods were the means by which Gandhi fought the English. Often, however, nonviolent disobedience led to violence and bloodshed, although Gandhi himself did his best to control the people.

The most famous demonstration of civil disobedience came in the Salt March of 1930, when Gandhi demanded the abolition of the state tax on the sale of salt. The salt tax, he felt, was the worst kind of taxation, since it hurt the poorest people in the country. Consequently, Gandhi organized a march to the sea to make his own salt. This 165-mile walk embarrassed the British and brought the plight of India to the attention of the world. During 1930 about 50,000 political offenders were jailed, including Gandhi and Nehru.

To publicize his boycott of English industrial goods and to encourage local village industry, Gandhi began what was to be known as the Homespun Campaign. He dressed himself in a homespun loincloth, took to spinning wherever he went, and lived on goat's milk. The issue of the evils of industrialization was one of the points with which Nehru, his disciple, did not agree. In September 1932 Gandhi went on a "fast unto death" against untouchability. This was another method of getting his way.

The Constitution of 1935

After Gandhi's popularity had gotten out of hand, the Government of India Act was passed giving complete self-government at the provincial level.

World War II

India was declared a belligerent by the British on the day the war broke out, without consultation with the Congress Party and against the wishes of the great majority of Indians. The Congress Party asked England for recognition of Indian independence, in return for which cooperation in the war was to be promised. This was rejected.

As the Japanese made gains in Malaya, Sir Stafford Cripps of the British war cabinet brought proposals to the Congress Party in March 1942, giving India more self-government and promising dominion status after the war was over. The Cripps mission failed, and the last and greatest nonviolent resistance campaign began. As a result, the Congress Party was outlawed and its leaders jailed. This led to violence: railroads and police stations were destroyed and government officials assassinated. By the end of 1942 order was restored, but 60,000 Congress Party members were jailed.

Although the Indian Congress Party refused to cooperate with the British, the contributions India made to the Allies were considerable. By 1945 India had an army of 2.5 million volunteers, the largest volunteer army ever assembled. Some of these men played a large part in the winning of Italian East Africa, and 70 percent of the one million troops that defeated the Japanese in Burma were Indian. Besides men, India contributed much to the Allied cause in the way of supplies and became a creditor nation. (At the end of the war it was owed, primarily by Great Britain, £1,250,000,000.)

INDEPENDENCE, PARTITION, AND THE EARLY YEARS 1947–1956

Why the British Granted Independence

One of the main reasons was, of course, the growing violence and nationalistic feeling in India. It was quite apparent that Britain could no longer rule India without holding it by military force and producing a great deal of hard feeling internationally. Britain could ill afford this after a world war of survival, and India was judged not worth the price.

The changing feeling at home was certainly a part of the decision to grant freedom. The most destructive of all wars had been fought to preserve the liberal and democratic world, and it seemed inconsistent for England to champion freedom in Europe and rule India by force of arms.

Hindus and Moslems

Hope that Hindus and Moslems might find a way of living

together was doomed as early as 1937 when local governments formed by the Congress Party shut out Moslems in some of the provinces. At this time Mohammed Ali Jinnah (Moslem League president after 1934) became committed to the concept of a Moslem nation of Pakistan.

In March 1946, the government of Great Britain dispatched a three-man mission under Cripps to bring about an immediate transfer of power in India, but the question of partition slowed down the process. That year rioting took place, in which Bengal and Bihar provinces alone suffered nearly 10,000 fatalities in six months. Finally the Congress Party agreed that no group should be compelled to accept a constitution against its will and, as expected, the Moslem majority areas voted for partition. On August 15, 1947, India was granted independence and divided into two separate nations.

The Problems of Partition

Pakistan consisted of two sections a thousand miles apart: West Pakistan (the Sind, the northwest frontier, Baluchistan, and the western part of the Punjab) and East Pakistan (the eastern part of Bengal plus the Sylhet district of Assam). National assets were divided on a ratio of 82.5 to 17.5 in favor of India. Everything (from railroad equipment and the national debt to criminals, lunatics, and office furniture) had to be divided, and Pakistan received its share only after Gandhi insisted.

The transfer of people who were located in split areas caused the most trouble. Rioting and religious wars broke out in the Punjab, which had been divided right down the middle. Approximately 12 million people moved (often fled) from one country to another, and estimates place the number of deaths through violence at 200,000 and others due to dislocation at 300,000.

Economic dislocation was another result of partition. East Pakistan grew 70 percent of the world's jute, but all the mills were in India. Pakistan received the better food- and cotton-growing areas and India the coal, metals, and industrial resources of the peninsula.

India received 82 percent of the population but only 69 percent of the irrigated lands.

The status of 562 princely states also caused problems. All the princely states joined either India or Pakistan, but trouble arose in Jammu, Kashmir, Hyderabad, Junagadh, and Manavadar.

The small states of Junagadh and Manavadar were predominantly Hindu and surrounded by Indian territory. They had, however, Moslem rulers, who joined Pakistan in 1947. The Indian government sent in forces and occupied the countries, granting a plebiscite that resulted in an overwhelming vote to join India. Hyderabad, the largest state in the Deccan and completely surrounded by Indian territory, was also Hindu with a Moslem ruler, and the Nizam felt powerful enough to hold out for independence. Armed Moslem forces terrorized the population, and Communists took control of many of the villages. After first trying an economic blockade, the Indian army took over the state in 1948.

Jammu and Kashmir

Pakistan had an excellent precedent in Indian action in Junagadh, Manavadar, and Hyderabad for taking over control of this area, which was predominantly Moslem (three-quarters) with a Hindu maharajah. In 1947 Pakistan invaded the area, and the maharajah quickly joined India. Indian troops arrived by airlift barely in time to save Srinagar, the capital. Nehru referred the case to the UN demanding a plebiscite and the condemnation of Pakistan as an aggressor. The two countries were at war for fourteen months until a cease-fire was arranged by the UN in January 1949.

Kashmir is valuable, for it has rich agricultural land and a lucrative tourist trade; it controls the headwaters of important rivers; and it is situated in a position strategic to both Pakistan and India.

Nothing was settled and war again broke out in 1965. The UN again sponsored a cease-fire, and China's involvement so worried the USSR that the Russians attempted to mediate the dispute, but the problem was not resolved.

The Death of Gandhi

Another result of the partition was the assassination of Mahatma

Gandhi on January 30, 1948. Fortunately for relations between India and Pakistan, he was killed not by a Moslem but by a fanatic Hindu who was confused and frustrated by Gandhi's attempt to stop the violence among Hindus, Moslems, and Sikhs. (In January 1948 he had begun a fast for the "reunion of hearts.")

The Government of India

India became a constitutional federal state. The sixteen states themselves were granted little power, for, unlike the United States, the residual powers were given specifically to the central government which has the power to seize and assume the functions of state governments in case of emergency. (This was done in 1959 in the Communist-controlled state of Kerala.) The constitution established a bicameral government, with executive power resting in a prime minister who is leader of the majority party in the House of the People, and a Federal Court of Appeals with powers similar to that of the United States Supreme Court.

At independence the Congress Party was the only large and important political organization. This party, which led India to independence and of which Jawaharlal Nehru became the head after Gandhi's death, was socialist and secular, favoring government control of basic industry (but not secondary industry) and democracy in its political creed and organization.

Jawaharlal Nehru

Born in Kashmir of the Brahmin caste in 1889, Nehru became a westerner when, at the age of fifteen, he was sent to England's Harrow School and then entered Cambridge at the age of seventeen. In 1916 Nehru began his political career when he met Gandhi and joined the movement for independence, during which he was imprisoned nine times, the longest from 1942 to 1945. In 1948 he became India's first prime minister and head of the Congress Party until his death in 1964.

A democrat and a socialist, prime minister of India, minister of atomic energy, minister of foreign policy and economic policy, he was by far the most powerful person in India. In a very real sense he was the father of modern India.

The Government of Pakistan

Pakistan did not experience the same stability of leadership as India. In fact, there were continual changes in government. At first Pakistan was under the rule of a governor-general and a constituent assembly. The first governor-general was Mohammed Ali Jinnah (1876–1948), the leader of the Moslem League and the man who was really responsible for the founding of Pakistan. He was not only governor-general but also head of the constituent assembly (formed in 1947). His death in 1948 left the country without a leader who could inspire loyalty and the necessary unity.

INDIA, PAKISTAN, AND BANGLADESH TODAY 1956–1979

Indian Politics

Upon Nehru's death in 1964, Lal Bahadur Shastri became prime minister. When Shastri died in 1966, he was succeeded by Indira Gandhi (Nehru's daughter but no relation to Mahatma).

The Congress Party started to lose control at the state level. In 1967 it lost eight out of sixteen provinces. Economic problems and a drought which caused severe food shortages were part of the cause. Then a decision in December 1967 that English should be the only official language until regions were in a position to accept Hindi led to riots and hundreds of deaths. In 1971, however, the Congress Party managed to regain two-thirds of the seats in the lower house.

Indira Gandhi came under increasing criticism for failure to solve economic problems. In 1975 a local court found Mrs. Gandhi guilty of violating election laws, and she was ordered to give up her seat in Parliament. Instead, she imprisoned the opposition, imposed strict censorship, and delayed elections.

When censorship was let up and new elections held in 1978, former deputy premier Morarji Desai and his splinter party—the Janata Party—took control of the government. Ever since, Indian party politics have been unstable and Desai's government fell on a vote of no confidence, and Mrs. Gandhi returned to office.

Pakistani Politics

In 1948 Ali Khan became prime minister (he had been Moslem League secretary, 1936–1947). A progressive and a moderate in relations with India, Ali Khan was assassinated by a Moslem fanatic in 1951. From 1951 to 1956 there were three prime ministers, each lasting about two years. Under the constitution of 1956 Pakistan was declared an Islamic republic and General Mirza was made its first president. The government was stronger at the provincial level but again lasted two years. In 1958 Mirza with the support of Marshall Ayub Khan took over complete control and declared martial law. Disorders finally forced him to resign in 1969 and the government was handed over to General Yahya Khan who ruthlessly restored law and order. Political changes reflected the government's inability to solve economic difficulties and the troubles in East Pakistan.

The first general elections ever held in Pakistan on the basis of "one man, one vote" were held between December 1970 and January 1971. The Awani League led by Sheikh Mujibar Rahman carried the East, and the Pakistan People's Party led by Zulfikar Ali Bhutto carried the West. (In 1978 Bhutto was convicted of the murder of a political opponent and sentenced to death.) East Pakistan demanded complete autonomy and civil war broke out.

Bangladesh

East Pakistan (Bangladesh) seceded from Pakistan on March 26, 1971. East Pakistan was the scene of brutal fighting between guerillas and West Pakistani troops. Several million refugees fled to India, and India entered the conflict on the side of Bangladesh. In two weeks the Pakistan Army was crushed and 93,000 prisoners of war were taken. On December 16, 1971, the Pakistani forces in the East surrendered and the next day a cease-fire was arranged in the West. Yahya Khan resigned in favor of Ali Bhutto. On April 17, 1972, the democratic government of Bangladesh was proclaimed with Sheikh Rahman as its first prime minister. (Bangladesh was recognized by Pakistan in 1974.) In August 1975 Rahman was killed in the first of a series of military coups.

The Economy of India

India's economy is 70 percent agricultural. The main exports are tea and jute. Most of the farms have fewer than five acres and India has a quarter of the world's population of cattle (see p. 284), indicating that cultural change comes even more slowly than economic. One of the problems of India's economic development has been an unwillingness to use harsh methods. For example, land reform was accomplished by abolishing *zemindar* landowners in 1953 and setting up a community development program under which the government gave advice and materials. The peasant could decide whether or not to accept this service. This method of economic improvement is necessarily slower than that in China or the Soviet Union for the people must be educated to want reform.

India's first five-year plan (1950) reflected all its problems. It proposed to:

1) Grow two stalks of wheat where only one had grown before.

2) Have one baby born where two had been born before.

3) Build new industries.

India began its fifth five-year plan with the first and third aims achieved, but the second far from accomplished.

Population Growth and Birth Control

Although India has spent £20 million on birth control clinics and has offered gifts of food, clothes, and cash to any man who would have a vasectomy, the population by 1978 was over 643 million. The average population density (in 1973) was 433.8 people per square mile, but this was less than many countries (the Netherlands had 838.8) and would not be serious if India were an industrialized nation. Unfortunately, birth control seems to be having no observable effect on a population growth.

Industrial Development

Since independence India has built an industrial base large enough for economic "take-off." Unfortunately its economic growth rate has just barely kept ahead of population growth, and in 1972, 250 million people were reported living below the poverty level (calculated at $5 per month consumption). Since then prices have risen 20-30 percent while incomes have remained the same, and the doubling of the price of oil seriously affected all "developing nations." (India imports two-thirds of its growing fuel requirements.)

Agricultural Outlook

Despite improvements in agriculture, India is still dependent on the monsoon rains and grain production is variable. During the past few years the monsoons have been flooding some places and avoiding others. Between 1957 and 1967, 30,000 students graduated from agricultural schools. The increased use of fertilizer and new seeds have been beneficial, but the statistics reveal the extent of the poverty of the soil: the U.S. has approximately the same amount of crop land as India but uses 8.3 million tons of nitrogen (India 2.0), 5 million tons of phosphates (India only 0.6), and 4.4 million tons of potash (India only 0.3).

The Economies of Pakistan and Bangladesh

Pakistan's economy is also based on agriculture (involving 58 percent of the labor force) and has developed one of the longest irrigation systems in the world. After 1960 Ayub Khan initiated land reform: 1500 acres was to be the maximum size of farms and any acreage over this was confiscated. Ali Bhutto introduced "Islamic Socialism" by nationalizing banks, life insurance companies, shipping and oil companies, and 40 basic industries. The loss of East Pakistan

deprived the economy of an internal market as well as jute exports.
Although all of the five-year plans have emphasized education, the fact that primary education will not be universal for boys until the end of 1979 and girls until 1984 indicates how slow progress has been.

Bangladesh is the principal world producer of raw jute but is faced with the difficulties of a one-crop economy and serious over-population (a density of 1360.5 people per square mile) ; 75 million people live in a country the size of Wisconsin. It has a literacy rate of only 15 percent (India, 30 percent) and the loss of many skilled workers seriously affected jute production. Most of the nation's industry and banks have been nationalized.

Subcontinent Relations

In 1971-72 Pakistan withdrew from SEATO and the Commonwealth. As early as 1966 it had been seeking support from China, and in 1968 it evicted the United States from the base at Peshawar.

Bangladesh became a member of the Commonwealth and eventually a member of the United Nations.

In 1976, diplomatic relations between India and Pakistan were finally resumed and so too was civilian air traffic—for the first time in eleven years.

The International Scene

India became the leader of the neutral nations, refusing to be committed to either the West or the East. It is an independent nation within the British Commonwealth but other than this has no alliances with any country. Despite the fact that it is extremely hard to maintain neutrality, India has been quite successful.

In 1951 India refused to condemn China as the aggressor in Korea but did provide some aid to the U.N. forces in the form of ambulance units. In 1955 India was present at the Bandung Conference of Asian nations and advocated peaceful coexistence with China, signing the Five Principles of Peaceful Coexistence submitted by Chou En-lai. At the Belgrade Conference of 1962 India was one of the few neutral nations that spoke against the Russian breaking of the atomic test ban. Since 1958, when serious border clashes first occurred and Tibet was annexed by China, relations with its northern neighbor have been strained. In August, 1971 India signed a treaty of friendship with the Russians who then supplied huge quantities of arms. Although India had been denouncing nuclear testing for years, in May of 1974 it exploded its own atomic device.

China

ANCIENT CIVILIZATION   2200–1000 B.C.

Information on the first known civilization in China, which developed near the Yellow River, is derived from the so-called "dragon bones," first discovered in 1899. These oracle bones were painted with Chinese characters and were used to ask the gods questions. Possibly there was an earlier civilization, between 2205 and 1523 B.C., known as the Hsia dynasty, but although there are many Chinese myths about it, historians have little evidence that it actually existed. It should be remembered, however, that for hundreds of years it was thought that the Shang dynasty was a myth.

THE SHANG DYNASTY AND THE BRONZE AGE
1523–1028 B.C.

The Shang was possibly the first and certainly the most civilized of a number of principalities located in the Huang Ho Valley. It is known to have had a system of writing using a brush on ivory or bronze, domesticated animals, and an organized army of over 5000 men using chariots.

The system of writing was perhaps the most important single contribution and was not lost with the end of the dynasty; some symbols are actually recognizable today, although most were simpler. The fact that the monosyllabic nature of the Chinese language has not changed accounts in part for the continuity of the writing system.

The practice of divination employing the use of oracle bones was combined with the worship of a major deity called Shang Ti. Ancestor worship (see p. 319) was probably begun during this period with the division of China into clans. (As early as the Shang the clan name [or family name] preceded the given name).

The downfall of the Shang came when a less civilized principality in the valley of the Wei called the Chou defeated the Shang ruler.

CLASSICAL CIVILIZATION   1000 B.C.—500 A.D.

Most of the chief characteristics of Chinese civilization were developed and/or strengthened during the classical era. Chinese political, religious, and social philosophy were established, the highly centralized system of imperial government was formed out of a host of petty principalities, and Chinese imperialistic expansion began.

THE DYNASTIES OF THE CLASSICAL PERIOD

The Chou Dynasty   1124–249 B.C.

This era is often referred to as China's feudal period for it was during the Chou dynasty that China experienced political chaos and decentralization resembling European feudalism. By 720 B.C. the reign of the Chou was weak, and power was distributed among principalities similar to feudal states. But there was more uniformity of culture than there was in Europe.

This was also the outstanding creative period of Chinese thought, as it was in many areas of the world; it corresponds in time with the height of Greek culture, the Hebrew prophets, and the flowering of Buddhism in India.

The Ch'in Dynasty   221–206 B.C.

The Ch'in is most famous for its contribution to China's political unity. The ruler called himself Chin Shih (first) Huang (emperor) Ti (deity of the Shang dynasty), and it was he who was solely responsible for the determined effort to unify and establish a central government over all China. He standardized weights, measures, and the writing system and laid out a network of roads. It is from the word "Ch'in" that China is named.

The price paid for unification was heavy. No freedom of thought was allowed, all books were burned except those on agriculture, medicine, and divination, and those who disagreed with the state were killed either by being buried alive or by forced labor on the Great Wall (completed in 204 B.C.).

The Han Dynasty   202 B.C.–220 A.D.

Liu Pang founded a dynasty (the Western Han) which lasted until 8 A.D. and then was revived (the Eastern Han) in 25 A.D. He immediately modified the severe laws of the Ch'in. Forced labor, however, continued. (Farmers usually had to spend at least a month out of every year in governmental construction projects).

The reign of Wu Ti (140–87 B.C.) was the height of the Western Han, witnessing the opening of the great silk route with Rome, the beginning of irrigation projects, the regulation of commerce and coinage, expansion into northern Korea, and explorations into Central Asia.

The Chinese invented paper and developed a calendar, and historical records of the dynasties were begun. During the Han, Confucianism slowly triumphed as the basis of the political structure of China. The Chinese became known as the "sons of Han."

The Six Dynasties Period   221–589 A.D.

The Han government disintegrated and China reverted to a

semi-feudal state in much the same way and for many of the same reasons that the Roman Empire collapsed.

POLITICAL AND RELIGIOUS PHILOSOPHY

Confucianism

Confucius (Kung Fu-tzu 551–479 B.C.) lived in the province of Lu and was a would-be government official of little significance. In his incidental career as a teacher, however, he was extremely important.

The main purpose of Confucius' philosophy and teachings was to bring social order into an era of political chaos and confusion and to return to the days of the founders of the Chou dynasty. The code became the most successful of all systems of conservatism, lasting 2000 years as the chief ideology of the world's largest country. Confucius believed that only through harmonious relations among individuals could true harmony between man and nature be reached.

The Five Relationships and the Classes of Society

Each person was to assume a specific place in society, with specific duties and modes of conduct known as *li* or propriety. This was accomplished by a system of superiors and inferiors. The Five Relationships of superiors over inferiors were prince over subject; father over son; husband over wife; elder brother over younger brother; and friend over friend.

The classes in society were ordered on the Confucian idea of a hierarchy of worth: first, scholars; second, farmers; third, artisans; fourth, merchants; fifth, slaves. Although their position varied throughout Chinese history, soldiers were not even on the social scale, on the assumption that "nice boys don't become soldiers." (This attitude is quite different in Japanese history.) Confucianism placed great emphasis on an intellectual and landed elite and depreciated the value of anyone in commerce or manufacturing. Consequently, it succeeded in creating a bifurcated social structure in which 80 percent were illiterate peasants and 20 percent landed upperclass. There was almost no middle class.

The Emperor

The emperor received the mandate of heaven, an authorization from the deity to reign, but he ruled by right of his virtue. Thus if he were not virtuous, he could lose his mandate. The ruler was considered to be the son of heaven; his only superior was God. He was therefore held responsible for all calamities, and consequently revolutions in China often occurred at times of famine or other hardships.

Emphasis on Paternalism

The emperor of the state was the father of society. The father in each family was the most important person and the family was the key social unit rather than the individual or the state. This was not true in Japan.

MAJOR CHARACTERISTICS OF THE CHINESE FAMILY:

1) The group was important not the individual.

2) Youth was subordinate to age.

3) Ancestor worship was emphasized (subordination of the living to the dead).

4) The wife was subordinate to the husband.

5) The daughter-in-law was subordinate to the mother-in-law.

6) Child-bearing, not love, was the reason for marriage.

Importance of Ceremony

Because of the strict relationships among people, Confucianism was based on ceremony and eventually became more form than substance. The Japanese succeeded in borrowing the ceremony and not the philosophy of Confucianism.

Mencius (Meng-tzu)

Mencius (373–288 B.C.) was a Confucian scholar who traveled from state to state preaching good government as Confucius had done and emphasizing the importance of education and self-improvement. He advocated a code of moral righteousness for all not just for the upper class. Mencius' most important contribution to Confucian theory was the clarification of the Right of Rebellion. He stressed the importance of the ruler ruling by good conduct; if he did not govern in this way, he could and should be overthrown. Once he had been overthrown, the mandate of heaven obviously would go to the conqueror.

Taoism

The other important philosophical movement in China was Taoism. Based on writings (the most important of which is the *Lao Tzu* or *Tao te ching*) by unknown authors at unknown dates (probably third century B.C.), Taoism advocates the subordination of oneself to nature's ways, for only in this manner can an individual lead a meaningful life. The search of the Taoist is to find union with nature, to find the way, or the *tao*. This is similar to renunciation of the world.

Taoism was in many ways the opposite of Confucianism, romantic rather than matter-of-fact, intuitive rather than orderly, mystical and vague rather than rational. Yet many Chinese were both Confucianist and Taoist—Confucian during times of peace and prosperity or while holding government office and Taoist during times of trouble and disorder or while at home in the country.

Ancestor Worship

Ancestor worship lasted, despite the introduction of the religious philosophies of Buddhism and Taoism, and Confucius encouraged it, believing that it would make people more aware of their responsibility to the family and their duties to their elders.

Yin and Yang

A belief in Yin and Yang persisted from early times and was

included in the philosophies of Confucianism and Taoism. Yang was positive and male, everything that was warm and active (represented by heaven), while Yin was negative and female, everything that was cold or wet or mysterious (represented by the earth). These were the two forces in the universe and were inseparable; therefore man and nature must be harmonious, and heaven and man were in partnership.

Buddhism

The religion from India (see p. 285), was not introduced until the end of the classical period and was adapted and changed by the Chinese to include Confucian ethics, Taoist beliefs, ancestor worship, and a multitude of gods.

THE CREATION OF THE CHINESE STATE

The formation of the central government of China and the establishment of the emperor as a hereditary leader was accomplished under the Ch'in dynasty. The imperial structure, with its all-powerful emperor and its efficient and disciplined bureaucracy, was the Ch'in's lasting contribution to Chinese history.

Uniformity was achieved by a common tax system, weights and measures, and a uniform written script that gave to China a language by which all could communicate. China was divided into provinces that could be administered from the central government, and irrigation and canal projects were begun. This was perhaps the time of the most profound and far reaching social upheaval in all Chinese history with the exception of the twentieth century.

Confucianism as the philosophy of government was later established during the Han dynasty, and an examination system as a means of recruiting government officials was introduced.

Territorial Expansion

During the Ch'in dynasty the area of land controlled was extended along the coast and below the Yangtze River and south as far as the Indochina border.

The Han dynasty is particularly famous for its imperialistic expansion—west into central Asia, north into Manchuria, and south into Indochina. At its height, it was equal in size and military might to the Roman Empire.

MEDIEVAL CIVILIZATION   500–1500 A.D.

One of the unique characteristics of Chinese history is its continuity. Although dynasties declined, decayed, and were rebelled against from within and invaded from without and finally overthrown, the basic characteristics of the Chinese way of life and government did not change. Although anarchy prevailed during the periods between great dynasties, Chinese culture was not destroyed. Although barbarians invaded and conquered the land, they themselves were conquered by Chinese philosophy and language, and their governments continued to be supported by Confucian doctrine, agricultural revenues, and forced labor. Although there were foreign commerce, migrations, and influence and although there were material innovations and discoveries, China remained essentially the same. During the medieval period, the greatest influence from the outside world was Buddhism, which the Chinese quickly accepted and adapted to their own use. But even Buddhism could not seriously challenge Confucianism or the structure of Chinese society. So although each dynasty during the medieval period varied in detail, in essence each was the same. The medieval era saw the revival, modification, and extension by the Sui and Tang dynasties of one of the most unique aspects of the Chinese imperial government— the civil service examination.

THE EXAMINATION SYSTEM

The Hans had originally introduced the examination system but from the time of the Sui and Tang dynasties it was to become the foundation of the Chinese government until it was finally abolished in 1900. No one could become an official of the government without mastering the works of the Chinese classics. There were five classics that were the most important, the earliest dating from the second century B.C., and they included songs, semihistorical writings, poetry, rites, and rituals. Combined with the *Analects* (the conversations of Confucious) and the *Mencius* (written by Meng-tzu) they constituted the examination and took years of study to master.

Effects of the System

Pro:

1) China was the first government to establish a bureaucracy based on merit (although the bottom ranks could be attained by purchase). An "intellectually unified nation" was produced which Edwin Reischauer in *East Asia* compares to the classical education which produced the ruling class of the British Empire in the nineteenth century.

2) It meant that the intellectual (so often the revolutionary in other countries) became the government's strongest supporter and contributed to the continuity of Chinese history and government.

Con:

1) It favored the rich since usually it was the wealthy who had the time to spend years in studies.

2) It was by nature conservative and backward looking.

THE DYNASTIES OF MEDIEVAL CHINA

The Sui   589–618

The Sui reunified China after over 350 years of civil chaos at the fall of the Han. In this respect it was similar to the Ch'in dynasty, although certainly not as bloody or as dramatic. It was a military regime that served its purpose of reunification and then collapsed.

The Tang   618–907

The Tang dynasty resembled the Han in the size of its empire and the brilliance of its civilization. It was a period of expansion into Manchuria, Mongolia, and Tibet. During the reign of Hsuan Tsung (712), schools were established all over China and the world's first newspaper was printed. Japan was so impressed by the dynasty's greatness that it borrowed wholesale from it, imitating everything it saw.

The Sung   960–1279

Political turmoil prevailed from 907 to 960, until the Sung dynasty finally was able to reunify and rule most of China proper (the eight provinces below the Great Wall, but not Vietnam, Central Asia, or the far north). After 1127, however, the Sung dynasty was pushed south of the Huai River.

The Southern Sung witnessed a flourishing of the arts (the dynasty is famous for its porcelains and paintings) and some attempts at economic reform were made. Trade was expanded, a better rice seed was introduced, gunpowder was used, and, most important, printing techniques were developed.

As civilian government grew, the military declined and Chinese cities prospered. Urbanization, however, led to several evils: absentee

landlordism in the countryside and a worsening of the position of
women (concubinage and the binding of feet).

The Yuan   1271–1368

Kubla Khan led the Mongols against the Sungs and successfully
established himself as ruler of all China. This was the first time that
China was completely under the control of a foreign dynasty, but
the Yuan was short-lived, for the Mongols were few in number,
hated by the southern Chinese, and quickly absorbed by the Chinese
culture.

This was the time of Marco Polo, and it is interesting to note
the contrast between Europe and China. In his travels, Marco Polo
stated that he had seen in China printed paper money, broad streets,
police patrols at night, public carriages, drains under the streets,
and landscaped roadsides—all of which he had never encountered
in Europe.

The Ming   1368–1644

A revolt in the south of China led by a poor farm laborer
established the Ming dynasty. The Ming saw a return to China for
the Chinese, the extension of the absolutism of the emperor, and
the growth of the influence of the eunuch. There was a vitality in
scholarship as well as extraordinary sea voyages (organized by the
eunuch, Cheng Ho) between 1405–1433 to India, the Middle East,
and Africa (the first voyage had 62 ships and 28,000 men).

Yet there was a quality of rigidity and resistance to change
which became increasingly typical of China and eventually became
one of the causes of the downfall of Chinese civilization in the face
of the Western impact.

MODERN CIVILIZATION   1500 to the Present

The modern history of China is really the story of the coming of the West in 1514, the dominance of the West by 1900, and the reaction to the West in the form of the Republican Revolution of 1911, the Nationalist Revolution of 1927, and finally the Communist Revolution of 1949. In 1500, China still thought of itself as the "Middle Kingdom," the center of the world. It still carried on foreign relations based on the tribute system, a sort of vassal relationship in which China would recognize the legitimacy of a neighboring state in return for tribute from that state. The Ming's fleets had sailed one hundred years before the first Portuguese ship reached China but, as John Fairbanks points out, "No Henry the Navigator came to the Chinese throne," and China failed to become a seafaring and commercial empire. To China, the rest of the world was barbarian and had nothing to offer. In a letter to George III of England in 1790, Peking announced that there was "nothing we lack, as your principal envoy and others have themselves observed. We have never set much store on strange or ingenious objects, nor do we need any more of your country's manufactures. . . ." This impression was not totally changed until 1900, and it was only then that China became fully aware of how archaic its institutions had become in contrast to those of the West (in comparison, see history of Japan). The hope, however, is that Napoleon's forecast of the future was mistaken: "Let China sleep; when she awakens the world will be sorry."

THE CHING (MANCHU) DYNASTY   1644–1912

The beginning of the Manchu reign in China is often cited as the commencement of the modern period, but it was not. The Manchus invaded and conquered China, but did not change its ways. China's imperial government remained essentially the same, although the Manchus set up a dyarchy in which there was one Manchu and one Chinese for every post. They attempted to maintain their dynastic identity and not be absorbed as the Mongols had been by Chinese culture. They forbade intermarriage between

Manchu and Chinese, retained Manchuria as an exclusive preserve
for themselves, limited the army to Manchurians, and increased
further the absolutism of the emperor.

The Chien-lung Period   1736–1795

This was the height of Manchu power. Chien-lung himself is
considered the greatest of the Manchus, equal to Catherine the
Great of Russia and Frederick the Great of Prussia, his contemporaries. A period of internal peace prevailed, with improvement
in the rural situation and religious tolerance. China stood in marked
contrast to Europe at the time and was certainly its equal if not its
superior. It was also a period of great physical extension—the Tarim
Basin area, Manchuria, Mongolia, Tibet, all were under China's
control, and even raids into Nepal were conducted.

The Coming of the West

The Portuguese arrived in China in 1514, followed closely by
the Spanish and the Dutch. From 1514 to 1644 there was little
direct trade, and when the Manchus came to power in 1644 they
prohibited trade by sea for forty years. From 1685 to 1759 there
was multiport trade, but by 1670 the Manchu government decided
that with the increase of foreigners, particularly British, who were
soon to dominate the trade, something had to be done, and the
factory system was introduced.

The Factory System

A system of trade regulations was established whereby foreigners, limited to the port of Canton, were not allowed to deal
with anyone other than one of the thirteen *cohongs* who were
representatives of the government. The *cohong* decided not only
what China would sell but also what it would buy and for what
price.

The regulations on foreigners were severe: they could not live
in China during the nontrading season, and during the trading

season they were forced to live outside of the city in factories or warehouses built for the purpose, and under no circumstances were they allowed to bring women with them. Their goods were taxed at whatever rate the government chose, and they were allowed no freedom of trade.

The purpose of the system, as far as the Manchu government was concerned, was to milk the trade and keep the barbarians under control.

Despite these restrictions the foreigners, particularly the British East India Company and the Americans, profited.

The Penetration of the West

The First Opium War   1840–1842

CAUSES

1) The Opium Trade

China was not interested in anything the British had to sell, but tea and silk were in great demand in London. The British were naturally opposed to paying in gold and by the eighteenth century found a commodity that the Chinese were happy to pay for—opium. The opium was grown in India and smugged into China. In 1729 200 chests (120 pounds per chest) were sold, and by 1838 the number had risen to 40,000. The result, of course, was that the Canton *cohongs* were losing out and the trading balance had shifted—now gold was being drained out of China. The Manchus, since they could not profit from the trade, tried to stop the opium importation. The government succeeded in getting the British to turn over 20,000 chests to the Manchu officials, but they could not force the British to sign a bond guaranteeing that there would be no more opium sold in China. This precipitated the war.

2) Lack of Diplomatic Equality

Foreigners were definitely considered and treated as inferiors by the Chinese. There was no communication with the dragon throne unless the emperor invited it, and even this invitation involved the humiliating *kowtow* (prostrating oneself three times and bowing the head nine times to the floor), which most Britishers and Americans refused to perform.

3) Clash between Legal Systems

The Chinese believed in the doctrine of responsibility: someone had to pay for a crime, whether it was manslaughter or murder. For example, in 1821 a jar fell off a ship and killed a woman in a sampan. All trade was halted until the American ship surrendered a man to be strangled by the Chinese.

The war did not last long, for the British with their gunboats, rifles, and cannons were definitely superior to the Chinese with their spears and junks.

THE TREATY OF NANKING

The treaty of 1842 ended the factory system and established what was to be known as the treaty system. It opened five ports to trade, gave Hong Kong to the British, and promised diplomatic equality along with an indemnity of $21,000,000.

Immediately, other treaties followed with other countries—the United States, France, Holland, and Germany. Each nation was granted a most-favored-nation clause, which meant that anything one nation received the other nation would also receive.

The Second Opium War   1858–1860

CAUSES

1) The primary causes of the second war were that the Chinese refused to accept the basic premise of the Treaty of Nanking—diplomatic equality—and that the treaty had never determined the status of opium nor had there been a settlement on whether foreigners were to live in or out of the cities.

2) The Chinese were also annoyed. The coolie trade, or the kidnapping of Chinese by Westerners to be used as cheap labor, was on the increase. There was piracy along the coast, and the Portuguese had established a protection racket.

THE TREATY OF TIENTSIN

All of the first gains were preserved by this treaty of 1858, and in addition eleven new ports were opened, opium was legalized, the tariff was fixed at five percent, diplomats were allowed to reside in Peking, and foreigners were permitted to navigate up the Yangtze River.

The treaty did not actually end the war; it took two more years of fighting to have the treaty ratified in Peking, but by 1860 the first chapter of the pressure of the West had ended.

Spheres of Influence

After 1898 China was divided into spheres of influence: Britain—the Yangtze Valley; Russia—Manchuria and Port Arthur; Japan—Korea and the Ryukyu Islands; Germany—Kiaochow Bay; and France—the three southern provinces of Yunnan, Kwangsi, and Kwangtung.

In 1899 and 1900 came the Open Door Notes of the United States. Secretary of State Hay called for the treaty powers to refrain from staking out exclusive trading rights and leave the door open for trade. Perhaps United States action slowed the process of cutting China into many different colonial areas, but probably the major reason for China remaining free was the bitter rivalry among European nations.

Reaction to the West

The Taiping Rebellion   1851–1864

The Taiping rebellion marks the opening phase in a revolutionary process, and it is in this framework that it is important. It was the beginning of a revolution that would eventually affect all aspects of Chinese society from the economic to the ideological.

Led by Hung Hsiu-chuan, a man who considered himself the younger brother of Christ and who aimed at the overthrow of the Manchus and the establishment of the "Heavenly Kingdom of Great Peace," this was the first foreign-influenced ideology to be successful since Buddhism.

At first the Taipings were remarkably successful, taking Nanking in 1853, moving thirty miles south of Peking, and consolidating the lower Yangtze valley area.

The rebellion is unique, for it not only professed a pseudo-Christian doctrine but also used military tactics such as guerilla warfare and fifth columns. It advocated economic reforms, redistribution of land, and a type of socialist state. It also advocated equality of women and language simplification. There are many similarities between the rebellion and the Communist Revolution in 1949.

Corruption and dissension among the leadership were two of the reasons for failure, but more important was the fact that the Taipings professed an ideology unsuitable for enlisting the support of the educated gentry. The educated began to mobilize opposition and organize local militias to put the Taipings down, asking for and receiving aid from Europeans.

RESULTS OF THE TAIPING REBELLION

1) It further weakened the Manchus, for it led to more foreign intervention and growing decentralization of China, with the development of native Chinese militia from local provinces under the command of the gentry.

2) The Manchus tried to restore Confucianism in the government, to improve the bureaucracy, to reorganize the military by incorporating some Western techniques, and to deal with the West on its own terms by establishing a foreign bureau and an interpreters' college. But the adoption of Western institutions began to undermine the very thing the adoption was supposed to build up.

The Reform Movement 1895–1900

Desire for reform was not only caused by further penetration by the West but also by the impact of the Japanese victory over the Chinese in 1895 (see p. 363). This was the first event that impressed a considerable number of Chinese, for here was an example of the modernization of an Asian country and the final proof of the weakness of China.

HUNDRED DAYS OF REFORM (JUNE 14–SEPTEMBER 16, 1898)

1) Kang Yu-wei, a member of the bureaucracy, was chiefly responsible for influencing the Emperor Prince Kung to make the reforms. These reforms included a new education system, a Western army, and the cleansing of government by the abolition of some of the more corrupt offices.

2) The reforms were in direct conflict with the desires of Empress Dowager Tzu Hsi, who was the real power in China, for the doing away with loyal if corrupt officers as well as the undermining of the Manchu nobility threatened her position. She immediately plotted against the prince and overthrew him, and on September 26 all reforms were abolished, the emperor was arrested, and she put an end to voluntary reform.

The Boxer Rebellion   1900

The Boxer Rebellion was another phase in the revolutionary process. It was symptomatic of the growing unrest and the increasing antiforeignism and was the last desperate effort to drive out the foreigners.

Led by a group that called itself the Fists of Righteous Harmony, the rebellion was supported quietly by the throne. It was directed against all foreigners and any Chinese who had come under the influence of the West (particularly Christians). The foreign legations in Peking were attacked, and 242 Westerners were killed as well as several thousand Chinese converts. The Western governments immediately sent an allied army (the greatest number of men to relieve the legations was sent by Japan—80,000). With this, the movement collapsed.

THE EFFECTS OF THE BOXER REBELLION

1) An indemnity of $333,000,000 was demanded, forts were dismantled, the foreigners occupied thirteen places around Peking, officials were punished (many were ordered to commit suicide), and a genuine Chinese foreign ministry was demanded.

2) It convinced many of the most conservative bureaucrats that things had to be changed, and it indicated the lack of central authority of the government.

3) Reforms by the Manchus (1901–1910) were instigated. Schools were established, the examination system was abolished, and students were sent abroad to study. A new army was created, modeled after the German system. A constitution was promised (copied from the Japanese) and drafted in 1908, and provincial assemblies were put into operation in 1909 and a national assembly in 1910. Railroads were built, but this led to a contest between central and provincial power. The early reforms had been within the Confucian system. These reforms were not, and the Manchus soon found that drastic change was undermining the very foundations of their government.

THE REVOLUTION OF 1911

Causes of the Revolution

Lack of Leadership

In 1908 Empress Dowager Tzu Hsi died, and her heir was a three-year-old boy who was controlled by the seventy-three-year-old, corrupt, and inefficient Prince Ching. Growing pressure from provincial assemblies and financial problems, along with a lack of central control, further weakened the Manchu government. It was only a matter of time before it would fall.

Revolutionary Developments

By the reforms of 1900–1908, new revolutionary groups had been created in China. The students educated abroad returned and demanded radical change not just reform. The army trained in Japan, the Chinese who lived in treaty ports beyond the reach of Manchu authorities, and the Chinese who lived overseas all demanded immediate change.

Revolutionary societies developed. The most important was the Teng Meng-Hui (the Together-Sworn Society), formed in 1905 by Sun Yat-sen. This was the party that was later to become known as the Kuomintang (KMT) or the Nationalist party. By 1912 its membership was approximately 300,000.

Sun Yat-sen and the Three People's Principles

Sun was the man who knit these revolutionary groups together. He was definitely a product of Western influence himself. Born in 1866 in south China of upper peasantry, he was sent to school in Honolulu, where he became a Christian, and he then attended the Hong Kong College of Medicine.

In 1905 he organized the Teng Meng-Hui and issued a manifesto that called for the driving out of the Manchus, restoring China to the Chinese, establishing a republic, and equalizing land ownership. His Three Peoples' Principles were formulated at this time and were what he considered the essence of revolution—nationalism, democracy, and people's livelihood. (This is what the Communists advocated in 1949 and the basis on which they claim Sun, as well as Marx and Lenin, as their ideological father.)

Sun also mentioned that the revolution would have to pass through several periods:

1) military government,

2) government by provisional constitution, in which the party would lead,

3) the final stage of a democratic republic.

The Revolution Itself

On October 10, 1911, the Wuchang uprising took place. In May of that year the Manchu government had decided to nationalize all trunk railroads. This led to local opposition in Wuchang, Hanyang, and Hankow. By accident a bomb went off in Hankow, men were arrested by the Manchu authorities, and lists of army officers involved in revolutionary activities were found, which meant that the officers had to mutiny or be caught by the government. The rebels set up a new republic in the south of China with Sun as president, but their forces were unable to take the north.

In the meantime the Manchu government had turned to the leader of the army, Yuan Shih-kai, to save them. They made him premier in November 1911, but then Sun offered him the presidency of the republic if he would turn against the Manchus. He accepted, and on February 11, 1912, the abdication edict of the Manchus was issued, transferring imperial power to Yuan, while Sun transferred republican power to him.

The Failure of the Revolution

The revolution removed the Manchu dynasty, but did not put in its place a viable political machine. Instead, a phantom republic was created by Yuan which was in reality a military dictatorship. By 1913 he had ended any pretense of republicanism by dissolving parliament and the KMT.

What unity there was in China quickly disappeared when Yuan died in 1915. China then broke into a score of regimes dominated by military men. The period from 1915 to 1927 is known as the era of warlordism, and even Sun became a warlord in Canton. World War I found China at the mercy of warlords and foreign powers. In 1915 Japan presented Twenty-one Demands (see p. 364) to which China was forced to submit.

There were, however, signs of intellectual change. The May 4, 1919 Incident was a mass demonstration by students against foreign representatives and a boycott of all Japanese goods, and the results were the refusal by the Chinese to sign the Versailles Treaty and increased anti-Westernism. The other important result was the fact that it made the students more conscious of the situation in China and more determined to do something about it.

It was at this time that Marxism-Leninism also appeared in China. The first Marxist study group was formed in 1918, and the Chinese Communist Party (CCP) was organized in 1921.

THE NATIONALIST REVOLUTION

The Triumph of the KMT

Russia had accomplished an impressive revolution with a tightly organized and highly disciplined party. Immediately afterward it had renounced its spheres of influence in China. Sun was impressed by both actions, and negotiations were begun with the Soviet government to help reorganize the KMT.

The Sun-Joffe Statement   1923

An agent of the Soviet Union, Joffe, was sent to Canton, and in return for the USSR's collaboration and aid Sun agreed that Chinese Communists could join the KMT as individual members. A veteran revolutionary agent of the Communist International, Borodin, was then sent to advise Sun in Canton on organization, training, and methods, thus creating a modern totalitarian party capable of taking over all of China. The military was also reorganized: Chiang Kai-shek was sent to Moscow for training and brought back to head the Whampoa Military Academy.

Sun's Death and Disunity

In 1925 Sun died, and open factional conflict broke out in the KMT between Wang Ching-wei, the new chairman of the government who was a leftist, and Chiang Kai-shek, head of the military forces. In March of 1926 Chiang carried through a coup d'état for leadership of the party when Borodin, the strong man behind Wang, was out of town. Wang fled and Chiang made a temporary compromise with Borodin.

The Northern Expedition

In the summer of 1926 the campaign against the warlords for the reunification of China under Chiang's direction was begun. By March 1927 Nanking and Shanghai had been taken by Chiang, and Hankow and Wuchang had been seized by the left wing of the KMT, which set up a government independent of Chiang's control in that area. Chiang therefore established his own regime in Nanking. Fortunately for Chiang, the left wing of the KMT split when the Soviet Embassy in Peking was raided and documents were found that showed Russian domination of the Chinese Communists. The

Hankow regime then fell to Chiang, and Borodin and his advisers fled to Moscow. The Northern expedition had turned out to be a three-way struggle—Chiang versus the Communists and Chiang versus the warlords. By the end of 1928 Chiang was in the saddle, Nanking was declared the new capital of the new China, and most of China had been unified.

The Achievement of the KMT

Not until 1943 did the Chinese succeed in doing away with extraterritoriality, although by 1937 foreign concessions had been reduced from thirty-three to thirteen and by 1933 the government had regained control of the tariff.

Economic reforms were initiated under T. V. Soong (the brother of Mme. Sun Yat-sen and Mme. Chiang Kai-shek).

In 1935 the currency was unified and communications were improved, but nothing was done about either the supervision of agricultural rents (although the government promised in a land law of 1930 to limit rent to 37½ percent of the crop) or the redistribution of lands. Emphasis was purely on technical improvements, and a high percentage of the annual budget was dedicated to military rather than economic needs. This, in part, reflected the military nature of the origins of the regime as well as the growing threat of war with Japan.

THE GROWTH OF COMMUNISM

The Early Period   1921–1923

In July 1921 the Chinese Communist Party was founded in Shanghai. Chinese students studying abroad had been exposed to Marxism, but there was very little interest in the ideology before the Russian revolution. Lenin's theory of imperialism (see p. 183) had great appeal to the Chinese for it explained the problem of colonialism and offered the country hope for the end of capitalist exploitation.

CCP–KMT Cooperation   1923–1927

The decision of the Communists to enter the Kuomintang caused considerable debate among the Chinese, but Moscow insisted upon it for the Chinese Communists were weak and this was believed to be the best way to spread their influence.

By the spring of 1927 both the KMT and the CCP had achieved what they wanted from the union—that is, the KMT possessed a party apparatus and military organization and the CCP had gained popularity through its work with the peasants and laborers.

Period of Insurrection   1927–1931

During the Northern expedition, the Communists were forced underground after the break with the KMT in 1927. Their work was concentrated primarily in the cities and with the labor unions, but in the 1930s the shift toward a peasant base was already being advocated.

Period of the Kiangsi Soviet   1931–1935

This was the critical transitional period, for the CCP had been forced into the countryside by Chiang's army. A Soviet republic was organized in Kiangsi in the south of China, with Mao Tse-tung as president.

This was also the time when Japan had taken over Manchuria and by 1933 was below the Great Wall. Chiang was willing to trade space for time in order to overcome his internal problems, and he signed the Tangku Truce with the Japanese, demilitarizing the area from Peking to the Great Wall. Then he turned to what he considered to be his greatest problem—the Communists—and in 1933 and 1934 conducted five extermination campaigns. The Chinese Communists were finally forced to flee from the south of China in 1934 and began the Long March to the north through the foothills of the Himalayas.

The Long March

About 180,000 Communists were in Kiangsi: 100,000 of these defied orders from Moscow and fled the area. Less than 20,000 survived the six-thousand-mile march, and they fought fifteen major engagements against the Nationalists en route.

The results of the march were the following:

1) During this period Mao became the unquestioned leader of the CCP.

2) The Communists were driven into the northern province of Shensi, where they became completely dependent on agrarian support. This dependency caused them to alter their program and in the end was the very thing that won for them mastery over the country of China.

3) Those who were fit survived. The 20,000 men who survived the Long March became the hard core of the Chinese Communist leadership, creating a bond that was not broken by factionalism and ambition until 1968. Mao Tse-tung, Chou En-lai, Chu Teh, and Liu Shao-chi were all to become leaders of Communist China as they had become leaders of the march.

THE TRIUMPH OF COMMUNISM

The Yenan Period and World War II (1935–1945)

The Kidnapping of Chiang Kai-shek 1936

Following his kidnapping by a northern warlord, whose troops Chiang had gone to inspect, and the negotiations carried on by the Communist Chou En-lai in order to force him to declare war against the Japanese, Chiang finally realized that he must do something about the Japanese situation, and an agreement was concluded for a united front between the Communists and the Nationalists against the Japanese.

The United Front against the Japanese

The united front policy was a Communist offer in February 1937 to abandon the system of soviets in favor of the Nationalist government, to subordinate the Red Army to the command of the Nationalist Army, and to end their policy of landlord extermination. They did this for several reasons:

1) The USSR, wanting to keep the Japanese out of Siberia, had ordered the Chinese Communists to cooperate with the Nationalists.

2) Relief from another planned bandit suppression campaign of Chiang's, which might have exterminated them completely.

3) It enabled them to pose as advocates of the interests of the people and to extend their area of control.

The War against Japan

On July 7, 1937, the Japanese attacked Marco Polo Bridge. By the end of 1937 they had overrun Nanking, and by 1938 Hankow was taken, a seacoast blockade was established, and all major treaty ports and the main lines of communication were in Japanese hands. China was trisected.

The Japanese-controlled areas were all provided with puppet regimes (Wang Ching-wei, the leftist whom Chiang had overthrown, was one of them), but the Japanese were unable to win the population or economically to integrate the south of China with the north.

The Nationalist-controlled areas were the largest, containing nearly one-half the population of China, but they had been pushed into the country, leaving the areas of their major support and their sources of income from trade. They were without industry or communications and were in the most conservative areas of China. Inflation immediately occurred (in 1945 the Chinese dollar was equal to one one-thousandth of its value in 1936). Inflation lowered the morale of the intelligentsia (who were dependent upon fixed incomes) and led to defection, which in turn led to more active attempts on the part of the Nationalist government to control thought, simply adding to the corruption and the disaffection with the regime. The army became obsolete, relying solely on old methods of positional warfare; the peasants were more heavily taxed; and the conservative landlords became the pillars of government. The conditions themselves, in contrast to the Communist-controlled areas, were enough to defeat the Nationalists.

The Communist-controlled areas were rosy compared with the Nationalists. The Red Army did very little fighting against the Japanese, reserving its greatest strength for the Nationalist war that was to follow. In the areas of Communist control, economic and social reforms were put through under Mao's doctrine of the "New Democracy." Moderate economic and political reforms including a ceiling on rent of 33½ percent, a self-sufficient industrial base, a political system whereby no more than one-third of the government were known Communists, and a mass cultural movement to educate the people were all established. The statistics prove the success of the Communists' wartime policy. In 1937 the Communists controlled 40,000 square miles of territory and one and a half million people; by 1945 they controlled 225,000 square miles and 85 million people.

The Civil War   1945–1949

During World War II the civil war had already begun. Both the Nationalists and the Communists did everything they could to check the other. The CCP moved into Japanese-controlled areas at the expense of the KMT, and the KMT blockaded Communist areas to prevent trade.

The five essentials of Maoist strategy that were to win him China were:

1) a fixed territorial base from which to expand;

2) a highly indoctrinated Red Army using guerilla tactics;

3) basing the strength of the party on the peasants and winning them over by land reform;

4) making sure that the party leadership was strong;

5) ensuring that the Communists were entirely self-sufficient and independent of any outside aid (even from Russia).

V-J Day led to a scramble for north China. The Nationalists immediately occupied (with United States aid) the major cities of China, but they also wanted to occupy Manchuria. The Communists moved into south Manchuria and the battle began.

The Marshall Mission

In January 1946 U.S. General George Marshall was sent "to end the civil war and to build a strong, united, democratic China." He was able to establish a cease-fire, but in January 1947 the mediations collapsed.

The story of the triumph of the Communists at this point is a military one. In 1948 the Communists took Mukden, and Chiang lost some of his best troops; from then on the Nationalists went downhill. In January 1949 the Communists crossed the Yangtze, and by April Nanking had fallen. That autumn Chiang fled to Taiwan. On October 1, 1949, the People's Republic of China was declared.

The Failure of the KMT

Domestic shortcomings of the Nationalists were certainly part of the reason for their failure. They had not satisfied the peasants; they had not satisfied those who demanded China for the Chinese and a strong unified country; and they had had to fight Japanese aggression along with inflation and political corruption. They had staved off defeat but in doing so had lost the energy needed for rejuvenation.

The Communists had the advantages of the support of the rural areas, an armed force based on a guerrilla army, and a unified and dedicated political and military command.

Chiang's mistakes were many. He believed that reforms must wait on unification, and he made no effort to present the people with an attractive postwar program. He was not a great military strategist and refused to give command to those better equipped than he; although he was superior in both numbers and arms, he overextended his troops, did not use his air force, and directed battles from miles away.

The Communist victory was not a popular revolution. Instead, it was a "slow defection because of the lack of another alternative." Once the KMT alienated the intelligentsia of China, the CCP won.

CHINA SINCE 1949

Mao and Chou

MAO TSE-TUNG

Until his death in 1976, Mao was secretary of the Chinese Communist Party and chairman of the Politburo—the top man in China.

Born in 1893 in Hunan province, the son of a sadistic and wealthy peasant, educated in a classical tradition and then in technology, Mao became a library assistant in the University of Peking. In 1921 he was present at the formation of the Communist Party, and in 1925 he directed the peasant department of the CCP, where he first became convinced of the necessity of working through the peasant in China. He became leader of the Party on the Long March and was definitely responsible for the New Democracy and the United Front policy. In 1949 he became chairman of the Central Government of the Chinese People's Republic as well as secretary of the Party. In 1959 he retired as head of the government, but, as in Russia, real power lies within the Party.

CHOU EN-LAI

Until his death in 1975, Chou was premier of the Government, Minister of Foreign Affairs, and member of the Politburo—the second man in China.

Chou was raised in a Cantonese family who had been members of the government under the Manchus. He was educated in Japan and then Paris and there became a Communist. In 1919 he was imprisoned during the student riots; in 1921 he was present at the founding of the CCP; in 1923–1927 he was chief of political training under Chiang Kai-shek; and in 1931 he sided with Mao. As foreign minister he negotiated the Sino-Soviet Treaty, the Geneva Conference, was the hero of the Bandung Conference, and handled international relations with consummate skill.

Cultural Revolution   1966–1969

The first great crisis within the Chinese administration occurred after 1968. The failure of the Great Leap Forward (see p. 344) and growing dissension between the "Maoists," who advocated the moral virtues of communism, and the faction represented by Liu Shao-chi, who placed technical and material development first, led to the "Cultural Revolution."

Mao turned to the army and General Lin Piao for support. Revolutionary committees and mass organizations such as the Red Guard Youth were established to purge the party and punish opposition leaders by public humiliation. By 1969 the military was in control under Mao; Liu (who had been slated as Mao's successor) had been stripped of his power; Lin Piao had been named Mao's successor.

The Succession

Factionalism and competition continued and became more apparent after the deaths of Chou and Mao. In 1971 Lin Piao was declared a traitor, and in 1975 Teng Hsiao-ping, who had been ousted during the Cultural Revolution, was reinstated by Chou En-lai, unseated as soon as Chou died, and finally in 1977 appointed deputy premier. By then Hua Kuo-feng—a compromise between the moderates and the radicals—had been named Chairman of the Communist Party, but the situation remains unstable.

The three groups contending for power in China are:

1) The "Shanghai Clique" or the radicals, who emphasize "reeducation" (mass indoctrination) and who have no trust of foreign countries.

2) The "Peking Pragmatists" (symbolized by Chou En-lai), who want concentration on industrial development and active diplomatic relations in hope of playing one nation off against another.

3) The "Military Group," who distrust civilian government and want to eliminate friction with the USSR.

The Economic Transformation of China

All statistics on China's economic growth are open to doubt. Although Chinese claims are often greater than actual achievements, some facts are known and others can be safely guessed.

Industrial Development

The development of industry has been the main concern of the Chinese five-year plans. Emphasis has been on heavy industry, particularly steel production, coal mining, and electric power output.

The first five-year plan, begun in 1953, was quite successful. Steel production is the best example: in 1952, 1.35 million tons of steel were produced; by 1955, 2.85 million; and by 1958, over 19 million tons, which exceeded the goal of the plan to quadruple steel production. Between 1951 and 1958 China's GNP went up 173.2 percent (in contrast to India's 120.3 percent). After 1960 China suffered from economic and industrial difficulties due to poor harvests and the sudden withdrawal of Soviet aid and technicians. In 1975 China produced 26 million tons of steel, and the value of its foreign trade had reached $17 billion (in 1950 it was $1.2 billion). The average factory worker earned $28 a month; the average peasant $14.

Agricultural Development

Although the Communists in 1949 immediately began an active antilandlord campaign, they at first continued the program of the New Democracy. As soon as most landlords had been tried and executed and most land redistributed, the government announced that individual ownerships was inefficient and began to collectivize, first introducing mutual aid teams and rural producers cooperatives and, by 1955, full-scale collectivization. Within two years 92 percent of the land was in collective farms.

Between 1952 and 1958 annual grain production was raised from 163 million tons to 250 million, but agricultural production growth was only 4 percent, while industrial growth was 17.6 percent.

In 1958, the Great Leap Forward was to begin and "true"

communism was to be established. The peasant was taken out of the collective and put into a commune. The objectives of this radical step are believed to have been:

1) The total mobilization of the 500,000,000 peasants into a massive human work force. The communes were approximately ten times the size of the collectives, and the workers were organized along military lines of companies, battalions, and brigades. Each person's activities were rigidly supervised.

2) An attempt to curtail both rural migration to the cities and rural unemployment, which has been an extremely serious problem.

3) The destruction of the family as the social unit. The communes were completely segregated. Children, wives, and husbands all lived in separate barracks and worked in separate battalions, and old people were assigned to "happiness homes" where they did "light" labor. Communal living was emphasized by eating, sleeping, and working in teams. Husbands and wives were allowed to be alone only at certain times of the month and for only brief periods. (This may have been an attempt to curtail the population growth as well as to break down family solidarity.)

4) A means of acquiring more capital for industrialization. Mess halls facilitated rationing, and the communes were to be self-sufficient units, producing the necessities of life and giving the unskilled worker some training in industry.

5) Another objective was the control of the ideological training of the Chinese masses. The rigid control offered excellent opportunities for indoctrination, and the worker had to take part in ideological sessions.

The communes have not proved as successful as the government hoped, but they have not yet been abandoned, although more freedoms have been allowed and incentives and private plots have been introduced. The Great Leap Forward collapsed partly because of inefficient use of manpower, loss of an incentive system, and lack of management. Grain production may have declined since 1958.

Population Statistics

Like most Asian countries, China faces a population problem. The 1953 census was 583 million people, with an annual rate of increase of 13 million. This means that by 1974 China had a population over 800 million (the Revolutionary Committee published the figure of 732 million). In comparison India had 600 million, the USSR 250 million, the U.S. 210 million. Although some attempts have been made to extend the practice of birth control, Mao believed that the greater the population, the stronger the nation.

Social Change

New railroads, highways, irrigation systems, local industries, health clinics, and "barefoot doctors" who work among the common people have certainly bettered the life of the Chinese, but again there are no definitive figures. Confucian social concepts have been discarded, and children are expected to obey the state, not their parents.

Education was seriously affected by the cultural revolution. Schools were established for officials who must attend a fourteen-week session to be cleansed of "bureaucratic habits." In 1975 only 167,000 people or 1.5 percent of secondary school graduates were admitted to universities and these had to be approved by committees of workers and peasants not by competitive examination. (In the United States 1.5 million people or 50 percent go on to higher education.) Graduates of secondary schools were sent to the country for two years of manual labor before they were allowed to go to the university.

The Communists in China, as in Russia, have employed "socialist realism" as the basis of all art. In the use of radio, newspaper, and mass organization, the Chinese revolution has surpassed most others in propaganda techniques.

Foreign Relations

The period from 1949–1954 was fundamentally one of aggressive expansion. The major examples of this policy were Korea, Tibet, and Indochina.

KOREA

By November of 1950 China had sent over a million men to fight in Korea. The motivations may have involved both fear of United States control of Korea through Japan and the need for a "cause," since China was plagued with enemies from within and without. Undoubtedly, China was closely tied with the Communists in Korea ideologically, but also Korea was considered vital to security as a necessary buffer area.

TIBET

In 1950 the Red Army invaded and took control of Tibet, which had traditionally been a part of the Chinese empire. This was not looked upon as an international affair by China, since the invasion was considered a necessary step in the reunification of the country.

INDOCHINA

China supported the Vietminh rebellion in Indochina, giving sufficient aid to tip the balance against the French. Advisers, equipment, and training facilities were made available to the Vietminh in southwest China, and a strategic railroad to the Indochina border was quickly completed.

The first sign of a shift in tactical policy came with the Korean truce on July 27, 1953, and became quite evident with the Geneva Conference. The period from 1954–1958 was not one of aggressive warfare but instead of "peaceful coexistence." There are several possible explanations for the shift in policy:

1) Aggression in Korea had resulted only in a military stalemate and was costing China important outlays of economic resources: 39 percent of the budget was spent on the military in 1950, and this was hindering internal progress.

2) Stalin's death and the de-Stalinization program may have encouraged Mao to initiate a less aggressive policy.

3) By 1955 at the Bandung Conference, it was quite evident that Asia was not only reacting to Western imperialism but also to Communist imperialism.

A conference was held in Geneva in 1954. The countries represented were Communist China, Vietnam, Cambodia, Laos, France, the United Kingdom, the United States, and the Soviet Union. The fate of Southeast Asia was determined. Korea remained divided at the thirty-eighth parallel, and elections for reunification were promised. Vietnam was temporarily divided along the seventeenth parallel, with the north going to Ho Chi Minh and the south to Bao Dai. South Vietnam, Laos, and Cambodia were not to participate in any military alliances and not to allow foreign military bases on their soil.

At the Bandung Conference in 1955 Chou En-lai announced that China would become the defender of peace, the defender of Asia. China would "seek common ground and not create divergence." China would base its new friendship on the Five Principles, which included territorial integrity and sovereignty, nonaggression, noninterference, equality and mutual benefit, and peaceful coexistence. Cultural exchange was encouraged. In 1955 alone China sent groups to twenty-four countries and received groups from thirteen.

But by 1958 China had reverted to a hard policy and an emphasis on "Stalinism." China, not Russia, was to be the leader of militant Communism throughout the world. The offshore islands, controlled by Chiang Kai-shek, were shelled, and the Tibet revolt of 1959 was crushed. That same year troops were sent into mountain areas claimed by India. In 1964 China placed further pressure on India by fanning the Indian-Pakistan controversy over Kashmir and directing attention and aid toward the Viet Cong in Vietnam. China's nuclear capacity, developed since 1964, gave it further prestige in the eyes of its neighbors.

Since 1971 with admission into the United Nations and with United States attempts to restore relations, a more moderate international stance has been taken, and China has returned to a policy of cultural exchange. Perhaps the most impressive example to date has been the Chinese Exhibition in 1973 in Paris and London of the archeological treasures uncovered since 1949.

Sino-Soviet Relations

The relations between Moscow and Peking were crucial to China between 1950 and 1960. In 1950 the Sino-Soviet Treaty was negotiated. Directed against the Japanese (and the United States), it gave military and economic aid to China. In return, joint stock companies and joint railroads in Manchuria were to be maintained. (These were terminated at the death of Stalin and control of Port Arthur was resumed by China.)

At first Soviet technicians and loans were necessary, but there was evidence that China was using its trade surplus with Russia to pay for assistance (in 1958 China exported $900 million worth of merchandise to Russia and imported $600 million) and that the loans were bankrupting the country. In technical assistance only about 80,000 advisers were sent but many Chinese were trained in Russia; military assistance in weapons came slowly; and the USSR was reluctant on the question of atomic weapons. Approximately 250 industrial projects were aided by Russian finances.

In 1958, however, the first ideological split between the two countries occurred over the issue of the communes. In 1960 there was controversy over the question of peaceful coexistence and revolutionary change. Although China agreed to an official statement of compromise, evidence of a breach and a challenge to the leadership of the Soviet Union was clear, and Russian technicians were withdrawn. By 1963 the war of words had become more and more severe. In 1969 military clashes along the Amur River and in Central Asia took place, and the Chinese began building air-raid shelters. This tension increased during the 1970s, particularly with China's invasion of Vietnam in 1979.

Sino-American Relations

From 1949 to 1972 the United States did not recognize the Communist government of China; carried on no diplomatic or trade relations; and was bound by treaty to support the Nationalist forces on Taiwan (Formosa). The U.S. was portrayed by the Chinese as a "paper tiger" whose defeat would mean the fall of imperialism.

With President Nixon's visit in 1972 China and the United States moved closer together, partial diplomatic recognition was achieved, and trade between the two countries was reestablished. But the United States is still bound by treaty to support Taiwan, and the Chinese will not establish full diplomatic relations until the United States resolves its interpretation of the Two Chinas policy.

Japan

ANCIENT AND CLASSICAL CIVILIZATIONS
660 B.C.–500 A.D.

Japan has no ancient and little classical history. By 500 A.D. it had not yet developed a mature civilization, but certain characteristics had evolved that were to influence later Japanese history. The first Japanese, probably from Korea, drove the Ainu, the aboriginal inhabitants of the islands, into the north of Japan. Although there was a certain amount of influence from Korea, Japan was geographically and culturally isolated at a time when other peoples were migrating, transmitting cultures, and intermarrying. For this reason Japan developed a uniformity not found in many countries. Its people became homogeneous—a mongoloid type with no significant additions to the blood for over a thousand years. It eventually developed a homogeneous culture as well, which remained intact until the Western occupation of Japan in 1945. Japan's isolation from the outside world made the periods of foreign contact generations of frantic borrowing, but at the same time reaction to outside influences made Japan even more determined to preserve the native elements of its culture—the emperor and the religion, Shintoism.

SHINTOISM

Little is known about the origins of the native religion of Japan. Shinto itself means *way of the spirit,* and it was originally and still is a form of pantheism, a simple faith concerned with the powers

351

of nature. Anything that is a part of nature is awe-inspiring or *kami*; a tree, or a rock—each has a spirit. It does not involve great reaches of the mind, a definite idea of the soul, or a speculative philosophy, only a strong sense of the beauty and richness of the environment.

The concept of the emperor sprang from Shintoism. The ancestor of the imperial line was believed to be the sun goddess. The emperor, therefore, was considered divine or semidivine. This theory was pursued to its fullest by the militarists of Japan in the 1930s and 1940s in order to arouse devotion and a sense of obedience in the people.

The chief sin of Shintoism is uncleanliness. Death, wounds, diseases, and lack of personal hygiene were considered not only unclean but also ungodly and could be cured only by ritualistic ceremonies. Therefore the Japanese were a very clean people, but they never developed a scientific attitude toward sanitation or medical care for their sick and wounded.

Early Shintoism did not involve ancestor worship. This was imported from China. There was no organized church as such, although there were Shinto priests. There was no concept of sin in the ethical sense, only in the ceremonial, and prayer was made outside a shrine after offerings and personal purification had taken place.

THE YAMATO CLAN AND THE CREATION OF THE EMPEROR

During the early period of Japanese history, the people who had settled on the islands lived in clans and fought among themselves. Gradually, certain clans in Kyushu began to extend their power, reached the province of Yamato, and established a central state there. According to legend, the emperor Jimmu celebrated his conquest in 660 B.C., (probably nearer the time of Christ). In order to maintain the supremacy of the Yamato sovereigns, the *Kojiki* and the *Nihon-shoki* 712-720 A.D., were compiled, recording the history of the imperial line from its mythical origins.

envoy from Korea was sent in 405 A.D. to educate the heir-apparent in the Chinese language and script. This prepared the way for the rapid absorption of Chinese culture more than a century later.

MEDIEVAL CIVILIZATION 500–1500 A.D.

It was not until 550 A.D. that Japan, through the influence of Chinese-Buddhist missionaries, became fully aware of the existence of the outside world. It was then that it began to borrow extensively from the Tang dynasty in China in hopes of creating a comparable civilization. Although the history of the medieval era from 618 to 906 A.D. is a record of this borrowing, Japan was not simply an imitator, for the remaining 600 years were spent in developing a culture that was truly Japanese. The medieval history of Japan is therefore most significant, for it was during this period that Japan developed its art, its language, and its social and political structure. National characteristics that were to make Japan unlike any other Eastern nation were also developed—its sense of conformity, its acceptance of hereditary authority, its devotion to the soldier, its ideal of self-discipline, and perhaps most important, its sense of nationalism and the superiority of the political unit over the family.

BORROWINGS FROM THE TANG DYNASTY 618–906

When Japan became aware of the brilliance of the Tang dynasty, it immediately began to send missions of specialists to investigate and bring back the glories and achievements of China. Obviously what was gained was not a real picture of China, for both distance and language changed the image. The final result was the borrowing of the forms of Chinese culture rather than the essence. This slavish imitation often led to the borrowing of things that were not suitable to Japanese society and had to be modified. The process was to be repeated in 1868 with Western culture.

The Imperial Ruler

Japan borrowed the imperial concept from China but retained the notion of the ruler as a high priest. Eventually this imperial ideal began to disappear, and although the emperor retained his title, he lost his imperial powers and became ruler in name only.

The Role of Women

Before 600 A.D. Japanese women often held important positions in society (it is even believed by some historians that many of the clans were matriarchal), but with the introduction of Confucian philosophy the position of Japanese women sank to an even lower scale than in China.

The Development of Central Government

The Japanese modeled their entire central governmental organization on that of China, including all the bureaucratic red tape and the hierarchy based on rank and scholarship. The central government was too big and too complicated for the needs of Japan, and a good example of borrowing form without essence is the fact that Japan retained bureaucratic rank without the Chinese emphasis on scholarship. In the building of Kyoto in 794, Japan imitated down to the last detail the capital city of the Tang, Ch'ang-an.

The System of Writing

Another disastrous innovation was the Chinese system of writing. Japanese could have easily been written phonetically, and a system of phonetics might have developed had not Japan adopted the Chinese characters, which were entirely unsuited, since Chinese was a monosyllabic language with no written inflections. Eventually Japan developed a system of writing that included both Chinese characters and phonetics.

The Confucian Class System

Japan also borrowed the Confucian class system but made it more inflexible and more unsuitable, for the scholar never became first in importance. The traditions of clan loyalty and hereditary rights were too strong, and in most cases scholars were given the humble clerical jobs. During the feudal era the military assumed the primary social position and retained it until after World War II.

The Arts

The one area Japan seemed capable of really profiting from was in the arts. Here Japan borrowed wholesale for a while and then perfected and developed its own style. The long horizontal scrolls of narrative are unlike any others in the world. In sculpture, Japan used a new technique in wood, and in painting an interest in humanity developed.

Buddhism

Buddhism, although Indian in origin, came to Japan from China. Japan later made its own modifications and innovations such as Zen, which stressed the virtues of mental concentration and physical self-discipline.

THE LOSS OF POWER BY THE COURT AND THE DUAL SYSTEM OF GOVERNMENT

The Fujiwara Clan

A dual system of government in which the emperor held the power in name but someone else held it in fact developed when the Fujiwara family won complete mastery over the imperial family through intermarriage. A daughter of the Fujiwara clan would marry the emperor and then as soon as a son was born persuade her husband to abdicate. Naturally, the head of the Fujiwara family would then act as regent for the small boy.

The Fujiwaras retained a monopoly of all high court posts from the seventh century to the early nineteenth century. But the court did not always retain the power in Japan.

The Military Aristocracy

In the countryside noble families and Buddhist monasteries became autonomous centers of authority. By the eleventh century real power passed to a rising military aristocracy. Tax-free estates grew up as the emperor had to give away more and more land in hopes of gaining loyal support against disruptive clans. When knights had to be called in to settle disputes between court factions in the capital, the beginning of military rule in Japan was not far away.

The Shogunate

Two military clans, the Taira and the Minamoto, began to compete for power in Japan around 1150. The Taira defeated the Minamoto in 1160 and settled in the capital, taking over the position of prime minister and controlling the government until 1185. The Minamoto retaliated by crushing the Taira in a war that lasted from 1180 to 1185. Minamoto Yoritomo, leader of the clan, did not attempt to control Kyoto, the capital; instead he built his capital in Kamakura and, assuming the title of *shogun* (generalissimo), created the first military dictatorship in Japan. This was the beginning of 700 years of rule by warrior aristocrats.

But even the shogun was unable to create an effective central government for long, for in 1219 the Minamoto line ended, and the Hojo clan became regents of Japan, ruling through a puppet shogun. In other words, the emperor was controlled by the Fujiwara, the government was controlled by the shogun, and the shogun was controlled by the Hojo regents. This was more than dual control: it was a tripartite government.

FEUDALISM AND THE MILITARY TRADITION

The Minamoto Period

The ethical or chivalric code was first established. The concept of a warrior's duty to his master was introduced. This is significant, for it also implied that there was a loyalty greater than that owed to one's family.

Zen Buddhism was created and became practically an official religion under the Ashikaga.

During this period the custom of suicide, of self-inflicted death preferable to capture, of death better than disgrace, was developed.

The Mongol Invasions

The failure of the Mongol invasions in 1281 further increased the prestige of the warrior class but revealed the growing dependence of the shogunate upon this military element in society.

The Ashikaga Shogunate   1338-1615

This period was essentially feudal for after defeating the Minamoto, the Ashikaga clan was never able to achieve central control of Japan. From 1467 on there were constant civil wars and shifting feudal allegiances. Feudal lords known as *daimyo* rose to power, and eventually war led to the financial ruin of the court aristocracy. (One emperor was reduced to selling calligraphy in order to keep himself alive.)

Although this was a period of political chaos, it was also an era of great art in the form of architecture, painting, and drama.

Trade and manufacturing flourished, and it was a time of migration
to the Philippines and Southeast Asia and contact with Europeans
through Christian missionaries. (By 1580 there were approximately
150,000 Japanese Christians and in the early 1600s twice that
number.)

MODERN CIVILIZATION   1500 to the Present

*The modern history of Japan should be divided into four major
periods: the first from 1615 to 1868, the Tokugawa regime; the
second from the Meiji Restoration in 1868 through World War II;
the third from the beginning of the occupation to 1952; and the
fourth from 1952 to the present. During each of these periods change
in Japan was overwhelming.*

THE TOKUGAWA REGIME   1615–1868

Japan ended the medieval period in some ways more modern
than it was to be for the next 250 years. It did not have political
unity, but it had witnessed a lively cultural development, an expanding economy, and a growing sense of its own importance in relations
with the outside world. In 1615, however, the Tokugawa Shogunate
claimed control of Japan and attempted, until its downfall in 1868,
to halt the expansion of Japan, to close the door to foreign influence,
and to maintain the domestic status quo.

The Rise to Power of the Tokugawas

The story of the success of the Tokugawas was, of course, a
military one. A daimyo by the name of Oda Nobunaga seized the
capital and most of central Japan. After his death, his general
Hideyoshi defeated the Satsuma clan in 1587 and by 1590 controlled
most of eastern and northern Japan. In 1597 Hideyoshi died, and
Tokugawa Ieyasu, one of his vassals, destroyed his family and took

over control of the rest of Japan.

Ieyasu's main purpose was to keep his own family in power and to maintain political stability. He thus created a system that remained almost unchanged for two and a half centuries.

The System of Control

A system of checks on and controls over the population was established. An extensive and efficient secret police patrolled Japan, and members of important, if unrealiable, families were held as hostages in Edo (Tokyo), the capital. The inner circle of people around Edo were those whose loyalty could be depended upon, and the outer circle were kept under constant surveillance and strict control.

The Confucian class system was rearranged and strictly maintained: first was the warrior or the *samurai*; second, the peasant; third, the artisan; and fourth, the merchant. No one could leave his employment and no one could change his class by law. The peasant was forced to hand in his arms, and the sword could only be worn by the samurai. The system was entirely artificial and real wealth was still in the merchant class, but it was an effective means of maintaining the status quo.

The warrior code of *bushido,* the unwritten ethical code of the samurai, was reestablished to control the warless warriors.

Japan was closed to the rest of the world. Foreign trade was eliminated, except for a restricted Dutch port; Japanese were not allowed to travel abroad; and those who lived overseas were not allowed to return. Christianity was outlawed, and many Japanese Christians were martyred. Punishments for Christians who would not renounce their faith were severe, including crucifixion. Priests, however, were exposed and often banished. The dramatic end to Christianity in Japan came in 1637 when an economic revolt led by Christians near Nagasaki took place and 37,000 were slaughtered.

The Downfall of the Tokugawas

The new economic system was probably one of the most important causes for the downfall of the Tokugawas, for as the nation began to build a more complex economic system with exchange based on money instead of rice, the feudal landowners and the samurai classes went further and further into debt to their social inferiors, the merchants. Many of the poorer samurai were among those who led the opposition to the Tokugawas.

The opening of Japan by U.S. Commodore Matthew Perry in 1854 proved the Tokugawa regime militarily impotent. By 1858 treaties were concluded that allowed foreigners permanent residence at five ports and at Osaka and Edo, and unrestricted trade relations were sanctioned.

The samurai of the outer circle were the most important cause of the Tokugawa fall from power. For two and a half centuries they had been forced to recognize the regime, but now there was hope, for the coming of the West had proved that the Tokugawas were vulnerable to attack.

In 1867 a bloodless revolution took place when the new shogun voluntarily surrendered the rule of the country to the emperor. Until 1868 there was some fighting between Tokugawa and imperial forces, but 700 years of military rule had ended.

JAPAN BECOMES A MODERN NATION   1868–1945

The imperial revival or the Meiji Restoration of 1868 ushered Japan into the modern world. The contrast between Japan's reaction to the threat of Western control and China's reaction is staggering. The explanation for Japan's much more rapid progress in modernizing the country and in driving out foreign control is found in a combination of two factors. One, the Meiji government was politically unified and efficiently administered by young and talented leaders, while the Manchu dynasty, after 200 years of strong rule, was decaying; and two, Japan had had a tradition of borrowing in the past, recognizing the superiority of other nations and quickly imitating them, while China had for centuries thought of itself as the center of the world without equal.

The Meiji Restoration   1868

The imperial restoration, named after the young Emperor Meiji, did not really restore authority to the throne. The system of dual control continued, and the leadership of the new regime was actually taken over by a group of young samurai.

The altering of the political and social structure of Japan was the first thing the Meiji Restoration accomplished. The feudal system was eliminated by decree in 1871 when an imperial edict abolishing all fiefs and transferring all taxes to the national government was proclaimed. The samurai were deprived of their economic and military privileges. In 1873 they were forced to commute their pensions to money bonds, and in the same year universal military conscription was passed by the government. In 1876 the samurai could no longer wear their swords, the final act that was to make them ordinary citizens. Obviously, the samurai fought this change. The Satsuma Rebellion of 1877 was the last attempt by the warriors to reassert their historic position. They were defeated by the government's peasant conscript army.

Political parties were formed by the discontented samurai who were not in power. The Liberal Party, formed by Itagaki, and the Progressive Party, formed by Okuma, were nevertheless soon destroyed by the government either by political suppression or by splitting their party leadership or the party itself. The result was that from the very beginning no strong political parties existed to oppose the government in Japan.

The Meiji Constitution (1889), written by Prime Minister Itu, was given as a gift to the people from the emperor. It in no way altered the structure of power, for the *diet* (parliament), consisting of a House of Peers (appointed by the emperor and elected by the nobility) and a House of Representatives (elected by the political parties), had very little actual power. Real authority remained in the hands of the cabinet or the obligarchy.

The early Meiji period was an age of reform. Many significant changes and additions were made to Japanese society.

1) The Japanese army was patterned after the German system and the navy after the British. The army and the navy were in theory to remain independent of politics.

2) One of the most important and influential reforms was put through in 1871, when education was made compulsary for nine years. Because of this reform Japan became one of the first nations to have a literate population. By borrowing from the French and thus establishing a highly centralized and controlled system that was geared to the needs of the nation, the government had at its disposal a powerful means of molding public opinion and persuading the populace to accept whatever policies it decreed and whatever image of the outside world was deemed politically advisable. It was for this reason that the Japanese went into World War II with little notion of the real strength of the United States.

3) Every Western nation contributed its share to the reforms and innovations of the Meiji: The United States, its postal service and its notion of public education; Great Britain, its cotton mills and mint, its railroad system and its navy; France, its administrative and educational systems and its criminal code; Germany, its pattern for local government and its constitution and cabinet system as well as its army; Italy, its sculpture and painting.

4) Unlike China, Japan began a rapid program of industrialization, with the expressed objective of building a modern nation. The government immediately began forced industrialization, and the necessary capital was found not only by taxing the peasant but also through a sudden demand on the world market for silk. When the government decided to sell its industry to individual citizens, manufacturing soon fell into the hands of a few wealthy families who formed monopolies known as *zaibatsu*. (The Mitsui family, for example, became so wealthy and so powerful that it employed 1,800,000 people in Japan and another 1,000,000 overseas.)

Foreign Relations

The Sino-Japanese War   1894-1895

The cause of this war is open to debate. Some historians believe that political leaders precipitated the war in an effort to stop political opposition at home; others believe that it was entirely the rivalry between China and Japan over Korea; and still others say that Japan was attempting to show its strength to the outside world.

RESULTS OF THE WAR

1) A resounding Japanese victory.

2) The Treaty of Shimonasiki, 1895: Korea was declared to be independent, and Japan was given Formosa, the Pescadores, and a huge indemnity. The Liotung peninsula was given back to China as a result of Western pressure, and this inflamed Japanese nationalism.

3) Japan was recognized as an important nation. By 1899 all occidentals were once again subject to Japanese law, and in 1900 Japan fought with the West against the Boxers in China. Perhaps the most significant proof of Japan's importance was the Anglo-Japanese Treaty of 1902. Not only did this break Britain's own isolation, but it also signified to the world that Japan had become a westernized nation. By 1911 Japan had also succeeded in terminating all tariffs imposed by treaties with the Western world. China did not eliminate its fixed tariffs until 1933 and did not eliminate extraterritoriality until 1943.

The Russo-Japanese War   1904-1905

This was definitely a conflict waged for imperialistic motives. Japan wanted to prevent Russian control of Korea, and most nations supported Japan (the United States and Great Britain provided money). In 1904 Japan attacked Port Arthur and in the Battle of Mukden in 1905 won overwhelming victory and initiated negotiations for the end of hostilities.

RESULTS OF THE WAR

1) The Portsmouth Treaty, 1905: Japan gained rights in

southern Manchuria and the southern half of Sakhalin Island, as well as recognition of its position in Korea, which it annexed in 1910.

2) The war amazed the world, for here was an Eastern nation, a small island, that had defeated the largest Western nation. To much of the world this was proof of what industrialization could do, and it was proof to non-Westerners that the white man was not as superior as he tended to assume.

World War I

Japan was on the side of the Allies, doing no fighting but profiting by taking over property, mining, and land controlled by the Germans in China. In 1915 Japan presented the weak Chinese government with 21 demands, which included a 99-year lease on Port Arthur instead of a twenty-five year one; control of industry and mines in Manchuria; and Japanese military advisers in China.

By the Treaty of Versailles, Japan gained the German Pacific islands as mandates and a seat on the League of Nations' council.

The Road to Totalitarism

The Liberal Era of the 1920s

From 1890 to 1918 the clans of Choshu, Sutsuma, and Hizen had dominated the government, but during the 1920s political parties had a chance to share in the government of Japan, for the old oligarchs had died out and the army had lost some ground for the first time because of a costly failure in Siberia during the Russian Revolution and also because of the general world attitude toward disarmament. Hara Kei (1918–1921) was the first party premier.

In 1925 a universal suffrage act was put into effect and in 1924 the army and the navy were reduced in size; earlier in 1922, at the Washington Naval Conference, Japan had agreed to limit her growing navy on a 5–5–3 ratio with the United States and Great Britain.

Signs of Change

The liberalism of the 1920s was for the most part limited to the cities. Although the army was reduced, ROTC programs were increased. A strict Peace Preservation Law designed to control thought by complete censorship of the press was passed, and prime ministers were regularly assassinated. The military was still immune from civilian and political control and in actual fact held a veto power over the cabinet. The transition to militarism was not unexpected, for Japan had had seven centuries of rule by the sword, her oligarchs were all ex-samurai, and there was a history of devotion to the military and the emperor

The army became more and more extremist and broke into two factions:

1) The Control Faction made up of high-ranking officers advocated a reconstruction of society along totalitarian lines and expansion into China and Southeast Asia. This group eventually won control of Japan.

2) The Imperial Way Faction consisted of younger, lower-ranking officers who were against capitalism, against parliament and political parties, and for direct and immediate action and expansion into Russia.

Outside Influence

DISILLUSIONMENT WITH DEMOCRACY

There was no disarmament, and democratic governments seemed to be failing all over the world. The greatest democracy of them all, the United States, had deeply insulted the Japanese when in 1924 it abrogated the "Gentlemen's Agreement" (by which Japan had agreed to limit Japanese workers immigrating to the U.S.) and officially barred all Asiatic migration into the country. Fascist totalitarian regimes, on the other hand, were proving quite successful, and also friendly toward the island nation.

THE DEPRESSION OF 1929

The collapse of international trade started Japan's own depression. A small country like Japan, which was completely dependent on the outside world for many raw materials as well as for a market for its goods, was entirely at the mercy of the tariff policies of other nations. Japan's price level fell 35 percent as compared with 27 percent in the United States. Its export trade decreased 27½ percent, and the export of raw silk fell by 50 percent in 1930. The price of rice fell drastically, and this ruined both peasant and landlord.

THE CHANGES TAKING PLACE IN CHINA

The rise of the KMT (Nationalists) posed a serious threat to Japan's control and interests in Manchuria.

The Manchurian Incident   1931

The military of Japan decided to take matters into their own hands and start their own imperialistic war. They did not have the backing of the civilian government, and the fact that they were able to get away with it proved the weakness of the party government of Japan and led the country into a war that was to last fourteen years.

In September 1931 Japanese army units, stationed in Manchuria to protect Japanese interests there, started out on their own conquest of all of Manchuria. The pretext for the Manchurian Incident was a trumped-up charge that Chinese agents had attempted to blow up a railway line.

Early in 1932 the Lytton Commission was sent by the League of Nations to investigate the incident and sharply criticized Japan's actions, but it had no power to do anything; and Japan's answer was simply to withdraw from the League (establishing a precedent that Italy, Russia, and Germany soon followed).

The End of Civilian Government   1932–1936

After the prime minister and various members of the cabinet had been assassinated in May 1932 by radical members of the army, party government collapsed. A compromise national government was established in which the military element increased and the party element slowly dwindled in number throughout the 1930s.

The showdown between military and civilian elements in the cabinet came on February 26, 1936, when young officers of the Imperial Way Faction mutinied and martial law was declared in Tokyo by the Control Faction. This was followed by a series of trials in which 13 officers and 4 civilians were executed. The significance of the event was the final intimidation of the population and their realization that only the military could control the military. In 1940 all parties were disbanded and the Imperial Rule Assisting Association, which was a military dictatorship, emerged. In 1941 General Tojo Hideki became prime minister, ending any pretense that the government was not a military dictatorship.

The China Incident
This was war, although undeclared, against China. In July 1937 Japanese troops overran the northern cities of China and established their control. A long and drawn-out battle was waged at Hankow, and finally in October the Japanese succeeded in capturing the city. The Japanese then began their move toward Chungking.

WORLD WAR II   1941–1945

At first Japan did not intend to go to war against the West. The outbreak of war in Europe seemed a welcome event, for Japan had joined Germany in the Anti-Comintern Pact in 1936 and Germany was certainly keeping the rest of Europe's minds off Japanese affairs. The surrender of France in 1940 gave the Japanese the opportunity to gobble up French Indochina; they had signed a neutrality pack with the Soviet Union, which meant they did not have to worry about their Siberian flank.

Why Japan Went to War

There are many possible explanations for the decision to enter the war. For one thing, the United States refused to condone Japanese aggression into Indochina; the U.S. froze all Japanese assets in the United States in July 1941 and put an economic embargo on Japan as well. For another, the Tripartite Pact of October 1940 in which Germany, Japan, and Italy agreed to aid one another if attacked by a power not involved in the European or

Chinese conflicts appeared to protect Japan against United States technological superiority. The military was faced with a costly stalemate in the China war and needed further victories to sustain their political position at home and their aggressive policy abroad. The Japanese were also victims of their own propaganda, which was aimed at convincing them that they were superior to the Western world.

When Tojo became prime minister in 1941, the Japanese government became committed to a policy of military action against the United States if diplomacy should fail. War at this point was almost inevitable, for neither the Americans nor the Japanese would yield over the issue of Japan's withdrawal from China, which the United States insisted upon before it would unfreeze Japanese assets or lift the embargo.

The War Itself

Pearl Harbor, December 7, 1941, was followed by amazing Japanese successes against the British in Singapore and the Malay peninsula. In 1942 the Philippines fell, followed closely by the Dutch East Indies and most of Burma. The main Japanese objective was to secure control of a wide perimeter around the home islands and to carve out an empire in Southeast Asia. The plan failed, partly because the Japanese were too successful in their first steps and attempted to expand the perimeter. They struck at the Coral Sea in the spring of 1942 and were defeated, and then at Midway in mid-1942 they lost their crucial aircraft carrier force. After this battle they never again regained the initiative and were on the defensive. They also failed in their efforts to establish an economic empire in Southeast Asia. The very forces of nationalism, which they had deliberately set in motion, turned against them.

Defeat and Surrender

In July 1944 Koiso replaced Tojo as prime minister and constructed the Supreme War Council in an attempt to harmonize political, economic, and military elements. The council consisted of the foreign minister, the prime minister, the ministers of the army and navy, and the chiefs of staff of the army and navy. The defeats of 1945 brought the eighty-year-old Admiral Suzuki to power, and he became a wavering advocate of peace.

On August 6 the first atomic bomb fell on Hiroshima; on August 8 Russia declared war on Japan; on August 9 Nagasaki was hit with the second A-bomb. On August 9 the Supreme War Council was deadlocked three to three on whether or not to accept the Allied terms of surrender. The army minister and the two chiefs of staff voted against it. That night Premier Suzuki called another meeting of the War Council and dramatically called upon Emperor Hirohito to vote. The emperor voted for acceptance of the Allied terms of unconditional surrender. The United States tacitly agreed to allow the emperor to remain on the throne.

Although the military extremists still did their best to change the decision, they were unable to do so, since most of the cabinet was behind it and all of the nobility backed the emperor's decision. Consequently, if the militarists had attempted a coup, there would have been no one they could have put in Hirohito's place.

On August 15 the surrender proclamation was issued, and on September 2, on board the *U.S.S. Missouri* in Tokyo Bay, Japan formally surrendered.

THE UNITED STATES OCCUPATION OF JAPAN 1945–1952

From September 1945 to April 1952, Japan was occupied by the United States. The aims of the occupation were to demilitarize by disarming and punishing, to decentralize, and to democratize. What the military occupation accomplished was one of the most profound revolutions in the history of the twentieth century. Nor could this have been done without the cooperation of the Japanese people. When, in August 1945, Emperor Hirohito announced that the Japanese should unite their "total strength to be devoted to the construction for the future, cultivate the ways of rectitude, foster nobility of spirit, and work with resolution" in order to "enhance the innate glory of the imperial state and keep pace with the progress of the world," the Japanese obeyed the imperial mandate and cooperated with their conquerors in a fashion unique in history.

Punishment and reform were accomplished between 1945 and 1948; reconstruction was begun between 1948 and 1950; and revision as well as reversal took place after 1950, when Japan suddenly became the friend and ally of the West and not the enemy.

Thirty thousand men occupied Japan, headed by General Douglas MacArthur. The group of men who had fought under MacArthur at Bataan and the General himself were really responsible for the ruthless but usually successful reforms.

Punishment and Disarmament

Demilitarization was one of the failures, for the repatriation of Japanese troops and civilians from overseas, the destruction of major industries with war potential, and the dismemberment of the empire led to serious economic problems in Japan. Those who had led Japan to war were tried for war crimes by an international tribunal (1946–1948). This did not accomplish its purpose, for Japan had no fascist party nor definite organization that had led it into war, and given the dual nature of the Japanese government, it was difficult to pinpoint responsibility.

Key Reforms

The Constitution

The constitution was written by MacArthur's staff with the help of Japanese advisers and was constructed and presented to the Japanese people in much the same manner as the Meiji constitution. There are five major differences between the Meiji constitution and the MacArthur constitution:

1) Redefinition of the emperor's position—he was no longer divine and this was publicly announced by Hirohito himself.

2) Transfer of basic political powers out of the hands of the oligarchy into the hands of the Diet; under the new constitution, both houses are elected, with the prime minister selected from the Diet. A party government based upon parliamentary majority was created.

3) For the first time citizens were protected by a bill of rights, which included academic freedom, equal education for all, rights of labor, and women's rights, as well as freedom of speech, religion, and so on.

4) The judicial system was altered and made independent of the executive. A supreme court was modeled after that of the United States.

5) Article 9 of the constitution called for the renunciation of war and made a standing army illegal. This was reinterpreted so that a police force and then a self-defense force were considered constitutional. In 1975 the self-defense force had 232,000 troops and over 1000 jets.

The Economy

Land reform was one of the most drastic and successful of all the reforms put through by the occupation. All nonresident farmers had to sell their land, except for 2.5 acres, to elected local land commissions, who then sold the land to tenant farmers at fixed prices. The purchaser had thirty years in which to pay. Rent was fixed at 25 percent of the rice crop. The results of this reform were that 5 million acres changed hands and that only 10 percent of Japan's farmers remained tenants, while approximately 80 percent had been before.

In 1946 a trade union law was passed that gave people the right to join unions, bargain collectively, and strike.

An attempt was made to dissolve the large family industrial monopolies of Japan. Their assets were frozen and a liquidation commission was established. This was one of the reforms that did not succeed; the *zaibatsu* reconsolidated themselves, and their financial power became greater than ever before.

Educational Reform

An effort was made to decentralize control of education, to purge teachers and textbooks, and to revise the curriculum. The educational reform did not really succeed in decentralization of the school system; the local boards are now appointed by the mayors of Japan. But education is no longer a tool of the state.

Peace with Japan

In 1949 the United States decided to sign a separate peace with Japan. The Japanese were hesitant to accept this for it meant taking sides in the cold war. They feared the Russians because in February 1950 the USSR had signed the Sino-Soviet Treaty, which was directed against Japan. In June 1950 the Korean incident began, and Japan's fears of invasion from the mainland increased. In August the government announced that it would choose the West rather than remain neutral in the cold war.

In 1951 at San Francisco, a meeting of all nations involved in the war against Japan was called to sign a treaty of peace. On September 8, 1951, forty-nine nations signed the treaty (China, India, and Burma did not attend the meeting; the USSR came but did not sign), and the United States concluded a security pact with Japan. Japanese independence and full sovereignty were granted on April 28, 1952. On April 29, 1952, Japan signed a separate peace with Taiwan. The USSR peace declaration was not agreed upon until 1956, after a bitter struggle between 1951 and 1955, during which time Russia vetoed Japan's entrance into the UN.

JAPAN   1952 to the Present

Social and Cultural Changes

One of the greatest changes between prewar and postwar Japan was social mobility. Equal education (Japan is almost 100 percent literate), destruction of wealth during the war, the changed attitude toward superiority, and the weakening of family control have all contributed to this.

Intellectually Japan has changed. Widespread devotion to pacifism and internationalism is found among the intellectuals. Radicalism is also prevalent. Although there is historic fear and dislike of Russia, there is still a great deal of admiration for the Chinese, and although less than one-third of the people vote socialist or Communist, support for the left may be as high as 90 percent among the intellectuals.

Another major change has been urbanization. An expanding economy and a small population growth produced a labor shortage; farm labor was reduced from 50 percent in 1945 to less than 20 percent by 1970. By 1972 one out of every four people lived in the Tokyo-Osaka area.

Economic Growth

Japan made an amazing economic recovery after the war. Its population problem was acute with the addition of 6 million Japanese from abroad and a birthrate of more than a million a year. The government successfully controlled the problem by legalizing abortion and maintaining offices of information on birth control throughout the country.

By the end of the occupation, production in industry was above the prewar peak of 1934–1936 and continued to rise at an unprecedented rate until the mid-1970s. The Korean War caused a boom that made it possible for Japan to accumulate capital, buy new machinery, and raise its standard of living.

Japan was dependent from 1946–1963 on aid of $4.8 billion from the United States, but by 1970 it had the third highest GNP in the world. Japan's per capita income rose from $146 in 1951 to $395 in 1960 to over $2000 in 1972. (In relation to other industrial countries, however, this is fairly low.)

The oil crisis in 1973 (80 percent of Japan's oil comes from the Middle East) combined with staggering inflation has emphasized Japan's dependence on imports. Its rate of growth which was

11 percent in 1973 dropped as low as 2.6 percent in 1974; and Japan experienced a trade deficit for the first time since 1968. But in 1977 exports exceeded imports by $9 billion.

Japan's greatest problem, however, is pollution. According to Edwin Reischauer, it is as "if half the population of the United States and one-fourth of its industry had been crammed into the single state of California."

The Political Scene

Japan is the only country outside the European heritage to have created what appears to be a stable democracy, but its government as yet has not been totally tested by either economic or international crises.

In 1947 the two conservative parties—the Liberals and the Democrats—were so opposed to one another that the Democrats went so far as to join with the Socialists in a coalition that could only fail.

The leader of the Liberal Party, Yoshida Shigeru, became prime minister again in 1948 and retained power through 1954. Yoshida was the ideal man for the post during the occupation years, for he had been against the rise of the military in the 1930s; he had refused to be ambassador to Washington because of Japan's Manchurian policies; and he had been an advocate of peace during World War II (he was imprisoned for two months for his attempts).

In 1955 the left and right wings of the Socialist Party joined, and in response the two conservative parties merged as the Liberal-Democratic Party (LDP). Between 1952 and 1960 the conservative vote declined and the Socialist vote increased. Ironically this was partly a reflection of the LDP's success in industrializing Japan (fewer farmers and a bigger urban labor force). The Socialists during the period resorted to violence over such issues as:

1) the creation of a military defense force;

2) centralization of education;

3) the United States Security Treaty. In 1960 the treaty was revised to be more favorable to Japan, but the Socialists wanted it discontinued altogether.

Although the conservatives continued to lose votes after 1960, relative to the Socialists, who were again split, they have maintained their strength. The Communist party, however, has been on the increase since 1969.

Prime Ministers of Japan

Yoshida	1946–1947	Liberal
Katayama	1947–1948	Socialist coalition
Yoshida	1948–1954	Liberal
Hatoyama	1954–1956	Liberal-Democrat
Ishibashi	1956–1957	Liberal-Democrat
Kishi	1957–1960	Liberal-Democrat
Ikeda	1960–1964	Liberal-Democrat
Sato	1964–1972	Liberal-Democrat
Tanaka	1972–1974	Liberal-Democrat
Miki	1974–1976	Liberal-Democrat
Fukuda	1976–	Liberal-Democrat

The International Scene

Relations with the United States

Japan imports more from the United States than any other country, and since the end of the 1960s the U.S. has become Japan's biggest customer. Japanese-United States relations were seriously strained in 1971 when the U.S. placed a 10 percent surcharge on all imports and devalued the dollar by allowing it to float on the world market and when the U.S. introduced a major change in its China policy without first consulting Japan. Relations have improved since Okinawa was returned by the United States to Japan in 1972.

Relations with Asia and the Soviet Union

Japan slowly reestablished relations with Southeast Asia but it was a long uphill battle against resentment and fear (not until 1965 was trade with South Korea reestablished). By 1972, 25.4 percent of Japan's trade was with the non-Communist countries of Asia. Japan's favorable balance of trade in Southeast Asia has caused anti-Japanese feeling to appear again.

In September 1972 Japan normalized relations with China, although some trade had been conducted before this, and in 1978 the two countries signed a treaty of peace and friendship. Japan's relations with the USSR have always been cautious, but Japan agreed to give technological assistance in Siberia and hopes for the return of the Kuril Islands that the Soviet Union occupied following World War II.

Southeast Asia

ANCIENT, CLASSICAL, AND MEDIEVAL CIVILIZATIONS

To talk about Southeast Asia as a whole is not as superficial as speaking of Africa as an entity. During the period before the coming of the West in 1500, China (and Confucianism and Mahayana Buddhism) conquered Vietnam, and the two proselytizing faiths—Hinayana Buddhism and Islam—spread from India into Cambodia, Ceylon, Laos, Malaya, Burma, Indonesia, and even as far as the Philippines. In parts of Southeast Asia, therefore, there is a cultural unity as well as an incredible diversity.

Throughout history Southeast Asia has been the scene of repeated cultural and military invasions: the Indian, the Chinese, and the Arab during the early periods; the Western European, the Japanese, and the American in the modern era. The most remarkable aspect of the early infiltrations is that China played such a relatively minor role, compared to the part it would play in the twentieth century.

Until well into the medieval period, Southeast Asian areas remained in small tribal groups, often at war among themselves and sometimes under the political domination of the empires to the north. The Southeast Asian style of life was never completely smothered by the Indian and Chinese: totemism continued and women were never reduced to the status of those in India and China.

BUDDHISM

Although Buddhism originated in India, its pure and original form (see p. 285) is found today only in Southeast Asia. The aspect of Buddhism that had the greatest impact was the development of monasteries. Buddhism became a monastic religion because the aim of the believer was to detach himself from life. The monk's main function is to serve as an example of the Buddhist way of life. Simplicity is his aim. Most are celibate, and their only possessions are a robe, an alms bowl, a needle, a string of 108 beads, a razor, and a filter to strain insects out of water. Unlike the Christian monk they do no manual labor and they can eat only before noon and this food must be begged for. For this reason, they have proved to be an economic drain in Southeast Asia (particularly in Burma and Thailand).

MALAYA

The Malay peninsula was settled by peoples of Malay stock, but two groups of people were believed to have been there first— the Negritos and the Sakai.

Like most of Southeast Asia, Malaya was subject to Indian influence at the beginning of the Christian era. The Indians were primarily traders, priests, and scholars—not conquerors—and a Malay-Hindu upper group was established and a state formed.

In the eleventh century Islam arrived, and the Malayan states became sultanates. Some sultans were vassals of other sultans, and all paid tribute to China or were controlled by Indonesian principalities (primarily in the fourteenth century). Malacca, founded in 1403 by a refugee from Malaya, became the center of Moslem influence.

THE PHILIPPINES

Before the coming of the Spanish and Portuguese, the Philippine Islands (a group of 7000 islands, its two largest being Luzon and Mindanao) had been controlled by a number of Malay principalities which were absolute monarchies whose subjects ranged from free peoples to slaves acquired in wars with neighboring principalities. Islam reached only the southern island of Mindanao (which was to lead to serious separatist movements in modern times).

CAMBODIA

The descendants of the Cambodians were the Khmers, a civilization ruled by god-kings who controlled what is today Cambodia, Laos, and the southern part of Vietnam (until 1757). Unlike the northern Vietnamese, the Cambodians (and Laotians) were influenced by Buddhism from India.

THAILAND (SIAM)

Thailand's people, the Thais, originally from Laos, intermixed with Khmers and by the eleventh century had established an independent state. In the fourteenth century the Mongol conquests in China led to heavy Chinese immigration into Siam and the establishment of a Chinese-dominated government in 1351. This government was an absolute monarchy. As in China the land was divided into provinces and ministries; there was no nobility; and the monarch appointed all offices of state and disposed of officials who did not suit him. Labor, taxes, and conscription were required of all subjects, but Chinese influence was only temporary. The Siamese government was subject to attacks from all sides, and in 1767 the capital was destroyed by Burmese invaders. Reunification followed, then dethronement of the monarch, and in 1782 the house of Chakkri was established with its capital at Bangkok.

BURMA

Burma, like other areas, was a conglomeration of tribes and

ethnic groups—the Karen tribes in lower Burma, the Shan tribes in the mountain plateaus, the Chin and Kachin tribes on the Indian-Tibetan borders. A Sino-Tibetan tribe, the Mons, ruled the greatest section of Burma before the eleventh century.

At the beginning of the Christian era the Indian merchant arrived in Burma. His faith, Hinayana Buddhism, the Pali script (derived from Sanskrit), as well as his customs, his art, and architecture were borrowed by the Burmese.

In the eleventh century the first kingdom of Burma was established. The many ethnic groups were unified under a Sino-Tibetan dynasty, the Pagan. The Pagan dynasty was destroyed by Mongol invasions from China.

On and off from 1287 to the middle of the eighteenth century, Burma's independence was challenged by invasions from Siam and China, but lasting Chinese influence was negligible. The military flavor of the current Burmese government is part of this heritage.

INDONESIA

The group of islands (the Larger Sunda Islands of Borneo, Sumatra, Java, Madina, and the Celebes; the Lesser Sunda islands; the Moluccas; and the island of New Guinea) known as Indonesia or the Spice Islands had witnessed two waves of Malay immigration that destroyed the tribal Negrito types on the islands.

In the eighth century the Indians came to the archipelago, first to Java, setting up their princely states, then to Sumatra. Two migrations of Indians seem to have come, one establishing Hinduism in the interior of Java and the other, Buddhism in the coastal areas.

In the twelfth century merchants from Persia, Arabia, and India arrived for the purpose of acquiring pepper from Sumatra and spices from the Moluccas. With the traders came Islam, and this became the dominant religion of the area.

In the fourteenth century Java, an agricultural state, gained control of the coastal trading states and established the empire of Majapahit. This was the first time that the islands were under one government. But the empire lost control over its vassal states, and the division between the agricultural inland areas and trading coast made it easier for the Dutch to gain control in the 1600s.

VIETNAM (ANNAM)

In 111 B.C. the Han dynasty of China annexed northern Vietnam (Annam) and this area was actually a part of the Chinese empire until 939 A.D., adopting its writing system, political institutions, Confucian philosophy, and eventually Mahayana Buddhism. Now and then China tried to reassert its control of the area but the Vietnamese fought against it, and Vietnam was generally only a tributary nation.

The southern part of Vietnam (the kingdom of Champa) was originally influenced by Indonesia and was only gradually defeated and absorbed by the north. By 1471 the north had virtual control of the south.

Buddhism played a less significant role in northern Vietnam than it did elsewhere since it was never allowed to grow into a power independent from the state.

MODERN CIVILIZATION   1500 to the Present

At the beginning of the modern era Southeast Asia was slowly brought under Western control; with the exception of Siam, the countries became colonies of the European powers. By the time total domination was established and effective economic exploitation begun, World War I had arrived and with it demands by Asians for independence. The idea of nationalism was a Western gift to Southeast Asia and was further intensified by the ideals of the war itself. Economic expansion, caused by the war, strained the Southeast Asian economy and led to further resentment on the part of the native-born against foreign control as well as the Chinese or Indian middleman. Throughout the period from World War I to World

War II Europe spent its energies in maintaining control of its colonies, but World War II brought drastic change in Southeast Asia. The Japanese occupied the areas under the slogan "Asia for the Asiatics." The Vichy French cooperated with the Japanese and further lowered European prestige. An Asiatic power, Japan, succeeded in driving the Westerners out, thus convincing Southeast Asia that it could be done. At the end of the war the withdrawal of the Japanese forces created a temporary power vacuum into which nationalist leaders stepped. By the time the Europeans returned, they had to face organized national resistance, and by 1955 almost all Southeast Asia was free. The great exception was the situation in Vietnam which was not resolved until 1975.

WESTERN DOMINATION

The Philippines under Spain

The 1521 Magellan arrived in the Philippines, and between 1556 and 1571 the Spanish established their rule of the islands. The Spanish created not only a new ruling class but also brought the Philippines into the Western cultural tradition, establishing Western law and the Christian faith. (The Philippines are 80 percent Catholic.) The area was ruled, however, as an appendage to the Spanish colonies in Central America, and it was not until 1862 that six ports were opened up to free trade. The opening of the ports led to prosperity for the Filipinos but increased dissatisfaction with Spanish rule, for they were still under strict political and cultural control.

Movements for Independence

José Rizal y Mercado (1869–1896), who had studied abroad, created the Liga Filipina in 1892. The organization demanded liberal political institutions and more educational facilities. Mercado was arrested, deported, and finally executed after his involvement in the Cuban Revolution of 1896.

With Mercado's arrest the Philippine nationalist movement

became more radical. Under the leadership of Emilio Aguinaldo, fighting broke out against the Spanish, and in 1897 a truce was negotiated but no reforms followed.

In 1898, during the Spanish-American War, Aguinaldo helped American troops drive the Spanish out of Luzon and then immediately declared the Philippines to be a republic. When the United States would not grant independence, Aguinaldo led military action against American troops throughout 1899. In 1900 the United States declared local self-government for the Philippines, and the last of Aguinaldo's followers surrendered in 1902.

Indonesia Becomes a Dutch Colony

Division in Indonesia facilitated foreign control. In 1596 the Dutch arrived; in 1602 the Dutch East India Company was formed, and the Portuguese were driven out of southern Moluccas; Spanish garrisons were wiped out; and inter-Javanese rivalries were played upon. By 1618 the fortress at Batavia (Jakarta) was built, and during the 1650s the Dutch subjugated the island's sultanates. By 1705 the Dutch East India Company had total control of Java.

The Dutch East India Company Rules the Spice Islands

In the eighteenth century the Dutch introduced agricultural exploitation, demanding forced deliveries from the local sultanates, whom they allowed to rule in name only. The Chinese were brought in as a favored economic group and became the intermediaries between the Dutch and the Indonesians.

Unlike the Spanish, the Dutch retained Malay law for the Indonesians, Chinese law for the Chinese, and, of course, Dutch law for the Hollanders. This did not encourage a Western cultural tradition.

The Netherlands Government Rules Indonesia

In 1796 the Netherlands government took control from the Dutch East India Company and established more direct rule of the area. Eventually it turned over the company's commercial monopolies to private individuals. Villages became responsible for taxes in kind and labor services.

Between 1811 and 1818, as a consequence of the Napoleonic Wars, the Dutch lost control to Great Britain. When European peace was established and the colonies returned, the Dutch met resistance from Javanese princes, which was not suppressed until the 1830s.

In 1830 a system was introduced whereby peasants were forced to plant crops for export and sale in Europe. The Dutch did bring new land under cultivation and introduce new agricultural plants such as tea, tobacco, and the cinchona tree (quinine), but the profits flowed into Dutch pockets, and by the 1850s liberals in Holland began to attack the system.

In 1860 the first steps were taken to abolish forced labor, and the agrarian law of 1870 forbade the sale of land to non-Indonesians. Land was in the hands of the village, not the private farmer, and thus no tradition of independent farming was developed. A new system of private plantations under European control brought no benefit to the Indonesian, and the European continued to gain sole profit from tin and oil.

By 1914 the economic situation in Indonesia was such that the Europeans controlled the capital; the Chinese were the middlemen and the Indonesians, with the exception of a small group of aristocracy, were the workers.

Indochina under France

Vietnam continued to suffer from division, and in 1673 it split into three parts, with three rival dynasties struggling for power. In 1789 the deposed king of Annam was reinstated with the help of the French, and in return France was allowed to maintain bases in the area. In 1801 France helped the king extend his control northward. Along with the French influence came Roman Catholicism opposed to a regime based on Confucianism. In reaction, the rulers of Vietnam began systematic persecutions of Christians which gave the French their excuse for military intervention and further political control.

In 1859 French troops captured Saigon and by 1862 the three provinces around it. They also "helped" King Norodom in Cambodia and established a protectorate in 1867. Between 1883–1885 there was war between China and France over control of Vietnam, which left the area to the French. In 1893 Siam, under British pressure, ceded Laos to France and in 1907 certain lands in Cambodia.

The colony of French Indochina, with a governor-general over the entire area, was thus created. The French followed the same policy as in Africa and the Middle East—a strong centralized rule, European ownership of production and the creation of a small number of new French citizens.

Burma Becomes British

Border troubles with the British East India Company in India led to war in 1824. In 1826, as a result, Burma lost Tenasserim, the coast of Arakan, and the Assam border area and was forced to allow a British resident in the capital city of Ava.

War was again waged in 1852, after the Burmese refused to allow British economic penetration. A third war broke out in 1885 and resulted in the destruction of the kingdom of Burma. However, the Burmese resisted with guerrilla warfare until 1895. In 1897 Burma was included in the administration of India.

The economic situation led to further antagonism on the part of the Burmese, for the Indian merchant was favored and soon became the moneylender and in time controlled the land, while the British owned the oil and teakwood. Buddhist monastaries also objected to British rule, for although Buddhism was not suppressed, it was no longer the state religion.

Malaya and the British

The creation of British Malaya was fundamentally the work

of Sir Thomas Stamford Raffles. In 1786 the British had acquired Penang. In 1819 Raffles gained the uninhabited island of Singapore by negotiation with the Sultan of Johore and created a free port, which not only prospered but was strategically located, for it controlled the Malacca Strait and the eastern approach to the Indian Ocean. In 1824 Britain exchanged, with the Dutch, Benkoelen on Sumatra for Malacca. (In 1511 the Portuguese had conquered Malacca and in 1641, the Dutch.)

Then began the penetration of the Malay peninsula itself. First came economic penetration, then treaties (1874), and, finally, total control.

By the beginning of the twentieth century there were three patterns of British rule in Malaya:

1) The Straits Settlement—a crown colony under a governor-general (who was also the most important power in all the areas)—which included Singapore, Malacca, Penang, the province of Wellesley, and the area south of Penang.

2) The Federated Malay States—under a British resident-general—which included the states of Negri, Sembilian, Selangor, Perak, and Pahang.

3) The Unfederated Malay States, which were protectorates.

The British introduced a plantation economy to Malaya and, as in their other colonies, used the Chinese and the Indian as the moneylender, the merchant, and the middleman. Eventually the Straits Settlement area became 80 percent Chinese, and this caused problems with the modern independence movement. To compensate, the British tended to favor the Malays culturally and politically.

Siam Remains Independent

The only country in Southeast Asia able to maintain at least partial independence was Siam. Its independence was due to a number of factors:

1) Siam had shrewd diplomats who successfully played England against France and persuaded the two nations that Siam was best left as a buffer zone.

2) Siam rapidly put through some timely domestic reforms and allowed liberal trading concessions to the British (in 1826) and the Americans (in 1833). It also opened up the country to foreign missionaries.

In 1851 a rapid program of westernization was begun under King Mongkut. The army and navy were modernized, currency reform was introduced, a foreign language school was built, communications were improved, hospitals were established, and extensive irrigation projects were begun. From 1868 to 1910 Mongkut's son, Chulalongkorn, created a ministry, an efficient tax system, and, most important, codified law. He also sent students abroad to study. Extraterritoriality had been granted, however, in 1835, but under Vajiravudh (1910–1925) Siam regained full sovereignty.

THE BATTLES FOR INDEPENDENCE

The Philippines

Under United States Control

Under William Taft, the civil governor, the Philippines had been granted local autonomy. Public health had been improved; education had been made free and universal (one-third of the children were enrolled); agrarian reform had made some headway, if only against church-held land. In 1907 the first representative assembly was granted.

Immediately after World War I Governor-General Francis Burton Harrison further increased Philippine representation by opening up most of the offices of the government to Filipinos. They now became the majority in the upper house as well as the lower house.

In 1934 an independence act was passed, promising independence in ten years after preparation. From 1934 the Philippines were to have commonwealth status; the United States was to control foreign affairs and defense only.

World War II

When the Philippines were attacked by Japan, defense was an American responsibility. Bataan surrendered in April 1942; Corregidor in May 1942. The Philippine government went into exile, but many of the government employees collaborated with the Japanese. Guerrilla resistance was led by tenant farmers organized into the Hukbalahap, controlled by the Moscow-trained Communist, Luis Taruc.

Independence

In 1946 the Philippines were declared independent under the following conditions: American bases were to be allowed; the United States agreed to pay $400,000,000 in war damages; and United States tariff on Philippine goods was free until 1954, to be increased gradually until a full tariff would be assumed by 1974. Nevertheless, the Philippines were not totally independent, for they were dependent on United States markets and economic interests.

Burma

Independence Movements

The British, unlike the French, made political concessions, but the tension between Burmese tenant farmers and agricultural workers and their Indian landlords and moneylenders increased during the 1930s. Serious uprisings led to the Burma Act of 1935, in which Burma was separated from India.

In the 1930s nationalist parties were formed. The Poor Man's Party (later the Freedom Block) was founded by Ba Maw, who became prime minister of the country in 1937, advocating rebellion against the British. (When the Japanese occupied Burma in 1942, they declared Burma independent under Ba Maw.) The Patriotic Party was founded by U Saw, who became prime minister in 1939. The Thakin Party was a group of students who were primarily critical of British education. Some of them became Marxists; others went to Formosa in 1941, where they were trained and organized by the Japanese for the conquest of Burma.

World War II

The Japanese occupation of Burma was not what the Burmese expected; all the major cities and much of the industry were destroyed by bombing, rice land was overgrown by jungles, and many water buffalo were slaughtered. In 1943 the Anti-Fascist League (AFPFL) was organized, as was the Communist Party.

Independence

At the end of the war negotiations were carried out between the British and General Aung San, head of the AFPFL. Aung San agreed to a peaceful settlement and called off the threatened general strike designed to force the British out of Burma. In 1947 the leaders of the AFPFL met to establish self-government. Independence was delayed, however, because U Saw, head of the Patriotic Party, endeavored to assassinate every member of the proposed government. He succeeded, with the exception of the vice-president of the AFPFL, U Nu, who was not at the meeting and who became Aung San's successor. In 1948 Burma was declared independent.

Indonesia

Independence Movements

Agitation for educational and commercial improvements and greater autonomy began in 1908 in Indonesia. In 1916 the Dutch created the *volksraad,* a council for the expression of public opinion. But even by 1928 the council was not representative of majority opinion for there were fifteen Dutch, four Chinese, one Arab, and thirty Indonesians (and of this thirty, ten were appointed by the Dutch government).

In the 1920s political "study clubs" led to the organization of the National Indonesian Party (PNI), with Sukarno, an engineer, as head. The party was dissolved by the government in 1929, and the Dutch created a prison camp in New Guinea for certain revolutionary leaders, while others were banished from Java (Sukarno was exiled to Flores and then to Sumatra). It was these revolutionaries who the Japanese freed.

World War II

Japan attacked in March 1942, and the Indonesians did not defend their country, welcoming the invaders as liberators. It soon proved, however, that Japan was not going to permit as much local participation as was originally hoped or promised, and some nationalists did not cooperate with the invaders. Sukarno, however, did.

The Wars of Independence

At the end of the war in August 1945, the Indonesian republic was proclaimed by Sukarno, and after six weeks he gained control. The British then arrived to evacuate the Japanese forces and recognized de facto the Sukarno government. This forced the British into the position of mediator with the Dutch.

In 1947 the Linggadjati Agreement was signed, giving Sukarno's government authority on Java, Madura, and Sumatra but retaining Borneo and eastern New Guinea for the Dutch. Dutch prisoners, who had been held as hostages by the nationalists, were freed; and the Netherlands immediately established an economic blockade of the three islands and sought to create rival puppet governments. In July 1947 war broke out; the Dutch won, and the United States took up the job of mediator. War continued, and in December 1948 the situation was brought before the United Nations. By the Hague Agreement of 1949, Indonesia was declared free.

Malaya

The first modern political activities occurred among the Chinese, who outnumbered the Malays in the cities and constituted about 44 percent of the total population. The KMT (Chinese Nationalist Party) founded branches in Malaya, and the CCP (Chinese Communists) followed suit in 1921.

World War II

In February 1942, Singapore and 85,000 British troops surrendered, and the Japanese occupied Malaya. The Japanese favored the Malays and heightened Malay distrust of the Chinese. The CCP organized the anti-Japanese underground movement.

Independence

In 1947 before a proposed Malay federation could be put into operation, Chinese Communisits led a planned military attack against plantation and mine owners, officials of the government, and the KMT members. They used 300,000 Chinese squatters who had been driven inland during the war as the center of their power. In 1950 the British sent in 18,000 troops; in 1952 they resettled 100,000 of the Chinese squatters. Finally, after a major military effort (35,000 British soldiers, an extra police force, the air force, and the expense of £100,000,000 a year) the military threat of the Communists was destroyed by 1954. In 1955 plans for the Federated Malay States could be continued and elections held.

Singapore

The merger of Singapore with Malaya would have meant the extinction of the majority position of the Malays in the Federation and the extension of Chinese influence into Southeast Asia. In 1955 there were serious riots in Singapore, and in 1957, under the leadership of Lim Yew-Hock, an independent state of Singapore was formed with internal freedom but with British control of foreign policy. In September 1963, a proposed federation, known as Malaysia, was approved by the British. The federation, within the Commonwealth of Nations, included North Borneo (Sabah) and Sarawak, Singapore, and the Federated Malay States. Singapore pulled out of the federation in 1965.

Indochina

Under the French

French policy was to exploit the economy of Indochina. In thirty years of rule the rice export tripled, but it was a Chinese monopoly; by 1939 the rubber industry exports equaled 78,000 tons and coal 2.5 million tons, but these were totally under French control. Indochinese goods were restricted by French tariff but the reverse was not true. The French destroyed the custom of communal lands in Vietnam which had traditionally supported the poor, and they not only dominated the economic scene but also the political scene, thus alienating the educated Indochinese.

During World War I, 100,000 Vietnamese were sent to France and they returned with revolutionary ideas. The fundamental influence toward nationalism, however, came from China. In 1912 the Nationalist Party of Indochina held its first meeting in Canton. In 1920 Ho Chi Minh (1892–1967), who had been trained in both France and China, organized the first Communist Party. By the beginning of World War II, however, the French administration had curbed the Communist Party (Ho Chi Minh was jailed 1931–1933) and destroyed the Nationalist Party.

World War II

The Japanese did not even pretend to liberate Vietnam and ruled through the Vichy French. Resistance movements sprang up, the Communist Party declared a united front, and in 1944, under the command of Vo Nguyen Giap (trained in China), they engaged in active battle. In 1945 the Japanese set up puppet governments under Bao Dai and the kings of Cambodia and Laos.

Independence and Division in Vietnam

In September 1945, the Nationalists established a government. After the Japanese surrender, the south was occupied by British troops and the north by Chinese troops. The Chinese immediately recognized Ho Chi Minh's government, but in the south the British sided with the French. War between the north and south broke out in 1946. In 1949 the French granted semi-independence within the French Union to Cambodia and Laos and set up Bao Dai as chief of state of Vietnam (both north and south). But despite his imperial descent he was the wrong choice. Bitter fighting continued until the truce of 1954, when the French pulled out completely; Laos and Cambodia were given total independence; Vietnam was divided at the seventeenth parallel; the Communists agreed to give up their projected invasion of Cambodia and Laos; and North and South Vietnam promised to allow civilians to move from one side of the border to the other and to hold elections in 1956 to reunite the area.

SOUTHEAST ASIA TODAY

Political Change since World War II

Communism

Since World War II Southeast Asia has been unstable, and 1975 saw the triumph of Communism in Indochina.

VIETNAM

No elections were held to reunite Vietnam in 1956, and by 1960 it was clear that the North Vietnamese Communists with the aid of the Vietcong (South Vietnamese Communists) were increasing their military and political activities in the south. The United States, in order to save the right-wing government in Saigon from collapse, began to expand its military commitment; in 1961 military advisers were raised from 685 to 2000 and the first combat support units were sent in. The Communists in turn decided on full-scale guerilla warfare. In 1962 the United States had an army of 11,000 men and was providing $500 million a year, but this was only the beginning of escalation. By 1969 the U.S. military force in the south was 541,500.

The year of the most savage fighting was 1968. In 1970 the war was spread to Cambodia and in 1971 to Laos. In 1972 the north invaded across the demiliarized zone and the U.S. resumed the bombing of Hanoi and mined the port of Haiphong. On January, 27, 1973, a cease fire was signed. The cease-fire and the Nobel prize which Secretary of State Henry Kissinger shared with North Vietnam's Le Duc Tho had very little meaning. Fighting continued, and by April 1975 the Communists occupied three-fourths of South Vietnam. In May Saigon fell and 35 years of war came to an end.

Thousands of refugees fled to the U.S. and Thailand. Vietnam was officially reunited in 1976.

LAOS

Laos was the scene of power struggles and civil war after 1954. From 1967 North Vietnam increased its military activities and government forces gradually lost ground despite massive U.S. aid (more aid per capita than any other nation). By 1975 the Communist Pathet Lao forces occupied most of the strategic areas and the coalition between the Pathet Lao and Prince Souvanna Phouma was clearly leftist.

CAMBODIA

From 1970 to 1975 there was civil war between the Khmer Rouge (Communists) and government forces (supported by the United States at the cost of $270 million a year). On April 17, 1975, the capital Pnompenh fell to the Communist forces who perpetrated a bloodbath and forced millions of city dwellers into the country announcing a return to agrarian ways. In 1979, Vietnamese forces invaded, and China retaliated by invading Vietnam.

OTHER NATIONS

Other countries were seriously unstable at the end of the Second World War. Not only was Malaya faced with Chinese Communist problems (see p. 391), but in Indonesia a Chinese minority caused a severe situation. Sukarno became more and more anti-Western and in 1965 Indonesia withdrew from the UN (reentered in 1967). An attempted coup by the Communist and the murder of six generals forced Sukarno in 1966 to turn to the military and General Suharto (who replaced Sukarno in 1967). From 1966 to 1967 over 300,000 Indonesians suspected of Communism were assassinated by Moslem students.

The Chinese populations in many Southeast Asian nations have caused instability for they have maintained allegiance either to the Nationalists in Taiwan or to the Communists in China, and they attempt to remain culturally distinct from the rest of the population by using the Chinese language and establishing their own schools.

The Philippines also encountered serious disorders after the war. During World War II the pseudo-Communist Hukbalahap Party had directed its energies as much toward killing its political rivals as killing Japanese (out of 25,000 killed only 5000 were Japanese). After the war they continued their program of slaughter and destruction, and the Communist leanings of the organization were more pronounced. By 1950 the Huks numbered 40,000 with about 2,500,000 reserves. Ramon Magsaysay (minister of defense and then president from 1953–1957) finally destroyed the Huks with the help of the military and with land reform—an attempt to satisfy agricultural discontent which had gained the Huks the support of the tenant farmers.

Thailand had suffered less of the ravages of war, for its government (headed by Pridi) was overthrown and Pibul, who was made prime minister, sided with Japan. Nevertheless the Communists proved a problem and in 1952 were rounded up. In 1957 they were released and in reaction the military staged a coup d'état.

Democracy

Most Southeast Asian governments would agree with Sukarno who said in 1957 that the "experiences of these eleven years have convinced me that the democracy we have adopted . . . is not in harmony with the soul of the Indonesian nation. This is what I call Western democracy—for that matter you may call it parliamentary democracy . . . an import democracy, not an Indonesian one." Most Southeast Asian nations are ruled by the military in fact if not in name. Even in Malaya the framework that makes democratic politics possible is provided by emergency regulations adopted in response to the Communist insurrection that started in 1948.

Economic and Cultural Problems

Poverty is the common denominator in all of Asia, and along with a need for improved methods of agricultural production and industry goes an extremely rapid population growth (in Malaya, for example, it is 3 percent a year and in Singapore 4 percent). In 1962 per capital income ranged from $50 per year in Burma and

Laos to $400 in Singapore.

Thailand with plentiful resources had a balance of trade deficit in 1972 of $400 million; Malaysia, on the other hand, has a favorable balance of trade (and a 70 percent literacy rate which helps account for its progress). In Malaysia, however, the Chinese and Indians have a disportionate share of the wealth and there have been serious civil conflicts. Burma has one of the lowest per capita incomes and was dependent upon foreign aid (it receives £300,000 a year from Britain), but the discovery of oil may improve the situation.

Japanese Involvement

Japan once again has a heavy economic stake in Southeast Asia and has been generous with its capital (in the 1970s Japan loaned Burma $10 million for off-shore oil exploration), but the whole issue of Japan's economic involvement is not resolved. Southeast Asia's balance of trade with Japan is extremely unfavorable, and anti-Japanese feeling was responsible for riots in Indonesia and Thailand in 1974.

American Involvement

What American withdrawal from Vietnam will ultimately mean to the economies of the nations of Southeast Asia remains to be seen. The Thais announced the withdrawal of American troops stationed in the country; yet since the establishment of bases in Thailand the United States (by 1975) had provided $670 million in grant assistance. In 1973 President Ferdinand Marcos of the Philippines announced that American bases were "eroding the integrity of the country." Yet the United States defense department was the second largest employer in the Philippines and spent about $150 million a year.

After American involvement in Vietnam ended, U.S. aid to Southeast Asia diminished. (In 1973, for instance, the U.S. gave Indonesia $233 million in economic aid; in 1974 $90 million.) But this must be balanced with the fact that during the period from 1965-1975 American trade with the area (excluding Indochina) more than doubled and business investments more than tripled.

Sub-Sahara Africa

ANCIENT AND CLASSICAL CIVILIZATION
1000 B.C.–300 A.D.

This chapter is limited to Sub-Saharan Africa because the area has developed separately from the northern and Mediterranean parts of the continent which are usually associated with the Arab Middle East. The people of the north were influenced by the Greeks, the Phoenicians, the Romans, and the Moslems and belong to the Mediterranean world. On the other hand, Africa south of the Sahara was relatively isolated by its vast expanse of desert. Almost nothing is known about tropical Africa before the Arab chronicles of the ninth century A.D. *and very little is known until the coming of the Europeans in the sixteenth century. Most of what historians know about pre-European Africa is based on archeological discoveries, since few African tribes or civilizations developed a system of writing and still fewer a calendar. Consequently, most of ancient and classical history is based on oral history (memorized by generation after generation) and artifacts (weapons, cooking utensils, and so forth).*

Historians now believe that humans originated in Africa and that until about 300,000 years ago the African was more advanced in tool making than anyone else in the world. African development, however, was not uniform. As early as 3000 B.C. *there were farming and neolithic tools in the Sahara (which was then a grasslands). Between 3000 and 100* B.C. *the "agricultural revolution" spread slowly into the south.*

During the ancient and classical period, Africa was never entirely isolated. Greeks traveled across the desert, and peoples from Indonesia, Malaya, and Polynesia reached Madagascar and penetrated the east coast of Africa. There are even indications of trade between east Africa and China, but the first civilization to influence African development fundamentally was the Egyptian. The Meroe civilization on the upper Nile and the Sudanic civilizations of west Africa were directly influenced by Egyptian political theories.

THE PEOPLES OF AFRICA

By about 8000 B.C. four racial types had appeared in Africa: (1) the ancestors of the modern Bushmen probably occupied most of the drier areas of the east and south; (2) the Pygmies' ancestry is not clear, but probably developed in the forests of the Congo and Guinea; (3) a race akin to the Caucasian (called proto-Hamite) appeared in the north and east; and (4) the Negroid emerged in the west central forested regions and soon became the dominant physical type. There are three main groups: the west African Negro; the Bantu, who are a linguistic, not a racial, grouping but do seem to be somewhat lighter-skinned than the west African Negro; the Nilotes of east Africa, who are tall, slender, and long headed.

THE MEROE OR KUSH CIVILIZATION   800 B.C.–300 A.D.

In 666 B.C., in the face of an Assyrian invasion, the pharaoh of Egypt retreated southward up the Nile to Kush, establishing Egyptian influence in the Kush area (what is today the Sudan).

Around the sixth century B.C. Kush began to push its frontiers southward into the wooded areas of Africa and founded the new capital of Meroe, henceforth ruling over a mixed population of Caucasians and Negroes. The Meroe had an Iron Age civilization and were able to defend themselves from Egyptian pressure in the north and expand into the south.

We know very little about the Meroe, but they seem to have been a trading civilization (Indonesian plants were introduced) and were directly influenced by Egyptian ideas. Their kings were considered to be divine.

AXUM

By the middle of the first century A.D., Meroe society was in decline, probably because of the rise of a rival trading empire, Axum.

Axum, located in the north corner of the Ethiopian highlands, was the great ivory market of northern Africa. During the second and third centuries A.D. its power rose, and by the fourth century it had conquered Meroe and burned the city to the ground. During the fourth century Axum became Christian (the Coptic church) with strong political and religious links with Byzantine Egypt.

MEDIEVAL CIVILIZATION   300-1500 A.D.

Africa's medieval period saw great kingdoms flourish in the Sudan (stretching from present-day Sudan to the west coast of Africa), the movement of the Bantu-spreading tribes into the south, and the creation of wealthy Moslem city-states on the east coast of Africa.

There is evidence of regular contact between Mediterranean and Sub-Sahara Africa. The western Sudan exported gold, ivory, and slaves to the north in return for luxuries and salt. With the Arab invasion of northern Africa, Islam penetrated below the Sahara, and eventually the Sudanic civilizations became Moslem. (The split in Nigeria between the Moslem north and the south is indicative of this conversion.) But no single empire rose to control the African continent; no single religion gave a cultural unity; and, although the majority of languages are derived from Bantu, no single language predominated.

SUDANIC STATES

From the Red Sea to the mouth of the Senegal River, African

peoples formed states "so similar that they must have been derived from a common source." There is little doubt that the ideas of ancient Egypt, transmitted through Meroe, formed the basis of these Sudanic civilizations, but there was also a southwest Asian influence that must have come from Axum.

Ruled by divine kings concerned with the fertility of the land, the Sudanic state was not feudal, for power was not hereditary but wielded by officials who held office at the king's pleasure and were transferred, promoted, and demoted at his bidding.

The Sudanic states are believed to have been parasitic growths fastening themselves upon existing agricultural societies, probably with the aid of cavalry warfare.

Ghana

The greatest of early Sudanic civilizations was Ghana, founded in the fourth century A.D. on the main caravan route to north Africa. At its height in the tenth century Ghana's capital city had a population of close to 30,000 people and controlled an area extending from the Atlantic Ocean almost to Timbuktu.

Berbers from the desert moved against Ghana in 1062, but not until 1076 were they able to capture the capital. Yet the nomads were unable to benefit from their conquest, for they soon began fighting among themselves, and Ghana became independent once again. However, the kingdom was never able to recover its trade or repair the damage done to its agriculture, and the empire began to break up into tribal units.

Mali

With the decline of Ghana, Mali (which probably had been a subject nation) grew, and the Mali empire was firmly established in the upper Niger River valley by Sundiata (1230–1255). Sundiata adopted Islam and Mali became a Moslem kingdom. By the fourteenth century Mali controlled the upper Niger west to the Atlantic and all the land north of the forest and east along the Niger to

Hausaland, and during that century Mansa (king) Musa made a pilgrimage to Mecca where he impressed the medieval world with his wealth and generosity.

Kanem-Bornu

In the Lake Chad area the kingdom of Kanem-Bornu was established and lasted 1000 years (until defeated by Europeans at the end of the nineteenth century). At its height it was larger than France and Britain combined.

Songhai

Mali collapsed when one of its vassals, the King of Songhai, broke away in the fifteenth century and eventually captured Mali territory, ending up with an empire even greater than Mali. The capital of Songhai was Goa, and its wealth was based on control of the salt mines. King Mohammed Askia's reign (1493–1528) was exceptional. The city of Timbuktu became his center of learning, a university was built, and clerics, judges, and scholars flourished under his patronage. Songhai fell to the Moroccans in 1591.

EAST AFRICA

Moslems had little influence in east Africa until the thirteenth century. Although they occupied the coastline and most of the land along the eastern frontier of Abyssinia (Ethiopia) and although by the tenth century a series of Moslem trading states had been built, Christian Abyssinia was able to dominate them and force them to pay tribute. (Ethiopia became Christian during the fourth century A.D.)

This domination eventually led, in the fifteenth century, to religious wars between Abyssinia and the Moslems. Ifat, the largest Moslem community, was destroyed in 1415 and the Moslems retreated temporarily to Yemen, across the Red Sea.

From the fourth to the tenth century, Bantu Negroes were spreading into Tanganyika and Kenya, and the number of Arab colonists was extremely small. From the middle of the thirteenth century, however, to the coming of the Portuguese, wealthy Moslem states grew up along the coastline and experienced a period of prosperity, trading in slaves and ivory. The Portuguese left no deep mark on east Africa. The essential cultural and commercial contact was Islamic.

THE WESTERN FOREST REGIONS

By the thirteenth century a growth of population in the Sudan led gradually to the infiltration of the forest lands; the governments of the forest regions were modeled on the older Sudanic states. North of the Gold Coast forest the Akan state of Bonot Banda was founded, but it was not until the fifteenth century that the forest was penetrated. The city of Ife, close to the edge of the forest, was the dispersal point for the Benin dynasty, which controlled the Nigerian forest lands. The Oyo, who held supremacy in the area in the seventeenth century, also had their center to the north of the forest.

These Guinea states were patterned after the Sudanic civilizations. They were urban in character, for the nucleus of each was a town surrounded by a wall. They established an extensive network of trade routes and exported gold dust, kola nuts (one of the few stimulants tolerated by Islam), and ivory. They imported salt, which came from the sea and the Sahara via the Sudan, and horses and cattle.

THE SOUTHERN SAVANNAS

Probably around the eighth century, civilization developed in the southern savannas (near Katanga). Again trade seems to have been the motivation, and gold was mined and exported east along the Zambesi River.

MODERN CIVILIZATION   1500 to the Present

Africa's modern history did not really begin until the opening up of the continent in the late nineteenth century by the Europeans. From 1450 to the 1880s most African states traded with Europe and the United States as independent nations and were powerful enough to deter invaders.

Sub-Sahara Africa was the last of the areas of the world to experience the impact of European peoples and ideas. For one thing, Africa had less to offer Europe than the East (only ivory and gold), and because of climate, disease, and lack of communications, Europeans were prevented from entering Africa and producing what they wanted. It was not until the seventeenth century, with the increased demand for slave labor on plantations in the New World, that Europe's interest in Africa began to grow. Yet three centuries of European trade in slaves on the coasts of Africa resulted in little penetration of Western influence. Ironically, it was not until the antislavery movement in Europe (in 1807 the slave trade was outlawed in Great Britain) had won great victories that European culture began to affect the indigenous civilizations of Africa. The exploration of inner Africa at the beginning of the nineteenth century was a manifestation of new European humanitarianism, of missionary zeal to convert the dark continent to Christianity, and of the effort to establish legitimate trade in place of the slave trade. But even as late as 1874 Ashanti was the only kingdom to have fought a European army, and little had been done to bring Africa into European hands; only a very small portion of the continent was actually under Western rule. It was not until Belgium and Germany became interested in Africa in the 1880s that the scramble for colonies began, and by 1914 almost all Africa was under European political domination.

During the years between the two world wars Europeans controlled everything, no African was in a position of responsibility, and there was little financial assistance to stimulate economic development. With the Second World War and its need for strategic raw materials and foodstuffs Africa suddenly became important, and Africa and its people began to change. With westernization came inevitable reaction and challenge to Europe's political domination of Africa. The disintegration of the colonial system began in 1957, when the British colony of the Gold Coast became the independent state of Ghana. By 1961 most of Africa was independent and faced new and often more serious problems.

THE COMING OF THE PORTUGUESE

Henry the Navigator (1394–1460) of Portugal had a scheme to circumvent the Islamic middleman by traveling around Africa to the Far East. In 1444 the Portuguese reached Cape Verde; by 1471 they were at the Gold Coast and building forts to protect their rights to the gold they found there. In 1488 Bartolomeo Diaz rounded the Cape of Good Hope, and in 1497 Vasco da Gama made his famous trip to India.

Angola

The Portuguese discovered the kingdom of the Bakongo, one of the largest states in Africa (it had a population close to 2.5 million). The Bakongo kingdom was a typical Sudanic state. Around the state were clusters of small states owing nominal allegiance to the Bakongo (one of these was Angola).

Missionaries were sent in 1490, and the king of Bakongo was converted to Christianity. From 1491 to 1543 an "ardent and enlightened" Christian sat on the throne, but the Portuguese were more interested in the slave trade than in the establishment of a Christian state, and by 1660 they were at war with the Bakongo. By the eighteenth century there was no Christianity and no state. When relations (which had been very good) worsened with the Congo over the slave trade, the Portuguese looked to the bordering kingdom of Ngola (Angola) and by the end of the seventeenth century the whole area was in Portuguese hands.

Mozambique

The Portuguese took control of Sofala at the beginning of the sixteenth century and soon came into conflict with the Vakaranga people (whose ruler was known as Monomatapa), who controlled the Zambesi River valley, the north and east parts of the southern Rhodesian plateau, and the lowlands of southern Mozambique. In 1560 the Portuguese occupied territory ruled by the Monomatapas. The military strength of the Portuguese and their assistance against the rising power of the Changamires made the Monomatapas dependent upon them, and by 1629 the Monomatapas had become Portuguese vassals. This, of course, meant the end of the kingdom and intermittent Portuguese control in the area.

The Portuguese Achievement in Africa

Although the Portuguese were the first Europeans to arrive in Africa, they made no significant contributions to African history from the fifteenth century to the end of the eighteenth century. To Angola they exported their own Portuguese criminal classes and then used them to incite natives to fight among themselves so as to make it easier to carry on the slave trade. In Mozambique the situation was less bloody, for it was gold rather than slaves that the Portuguese were interested in, but again exploitation was the theme of Portuguese control.

The opening up of trade and slave routes by the Portuguese did, however, bring Africa into contact with the outside world and with its own peoples. Moreover, the Portuguese did introduce new plant foods (coffee, tobacco) from South America.

THE SLAVE TRADE

The need for labor on the sugar plantations in the New World led to the growth of European interest in Africa. The Europeans sailed to the Gold Coast and bought their slaves from African kings or merchants. The slave trade was pioneered by the Dutch, who had ousted the Portuguese from the Gold Coast by 1642. Soon, however, the British and French became interested, and by the eighteenth century they handled the major portion of the trade. (England controlled more than 50 percent.)

Effects

One result was depopulation which was not as great in West Africa as in Angola and East Africa, but by 1600, 900,000 slaves had been taken to America; during the 1600s, another 2,750,000; during the 1700s, 7,000,000 more; and by 1900, another 4,000,000. For every West African on a plantation in the New World, it is estimated that one died in the slave wars or en route; for every East African taken by the Arabs, five to twelve died.

The slave trade moved the centers of African wealth and trade from the Sudan to the coast.

Tribal war and conflict in the interior were also results of the slave trade. At first the slaves who were sold to Europeans were probably slaves in the African communities, but with the increased demand, chiefs resorted to the use of their newly purchased firearms to raid one another's tribes for slaves.

The Antislavery Movement

In 1807 the British Parliament passed a bill outlawing the slave trade, but England felt the need for suppressing the trade not only among its own people but also, for commercial reasons, among the other European nations. Legitimate trade could only be developed after the more profitable and much easier slave trade had been eliminated.

In 1808 the United States followed suit; in 1814 so did the Dutch; and after the Napoleonic wars most other European nations, except Spain and Portugal, outlawed the slave trade. Great Britain set up naval patrols and persuaded or forced African rulers to outlaw the export of slaves, but it was not until the United States Civil War in 1865 and the final abolition of slavery in Cuba and Brazil in the 1880s that the picture really changed.

The antislavery movement was part of a larger humanitarian movement in which the revival of Christianity played a major role. Missionary activity in Africa began to gather momentum in the 1850s and had spread rapidly by the 1870s.

EXPLORATION

Commercial and missionary interests led to the opening up of Africa. The geographical exploration of the interior started in the 1790s, but it took eighty years to learn the main facts about the continent.

The British led the way in the exploration of Africa, for it was in the pay of the British government that Mungo Park sailed most of the course of the Niger in 1805; Denham and Clapperton explored Bornu and Hausaland in 1823–1825; the Lander brothers followed the lower Niger to the sea in 1830; and the German Heinrich Barth explored central and west Sudan in the 1850s.

The French contributed little despite their interest in Senegal. René Caillié's journey in 1827 was the only one that compared with the British feats, and it was a private venture.

Some of the earliest pioneers in east Africa were German (Knapf and Rebmann located Mount Kilimanjaro), but again exploration of the south and east was done primarily by the British. The Royal Geographical Society financed David Livingstone's trip to Victoria Falls in 1853, Burton and Speke's trip to Lake Tanganyika in 1858, and Livingstone's expedition of 1859–1864. David Livingstone was probably the symbol of his age, for he was both a medical missionary and an explorer, and it was his task to look for trade routes that would permit English manufactured goods to supplant the slave trade.

POLITICAL ANNEXATION AND THE SCRAMBLE FOR COLONIES

Not until the 1880s did the European nations become involved in schemes for political annexation in Africa. Two countries, which had heretofore not been interested in Africa, suddenly entered the picture.

King Leopold of Belgium decided to develop the Congo as his commercial monopoly, and as Roland Oliver and J. D. Farge said in *A Short History of Africa,* "Probably it was Leopold, more than any other statesman, who created the 'atmosphere' of scramble." Between 1883 and 1885 Germany annexed southwest Africa, Togoland, the Cameroons, and East Africa.

At the Berlin Conference of 1884–1885 the actions of Germany and Belgium were legalized and an international code for the partition of Africa was established. This attempt at internationalism failed because there was no machinery to enforce international law, and in the fifteen years following the conference, the entire continent with the exception of Ethiopia and Liberia was divided among the great powers.

The Process of Acquisition

Treaties granting rights to European powers were signed by the tribal chiefs of the interior, who the Europeans insisted had the authority to convey land, grant mining concessions, and so forth. (By tribal law they had in fact no such power.)

The system of indirect rule was established in most territories whereby the Europeans built up the power of the chief and ruled through him. By this means a labor force was acquired to work the mines and plantations.

French Interests

France had turned to west Africa in order to compensate for the loss of empire during the Napoleonic wars. In 1854 Senegal was developed as a French colony and as a base for the French conquest of the western Sudan. Logically, France should have expanded quickly into west Africa. By 1883 the French had fought their way to the upper Niger but did not succeed in reaching Timbuktu until

1893, for the western Sudan had witnessed a new advance of Islam and the Mande tribes were too strong.

British Interests

Initially British interests had been on the western coast of Africa. Sierra Leone was colonized by the British at the end of the eighteenth century and Freetown was established. It was a private venture of antislavery humanitarians. (Liberia was the American equivalent in 1821 and Libreville the French copy of Freetown in 1849.) By 1860, 70,000 Africans freed from slave ships had settled in Sierra Leone, and the British were convinced that the most effective way to stop the slave exporting was to establish rule over the coast. But it was not until 1874, after the Danes and the Dutch had handed over their forts and the British had defeated the Ashanti, that the Gold Coast was declared a British colony. In 1851 Lagos was captured, and in 1861 it became a colony.

From 1886 to 1892 British African policy was based on the retention of Egypt at all costs. This meant that Britain was willing to allow French expansion in the west, despite the fact that it involved the encirclement of four British spheres on the coast. Great Britain instead turned to the east coast of Africa, although it was commercially almost valueless.

South Africa

South Africa was the one exception in the period prior to the scramble for concessions.

A small Dutch colony had been planted at the Cape of Good Hope in 1652 in order to supply food for passing ships. The Dutch East India Company found it necessary to attract colonists to the Cape in order to create a labor force and to defend the settlement against the Bantus, who had moved into the south. However, the settlement soon became too large, and opposition grew to the company's rule. Some of the colonists decided to seek liberty and a new life in the interior. These colonists, known as the *Trek-Boers* (migrant farmers), moved east to Natal and established the Boer republics of Fraaff Reinet and Swellendam. In 1779 they first came in conflict with the Bantu tribes (the Infidel Wars).

THE ZULUS

The advance of the Boers cut off new lands available for the Bantu tribes, forcing the various tribes to fight among themselves for the remaining land. The victor of these wars was the Zulu clan in northern Natal, led by Shaka, who created a Zulu empire. (Two areas that withstood Zulu pressure were Swaziland and Basuto.) It was not until 1838 that the Zulus were challenged by the Boers.

During the Anglo-French wars of 1793–1815, the Cape came under British control and so did the independent Boer republics of Swellendam and Fraaff Reinet in 1795.

THE GREAT TREK

The Boer farmers were as unhappy under British rule as they had been under the Dutch East India Company. When British humanitarian colonial policy favored returning disputed frontier land to the Bantus in 1836, the Boer farmers decided on a second trek.

The Great Trek (1835-1837) was the exodus of the Boers living along the frontier to the lands across the Orange River, where they established the virtually independent republics of Natal, Transvaal, and the Orange Free State. In December 1838, the successor of Shaka, King Dingane of the Zulus, was defeated by the Boers, led by Andries Pretorius, and the Afrikaners were able to settle in Natal. (In 1879 another war was fought against the Zulus, but this time by the British.)

THE BOER WAR

The Boer republic of Natal was established in 1839 but was annexed by the British in 1845. The Transvaal and the Orange Free State became independent republics in 1852 and 1854, but they were so poor that they were incapable of coping with the wars of the Bantus. Despite Boer opposition the ideal solution, according to the British, was a federation of the British colonies and the Boer republics.

In 1877 the Transvaal was annexed, and the British found

themselves at war with both the Zulus and the Boers. In 1881 the British decided that the Transvaal was not worth the military effort and recognized its independence once again.

Hostility between Boer and British was further increased by British (Anglican) missionary work, for the Boers were strict Calvinists and believed in racial segregation.

The discovery of gold in the Transvaal in 1886 again caused trouble. Kruger (president of the Transvaal from 1883 to 1902) and Rhodes (a British settler in South Africa, who had acquired mining rights in the Kimberley diamond mines and was prime minister of the Cape Colony, 1890–1896) soon clashed. Rhodes succeeded in encircling the Transvaal and persuading Great Britain to annex Bechuanaland in 1885, to declare a sphere of interest extending from Bechuanaland to the Zambesi River in 1888, and to acquire Northern Rhodesia and Nyasaland in 1889–1890. But Rhodes had to fight the Portuguese in Mozambique and to overcome an uprising of the Matabele and Mashone tribes (1897) in order to achieve his policy of encircling the Transvaal.

Kruger retaliated by building a railroad to the Portuguese port at Delagoa Bay, and Rhodes answered by attempting to instigate a revolution in the Transvaal, supported by hired mercenaries. The Jameson Raid of 1896 failed, and this ruined Rhodes' political reputation and career.

Gold, however, continued to attract English settlers into the Transvaal, where the Boers treated them as second-class citizens. War between Boer and British came in 1899. In 1902, after three years of inglorious war in which the Boers were regarded as the heroes by the rest of the world, the Boers sought peace, and the independent republics and the British colonies became a federation.

By 1902 the scramble was over, and the only Sub-Saharan countries that remained independent were Ethiopia (which had defeated the Italians and limited their expansion to the coastlines of Eritrea and Somalia) and the American-influenced republic of Liberia.

THE COLONIAL PERIOD

The First Years of Colonial Rule

Once the colonial powers had taken their share of Africa, they lost interest in the development of their acquisitions. In nearly every territory only a serious military crisis brought reinforcement or economic grants-in-aid. With the establishment of civil administration over a colony the grants-in-aid ended, and the colonial administration was generally expected to pay for itself out of custom duties and taxes.

During the first years of the colonial period, the great powers had no positive policy and were concerned only with maintaining peace and security and making their territories economically self-supporting. Since taxation was to be the basis of self-sufficiency, some European nations encouraged African production and others encouraged white immigration. Which policy they followed generally depended on the governor of the territory. For example, the British government encouraged European plantations in Kenya and Nyasaland but not in Uganda, and it disallowed them in west Africa.

Between the World Wars

A Change in Attitude

The great colonial powers suddenly were no longer as self-confident as in the past, and they began to feel that colonialism required a goal, a justifying moral, and a political philosophy. After the war the decision to break up the German empire also had to be rationalized. Togoland and the Cameroons were divided between France and Britain; southwest Africa went to the Union of South Africa; German east Africa was divided between Britain and Belgium. These territories became mandates under the League of Nations, and the trustee nation had the obligation to govern justly and to carry them forward economically and politically. They were viewed as "a sacred trust of civilization."

This view implied an extension and change in the functions of the colonial governments. Education is perhaps the best example. In all of the colonies there was some attempt to educate the natives.

1) Britain used the already established missionary schools, ensuring that about one-quarter of its Africans received from two to four years of education—some received from eight to twelve.

2) Belgian policy was similar, although the emphasis was on primary education.

3) France made no use of the missions, but established state schools for the select minority.

Throughout Africa most of the European powers followed the doctrine of assimilation, the philosophy which assumed that the Africans would grow into citizens of the European country. Britain was an exception, for it never assumed that the African would become a Britisher. This is perhaps one of the reasons why Britain accepted independence as an ultimate goal much more readily than did Portugal, France, or Belgium.

Economic aid, however, did not come, although railroads were built by most colonial powers. Nor did European private investment flourish. With the exception of South Africa, Europeans did not migrate to Africa readily (by the 1930s there were only 60,000) and the few who did had neither skills nor capital. The only exception to this was in the mining industry (which consumed two-thirds of European investment), but this was limited to South Africa, the Rhodesias, and the Katanga province of the Belgian Congo. Only in these territories did secondary industry develop (by the mid-1930s South Africa accounted for more than half of Africa's international trade).

World War II

The Great Depression of 1930–1936 led to the realization on the part of the European governments that they could not depend on private investment in Africa to develop their colonies, and then World War II followed and changed both Europe's and Africa's attitude toward the nature of colonial responsibility and the right of Europeans to be there at all. During the war Africa became important as a future supplier of industrial raw materials and unprocessed foodstuff. The need for raw materials (the value of the Congo's exports increased fourteenfold) and greater private investments led to rapid economic change in Africa. Europe (particularly the British) also felt a moral obligation to the colonies, and this ultimately led to political and social change in the form of the founding of universities, the training of doctors, and the liberalizing of political control. Results of the change varied from colony to colony according to the mother country's colonial aims and the number and influence of European settlers in each colony.

Here again education is a good example of varied colonial achievement. From 1946 to 1954 the number of children in school increased in British Ghana, from 147,447 to 521,989; in the Belgian Congo, from 885,038 to 1,138,700; in French West Africa, from 107,470 to 284,441; and in British Nigeria, from 614,173 to 1,114,985. By 1954 twenty-five universities and technical schools had been established, but this figure is misleading for ten were in British territories, ten in the Union of South Africa (only three of which were for blacks), three in Liberia, and only one in Belgian and French territories.

Europe's exhaustion following World War II, Asian independence, which was granted at the end of the war, the increasing number of Africans who left their villages for the cities, the mounting discontent caused by postwar inflation and demobilization, and the growing number of young Africans who had been educated in the Western liberal tradition—all these factors led to the rise of political agitation among Africans and the demand for independence throughout Africa. Only the British, however, relinguished authority willingly and with more success than the other European nations involved in Africa.

INDEPENDENCE

South Africa

South Africa had become a self-governing union in 1909 within the British Commonwealth of Nations, and in 1923 Southern Rhodesia had gained virtual self-government, but in both cases self-government was for whites only.

The three Bantu territories—Basutoland, Bechuanaland, and Swaziland—remained under British protection because of South Africa's attitude toward nonwhites. After 1948 the majority of the electorate in the Union voted for *apartheid,* the principle of total separation between white and black.

In May 1961 the South African government broke with the British Commonwealth on the issue of apartheid, stating that no nonwhite would have a share in politics and that the Bantus would be confined to separate areas.

Southern Rhodesia

From 1923 to 1963 Southern Rhodesia had two main aims:

1) To stay out of the Union of South Africa;

2) At the same time to maintain power in the hands of the white minority.

With this purpose in mind a federation of the two Rhodesias and Nyasaland was proposed, with hopes of getting rid of British surveillance and of creating a bloc strong enough to stand against the Union of South Africa.

After World War II white Southern Rhodesians renewed their campaign, stressing the economic advantages of the union, and in 1953 the British government finally agreed to this policy, which most Africans in the three territories were opposed to. The situation could not long remain static, with 300,000 Europeans and 7,000,000 Africans. The federation called itself a partnership of black and white in government; this was definitely a misnomer. Only fifteen out of fifty-nine seats in the federal assembly were reserved for African interests, and only twelve of these were actually held by Africans.

On December 31, 1963, the union broke up. Nyasaland became the independent state of Malawi and Northern Rhodesia became the independent state of Zambia. Southern Rhodesia remained a white self-governing colony. In 1965, in defiance of both the British government and world opinion, Rhodesia declared its independence unilaterally.

The Sudan

In 1953 the Sudan received from Great Britain and Egypt the agreement that it could decide its future after a three-year transitional period. In 1956 it voted to become an independent republic (see p. 35).

West and East Africa

There had been reactions in west and east Africa to colonial control and alien pressures before World War II. In 1915 a rebellion led by John Chilembwe in Nyasaland had a political-religious orientation (the Mau Mau uprising of 1952–1956 in Kenya was also a pseudo-religious and political movement), and in British west Africa the newly educated Africans formed political associations and hoped to convert the legislative councils into African parliaments. In the French colonies, authority had always been centered in France, and therefore African intellectuals sought to secure greater influence in Paris. During the 1930s they had little support and no means of influence.

With World War II, however, the French Africans' attitude changed. During the war French territories had been controlled by the Vichy government, and this produced a severe shock among the Africans. In French Equatorial Africa, Africans led by Félix Éboné joined the Free French movement and, in Brazzaville in 1944, declared that Africa's future would be decided by Africans. This led to the establishment of the French Union after the war, in which Africans were to be partners in government, and more important, it led to decentralization within the French colonial empire. An interterritorial party was founded (the Rassemblement Démocratique Africain), which continued agitation in France (between 1948 and 1950 it was suppressed because of its militant association with Communism), but what happened in the British colonies changed the French Africans' outlook.

British West Africa

In the British colonies on the west coast, World War II had led to an increase in income, more contact with the outside world (particularly among Africans fighting in the Burma campaign), and a desire for independence. When the war ended there was growing agitation for independence; there was economic discontent (new wealth but nothing to buy); and there was a growing demand that Britain fulfill the ideals laid down in the charter of the United Nations. Great Britain, however, continued to move slowly, and Africans became increasingly frustrated.

On the Gold Coast in 1948 in response to this frustration, there was boycotting and rioting. Kwame Nkrumah returned from England to organize political opposition, and in 1949 the British agreed to an all-African committee to devise a new constitution for Ghana. Nkrumah, however, was not satisfied and demanded self-government. In 1957 it was granted, and this was the beginning of the end of colonialism in Africa.

Independence followed in most of the British colonies but at a slower pace than in Ghana since many of Britain's African colonies faced special problems. Nigeria was separated into three districts, and therefore time was needed to form some kind of a federation. Sierra Leone and Gambia were poor and small.

British East Africa

Britain's colonies on the east coast also had a variety of problems which slowed the pace of independence. Uganda had four kings (the kingdoms of Toro, Bunyoro, Ankole, and Buganda) who all claimed power. Kenya had a white settler problem, and in 1953 the Kikuyus (about 1,200,000 natives) had formed a terrorist organization called the Mau Mau and revolted against white supremacy in the highlands; Tanganyika was a huge trust territory with a small population and at least 120 different tribes.

French Africa

In 1956 the French granted more local autonomy, but this did not satisfy the new nationalists inspired by Nkrumah and the independence of Ghana. In 1958 French colonies were given a choice of independence or remaining within the French Community (a position similar to being in the British Commonwealth). All except Guinea voted to stay in the Community. But the example of Guinea and the influence of its president, Sékou Touré, led to the withdrawal of nine of the fifteen nations forming the French Community. By 1960, practically all French African colonies were independent, some within and some outside, of the Community.

The Accra Conference

Ghana decided to direct all its resources against colonialism, and in 1958 the first African conference (representing twenty-eight territories) met. Nkrumah announced that "Our task is not done and our own safety not assured until the last vestiges of colonialism have been swept from Africa."

The Congo

Independence in the Belgian Congo was the pan-African movement's "greatest triumph and its most serious test." It was also an example of the disruptive force of tribalism.

The Belgian Congo had been under strict paternalistic control since 1885, but in 1955 the Belgian government finally bowed to nationalistic pressure and allowed a few political groups to exist. In 1958 Patrice Lumumba began to agitate for independence, and in 1960 the Belgian government granted free elections and independence.

Lumumba became the first premier, with Kasavubu as president. Conflict between the two men developed, since Lumumba tended to be pro-Russian and Marxist, and Kasavubu was more favorably inclined toward the West. In a heavily tribal country the government was totally dependent on the army, which was still led by Belgian officers. When the army mutinied against their officers the regime collapsed, and the Congo broke into warring tribes. The province of Katanga, led by the pro-Belgian Tshombe and supported by Belgian mining interests, declared its independence, and the Africans turned to the UN for support.

The years 1960–1961 witnessed chaos, murder, and war in the Congo, in which Lumumba was killed (February 1961) and UN troops endeavored to maintain the peace and crush the independence of Katanga by force of arms. The situation was temporarily solved and the country united under Premier Cyrille Adoula in 1962, but UN troops remained for two more years.

Ironically, Tshombe, the separatist leader of Katanga, was made premier of the Congo in 1964. That same year UN troops withdrew, but the Congo's troubles were far from over. Tshombe was not trusted by many African leaders: he had been on good terms with some of the most hated white men, and the rebels who were pro-Lumumba held him responsible for their hero's death, and the rebellion continued. From one of the wealthiest colonial territories, the Congo was reduced to one of the least solvent and stable. When the rebels took Stanleyville at least 58 whites were massacred, but the entry of United States and Belgian paratroopers saved the lives of thousands.

At the end of 1965 Mobutu (who had been second in command under Lumumba) took over control and successfully stamped out rebellion and opposition and put the Congo (later renamed Zaire) back on a solvent and stable course.

Portuguese Africa

The Portuguese were among the last to give up their colonial empire in Africa. It was not until 1973 with the overthrow of the right-wing dictatorship in Portugal that the nation was willing to relinquish its colonies. But Portugal had in no way prepared Mozambique and Angola for independence. The two countries' commercial and bureaucratic offices were staffed by whites and neither country had time to prepare for freedom (Mozambique, for example, had nine months where Ghana and Nigeria had almost ten years). Angola with three black nationalist groups was torn by civil war in 1975, and with outside intervention has become communist.

The Independent Nations of Sub-Sahara Africa

NATION	COLONIAL POWER	DATE OF INDEPENDENCE
Angola	Portuguese	1975
Basutoland (see Lesothso)	—	—
Bechuanaland (see Botswana)	—	—
*Botswana	British	1966
Burundi	Belgian	1962
Cameroon	French	1960
Cape Verde Islands	Portuguese	1975
Central African Rep. (Emp)	French	1960
Chad	French	1960
Comorro Islands	French	1975
Congo	French	1960
Congo (see Zaire)	Belgian	—
Dahomey	French	1960
Equatorial Guinea	Spanish	1968
Eritrea (part of Ethiopia)	Italian	1952
Ethiopia	—	—
Gabon	French	1960
*Gambia	British	1965
*Ghana	British	1957
Guinea	French	1958
Guinea-Bissau	Portuguese	1974
Ivory Coast	French	1960
*Kenya	British	1963
*Lesotho	British	1966
Liberia	—	—
Madagascar (see Malagasy Republic)	—	—
Malagasy Republic	French	1960
*Malawi	British	1964
Mali	French	1960
Mauritania	French	1960
*Mauritius	British	1968

*Nations are starred if they are members of the British Commonwealth.

NATION	COLONIAL POWER	DATE OF INDEPENDENCE
Mozambique	Portuguese	1975
Niger	French	1960
Northern Rhodesia (see Zambia)	—	—
Nyasaland (see Malawi)	—	—
Rhodesia	British	1965
Rwanda	Belgian	1962
Sao Tome and Principe	Portuguese	1975
Senegal	French	1960
*Sierra Leone	British	1961
Somalia	British & Italian	1960
South Africa	British	1910
Southern Rhodesia (see Rhodesia)	—	—
Sudan	British & Egyptian	1956
Sudan (see Mali)	French	—
*Swaziland	British	1968
Tanganyika (now Tanzania)	British	1961
*Tanzania	British	—
Togo	French	1960
Togoland (joined Ghana)	British	1960
*Uganda	British	1962
Upper Volta	French	1960
Zaire	Belgian	1960
Zambia	British	1964
Zanzibar (now Tanzania)	British	1963

*Nations are starred if they are members of the British Commonwealth.

The Leaders at Independence

The leaders of the countries of Africa at the time of independence reveal the diversity and the depth of nationalistic feeling characteristic of the continent.

FELIX HOUPHOUET-BOIGNY

Félix Houphouet-Boigny of the Ivory Coast was not from a poor and illiterate family as were Nkrumah and Nyerere; he was the son of a wealthy chief. He was one of the few leaders in ex-French territories who was dedicated to the French Community, yet he could not keep his own country in it.

KWAME NKRUMAH

Kwame Nkrumah, ex-president and prime minister of Ghana, was the most typical leader of his time. Educated abroad, he had a British university education and a master of science degree, became a fervent anti-colonialist, and an exceptional prime minister. His Pan-African ambitions proved his undoing: he became dictatorial and was ousted by a military coup.

KENNETH KAUNDA

Kenneth Kaunda of Zambia was the son of a preacher and a strong advocate of Gandhian nonviolence. He was a dedicated Pan-Africanist and believed in protecting the rights of white settlers. By the end of the 1960s, however, he had been pressured into giving support to African liberation forces operating in Rhodesia, Angola, and Mozambique, and the establishment in 1973 of a one party government may be a reflection of the difficulties he faced.

JULIUS N. NYERERE

Julius K. Nyerere of Tanganyika acquired a master of art in history and economics from the University of Edinburgh. He had been a teacher and maintained peace between white and black in Tanganyika, but union with Zanzibar (1964) resulted in the "moderate" Nyerere becoming more and more radical.

JOMO KENYATTA

Jomo Kenyatta of Kenya was first educated in a Church of Scotland mission school. His career was in many ways the most varied of the influencial leaders. He traveled abroad, attended the London School of Economics, wrote a book on anthropology, was arrested in 1953 for his connection with the Mau-Mau uprising, and not released until 1961. He headed Kenya's government from independence to his death in August of 1978.

THE IMPACT OF THE WEST

Traditional African Culture

The African tribe was organized and highly developed in politics, human relations, and culture. The chief's power varied from tribe to tribe, but in almost every case it was not absolute, for religious men (witch doctors) and tradition influenced his decisions.

In African culture there was no written law, and power rested primarily on the control over people rather than ownership of things. Chiefs, for example, usually lived in the same type of dwelling and wore the same clothes as their subjects, but they invariably had more wives, more children, and more people who owed them special duties. Land was not a saleable product, and there was relatively little difference in wealth among Africans in a particular village. Group responsibility was more important than individualism, and usually the tribe was a kin group that lived together in a village.

Polygamy was a common practice, and *bridewealth* (cattle or produce paid by the groom's family to the bride's family) ensured that the bride had a certain amount of protection and independence. (If she was mistreated by her husband, she could return to her own family, and her family was not obligated to return the dowry.) Even the late Tom Mboya of Kenya paid a "brideprice" of sixteen cows for his wife, Pamela Odede (an American college graduate).

Religion was often a highly developed ritualistic system, involving ancestor worship and spirit worship, in which the duty of the witch doctor was to manage the spirits. Religion was one of the elements that bound clans together.

Cultural and Economic Impact

The cultural and economic impact of the West upon Africa

is best epitomized in the words of Henry Morton Stanley: "There are 40 millions of people beyond the gateway of the Congo, and the cotton spinners of Manchester are waiting to clothe them. Birmingham foundries are glowing with the red metal that will presently be made into . . . trinkets that shall adorn those dusky bosoms, and the ministers of Christ are zealous to bring them, the poor benighted heathen, into the Christian fold."

The Influence of the European Trader

The slave trade had little cultural influence, except perhaps to give Africans a preconceived notion of Western materialism. In some cases Africans, in order to regain freedom from Western domination, tried to adopt Western ways, but this was not usually the case.

The Influence of the Missionaries

The missionary deliberately set about to change the African way of life by education, medicine, and religion. Educated Africans moved away from their traditional culture; medicine changed the Africans' attitude toward illness, family, and agriculture. Christian converts became isolated from their kin group because they could no longer participate in religious rituals.

The Influence of the Colonial Administrators

Working for the white settler on a plantation or in a mine undermined the African way of life. The introduction of wages and a money economy weakened the influence of the father, since sons who earned their own money could challenge his authority, and decreased the size of families and the number of wives a man could afford, since today bridewealth is often paid in cash, not kind.

The Europeans deprived chiefs of their traditional authority and established Western notions of law and order that outlawed many of the traditional ways.

The destruction of the old way of life has been more rapid than in most civilizations, and the reaction has been varied. Some tribes have lost their traditional rules of conduct without working out new ones. In 1948–1949 in Elizabethville (Congo), 88 percent of the cases before the police courts were instances in which Africans had not done things in the "western way," for example, cases of polygamy and breaking of labor laws.

The establishment of colonies by different European powers created the economic isolation of people who live side by side, and most of the boundaries of the states of Africa are the result of the accident of Western colonization. They do not necessarily represent ethnic, linguistic, or economic divisions.

As in the West urbanization and industrialization have been the instruments of vast social change and the seedbed of many problems, but the full impact was just beginning to be experienced by the 1970s. The African was separated from the traditional kin group, and was exposed to Western ways as well as the ways of other tribes.

Western education, either at home or abroad, has been the most significant force in undermining traditional African culture. The concepts of nationalism, of the importance of individualism and of progress through science have all had their effect on Africa as on the rest of the non-Western world.

AFRICA TODAY

Political Problems

Tribalism

Africa is composed of hundreds of different tribes with diverse cultures and languages. There is a desire to unify these tribes which often cuts across existing national boundaries. For example, the Bakonga live in three areas, northern Angola, Zaire, and Congo. The Ewe spread across the boundaries of Ghana and Togo, and the Masai of Kenya also live in Tanzania. There are many Africans who have little loyalty to their nation and still think of themselves first of all as part of the tribal people to which they belong.

Nationalism, the legacy of the West, found a strong rival in tribalism, the heritage of Africa, and it became one of the most serious problems faced by the new nations. Prime examples of the fearful consequences of genocide are manifest in the civil war in the Congo (see p. 418) ; war in Rwanda between the Batutsi and the Bahutu in 1964 in which tens of thousands were killed; Milton Obote's attempt (1966) to destroy the position of the Buganda in Uganda; the assassination of one of Africa's finest leaders, Tom Mboya of Kenya, in 1969; the bloody Nigerian conflict (1967–1970) in which Biafra tried to secede and the Ibo people were decimated; and in 1972 the massacre of some 200,000 Bahutu in Burundi by the Batutsi tribe. Tribal war, moreover, contributed to the rise of military government.

Militarism and One-Party States

In almost all African countries, economics—the immediate need to improve the lot of the masses—has caused political change. In general one-party states with socialistic programs have been adopted. Civil services, trade unions, and communications were brought under government control and opposition was ruthlessly crushed. Internal stability was purchased at the price of democracy. As early as 1956 Nkrumah of Ghana announced that "Even a system based on . . . a democratic constitution may need backing up . . . by emergency measures of a totalitarian kind." Nyerere of Tanzania announced that there could be "no room for difference or division." African tradition says that "the elders sit under the big tree and talk until they agree," which bears similarities to Lenin's theory of "democratic centralism" (see p. 179).

Since 1965 the military has overthrown civilian governments throughout the continent. Between November 1965 and February 1966, there were six revolutions: the Congo (Zaire) with Mobutu; Dahomey where the army took over for the third time in two years; the Central African Republic; Upper Volta; Nigeria where the prime minister was assassinated as a result of a military coup; and Ghana with the bloodless overthrow of Nkrumah. In November, 1966 the army took power in Burundi and in 1967 in Togo. Obote used the army to produce political change in Uganda in 1966 but in doing so he created the situation in which he himself was overthrown by the military, led by Idi Amin in 1971. The army intervened in Sierra Leone in 1967 and again in 1968 but in this case the army stepped down and civilian government was returned.

1973 was the first time since the independence movements that Africa had no coups, no assassinations, and no civil war, but after the terrible droughts of 1973–74 there were coups in Niger, Upper Volta, and Ethiopia. With the independence of Angola in 1975 once again there was civil war with factions aided by the USSR, Cuba, China, and the West, and the situation remains unstable. In 1978 leaders in the Congo and Nigeria were assassinated.

Economic Problems

One-Crop Economies

Many countries have their wealth and economic future tied in a one-crop economy and are consequently totally dependent upon the price of that crop on the world market. For example, Gambia depends on groundnuts for 90 percent of its exports; Ghana depends on cocoa, Uganda on cotton, Tanzania on coffee and mica, Cameroon on cocoa and coffee, and Somalia on fresh fruits and nuts. Even Rhodesia is almost completely dependent on the copper market.

Uneven Distribution of Wealth

South Africa, Rhodesia, Zambia, and the Katanga province of Zaire have the lion's share of gold, industrial diamonds, cobalt, copper, platinum, and uranium. Liberia is rich in iron ore, rubber, and timber, and with the discovery of oil Nigeria has prospered. (In 1960 agriculture accounted for 80 percent of Nigeria's total exports; by 1972 only 17 percent.) The Ivory Coast has a variety of natural resources and is the richest and potentially most self-sufficient nation in former French West Africa.

Landlocked Chad is at the other extreme with 96 percent of its people engaged in subsistence agriculture. Of the countries in equatorial Africa only Gabon is an economically viable state.

Dependence on Other Nations

Malawi is dependent on trade outlets through Mozambique to the Indian Ocean and on employment in Rhodesia and South Africa. Zambia has finished a road and is constructing a railroad which will ease its position, but the ex-British protectorates in South Africa are still totally dependent on the "white south." Most of

Rhodesia's trade in the past has gone through Mozambique, but this situation changed drastically with the independence of the former Portuguese colony.

The Exodus of the Whites

It is not surprising that black Africa established a racialism of its own. Some of it has been violent, some more moderate, but the result has created economic problems and in some cases chaos. Over a half million whites have pulled out, and disruption of industry and rail service, delays in cargo shipments, and, more seriously, a decline in food production have been the results (between 1970–73 food production declined by 7 percent).

In Zaire 30,000 white traders were expelled. In Kenya the government issued non-negotiable, one-time offers to buy out the white settler who had no choice but to accept. In Tanzania also most whites knew that they would no longer be welcome and sold their farms. In Ethiopia with the fall of Emperor Haile Selassie the military took over most business firms and 10,000 Europeans exited. The exodus from Angola and Mozambique in 1975 was a flood, leaving the country with no skilled administrators. The most radical case occurred in Uganda where 50,000 Asians were expelled with no compensation, and the country was left with no plumbers or electricians.

Extremism and Instability

Uganda under Amin confiscated property, introduced "Police Safety Units," and citizens vanished without trace. This has naturally led to the exodus of skilled blacks and totally curtailed the tourist trade.

The civil war in Angola more than halved the area's output in oil, coffee, and diamonds. Tanzania's widespread nationalization has meant little foreign private investment.

Other Problems

The forces of nature are unfavorable in many parts of Africa. Droughts, like that in the belt stretching from Senegal to Ethiopia in 1973–74, have been devastating. Yellow fever and sleeping sickness still plague large sections. Like all developing nations, there is a shortage of skilled labor, education, sanitation, power, transportation, and investment capital.

Education

Most of the countries suffer from illiteracy. The Ivory Coast has a literacy rate of only 20 percent; and relatively rich Liberia spends very little on education and has only a 15 percent literacy rate. Even in the ex-British colony of Kenya, the literacy rate is only 50 percent although Sierre Leone's is 80 percent. The Sudan has a low literacy rate which is complicated by the fact that the people speak 171 different languages. Somalia has the lowest literacy rate in Africa and the highest birth rate—not a very promising combination of statistics.

Population Statistics

Head counting is particularly unreliable. A guess would be that in 1920 Africa had 140,000,000 people; by 1969, 390,000,000. What is certain is that as a whole Africa has 20 percent of the land surface and only about 9 percent of the population of the world. This is deceiving, however, because under present economic conditions, certain areas (like former French West Africa) are badly overcrowded, and others are uninhabitable.

Pan-Africanism

The prospects of forming a "United States of Africa" are dim. Africa is a huge continent with poor communications, large areas with little population, and a fragmented economy. The principle of the sovereignty of each individual country has already been firmly established.

In 1963 the Organization of African Unity (OAU) was formed, and although it was helpless in Nigeria it did mediate Somalia's border disputes with Kenya and Ethiopia in 1968.

There has been progress toward international economic cooperation: the East African Community (Kenya, Uganda, and Tanzania) was formed in 1967 and in 1973 an Economic Community
for West Africa (Mali, Mauritania, Ivory Coast, Senegal, Niger,
Upper Volta, and Dahomey) was created.

The explosive force which holds the OAU together is white
control in South Africa and Rhodesia, but here there is no total
unity of direction to be taken by the leaders of black Africa.

Foreign Relations

Except for Angola, Africa has not become a battleground for
the big powers. Foreign aid has been balanced in a rather interesting
way: China and the United States helped to link Zambia with
Tanzania; Britain and the USSR supplied assistance to the federal
forces in Nigeria; and Russian aid to Nigeria was balanced by
American aid to Zaire.

Africa's relations with the Arab world have changed. Many
African nations have been successfully woed by the Arabs, despite
Israeli economic and technical assistance, and the OAU is asking
the Arabs to place an oil embargo on white dominated Africa.

Unresolved Problems

In 1973 Rhodesia had 5.5 million Africans and 267,000 Europeans, and South Africa had approximately 10,500,000 Africans
and "colored" and 3,000,000 whites. Both countries evolved policies
to subordinate the African majority.

South Africa

Apartheid involved total segregation—political, geographical,
and social. All nonwhites were disenfranchised, trade unions were
forbidden, and Africans were tied to their jobs. South Africa is
under intense international pressure and increasing internal conflict.
In 1973 blacks paralyzed the city of Durban and won across-the-

board wage hikes and the seven Bantu groups of Southwest Africa (Namibia) formed a federation demanding independence. In 1976 more than 300 people were killed in riots, and in 1978 the government finally desegregated the theatre and the opera. Independence for Southwest Africa seems assured but racial trouble in South Africa continues.

Rhodesia

The government had white supremacy policies similar to South Africa's. In 1965 Rhodesia broke with England; in 1966 the UN authorized Britain to use force against tankers carrying oil to Rhodesia (it didn't) and economic sanctions were introduced by many nations (generally unsuccessfully). Guerilla raids from the north caused the closing of the borders with Zambia and made Rhodesia more and more dependent on South Africa.

Britain refused to recognize independence until an agreement was reached with the Africans, and South Africa, in order to lessen its own problems, put pressure on Rhodesia for a black-white compromise. Prime Minister Ian Smith's proposal (1976) to shift power to the country's blacks by 1978 was not accepted by the liberation movements. In 1978–1979 Smith unilaterally made an agreement with three major black leaders who do not represent the two liberation movements in the country. Since the liberation movements control one-third of Rhodesia, the outcome is certainly not resolved, despite elections in 1979.

Selected Bibliography

The following are useful reference works for world history:

Bowle, John. *Concise Encyclopedia of World History,* 2nd ed. London: Hutchinson, 1971.

Langer, W. *Encyclopedia of World History,* 5th ed. Boston: Houghton Mifflin, 1972.

The following atlases are recommended:

Cole, J. P. *Geography of World Affairs,* 4th ed. New York: Penguin, 1972.

McNeill, W. H.; Buske, M. R.; and Roehm, A. W. *The World: Its History in Maps.* Chicago: Denoyer-Geppert, 1963.

Palmer, R. R., ed. *Atlas of World History.* Skokie, Ill.: Rand McNally, 1962.

The best general surveys of world history are the following:

McNeill, W. H. *The Rise of the West: A History of the Human Community.* Chicago: University of Chicago Press, 1963.

Stavrianos, Leften S. *The World since 1500,* rev. ed. Englewood Cliffs, N.J.: Prentice-Hall, 1970.

McNeill also has *A World History,* 2nd ed. (New York: Oxford University Press, 1971) and Stavrianos has *Man's Past and Present, A Global History* (Englewood Cliffs, N. J.: Prentice-Hall, 1971). H. G. Wells, *The Outline of History,* 1st ed. (Garden City, Doubleday: 1920) is a classic.

Other analyses are the following:

Bowle, J. *Man through the Ages.* Boston: Little, Brown & Co., 1962.

Durant, Will H. *The Story of Civilization,* 1st ed. New York: Simon and Schuster, 1935.

Toynbee, A. J. *A Study of History,* new abridged ed. with Jane Caplan, New York: American Heritage, 1972.

Interpretations of the contemporary world from a global viewpoint are:

Dean, V. M. *The Nature of the Non-Western World,* rev. ed. London: Mentor Press, 1966.

Carr, E. H. *The New Society,* New York: St. Martin's, 1965.

Jaspers, K. *The Future of Mankind.* Chicago: University of Chicago Press, 1961.

Heilbroner, R. L. *The Future as History.* New York: Harper & Row, 1960.

Thomson, D. *World History 1914 to 1968,* 3rd ed. New York: Oxford University Press, 1969.

Selected Bibliography for the Middle East

Prehistoric Period

Childe, V. Gordon, *Man Makes Himself.* London: Mentor, 1958.

Hawkes, J. and Wooley, L. *Prehistory and the Beginnings of Civilization.* New York: Unesco, 1963.

Ancient and Classical Period

Frankfort, H. *The Birth of Civilization in the Near East.* New York: Barnes & Noble, 1968.

Frankfort, H., et al. *Before Philosophy.* Gretna, La.: Pelican, 1963.

Geer, J. *How the Great Religions Began.* London: Signet Key Book, 1954.

Hitti, P. K. *The Near East in History.* New York: Van Nostrand Reinhold, 1961. This is the best general survey.

Medieval Period

Gibb, H. A. R. *Mohammedism.* New York: Oxford University Press, 1961.

Hitti, P. K. *The Arabs: A Short History,* rev. ed. London: Gateway, 1968.

Lewis, Bernard. *The Arabs in History.* New York: Harper & Row, 1958.

Modern Period

Atiyah, E. *The Arabs,* rev. ed. New York: Penguin, 1958.

Fisher, S. N. *The Middle East,* rev. ed. New York: Knopf, 1969.

Gibb, H. A. R., and Bowen, H. *Islamic Society and the West.* New York: Oxford University Press, 1963.

Kerr, Malcolm. *The Arab Cold War, Gamal abd al-Naser and His Rivals 1958–1970,* 3rd ed. New York: Oxford University Press, 1971.

Lerner, D. *The Passing of Traditional Society: Modernizing the Middle East.* New York: Free Press, 1967.

Lewis, B. *The Emergence of Modern Turkey.* New York: Oxford University Press, 1961.

Safran, Naday. *The United States and Israel.* Cambridge, Mass.: Harvard University Press, 1963.

Thomas, L. V., and Frye, R. N. *The United States and Turkey and Iran.* Cambridge, Mass.: Harvard University Press, 1952.

Thompson, J. H., and Reischauer, R. D., ed. *Modernization of the Arab World.* New York: Van Nostrand Reinhold, 1966.

Selected Bibliography for Western Europe

Ancient and Classical Periods

Boak, A. E. R. *A History of Rome to 565 A.D.,* 5th ed. New York: Macmillan, 1965.

Bowra, C. M. *The Greek Experience.* London: Weidenfeld and Nicholson, 1957.

Childe, V. Gordon. *What Happened in History.* New York: Penguin, 1965.

Finley, M. I. *The Ancient Greeks: Their Life and Thought.* New York: Viking, 1963.

Grant, Michael. *The World of Rome,* new ed. Cardinal, 1974.

Kitto, H. D. F. *The Greeks*. New York: Penguin, 1961.

Tarn, W. W. *Alexander the Great*. Boston: Beacon, 1971.

Medieval Period

Bloch, Marc. *Feudal Society*. Chicago: University of Chicago Press, 1961.

Ferguson, W. K. *Europe in Transition, 1300–1520*. Boston: Houghton Mifflin, 1962.

Huizinga, J. *The Waning of the Middle Ages*. Edward Arnold, 1924.

Southern, R. W. *The Making of the Middle Ages*. New Haven: Yale University Press, 1953.

Strayer, J. R., and Monro, D. C. *The Middle Ages: 395–1500*, 5th ed. New York: Appleton-Century-Crofts, 1970.

Modern Period

Aron, Raymond. *The Century of Total War*. New York: Doubleday, 1954.

Ashton, T. S. *The Industrial Revolution 1760–1830*, rev. ed. New York: Oxford University Press, 1962.

Bainton, R. H. *Here I Stand: A Life of Martin Luther*. Nashville: Abingdon, 1950.

Bowle, John. *The Imperial Achievement: The Rise and Transformation of the British Empire*. Boston: Little, Brown & Co., 1974.

Braudel, Fernand. *The Mediterranean and the Mediterranean World in the Age of Philip II*. New York: Harper & Row, 1973.

Brinton, Crane. *The Anatomy of Revolution*. Vintage, 1957, 1965.

Bullock, A. *Hitler: A Study in Tyranny*, rev. ed. New York: Harper & Row, 1962.

Butterfield, Herbert. *The Origins of Modern Science*. New York: Macmillan, 1949, 1962.

Elton, G. R. *Reformation Europe, 1517–59*. New York: Harper & Row, 1963.

Fay, S. B. *The Origins of the World War*, 2nd ed. New York: Free Press, 1968.

Fisher, S. *The Passing of the European Age,* rev. ed. New York: Russell and Russell, 1967.

Gay, Peter. *The Enlightenment, an Interpretation,* 2 vols. New York: Knopf, 1966–69.

Gilmore, M. *The World of Humanism 1453–1517.* New York: Harper & Row, 1962.

Hayes, C. J. H. *The Generation of Materialism: 1871–1900.* New York: Harper & Row, 1941.

Hill, J. E. C. *The Century of Revolution 1603–1714.* Cardinal, 1974.

Holborn, Hajo. *The Political Collapse of Europe.* New York: Knopf, 1951.

Hughes, H. S. *Contemporary Europe: A History,* 3rd ed. Englewood Cliffs, N. J.: Prentice-Hall, 1971.

Lafore, L. *The Long Fuse: an Interpretation of the Origins of World War I.* Philadelphia: Lippincott, 1971.

Langer, W. L. *European Alliances and Alignments,* 2nd ed. New York: Knopf, 1950.

Lichtheim, C. *A Short History of Socialism.* New York: Praeger, 1970.

Ortega y Gasset, J. *The Revolt of the Masses.* London: Allen and Unwin, 1961.

Palmer, R. R. *The Age of Democratic Revolution: A Political History of Europe and America 1760–1800,* 2 vols. Englewood Cliffs, N. J.: Princeton University, 1959–64.

Palmer, R. R., and Colton, J. *A History of the Modern World,* 4th ed. New York: Knopf, 1971.
This is the best general survey.

Parry, J. H. *The Age of Reconnaissance: Exploration, Discovery and Settlement 1450–1650.* Weidenfeld and Nicholson, 1963, 1969.

Randall, J. H. *The Making of the Modern Mind,* rev. ed. Boston: Houghton Mifflin, 1954.

Sachar, H. M. *The Course of Modern Jewish History.* New York: Dell, 1958.

Smith, L. B. *The Elizabethan World.* Boston: Houghton Mifflin, 1967.

de Tocqueville, Alexis. *The Old Regime and the French Revolution.* New York: Doubleday Anchor, 1960.

Wright, Gordon. *The Ordeal of Total War, 1939–1945.* New York: Harper & Row, 1968.

Selected Bibliography for Russia

Ancient, Classical, Medieval, and Modern up to 1914

Florinsky, Michael T. *Russia: A History and an Interpretation,* 2 vols. New York: Macmillan, 1947, 1953.
This is the best study.

Florinsky, Michael T. *Russia, a Short History,* 2nd ed. New York: Macmillan, 1969.

Mazour, A. G. *Russia: Tzarist and Communist.* New York: Van Nostrand Reinhold, 1962.

Seton-Watson, H. *The Russian Empire 1801–1917.* Clarendon, 1967.

Vernadsky, George. *The Origins of Russia.* Clarendon, 1959.

Walsh, W. B. *Readings in Russian History,* 4th rev. ed. Syracuse, N. Y.: Syracuse University Press, 1963.

Russia 1914 to the Present

Carr, E. H. *The Bolshevik Revolution 1917–1929,* 7 vols. New York: Macmillan, 1951–64.

Fainsod, Merle. *How Russia is Ruled,* rev. ed. Cambridge, Mass.: Harvard University Press, 1963.

Grey, I. *The First Fifty Years: Soviet Russia 1917–1967.* Hodder and Stoughton, 1967.

Inkeles, A., and Geiger, K. *Soviet Society: A Book of Readings.* Boston: Houghton Mifflin, 1961.

Kennan, G. F. *Russia and the West under Lenin and Stalin.* Boston: Little, Brown & Co., 1961.

Lichtheim, C. *Marxism: An Historical and Critical Study,* rev. ed. Rutledge and Paul, 1964.

Nettle, J. P. *The Soviet Achievement.* Thames and Hudson, 1967.

Pares, B. *The Fall of the Russian Monarchy: A Study of Evidence.* Vintage, 1961.

Wolfe, Bertram. *Three Who Made a Revolution,* rev. ed. Boston: Beacon, 1964.

Selected Bibliography for North America

Allen, F. L. *The Big Change: America Transforms Itself, 1900–1950*. New York: Harper & Row, 1962.

Bemis, S. F. *A Diplomatic History of the United States*, 5th ed. New York: Holt, Rinehart & Winston, 1965.

Billington, R. A. *Westward Expansion*, rev. ed. New York: Macmillan, 1959.

Craig, C. M. *The United States and Canada*. Cambridge, Mass.: Harvard University Press, 1968.

Creighton, D. G. *Dominion of the North: A History of Canada*. New York: Macmillan, 1958.

Creighton, D. G. *Canada's First Century, 1867–1967*. New York: Macmillan, 1970.

Dangerfield, George. *The Era of Good Feelings*. Harbinger, 1963.

Franklin, J. H. *From Slavery to Freedom: A History of Negro Americans*, 4th ed. New York: Knopf, 1974.

Galbraith, J. K. *The Great Crash, 1929*. Boston: Houghton Mifflin, 1961.

Leuchtenburg, W. E. *The Perils of Prosperity 1914–1932*, 2 vols. Chicago: University of Chicago Press, 1958.

Link, Arthur, and Catton, William B. *American Epoch: A History of the United States*, 4th ed. New York: Knopf, 1973.

Morgan, Edmund S. *The Birth of the Republic 1763–89*. Chicago: University of Chicago Press, 1956.

Nevins, Allan. *Ordeal of Union*, 2 vols. New York: Scribners, 1947, 1966.

Rossiter, Clinton. *Seedtime of the Republic*. New York: Harcourt Brace Jovanovich, 1953, 1964.

Weinberg, A. K. *Manifest Destiny*. New York: Quadrangle Books, 1963.

Wiebe, Robert H. *The Search for Order 1877–1920*. New York: Hill and Wang, 1967.

Selected Bibliography for Latin America

Bemis, S. F. *Latin American Policy of the United States: An Historical Interpretation.* New York: Harcourt Brace Jovanovich, 1943.

Crow, John. *The Epic of Latin America.* New York: Doubleday, 1971.

Davis, R. T. *The Golden Century of Spain 1501–1621.* New York: St. Martin's, 1954, 1964.

Fagg, John E. *Latin America: A General History.* New York: Macmillan, 1963.

Gibson, C. *Spain in America.* New York: Harper & Row, 1966.

Hanke, Lewis. *History of Latin American Civilization, the Modern Era,* 2nd ed. Boston: Little, Brown & Co., 1973.

Herring, Hubert. *History of Latin America,* 2nd ed. New York: Knopf, 1961.
This is a good general history.

Hilton, Ronald. *The Latin Americans: Their Heritage and Their Destiny.* Philadelphia: Lippincott, 1973.

Keen, Benjamin. *Latin American Civilization, the National Era,* 3rd ed. Boston: Houghton Mifflin, 1974.

Needler, Martin C. *Latin American Politics in Perspective,* rev. ed. New York: Van Nostrand Reinhold, 1967.

Parkes, Henry B. *A History of Mexico,* 3rd rev. ed. Boston: Houghton Mifflin, 1960.

Schurz, W. L. *This New World: The Civilization of Latin America.* New York: Dutton, 1954, 1962.

Whitaker, Arthur, and Jordan, David C. *Nationalism in Contemporary Latin America.* New York: Free Press, 1966.

Worcester, Donald, and Schaeffer, Wendell. *The Growth and Culture of Latin America,* 2nd ed. New York: Oxford University Press, 1971.

Selected Bibliography for India

Ancient, Classical, and Medieval Periods

Basham, A. L. *The Wonder That Was India*. New York: Hawthorne, 1963.

Bary, W. T. de, ed. *Sources of the Indian Tradition*. New York: Columbia University Press, 1958, 1967.

Piggott, S. *Prehistoric India to 1000 B.C.* New York: Penguin, 1961.

Wallbank, T. Walter. *A Short History of India from Ancient Times to the Present*. Mentor, 1958.

Modern Period

Brecher, M. *Nehru: A Political Biography*. New York: Oxford University Press, 1959.

Brown, W. Norman. *The United States and India, Pakistan and Bangladesh*. Cambridge, Mass.: Harvard University Press, 1972.

Dean, V. M. *New Patterns of Democracy in India,* 2nd ed. Cambridge, Mass.: Harvard University Press, 1969.

Lamb, Beatrice P. *India: A World in Transition,* 3rd ed. New York: Praeger, 1968.

Nehru, Jawaharal. *The Discovery of India*. New York: Doubleday, 1960.

O'Malley, L. S. S. *Modern India and the West,* New York: Oxford University Press, 1941.

Panikkar, K. M. *A Survey of Indian History* 4th ed., New York: Asia Publishing House, 1971.

Spear, Percival. *India: A Modern History,* rev. ed. Ann Arbor, Mich.: University of Michigan Press, 1972.

Spear, Percival. *India, Pakistan and the West,* 4th ed. New York: Oxford University Press, 1967.
This is the best general survey.

Selected Bibliography for China

Ancient, Classical, and Medieval Periods

Bary, W. E. de, ed., *Sources of the Chinese Tradition*. New York: Columbia University Press, 1960.

Creel, H. G. *The Birth of China*. New York: Ungar, 1954, 1964.

Fung Yu-lan, *A Short History of Chinese Philosophy*. New York: Macmillan, 1948, 1966.

Goodrich, L. Carrington. *A Short History of the Chinese People,* 3rd rev. ed. New York: Harper & Row, 1959.

Latourette, K. S. *The Chinese: Their History and Culture,* 4th ed. New York: Macmillan, 1964.

Modern Period

Brandt, C., Schwartz, B., and Fairbank, J. K. *A Documentary History of Chinese Communism*. Cambridge, Mass.: Harvard University Press, 1952, 1959.

Ch'en, Jerome. *Mao and the Chinese Revolution*. New York: Oxford University Press, 1949.

Fairbank, J. K. *The United States and China,* 3rd ed. Cambridge, Mass.: Harvard University Press, 1971. This is the best introduction to modern China.

Fairbank, J. K., and Teng, Ssu-yü. *China's Response to the West*. Cambridge, Mass.: Harvard University Press, 1954.

Fairbank, J. K., Reischauer, E. O., and Craig, A. M. *East Asia*. Boston: Houghton Mifflin, 1973.

Harrison, James P. *The Long March to Power: A History of the Chinese Communist Party 1921–1972*. New York: Praeger, 1972.

Karnow, Stanley. *Mao and China from Revolution to Revolution*. New York: Viking, 1972.

Morse, H. B., and MacNair, H. F. *Far Eastern International Relations*. Boston: Houghton Mifflin, 1931, 1967.

North, Robert C. *Moscow and Chinese Communists*. Stanford, Ca.: Stanford University Press, 1953.

Perkins, Dwight. *Agricultural Development in China 1368–1968.* Chicago: Aldine, 1969.

Sheridan, James E. *China in Disintegration, The Republican Era in Chinese History 1912–1949.* New York: Free Press, 1975.

Selected Bibliography for Japan

Ancient, Classical, and Medieval Periods

de Bary, W. T., Tunoda, R., and Keene, D., ed. *Sources of the Japanese Tradition.* New York: Columbia University Press, 1958.

Latourette, K. S. *The History of Japan,* rev. ed. New York: Macmillan, 1957.

Reischauer, E. O. *Japan: The Story of a Nation,* rev. ed. New York: Knopf, 1974.

Sansom, G. B. *Japan: Short Cultural History,* rev. ed. New York: Appleton-Century-Crofts, 1962.

Modern Period

Benedict, Ruth. *The Chrysanthemum and the Sword.* Boston: Houghton Mifflin, 1946.

Borton, H. *Japan's Modern Century.* Ronald Press, 1955.

Fairbank, J. K., Reischauer, E. O., and Craig, A. M. *East Asia.* Boston: Houghton Mifflin, 1973.

Reischauer, Edwin O. *The United States and Japan,* 3rd ed. Cambridge, Mass.: Harvard University Press, 1965.
This is the best survey.

Reischauer, Robert K. *Japan, Government–Politics.* Nelson, 1939.

Sansom, G. B. *The Western World and Japan.* New York: Knopf, 1950.

Scalapino, R. *Democracy and the Party Movement in Prewar Japan.* Berkeley, Ca.: University of California Press, 1953, 1967.

Selected Bibliography for Southeast Asia

Elsbree, W. H. *Japan's Role in Southeast Asian Nationalist Movements 1940–1945.* Cambridge, Mass.: Harvard University Press, 1953.

Fairbank, J. K., Reischauer, E. O., and Craig, A. M. *East Asia.* Boston: Houghton Mifflin, 1973.
This covers only Vietnam and Korea.

Kahin, George M., ed. *Governments and Politics of Southeast Asia,* 2nd ed. Ithaca, N.Y.: Cornell University Press, 1964.

Kahin, George M., and Lewis, John W. *The United States in Vietnam,* rev. ed. New York: Dial Press, 1967.

Harrison, Brian. *Southeast Asia: A Short History,* 3rd ed. New York: St. Martin's, 1966.

Pratt, John T. *The Expansion of Europe in the Far East.* Sylvan Press, 1947.

Steinberg, David J., ed. *In Search of Southeast Asia: A Modern History.* New York: Praeger, 1971.

Taylor, George E., and Michael, Frank H. *The Far East in the Modern World,* rev. ed. New York: Holt, 1964.

Wint, G. *The British in Asia.* Russell and Russell, 1971.

Selected Bibliography for Africa

Bohannan, P., and Curtin, P. *Africa and the Africans,* rev. ed. New York: Natural History, 1971.

Davidson, Basil. *Black Mother, the Years of the African Slave Trade.* Boston: Little, Brown & Co., 1961.

Davidson, Basil. *African Kingdoms.* Alexandria, Va.: Time-Life, 1966.

Davidson, Basil. *Which Way Africa,* rev. ed. New York: Penguin, 1971.

Emerson, R. *From Empire to Nation: The Rise to Self-Assertions of Asian and African Peoples.* Cambridge, Mass.: Harvard University Press, 1960, 1967.

Fage, John D., ed. *Africa Discovers the Past*. New York: Oxford University Press, 1970.

Hatch, J. *A History of Postwar Africa*. New York: Praeger, 1965.

Hodgkin, T. *Nationalism in Colonial Africa*. New York: New York University Press, 1957, 1965.

July, Robert. *A History of the African People*. New York: Scribners, 1970.

Murdock, G. P. *Africa: Its People and Their Cultural History*. New York: McGraw-Hill, 1959.

Oliver, Roland, ed. *The Middle Age of African History*. New York: Oxford University Press, 1967.

Oliver, Roland, ed. *The Dawn of African History*, 2nd ed. New York: Oxford University Press, 1968.

Oliver, Roland, and Atmore, Anthony. *Africa since 1800*, 2nd ed. Cambridge University Press, 1972.

Oliver, Roland, and Fage, J. D. *A Short History of Africa*, 4th ed. New York: Penguin, 1972.

Wallerstein, I. *Africa: The Politics of Independence*. New York: Random House, 1963.

Wallerstein, I. *Africa: The Politics of Unity*. New York: Random House, 1967.

INDEX

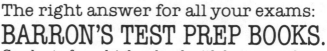

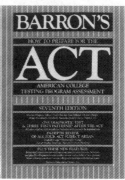

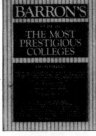